D0914891

BOOKS BY

C. E. LUCAS PHILLIPS

Cockleshell Heroes

Escape of the 'Amethyst'

The Greatest Raid of All

Alamein

ALAMEIN

'It all depends on *that* article' (Wellington before Waterloo, pointing to a British soldier)
The photograph is of a bren gunner of
The Royal Sussex Regiment before Alamein

C. E. LUCAS PHILLIPS

ALAMEIN

WITH ILLUSTRATIONS

An Atlantic Monthly Press Book

LITTLE, BROWN AND COMPANY

Boston *Toronto*

LIBRARY OF CONGRESS CATALOG NO. 63-8308

Second Printing

ATLANTIC—LITTLE, BROWN BOOKS
ARE PUBLISHED BY
LITTLE, BROWN AND COMPANY
IN ASSOCIATION WITH
THE ATLANTIC MONTHLY PRESS

PRINTED IN THE UNITED STATES OF AMERICA

Contents

List of Illustrations

PHOTOGRAPHS

(Those not otherwise acknowledged are reproduced by the courtesy of the Imperial War Museum, several having been specially extracted from the documentary film *Desert Victory*, made by the Army Film and Photographic Unit in the Western Desert.)

Maps and Diagrams

Drawn by Miss Audrey Frew, ARCA.

For old times' sake, Major R. S. Richmond, MC, RA, Instructor in Gunnery, has been good enough to rub the rust off my recollection of artillery procedure in Chapter Ten. Mr D. W. King, O.B.E., Chief Librarian of the War Office, has been a valuable 'Intelligence Officer' throughout my literary operations, and Mr L. A. Jackets, Head of the Historical Section of the Air Ministry, has unhesitatingly given me the fullest 'air support'. Miss Rose Coombes, Librarian of the Imperial War Museum, has helped my search for published and unpublished matter that is difficult of access, and the photographic staff of the Museum responded generously to my large demands, particularly in the skilful extraction of shots from that superb documentary film, *Desert Victory*, made in the desert by the Army Film and Photographic Unit. The Historical Section of the Cabinet Office and the German Military Historical Research Bureau have helped to clear up some points of doubt.

Lieutenant-General Sir Henry Wells, Major-General Sir William Gentry and others have guided me in the operations of 9th Australian Division and 2nd New Zealand Division respectively. Brigadier P. N. M. Moore, Brigadier G. R. McMeekan and Major J. F. M. Perrott have informed me in great detail on the methods and incidence of mine-lifting operations, which were so vital a preliminary to the victory.

The figures I have given for enemy tank losses must be regarded as approximate; no completely reliable record seems now available, but I have used the best ascertainable information.

Oxshott, C. E. LUCAS PHILLIPS
January 1962

Author's Notice

Accounts of the Battle of Alamein from the generals' point of view have been written by several hands, but, hitherto, no account appears to have been published from the point of view of the regimental soldier, other than personal narratives and regimental histories. In spite of its great fame, Alamein still remains a battle of which the combat operations are little known, even by many of those engaged in it. This book is an attempt to fill that gap in part and to present a general picture of the battle in the manner of the *peintre militaire*.

Hitherto, Alamein has been generally looked upon as a 'general's battle'. I hope that these pages will show, however, that, under the direction of a commander of the first order, it was very much a 'soldier's battle', in the great tradition of Waterloo, Blenheim, Agincourt and many another famous field. It was won by that series of 'dog fights', that 'real rough-house', that 'continuous strain of hard battle fighting' which Field-Marshal Montgomery expressly prescribed and for the success of which he relied upon the fighting qualities of one of the finest armies that this country and the British Empire have ever put into the field.

Nevertheless, it will be seen that Alamein was far from being the straightforward and almost fore-ordained victory which the Field-Marshal has made it appear to be. In fact, as Wellington said after Waterloo, 'it was a damned nice thing'. Although we could never have actually lost the battle, the prospect of a clear-cut and decisive victory hung in the balance (though not in the Field-Marshal's own mind) until the eleventh day.

I have devoted a considerable portion of the book to an exposition of the conditions and events preliminary to the battle, as I am anxious that the reader not familiar with these matters should, like

Montgomery's soldiers, go into the battle well briefed. For a like reason, I have added a very short glossary. Some recent ill-qualified criticisms, which require refutation, have impelled me also to expand on certain points more than would otherwise have been necessary.

In the main, I have confined myself to a straightforward narrative. The book is not a commentary (though comment there certainly is), nor have I strayed into the blind alleys of author's hindsight. But there is a personal reputation that has to be put right and I have taken occasion also to reduce to its proper proportions the legendary and wholly exaggerated image of Field-Marshal Rommel. One of the foundations of Montgomery's victory was his shrewd and exact appreciation of the mistakes that he knew Rommel would make. Hence the deliberate invitations to self-destructive counter-attacks.

This account has been compiled from all the available official records and various other authorities, which are set out in Appendix G. Among them is a considerable list of persons who have been kind enough to entrust me with their private diaries or journals or who have given me their personal narratives, in writing or verbally, often at considerable length and in great detail. Some have spent long hours with me in the close examination of maps and documents. To all I am very much indebted. Where I have not accepted personal accounts in full detail, I hope it will be understood that all have had to be checked with other information.

I have especially to thank Major-General Raymond Briggs for his painstaking and most valuable help at all stages, by no means confined to the activities of his own division; his expertise in tank warfare, his long experience of the desert and his acquaintance with all the leading actors on that dramatic stage have been a stimulus to the understanding of operations. Likewise Major-General D. N. Wimberley has contributed most generously and in great detail on operations generally and those of the Highland Division in particular. Field-Marshal The Viscount Montgomery has informed me on the considerations that governed many of his decisions and on a great deal else as well. Lieutenant-General Sir Oliver Leese, Bt, has thrown light on many facets of the battle and on the people concerned in it.

Part I

THE DESERT BATTLEFIELD

Chapter One

ON THE SPRINGBOK ROAD

Early on the morning of 1 July 1942, a British artillery officer, dressed in tropical shirt and shorts, was jolting down the 'Springbok Road', which led southward from El Alamein, to rejoin his regiment in the Western Desert. He knew that the regiment had just moved into the hollow depression known as the Deir El Shein, after a hair-raising all-night drive across the open desert to avoid capture by the advancing enemy forces under Rommel.

He was disobeying an order by General Auchinleck that certain officers should be 'left out of battle', in order that whole units should not be wiped out, but he knew that his regiment was likely to engage the oncoming enemy some time that day, that they must be tired, and he was damned if he would stay out.

He halted his small column of three vehicles to rest the drivers. Stepping out of his car, he stretched his legs, his desert boots sinking deep into the powdery dust, and smoked awhile, flicking the air with his handkerchief to keep off the soft-winged flies that came swarming round. The sun at this early hour was already hot.

After a minute or two a truck came slowly up from the south in a shroud of dust and stopped beside him. It was from a Free French unit stationed deeper in the desert. A French officer dismounted and saluted. He was tall and very handsome but clearly very worried.

'Can you tell me what is happening?' he asked. 'Is it true that the Boche has broken through?' He spoke perfect English, but his voice and face showed anxiety.

The British officer smiled. 'Good heavens, no! Everything is under control.' He really knew very little about the situation himself.

The Frenchman relaxed but was not fully reassured.

'You are sure about that?' he said. 'We've heard that the Boche are through on the coast road and making for Alexandria.'

'Well, I've just come from the coast road myself, saw the South Africans sitting tight at Alamein and everything is perfectly peaceful. Not a shot to be heard.'

The Frenchman looked more relieved and said: 'That's good news. We are cut-off by ourselves, you know, out at the other end of the desert and we don't hear much. We heard stories that there had been a complete collapse and the Boche was overrunning everything. So my CO sent me up to find out.'

'Well, you can go back and tell your CO that all is well and under control. Here we are and here we're jolly well going to stay.'

They chatted for a bit and the Frenchman then remounted his truck and turned about.

The British officer thought what a fine fellow he looked and felt very sorry for him and his comrades away by themselves and out-of-touch; and cut-off, he reflected also, from a country under the heel of a conqueror. The Frenchman was the only man he had met who was ill at ease. Though he himself had only a general idea of how operations to the westward were going, the British officer had a strong feeling of confidence. In spite of the long withdrawal from Gazala, in the latter stages of which he had taken part, morale was high among all whom he saw. How coolly, he recollected, 'Pasha' Russell had given his orders in that ticklish situation near Matruh!

No doubt was in his mind that Eighth Army was well collected and that the reins of command were in good hands. That there should be any questioning of the higher leadership was a thought that never entered his head.

Such was the author's own introduction to the Alamein 'line' and in a few hours he was in action against the German panzer divisions.

That day Rommel's long advance was brought sharply to a halt.

Chapter Two

THE DESERT

Rock, Sand and Sun – Desert Rivals –
The Men Who Peopled the Desert

ROCK, SAND AND SUN

The Libyan, or Western, Desert extends westwards from the Nile and southwards from the Mediterranean for perhaps 2,000,000 square miles. It embraces some of the most arid country on earth. Save for some little streams in the small Cyrenaican hills, no river of any sort waters its harsh and desiccated surface. Along the verge of the Mediterranean rain may fall several times in the winter, but a few miles inland there is rain only two or three times a year, and in the deep heart of the desert there may be none at all for several years. When it does fall, however, the desert may become a bog within an hour, making the movement of all wheeled vehicles impossible, a phenomenon which on two occasions was to save the flying remnants of Rommel's army from encirclement and destruction by Montgomery's pursuing divisions.

Thus we note very early that the 'sands of the desert' are for the greater part not truly sand, but dust. To the geologist, they are the 'mechanical products of sub-aerial erosion by exfoliation and wind abrasion.'[1] We shall see all too much of this gritty dust, churned to powder by tanks, guns, vehicles of all sorts and the bursts of shells, enveloping the battlefield of Alamein in clouds as thick as a fog.

1. Professor Fisher, *The Middle East.*

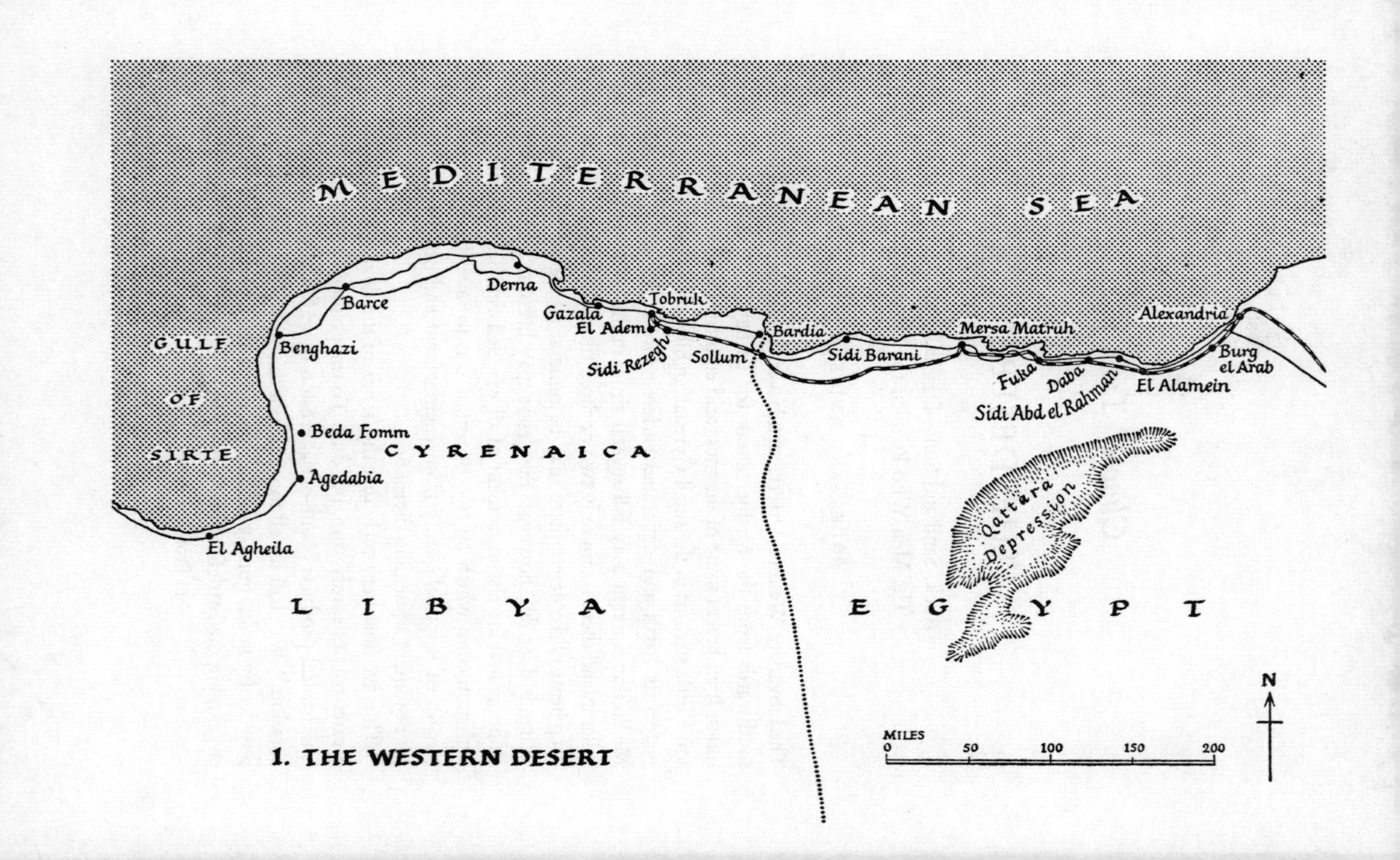

1. THE WESTERN DESERT

Far to the south there rolls the Great Sand Sea, known to the Arabs as 'the Devil's Country', almost impassable to anything but a camel, but over those portions of the desert where the armies fought there stretch great areas of rocky outcrop, stony wastes and loose sand. For the greater part this great waste has a complexion that is of a pale tawny hue flushed with pink, but near the sea, where limestone predominates, it is much paler and littered with whitish stones, and on the shore itself, where Montgomery, Leese and Coningham had their headquarters caravans, and where Winston Churchill and the soldiers of both armies bathed as opportunity was given, the sand is a blinding white against the brilliant blue of the Mediterranean.

For some miles inland rock continues to predominate, thinly overlaid with sand, so that it was terribly hard work for the soldier to scratch himself even the smallest trench or to hew out a shallow pit for a gun. As one journeys inland sand begins to predominate, getting softer and softer, deeper and deeper, so that one may dig easily, but to drive a vehicle becomes more and more difficult.

Here and there the desert erupts into low eminences of bare rock, as on Ruweisat Ridge, Miteiriya Ridge and the little hill called Tel el Eisa, where some of the bloodiest fighting of the war took place and where the harsh rock became littered with corpses rotting in the sun and smothered in black swarms of flies. The counterpart to those small elevations is provided by many *deirs* or 'depressions', gouged out of the desert's countenance, like deep scars. They are large areas of eroded and windswept soil. Some are shallow and saucer-like, as in the Deir el Shein, where 18th Indian Brigade fought a critical action with the Panzers. Others have steep, cliff-like perimeters providing, as in the Munassib Depression, a natural defensive fortress, assailable only by the hardiest troops, such as the North-countrymen of the 50th Division and the high-spirited Maoris from New Zealand.

Largest of all the depressions is that of Qattara, stretching for several thousand square miles, its floor 400 ft below sea level, much of it salty marsh and, because it was virtually impassable by anything but a jeep, providing a barrier to the wide-flanking movements which, in the earlier desert battles, had been the favourite manœuvre of the armoured divisions of British and Germans alike.

Apart from these occasional small elevations and ragged depressions, the greater part of the desert is, to the casual eye, almost quite flat. Not so, however, to the eye of the more experienced soldier, to whom an undulation of only three or four feet might give cover from observation by an enemy, and it was by the skill that he showed in taking advantage of these trifling undulations that the older hand in the desert was known. 'The desert,' he would say to the newcomer, against all the obvious evidence of unaccustomed eyes, 'is not flat.'

Possession of these mere ripples in the land surface, often too insignificant to be marked on even a large-scale map, was of high importance, as giving command over the enemy country. For the same reason, the lines of the 'forward defended localities' (FDLs) of the opposing armies were often far apart, sometimes several miles apart.

It is no surprise that in this great desert there is little life. A few nomad Arab occasionally wander across the waste and somehow manage to raise a little thin barley in the unpromising soil near the sea, but, apart from some scattered settlements along the coast and a few oases deep in the south, no man permanently lives there. After the infrequent rains, the hollow places of the desert become miraculously flushed with green and enamelled with many small flowers; campanulas, dwarf iris, sea lavender, ranunculus and little red poppies eagerly open their petals to the ardent sun. They mature quickly and quickly die. Along the sea-board there is an occasional stunted palm or a wild fig. Otherwise plant life in the desert is confined to a scattering here and there of small, prickly bushes of 'camel thorn', littered with the empty, white shells of snails.

Few animals of any sort are to be seen, but there are some lizards, a rare grey fox or jackal, the changeful chameleon, which the troops tried to keep as pets, the shy jerboa or desert rat, which the British 7th Armoured Division took as its famous emblem, a few larks and brisk little white wagtails, plenty of small scorpions and the black rotund scarab-like scavenging beetle, for which the troops had a rude name. Very occasionally a small herd of wandering gazelle may be seen in the winter, their elegant forms and graceful movements softening for a moment the harshness of the scene.

Dry, austere and monotonous, the desert is also very hot. Near the sea the fierceness of the sun is somewhat moderated, but far inland shade temperatures of 120 degrees are common, though in the northerly plateau, where the fighting took place, they seldom go much above 100 in whatever shade there might be. Despite the heat, however, there is a quality in the air (except at midday) which gives to the climate an exhilarating, almost a champagne quality. The soldiers and airmen who lived and fought there were, except for some special ailments, extremely fit and in lively spirits.

There is approximately an 8-hour day, the sun rising very quickly about 7.30 a.m., its globe huge on the flat horizon and the skyline crimsoned by the irradiation of the floating particles of dust. To the soldier, however, the 'first light' that comes about an hour before sunrise is of greater importance. The multitudinous stars fade, the vault becomes suffused with changing hues, shapes solidify and all movement must cease if the enemy is near. Towards midday the air begins to stifle, invaded by a torpidity that presses down upon one's head and shoulders. As the afternoon comes on, the face of the desert begins to palpitate in the heat haze under the brazen sun. Imaginary lakes, which the wandering Arab called 'Devil's Water', deceive the eye. Distant objects seem to float and move in space as the horizon becomes a quivering mirage and during these hours the soldier is unable to observe or reconnoitre accurately. An hour or two before sundown, as the landscape settles again into solidity, swirling sandstorms are apt to spring up, enveloping everything in a fog of dust.

Then, as the sun slips away and the scorched earth, having no moisture content to retain heat, rapidly cools, the evening breeze springs up and the flies give up their day-long torment; there is a sigh of relief by all living creatures, as though a burden has suddenly been lifted from their shoulders. Night falls and the vault overhead becomes thronged with a myriad stars, glittering with diamond brilliance. Unexpectedly, the nights become very chilly, especially in the winter, and as the troops stand-to at first light it is bitterly cold and the keen wind cuts like a knife.

To the newcomer who found himself alone and the young officer leading a column for the first time, the desert could be a place of real fear: no roads, no houses, no trees, no landmarks of any sort for hundreds of miles. He experienced for the first time the fear of being completely lost and meeting his end either in the arms of the enemy or in the malevolent thirstlands of the deep and empty desert beyond the fringes of the ranging armies. It was quite easy for the uncertain mind to break into panic. The deceitful mirages of the afternoon and the obliterating sandstorms added to the confusion of mind and senses.

By night, the difficulties were greatly increased and, when there was no moon, it was unwise to move more than a few yards from one's trench or truck or tent without taking a compass bearing and returning on the back bearing. Major-General Douglas Wimberley, commander of 51st (Highland) Division, when a newcomer to the desert, going out without a compass at night, took two hours to find his way from his caravan to the mess tent 400 yards away.

To overcome fear of the desert and to learn how to find one's way in its featureless wastes were the first points of training. Away from the coast, the maps, for the greater part, were completely blank spaces, marked only by the squares of the military 'grid', by which map references are given, or here and there by some small feature without significance to the unaccustomed. To locate any position with the precision needed for military operations was often a baffling difficulty. Even the most experienced men would disagree and the air pilot was no less perplexed. This aspect of desert warfare is, therefore, one that we should particularly notice, for in the Battle of Alamein it was to arise critically on several occasions and was to decide the fate of several attacks and the lives of many men. Battalions were required to attack an objective that was a mere pinpoint on a blank map; and the attacks were nearly always at night.

Much was done by artificial means to remedy the blankness of the desert. Cairns and trigonometrical points were erected in any area occupied. Tracks for the main supply routes were marked out with oil drums, but night movement remained hazardous. On a straight, undeviating course the compass and the speedometer would take one reasonably near to one's destination. The 'sun compass' – a simple gnomon mounted on a circular disc and fixed to the wing of a vehicle – was one of the hall-marks of the older desert hand.

DESERT RIVALS

Politically, until the defeat of the German-Italian armies, this Libyan or Western Desert was shared by Egypt and Italy. The boundary between their territories was marked by a 12-ft wide belt of barbed wire that ran from the sea at Sollum southwards for 400 miles, but it was soon to become rent and ragged as the battle flowed to and fro across it.

Beyond 'the wire', as this frontier was called by the British troops, lay the great bulge of Cyrenaica and westward of Cyrenaica was Tripolitania, both Italian colonies. In the early stages of the war the main pre-occupation of the British, whose small and sparsely equipped force was outnumbered by the Italians in the proportion of about ten to one, was to prevent the enemy from seizing Egypt and the Suez Canal, which were vital to Allied strategy in the global war. When it was seen with what unexpected ease the badly led Italians could be overcome, the grand aim was to defeat the enemy forces in both colonies and to march upon the capital city of Tripoli itself, 1,300 miles away. In the result, we went much farther. The grand aim of the enemy was to seize Cairo and Alexandria, when a yet vaster prospect would open up.

Until El Alamein, nearly all the fighting had been in Cyrenaica: between the neighbourhood of Sollum on the east and Agheila, gateway to Tripolitania, on the west. This was due to two facts – that between these two places there were few good defensive positions of any extent and that, the farther an army advanced from its main supply base, the weaker became its power to strike. To advance westward beyond Agheila represented a very severe strain on the supply system of the British, while to advance eastward much beyond Sollum presented a similar problem to the Axis forces.

THE MEN WHO PEOPLED THE DESERT

Such, in brief outline, was the desert in which the armies and their airmen lived and fought. It was, on the whole, a healthy life, but it was not a soft one. To men who lived entirely in the open the absence of rain, snow and mud was a blessing that more than compensated, however, for its lack of comforts. If the sand penetrated your food, your clothes, your hair, your vehicle parts and made red rims round your eyes, that was better than mud. If the heat was stifling at midday and made one dizzy in the afternoon, it was enjoyed at other hours.

The Australians, with their disregard of most outward forms of discipline, often wore little else but shorts and boots, and one might find that the only sign of a major's rank was a crown drawn in chinagraph pencil on his bare, brown shoulders. Indeed, on occasions one might see an Australian aircraft sentry, on the approach of a hostile aircraft, get to his feet and stand up to his mounted bren gun completely naked.

The worst of torments was the inescapable plague of flies. Soft-winged, silent, flying lazily without buzz of movement, they followed wherever man went. They crawled up your nose, fed on the moisture at the corners of your eyes, settled on your lips, flew into your mouth while you spoke. They relished sweat, and as you marched along you would see the back of the man in front of you completely blanketed with a black swarm. They swooped on all food as a hawk upon a partridge. While you ate your meal, one hand was employed continuously in waving them off, but they would, nevertheless, descend upon the morsel that you carried to your mouth. To the wounded who lay out in the desert till help came they were a hellish torture.

The flies enjoyed any particle of blood from the smallest scratch or prick on your body and, together no doubt with some food deficiency, were the cause of the 'desert sores' that infected most men after a few months; the daubs of 'gentian violet' with which the doctors treated these unpleasant sores were a common sight on men's faces, arms and knees. Because of the flies, hygiene was extremely important and in this, as in much else, Eighth Army had a high standard. In the battles of movement or on marches, one walked away to a flank with a spade, but when positions became fixed, as at El Alamein, latrines were dug and their sites frequently moved.

As in all deserts, water was the most precious of all elements. Its provision was a responsibility of the Royal Engineers, after medical tests. It was strictly rationed and was supplied to forward units in small water trucks equipped with sterilising and chlorinating apparatus, and the tank was kept under lock and key after issues had been made. All water was chlorinated and sometimes the only supplies available were saline; hence the milk curdled in the tea and sank to the bottom of the mug. In times of moving operations water was carried on the outside of each vehicle in a *chargal* of thick canvas, in which it kept reasonably cool.

Normally the ration was a gallon a day per man, which had to suffice for drinking, washing of oneself and one's clothes, cooking, and the radiator of one's vehicle. When far from water points the ration fell to half a gallon, and a man was then hard pressed. In the Alamein position, which was near to pure water supplies, the ration was generally one-and-a-half gallons.

If the unit was in a stationary position, half the ration went to the cookhouse. With care, a quart was sufficient for washing. After the morning wash it was left in your canvas camp basin (or the half of a petrol tin if not an officer) all day. For the evening wash the soap suds were skimmed off and it was used again. Another skim next morning and it was poured into a petrol tin to accumulate for washing clothes. Finally, after the sand had been allowed to settle, it was carefully decanted into the radiator.

The British soldier has usually been well fed, but in the Western Desert, though his food was ample, it was nearly always hard tack. Bully beef and hard biscuits was his staple fare, but he also had some tinned bacon, not very palatable, some tinned meat and vegetable ration, tinned butter, tinned milk and, of course, tea, which he brewed whenever he had the chance. Fresh provisions were unknown to forward troops, except for some occasional Egyptian onions. The quartermasters of the Highland Division usually managed somehow to get enough oatmeal for porridge by swopping it for the occasional rice ration. The harsh and acrid 'V' cigarette was, for most men, the only smoke.

On the few occasions when positions became fixed, units were able to establish cookhouses and distribute hot meals to their men, but the typical method of cooking in the desert was for a soldier, or a group of soldiers, to 'brew up' his own food in a billy-can, which was to be seen hanging from a hook on many a jeep and truck. Thomas Atkins brewed up by means of a 'desert fire', which was made by simply mixing a little petrol with sand in an empty petrol tin and setting light to it: an operation by no means without mortal danger to the unskilled. The desert fire could not, of course, be lit in close proximity to the enemy.

The Germans (but not the Italians) were better than we at providing forward tank crews and other forward troops with a hot meal. The German and Italian soldiers also enjoyed a more varied ration than ours, their tinned tomatoes and other vegetables, when we captured them, being found good. They, or at least their officers, also had good supplies of wines.

At night the soldier's bed was the ground and a very hard bed it could be where rock was predominant. When not in close contact with the enemy, most men and officers slept under a small bivouac sheet, or 'bivvy', or else underneath a lorry, and officers usually had a light Houndsfield bed, standing a few inches off the ground. Tank crews slept beside their tanks, sometimes under tarpaulins slung pent-wise from it. General Auchinleck, like an infantry officer in the front line, slept on the ground in the open and so did several other generals.

The soldier thus led a fairly hard but a healthy life. Apart from the prevalent desert sores, which were ugly, vexatious and stubborn, but only occasionally disabling, there were no widespread sicknesses, the principal being bowel diseases of varying degrees of severity (from mild forms of 'Gippy tummy' to the more deadly ones of amoebic and bacillary dysentery due to the multitudes of flies), some malaria, a certain amount of sandfly fever (a prostrating and sometimes fatal infection from the tiniest of flies) and a strange and widespread persistence of jaundice among officers.

For about three months of the year the weather was cool enough to wear battledress, but for the rest of the year khaki drill, or 'KD', was the rule. This meant shorts and shirt for most of Eighth Army and their comrades of the Desert Air Force, but many commanding officers required all officers and men to wear slacks instead of shorts. Slacks, though not so cool as shorts, were a more sensible dress in a climate where there were so many things to bite or scratch you and they greatly reduced the danger of desert sores and malaria.

The beret had not yet come in as the general headdress, except for the Royal Tank Regiment and some armoured-car units; the uniform wear, when it was not necessary to don steel helmets, was the impracticable fatigue or 'side' cap. Most officers, however, preferred the peaked Service cap. The Scottish and Australian regiments had their own special headgear. The jaunty bonnets or glengarries of the 'Jocks' of 51st (Highland) Division, who arrived shortly before Alamein, and the kilt worn by some of their pipers, gave a touch of *panache* to the otherwise drab scene.

A different sort of *panache*, however, was contributed by the officers of some of the older desert regiments, particularly of the armoured units. The delight of the cartoonist 'Jon' of *Eighth Army News*, these officers had acquired a notoriety for the informality of their dress. Corduroy trousers, civilian-style pullovers and coloured scarves were the hallmarks of a fraternity – for these 'old desert hands' of pre-Alamein were very much a fraternity, bound together by ties of comradeship in many a critical action – who took their campaigning in a gay and gallant spirit, and they were also the hallmarks of an army that was composed mostly of civilians. Their 'desert boots', low-cut, of suede, soled with rubber, became fairly general wear for officers throughout the army and set a fashion that afterwards became adopted in civilian life.

Most remarkable of all their garments, however, was the Hebron coat, usually called a *poshteen*, from its resemblance to the more elegant Indian coat of that name; it was a shaggy sheepskin garment worn to keep at bay the biting wind of the desert dawn and was the hallmark of the old desert hand. It was off-white in colour and could be seen a mile away.

Thus, sometimes the only article of military uniform worn by an officer was his cap. When General Montgomery was appointed to command Eighth Army shortly before Alamein, it was quite expected that, with his reputation for austerity and sharp words, he would sternly forbid this informality in dress; in fact, to some extent, he fell for it himself.

These few general observations will serve to show that the troops of Eighth Army led a very masculine and exclusive life. The desert was all their own and there was no one else in it but the enemy, who led a similar kind of existence. There were no billets, no pubs, no girls, no civilians of any sort and precious few 'amenities' or 'welfare' until one went back to the Nile Delta on local leave or rest or on a course. There was no home leave to Britain at all and before the end of operations many officers and men had been away from home for four years or even more. The flies, the all-penetrating sand, the heat, the hard tack, the tainted water were the background to daily life, and the ordeals of battle its forefront.

Yet the spirit of all was extremely high; men were all the fitter and their morale all the more buoyant for being cut off from civilian contacts and for being cast out in the great spaces on a great enterprise.

There has rarely been any army so bound together in a sense of comradeship and animated with so much pride in themselves as Eighth Army and the Desert Air Force in Egypt, and those who preceded them in title. They had a tradition all their own and of their own making. It was never quite the same after Africa. They were conscious that they were the only British troops fighting the Germans on land anywhere in the world and that the eyes of the nation were on them – the eyes of a hard-pressed nation groping in the black-out, severely rationed for food, clothing and all the

Montgomery in front of a Grant tank

Coningham discussing air support proposals with Montgomery.

Immediately after Montgomery had disclosed his plan to Corps and Divisional commanders on 15 September, the generals of 10 Corps discussed it among themselves. *L* to *R:* Briggs, Freyberg, Gatehouse, Lumsden, Gairdner

Leese, Montgomery, Lumsden, Walsh (holding map-board).

material amenities of life and enduring, in many cities and towns, the ordeal of the bomb by night.

All in all, therefore, the desert war was not a scene of fretful discontent and disillusion. There was a keen exhilaration and a sense of adventure in it. The arms of both sides were unstained by acts of barbarity or dishonour. There were no civilians. Soldier met soldier on land or in the air as in some vast amphitheatre reserved to themselves. If one had to make war, the desert was the ideal place. There was no mud, no snow, and ice, no restriction to free movement, no sense of confinement in the great space. One could fling wide one's arms and stretch far one's vision.

Chapter Three

THE FIGHT BEGINS

Early Operations – Ebb and Flow – The General Strategic Position – The Shape of the Army – The Air Arm – The Aspect of the Enemy – The 'Alamein Line' – Rommel Halted

EARLY OPERATIONS

Fighting had been in progress in the Western Desert since the autumn of 1940. Britain at that time, by treaty rights, maintained small armed forces in Egypt, as she did also in Palestine, Iraq and other territories in the enormous area known as the Middle East, over all of which General Sir Archibald Wavell, one of the most able commanders and the most noble-hearted of men, was Commander-in-Chief.

The Middle East, with its great oilfields, its control over the sea, air and land routes to the Indies and Australasia and its proximity to politically sensitive areas, was of immense importance to Britain and to the lands of the Commonwealth and Empire who, after the fall of France in June, faced the enormous strength of the Nazis and the Fascists alone. While the bulk of the British Army, scantily armed with old weapons after Dunkirk, hourly awaited the expected German invasion of England, only a small force of 36,000 men stood guard in Egypt.

With the fall of France, Mussolini, hoping to snatch some of the spoils of Hitler's victories, had dragged Italy into the war at the

German heels. Upon Wavell and his scanty, partially equipped forces in Egypt there thus suddenly fell a heavy responsibility; for, as we have seen, the Italian colony of Cyrenaica lay westward of the belt of barbed wire that fringed the Egyptian border, and its twin colony of Tripolitania stretched away yet farther west. Very large Italian land and air forces were assembled in these colonies, under the command of Marshal Graziani, far outnumbering all the British and Allied forces that Wavell had at his command in the whole of the Middle East.

It was fortunate, however, that the slender British forces in Egypt included an improvised 'mobile division' which, in so far as he had been permitted by an unsympathetic higher command before the war, had been trained in the spirit and the tactical elements of modern tank warfare by Major-General P. C. S. Hobart, one of the formative thinkers and practitioners in that adventurous field. This stripling 'mobile division', at that time commanded by Major-General M. O'Moore Creagh, was to become the celebrated 7th Armoured Division, known to friend and foe alike by its proud badge of the Desert Rat.

In September 1940, Graziani, hoping to add Egypt to Italy's crown, crossed the frontier with about 100,000 men, supported by an air force greatly outnumbering our own.

Advancing with extreme nervousness, he halted at Sidi Barrani, well within the frontier but still some seventy miles from the main British positions, and there, feeble of purpose, he built a series of fortified camps, manned by 80,000 men and 120 tanks.

On 9 December the British Cyrenaica Force[1] of 30,000 men, composed mainly of the 7th Armoured Division and the 4th Indian Division, under Lieutenant-General R. N. O'Connor, after a long, difficult and daring indirect approach march by night, descended into their midst and utterly routed them, capturing 38,000 prisoners, 73 tanks and 237 guns. It was an almost incredible and totally unexpected victory.

Exploiting with great audacity this sparkling success, which had been intended as a mere raid, the little general harried the demoralised

1. Later the Western Desert Force.

enemy right across Cyrenaica, with further enormous hauls of prisoners, tanks and guns, and finally, after a breathless forced march across the desert with the scantiest of forces, he cut off what remained of the Italian army at Beda Fomm, south of Benghazi, on 5 February, and forced their surrender. In the two months of an entirely extempore campaign he had captured 130,000 prisoners, 400 tanks and more than 1,200 guns; the cost to the British had been 1,744 killed, wounded and missing.

To the people at home, gripped in a hard winter, peppered by bombs, living on short rations and groping at night through the pall of the black-out, these sensational victories came as a tremendous tonic. O'Connor's campaign had been a brilliant example of *blitzkreig* tactics, pressed forward with great resourcefulness in the face of severe supply difficulties and shortages of equipment. But it had been waged against an enemy who from the outset had shown his inferiority alike in morale, equipment and training and it was to be the end of the easy successes.

O'Connor's small army paused with its van at Agheila, on the Tripolitanian border, and there seemed nothing to prevent them from marching victoriously upon distant Tripoli itself – a consummation which, if it could have been achieved before the arrival of the Germans, would have saved two years of further fighting in the desert, and completely altered the strategic situation in the Mediterranean. But political considerations put an end to such hopes.

Greece was now being threatened and we had promised in 1939 to go to her aid if called upon. We did so now, scraping together all the land, air and sea forces that we could, and O'Connor's advance, with all its dazzling prospects, was halted. Those who have since criticised Mr Churchill for this decision should bear in mind that it was not adopted by the War Cabinet until encouraging reports from Greece and from the Middle East had been received from Mr Eden, Field-Marshal Sir John Dill, Field-Marshal Smuts and Wavell himself, though the Chiefs of Staff at home were firmly opposed to it. Thus another Dunkirk, another Norway was the lot of our troops.

The obligations of honour led not only to a minor disaster in

Greece but also to a severe trial in Africa. O'Connor himself went on leave, 7th Armoured Division was sent back to the Delta and 6th Australian Division (newly arrived) to Greece. Their places were taken by a new commander and new, inexperienced divisions who had had no collective training in the desert; the solitary armoured brigade was a scratch force, equipped mainly with captured Italian tanks. Our air strength was also greatly reduced. Cyrenaica became a static command with the forces widely dispersed.

It happened that the moment when O'Connor's advance was allowed to fizzle out was just the moment chosen by Hitler to send a German armoured force to succour the desert Italians in their despair. To command them he sent Lieutenant-General Erwin Rommel. A new, dynamic and totally unexpected force burst upon the arid desert scene.

Rommel, who had made his name in the 'blitz' campaign against France as commander of an armoured division, was, whatever his defects, a leader and opportunist of great thrust and initiative. He caught the attenuated British forces near the frontier off their guard and inadequately supported in the air, and sent them hurrying back to the Egyptian frontier in April 1941. Virtually all the ground that O'Connor had won in the winter was lost and he himself, hurrying back from Cairo, was taken prisoner in one of these dramatic minor incidents that characterised the fluid desert war. Tobruk, which Rommel failed to capture, now began its epic siege.

The Germans, with two armoured and one infantry division, brought into the desert war two vital new factors: they brought troops who were vastly superior to most of the Italians then in the field – brave, highly trained, aggressive, resourceful and tremendously quick off the mark – and they brought a quantity of war equipment that was superior to anything that we ourselves had. This superiority was to become especially noticeable in the later models of their Messerschmitt fighter aircraft, their tanks, their anti-tank guns and their tracked and semi-tracked vehicles, and this superiority in equipment they enjoyed for the next eighteen months.

Outstanding in this array of fighting equipment were the tanks of 15th and 21st Panzer Divisions, formidable and efficient engines of war which, in the fighting that swayed backwards and forwards across Cyrenaica in this period, became factors of dominant tactical importance. They will be described later.

In all these eighteen months of ebb and flow our own armoured regiments, with their little 2-pdr popguns, their less resistant armour and sometimes (as with the Crusaders) their mechanically unreliable tanks, fought with dash, gallantry and often self-immolation against a heavier enemy and against highly penetrating anti-tank guns. But it was not only by this technical disadvantage that they were handicapped; for, no less damaging to their prospects in battle, was the deterioration that began to ensue in the tactical methods of superior commanders, who, in the handling of armour, forsook the fundamental rule of concentration of force.

Shortly after withdrawal to the Egyptian frontier, General Sir Claude Auchinleck succeeded Wavell as C-in-C Middle East, and on 26 September he reorganised the Western Desert Force under a new command which was designated Eighth Army, under General Sir Alan Cunningham. Very soon afterwards (9 October), as one result of extensive reorganisation of the Middle East air forces by Air Marshal Tedder, No. 204 Group, RAF, was reconstituted for the air support of the Army in the field, first as Air Headquarters Western Desert and then as the Western Desert Air Force, to become famous under the brilliant leadership of Air Vice-Marshal Arthur Coningham, known to all as 'Mary', because he was a New Zealander, though not a Maori. Both the British and the German-Italian armies and air forces became considerably augmented.

In November the new Army, supported by its comrades of the WDAF, began its first offensive, known as Operation 'Crusader'. In a long, confused and gruelling battle of tanks, infantry and air forces, marked by inferior generalship on both sides but resolved by the tenacity of the regimental officer and man, and by the personal intervention of Auchinleck, Tobruk was relieved, and Rommel, completely outfought and barely escaping complete destruction, was forced back to Agheila again, whence he had started. The credit for this half-forgotten victory is aptly expressed by General de Guingand's tribute to 'this gallant army who, although equipped with inferior tools, by sheer courage, dogged determination and spirit, defeated some of the finest and most experienced troops in the German Army.'[1]

Once again our forces, greatly extended, were reduced also in strength by the dispatch of troops to the Far East. The Axis air forces were heavily reinforced and air superiority changed hands.

Resilient and resourceful, Rommel, the 'Desert Fox', very quickly resumed the offensive and in January 1942 once more surprised the strung-out British with swift and penetrating strokes. This time, however, instead of going right back to the Egyptian frontier, Eighth Army formed a good defensive front halfway, with its northern flank near Gazala. Lieutenant-General Neil Ritchie was now in command.

This position Rommel attacked on 26 May with great vigour, with formidable new tanks and with air forces considerably outnumbering our own, and there was another long, bitter and critical battle in which Rommel once again escaped destruction by a hair's breadth; but by brilliant opportunism, profiting from the lamentable generalship of his opponents, he turned an impending defeat into a remarkable victory.

The British, not routed, nor even dispirited, but convincingly defeated in a tactical sense, were obliged by the speed of the German advance to abandon one defensive position after another, often fighting their way out after encirclement, as 50th Division and the New Zealanders did until, finally, on 1 July they stood at bay in the last defensive position of all short of the Nile and only sixty miles from Alexandria – El Alamein. They were saved from any greater disaster and kept as 'an army in being' by Auchinleck, who, while still bearing his large responsibilities as C-in-C for the whole of Middle East, personally assumed command of Eighth Army in the field for the second time.

The Battle of Gazala was a sharp tactical reverse for the British, due wholly to its mismanagement by the Army and Corps

1. *Operation Victory*. A vivid description of this battle is given in R. J. Crisp's *Brazen Chariots*.

commanders. To the good people at home it was hard news to bear. To Mr Churchill, closeted with President Roosevelt far away in Washington, the surrender of Tobruk by the commander of 2nd South African Division was a grievous blow, for the little maritime fortress, though its military importance was small, had in its first siege become a symbol of heroic resistance.

Egypt now seemed to be at the feet of the enemy and the whole Middle East seemed imperilled. The Navy vacated Alexandria and in Cairo precautionary steps were taken for the move of GHQ. Mussolini himself flew over to Cyrenaica (in a Red Cross aircraft, heavily escorted by fighters), ready for a triumphal entry into the streets of Cairo.

EBB AND FLOW

Thus, until the occupation of the Alamein position, the war in the desert had been swaying to and fro between Agheila on the west and Sollum on the east, with a great deal of severe fighting and with tactical successes won by both sides but with no decisive victory by either. There had been many audacious little raids and other minor operations by land and sea, chiefly by British forces, but they had no appreciable effect on the main course of events. Most of these side-shows were wasted effort. Far away in the south, however, the Long Range Desert Group, best of them all, living a hardy life in the lonely and waterless wastes of the deep desert, did very valuable scouting work and some useful raids.

In the air mastery had not yet been won by either side and the British and their enemies alike were bombed and machine-gunned from the air, requiring tanks and vehicles to be well dispersed on the ground, but otherwise having little influence on the battle as a whole. The effective integration of battlefield operations by ground and air forces had not yet been properly worked out. In contrast to the passive attitude towards hostile aircraft of troops in training at home, the desert soldier stood up to them and fired at them with whatever weapon he had.

The RAF's bombing of enemy ports and shipping was quite

another matter and, together with the unceasing attention by the Royal Navy to the enemy's supply ships and transports, was in due time to have a very considerable effect indeed on the course of operations.

THE GENERAL STRATEGIC POSITION

After this cursory review of the desert operations before Alamein, it is time that, in order to assess the value of the forthcoming operations, we looked briefly at the general strategic position in 1942 and took stock more exactly of those forces that were destined to play so decisive a part in the shaping of it.

Until the autumn, the year 1942 had marked the blackest possible days for the friends of freedom in their fight against the Axis forces throughout the world. Everywhere we were suffering heavy defeats, heartbreaking losses and even humiliations. Nearly all Europe was dominated by Hitler, the German forces were biting deep into the heart of Russia, the American fleet had been crippled at Pearl Harbour, Singapore had surrendered, the Japanese had swept victoriously over the lands and seas of the Far East, and the Americans and British were suffering enormous losses from the German submarines in the Atlantic. The skies of all the world looked black, relieved only by the small gleams of a few minor successes and the one larger success of the American naval victory over the Japanese at Midway Island in the Pacific. To the long list of calamities had now been added the loss of Greece and the tactical defeat of the British at Gazala.

In the Mediterranean an unceasing struggle was being waged by land, sea and air. The German-Italian forces held most of the northern shores. All the German land and air forces in the Mediterranean sphere were under the command of Field-Marshal Albert Kesselring, who was both Commander-in-Chief South and Air C-in-C, Rommel's Army, however, being expressly excluded. The British and their allies held Egypt and the Levant.

Between the two lay Malta, the little island heroically defying assault from the air and close blockade from the sea. Garrison and

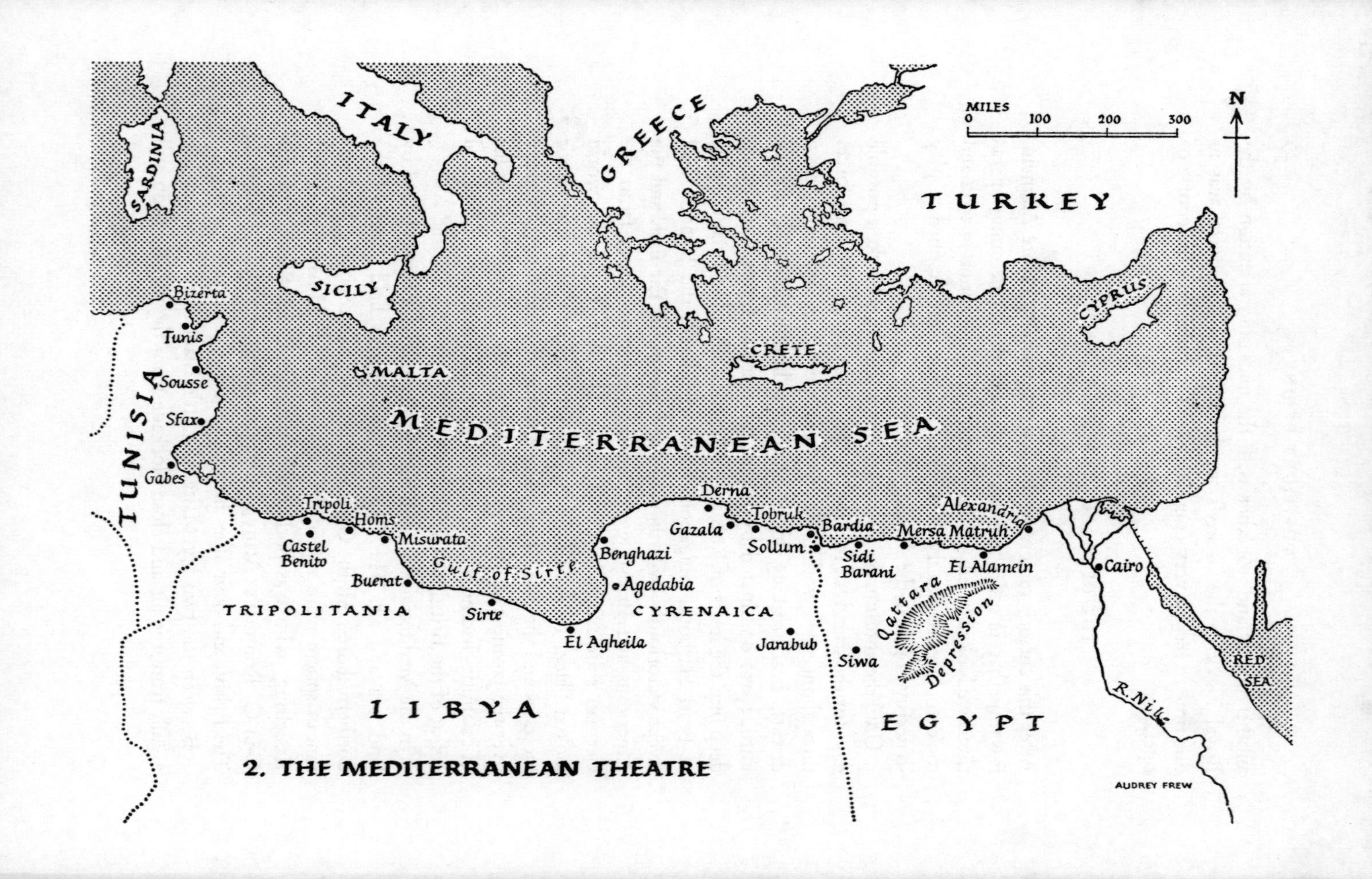

2. THE MEDITERRANEAN THEATRE

civilians were living stoically on semi-starvation rations. The Governor, General Lord Gort, VC, was pedalling about the bomb wreckage on a bicycle, to conserve the precious and precarious supplies of petrol brought to the island at fearful risk by our merchant ships and their escorts. We shall lay special emphasis on Malta, because its vital relationship to the desert campaign has not been generally understood. Strategically, not the least reason for requiring Rommel to be thrown back as quickly as possible was the need to save Malta – a requirement that was emphatically and repeatedly urged upon the military command in Egypt.

A thorn in the side of the enemy, Malta was of very great strategic importance to the whole war effort. Had it fallen to the enemy, virtually the whole of the Mediterranean would have been closed to us and we could no longer have fought our way through that sea, as we often did, thus saving forty-five days and 15,000 miles on the passage round the Cape. The island was also a vital staging post for aircraft reinforcements on their long flight from Britain.

What is of most interest to us, however, was Malta's close relationship with Egypt and the Western Desert and their mutual interdependence. From Malta there sallied out the submarines, light naval craft and aircraft that preyed unceasingly upon the enemy ships carrying supplies and reinforcements from Europe to the Axis forces in the desert. Correspondingly, the airfields and ports of the African coast, if in our hands, provided bases from which our air and sea forces could powerfully help the defence of the island. Of great importance among these were the airfields of Cyrenaica, particularly the Martuba group, from which the approaches to Malta were within the range of the RAF. These airfields were now, since Rommel's last advance, in the hands of the enemy, and the case of the little island was daily becoming more desperate.

That position was, of course, seen by the Germans and Italians as clearly as by the Allies. It was the agreed Axis policy that, after Rommel's success at the Battle of Gazala, he should halt on the Egyptian frontier, while Kesselring and the Italians mounted an attack on Malta with all the force at their command. With the removal of the main barrier to Rommel's reinforcement and supply, his army could be rapidly built up in sufficient strength to overcome Eighth Army and he could then sweep forward into Egypt. The British would be obliged to abandon the Mediterranean and the way would be open to a still more glittering prospect in the field of grand strategy; for the shape of Rommel's thrust into Egypt bore a significant relationship to the deeper thrust that the German armies were making through Russia towards the Caucasus. If both these thrusts continued and converged, all the vast oil fields of Persia, Irak and the Persian Gulf would be lost to the Allies, the Suez Canal would pass to the control of the Axis and the alarming prospect arise of the Axis joining hands with the Japanese.

The capture of Malta, if it could have been achieved, was, therefore, of capital importance both to Rommel's forces and to Axis strategy, and would have been calamitous to the Allies. Fortunately, Kesselring's intention was frustrated by Rommel himself who, having reached the Egyptian border, believed that he had Eighth Army on the run and that only one more effort was needed to overcome it decisively and to place all Egypt within his grasp. Hitler, promoting him to field-marshal, approved his proposals for pushing on and Mussolini consented. The assault on Malta was postponed and, indeed, never took place. It was one of Rommel's many errors of judgement. His strategic faculty was inferior to his tactical, which itself, though he had been an infantryman, was of high quality only in the handling of the moving armoured battle. As an American military critic, Brigadier-General S. L. A. Marshall, has said, Alamein, like Stalingrad and the Marne, was a 'monument of the supreme folly of over-extension'. All three, be it noted, were German follies.

Such in broad outline was the strategic outlook on the last day of June 1942 when Eighth Army hastened back into the Alamein position, only just ahead of the Germans, and as the Desert Air Force leapfrogged back to rear airfields.

THE SHAPE OF THE ARMY

For the benefit of readers not familiar with these matters, it will be helpful to our understanding of the events to follow to give a brief explanation at this stage of the structure and composition of the armies that temporarily peopled the desert at the time of Alamein. We shall look first at the British forces.

The basic formation of an army in the field was the division. Commanded by a major-general, it consisted at that time of from 13,500 troops in an armoured division to 17,000 in an infantry division, when at full strength, which was rarely the case. A division was in itself a balanced and complete army of all arms on a small scale, except for the absence or presence of the tank element.

The infantry division, at full complement, consisted of three brigades, each brigade being composed of three battalions. The assault strength of the battalion lay mainly in its four all-too-small 'rifle companies', supported by platoons equipped with anti-tank guns, small trench-mortars and the light, tracked bren-gun carrier. Thus the infantry had a variety of weapons but never enough bayonets in the assault.

Even at full strength, a battalion could put only about 450 men into an assault (half that number in the first wave). It was the rifle companies that usually took the brunt of casualties and after two major assaults the battalion was usually too weak for another. Each division had also a heavy machine-gun battalion, equipped with forty-eight Vickers guns.

Besides the infantry brigades, the division had three regiments of field artillery, totalling seventy-two 25-pdr guns when at full establishment, an anti-tank regiment Royal Artillery, and a light anti-aircraft regiment of bofors guns. All the artillery was under the direction of the Commander Royal Artillery (CRA), who was a brigadier and who could, at extremely short notice, concentrate the fire of all his field guns on one point if need be.

Until shortly before Alamein the army had no anti-tank guns, either in the artillery or the infantry, heavier than the little pre-war

2-pdr, but by the time of the main battle most of the 2-pdrs had been replaced by the new 6-pdr, a fine little gun that, at close quarters, could account for most enemy tanks then in the field, but which required steady nerves and stout hearts.

The division's fighting components were completed by its three field companies and one field park company of Royal Engineers, whose gallantry and steadiness in the dangerous minefields of Alamein were to open the gates to victory.

On the administrative side, the division had three field ambulances of the Royal Army Medical Corps, a unit of the Royal Corps of Signals, supply and transport companies of the Royal Army Service Corps (who in the fluid desert war often had to fight as well as to deliver ammunition, rations, petrol and stores), repair workshops of the newly-formed Royal Electrical and Mechanical Engineers, a red-capped unit of the Corps of Military Police, recruited largely from road scouts of the Royal Automobile Club and the Automobile Association, who in the minefields of Alamein behaved with exemplary courage, and other non-combatant elements.

The headquarters staff of a division consisted of a few General Staff Officers under a GSO 1, dealing with operations, and an administrative staff under an Assistant Adjutant and Quartermaster-General, both lieutenant-colonels.

An armoured division differed from an infantry division mainly in the fact that it consisted, normally, of one armoured brigade and one motorised infantry brigade. The armoured brigade comprised three 'armoured regiments' and one motorised infantry battalion. The infantry battalion went into action with the tanks, either on foot or in bren-carriers. The armoured regiments were drawn from the Royal Armoured Corps and might be either *battalions* of the Royal Tank Regiment or else cavalry or yeomanry *regiments*.[1] There was a subtle difference between the two. The number of tanks in each armoured regiment at the time of Alamein under the Middle East establishment, when at full strength, was fifty-two. The regiment (or battalion), in addition to its headquarters, was organised in three squadrons of four troops, with normally three tanks in each troop.

1. All became 'regiments' late in 1945.

Until Alamein, when the first Sherman tanks had arrived from America, the British tanks were at a large disadvantage in battle with the Germans', though much superior to the Italian M13's. The Crusader was mechanically unreliable, the old Matilda 'I' tank was too slow for desert warfare, the American Stuart (or 'Honey') was designed merely as a very fast 'light cavalry' tank. All were under-gunned, the British-made tanks mounting only a 2-pdr. Their armour-plating (except for the old Matilda) was somewhat inferior to that of the Germans in resistance and their guns could fire only solid shot. Thus our tanks had to close to about 600 yards before they could hope to kill, whereas the Germans could stand off at 2,000 yards or more and knock out our tanks as they approached. Only in the American Grant, some of which we received in time for Gazala, were we able to compete on nearly equal gun terms with the Germans, but the Grant suffered from the disadvantage that its 75 mm gun was mounted in a side sponson and so could not fire all round.

A very important element of the armoured division, paradoxical though it may appear, was its infantry brigade. This took two forms. One was the 'lorried infantry' brigade, who were ordinary infantry transported by lorries; The Queen's and the Royal Sussex were so equipped for 7th and 10th Armoured Divisions. The other was exemplified in 1st Armoured Division by 7th Motor Brigade; like the motor infantry battalions in each armoured brigade, they were specialised, highly mobile troops, who will be seen at closer quarters on several occasions.

Another special feature of the armoured division was its armoured-car regiment. It had no part in a pitched battle, but was for reconnaissance, exploitation in the pursuit, covering a withdrawal and so on. Otherwise, the armoured division was constructed much the same as an infantry division, with its own artillery, engineers and service elements, though there were slight variations in strengths and in equipment. They tended to adopt a cavalry terminology, so that, for example, the 'field company' of Royal Engineers became a 'field squadron' and a 'platoon commander' became a 'troop leader'.

These are the formations with which we need to be most familiar for an understanding of events. There were, however, many variations of the official establishments, either caused by battle or duly authorised. Thus the New Zealanders and 50th Division each had only two brigades, due to heavy casualties before Alamein, but, on the other hand, 7th and 10th Armoured Divisions each (at Alamein) had two armoured brigades and 7th had three armoured car regiments; several divisions had more than their official element of artillery, in which Eighth Army was particularly strong.

Above the division was the Corps, commanded by a lieutenant-general. Except for its headquarter staff, it had no prescribed establishment of troops and might consist of any number of divisions or unattached brigades and various 'corps troops'. At Alamein there were three corps – 10th, 13th and 30th. An important element of the corps troops were the Medium Regiments, Royal Artillery, equipped with 4.5-inch or 5.5-inch guns with fairly long ranges and firing projectiles of 55 lb and 100 lb respectively. They were worked very hard and did brilliant service.

The corps commander, once Eighth Army was properly reorganised by General Montgomery, had great resources for concentration and reinforcement of effort. Thus, with the remarkable flexibility of the British artillery, the Corps CRA could concentrate all the field and medium guns on one task, the Chief Engineer could similarly group all the RE resources, and the supply and transport columns could be pooled for one major operation (as happened on a large scale on one occasion).

Above the corps was the Army, which in turn had its own heads of arms and services and its own 'army troops' (as for example, the heavy anti-aircraft regiments), and various specialist units, such as 1st Camouflage Company, RE. The chief staff officer at both the Army and the Corps headquarters was a Brigadier General Staff (BGS) and a brigadier was also responsible for the administrative 'A' and 'Q' services.

Gatehouse expounding the battle plan to the HQ Squadron, 10th Armd. Div. on 23 October

Briggs and Custance before Kidney Ridge, 27 October

Morshead

Below: A Highland Division group. *L to R:* Urquhart (GSO 1), Wimberley (GOC), Denholm-Young (Chief Signals Officer), Alec Fraser (Div. Sigs.)

THE AIR ARM

For their support in the air Eighth Army had immediately at hand, and virtually part of itself, the Western Desert Air Force under 'Mary' Coningham. By the time of Alamein the Desert Air Force, as it was more usually called, had been considerably augmented and it included seven American squadrons – four of Mitchell medium bombers and three of Warhawk fighters. Its Order of Battle is given in Appendix B. The main fighter airfields were in the Amiriya region, near Alexandria.

In glaring contrast to the acid relations between Rommel and Major-General Hans Seidemann, the *Fliegerführer* Afrika, a close and intimate partnership was enjoyed between Eighth Army and the Desert Air Force – a partnership that became a brotherhood. The Army Commander said what the programme was and what he required in air support. Coningham resolved these requirements into tactical air terms according to his resources.

This close partnership between the Army and the DAF, however, must not obscure the contributions to the joint effort made by the other Air Forces under the command of Arthur Tedder as AOC-in-C. The Desert Air Force under Coningham, Air Headquarters Egypt under Air Vice-Marshal W. A. McClaughrey, the British and American heavy bombers of No. 205 Group under Air Commodore A. P. Ritchie and No. 201 (Naval Co-operation) Group under Air Vice-Marshal H. P. Lloyd all existed for different purposes, but when need arose Tedder applied them all to the common purpose. Thus No. 205 Group was frequently at Coningham's service; Coningham did not have operational command of it, but it was he who set the target pattern for Ritchie's Wellingtons. Similarly, he was able to enlist the invaluable flare-dropping Albacores of the Fleet Air Arm as lamplighters to illuminate the targets of our night bombers.

Tedder's forces had for some time been equipped with some American as well as British aircraft, manned by British or Dominion air crews, but American-manned squadrons began to arrive at the end of June. At the end of July, 57 Fighter Group arrived with their Warhawks (P.40's). Next month came the Liberators (B.24's) of 98 (Heavy) Bombardment Group and the Mitchells (B.25's) of 12 (Medium) Bombardment Group. In command of the Americans was Major-General Lewis Brereton, who was as keen a disciple of co-operation as Tedder.

The application of air power to the needs of the battle were constantly under Tedder's own eye and he relied upon team work among all his forces to achieve concentration of effort. He was a brilliant innovator in the functional handling of air forces, as Coningham was of their tactical use. From this, in spite of the mixed nationalities and equipments that made up his command, there derived the impression of a single cohesive force which was our greatest strength against an enemy who, in the Mediterranean as a whole, far outnumbered the Allies.

Behind the fighting formations of Eighth Army there gradually developed an impressive array of administrative and service establishments, both Army and RAF – workshops of all sorts, great supply depots, casualty clearing stations, General Hospitals in Cairo or its neighbourhood, dockyard services, reinforcements camps, training schools of every description. The greater part of these impressive base installations, which supplied Eighth Army with all its gear and tackle for victory, was the kingdom of Lieutenant-General Sir Wilfred Lindsell, one of the greatest of administrative generals.

THE ASPECT OF THE ENEMY

We must now look cursorily on 'the other side of the hill' and see the outlines of the enemy as they were at the time of Alamein, remembering that, basically, their organisation in divisions was similar to our own.

We have seen already with how little difficulty the small British army under O'Connor had defeated an Italian army that outnumbered them enormously. Later on, however, the quality of the Italian troops improved and the fashion of deriding them all is by no means a true indication of their qualities. Some of the divisions fought well on occasions. The best of their troops generally were their artillery: it was no fun being shelled by them. The Folgore Parachute Division was as good as the average German division and better at night work, at which the Germans, unlike the British, did not excel. The Bersaglieri had fought extremely well at Sidi Rezegh, and Trento could give a good account of themselves also.

Of the two armoured divisions – Ariete and Littorio – Ariete were the better and were well thought of by the Germans. These armoured divisions, if unable to stand up to British tanks for long in pitched battle with their inferior M13's, fulfilled many valuable tasks, took some of the burden off the Germans and, with their three machine guns and one 47 mm gun firing high explosive, were a serious threat to infantry. Although some of the Italian troops were undoubtedly of poor quality, it may be said in general that they could fight well at a distance, repelling British attacks more than once, but collapsed if their opponents got to close quarters.

There were three Italian army corps – 10th, 20th and 21st. The 20th, under Lieutenant-General De Stephanis, comprised the two armoured divisions and the Trieste, which was their motorised infantry division. There were eight Italian divisions in all, but they were of a lower establishment than a British division and usually below strength. An outline Order of Battle of the Italians is in Appendix D and of the Germans in Appendix C.

The heart of the enemy strength, of course, from early 1941 onwards, was the German element – the *Panzerarmee*. Above all, it lay in the tanks of the German Africa Corps (*Deutsche Afrika Korps*, or *DAK*), composed of 15th and 21st Panzer Divisions. These Divisions were armed with first-class tanks that had very resistant armour and guns that fired high explosive as well as solid shot, the latter often having a steel cap or a tungsten-carbide core for extra penetration. Their chief tanks were the *Panzerkampfwagen* Mark III and the *Pzkw* Mark IV, both very formidable fighting vehicles, to which various improvements were made as the war progressed. The emblem of the *DAK* was a palm tree and, of course, all German tanks and vehicles were sprinkled with the crooked cross of the reversed swastika.

For its infantry element, the *Panzerarmee* had the famous 90th Light Division, fine fighting troops composed largely of Panzer Grenadiers. Just before Alamein these were augmented by 164 Light Division (identified by the crossed swords that are the mark of Meissen porcelain), and by the tough Ramcke Parachute Brigade, who were composed of German air-force ground troops under Major-General Bernhard Ramcke. The Ramcke were not popular with German army units, as they were always demanding favoured treatment. The German infantry were equipped with a particularly vicious machine gun in the Spandau, the intimidating bursts of which resembled the fast revving-up of a racing car. It will crackle frequently through these pages. All the German formations, thanks to the Royal Navy and the RAF, were much below strength at most material times.

Tanks were not the Germans' only armoured fighting vehicles. As the war progressed they were equipped with an increasing number of guns of all sorts – field, medium and anti-tank – mounted on tank or other tracked chassis. These were the 'self-propelled' guns. The Italians had similar equipment. They were of great value for bringing quick artillery support to any point where it is needed.

Rommel's artillery, wheeled and tracked, by the time of Alamein included 109 guns of 'medium' calibre, against the British 52; and 26 pieces of heavy artillery (above 6-inch) to the British none. The British, however, had a superiority in field artillery. In the tactical handling of this artillery the Germans and Italians were very much inferior to the British, who in this department had attained a standard not known before.

The most formidable of all the enemy artillery was the famous 88 mm, manned by Flak Batteries of the Luftwaffe – the German air force. Originally designed as an anti-aircraft gun, the famous 88 proved also a devastating anti-tank gun, especially when it became equipped with its half-tracked tractor, which enabled it to come into action extremely quickly. Its 21-lb armour-piercing shot, faster than sound, could kill a tank at 3,000 yards (nearly three times farther than any British gun) and its air-burst high explosive, bursting a few feet above ground, was terribly lethal to men. On one occasion (witnessed by the author) a single 88 held up a whole armoured squadron for a time, picking off our tanks at long range as they topped a crest, and its flashless propellant made it impossible to locate. At the beginning of the Battle of Alamein the Germans had eighty-six of these 88s.

Almost equally formidable was the very similar 76.2 mm captured Russian gun, of which, on 23 October, the Germans had ninety-five, including thirty self-propelled models on Czech tank chassis. The British had an even better weapon than either of these in their 3.7-inch anti-aircraft gun, but never employed it in an anti-tank role.

These two German and Russian guns were the most formidable tank-killers in the world, but even the standard German 50-mm anti-tank gun had a performance some 40 per cent better than our little standard 2-pdr, though perhaps not quite as good as our 6-pdr when it at last arrived. The general (but not complete) superiority of German war material at that time was well exemplified by the petrol – or water – container that was subsequently to become world-famous and copied everywhere – the container which the British troops christened the 'Jerrycan'. It made a glaring contrast with our civilian-type petrol tin, which was made of flimsy, paper-thin metal; so wasteful was it that staff calculations allowed for 25 per cent loss by breakage and evaporation on a desert journey of 250 miles.

In the air there was less technical disparity, but neither the British nor the American aircraft had so high a performance as the Messerschmitt 109 F & G, which could overhaul anything we had. Nor had we a counterpart of the Junkers 87, the famous 'Stuka' dive-bomber, which dived straight down upon its victim with a fiendish scream; but the Stuka was largely an instrument of terror or of purely local and isolated destruction, less effective tactically against resolute troops than the allied bombers.

It will be seen from this cursory survey, therefore, that, although in the later phases of the campaign the British sometimes had a slight superiority in numbers (not very marked before Alamein), they were at some disadvantage with the Germans in certain particulars of equipment. Our inferiority in tanks was a reproach to the nation that had invented them and, indeed, it was not until the end of the war that, in the Centurion, we produced a tank that was probably better than any other in the world. But the Germans, we may remember, had been preparing for a long time.

What the British were always superior in was in supplies, particularly petrol, as our sea and air forces (to which in due time were added American aircraft) took their weekly toll of the Axis transports at sea. Both armies freely used the transport guns and stores that they won at various times from each other.

THE 'ALAMEIN LINE'

These were the armies that became locked together after the long withdrawal and pursuit from Gazala begun on 26 May. Both sides were very tired after the long running fight, but there was to be no let-up, for Rommel, sanguine and full of drive, was determined to maintain the momentum. The Battle of Gazala continued without any interruption in the fighting, its waves beating swiftly upon the rock and sandy wastes of the strip of desert to become famous as the 'Alamein Line'.

Long before the war this 'line' had been recognised in appreciations by the British General Staff in Egypt as peculiarly fitted for defence. It was the obvious last-ditch position for the protection of the Nile. On the instructions of General Wavell, who had inherited these reports, it had been reconnoitred by Lieutenant-General J. R. Marshall-Cornwall as early as 1940. In the next year General Auchinleck had entrusted its lay-out to Lieutenant-General W. G. Holmes. Its special feature was that it represented the shortest distance in the whole desert between two impassable features: on the north the sea and on the south the vast, untraversable Qattara Depression. Thus it had no flanks. The typical desert operation of a right or left hook round an open flank to take an enemy by surprise would be ruled out if the whole thirty-eight miles were occupied.

The position had been well selected by the reconnaissance parties, but the defence works were of an exiguous nature, being composed of a series of unfinished defence localities or 'boxes', separated from

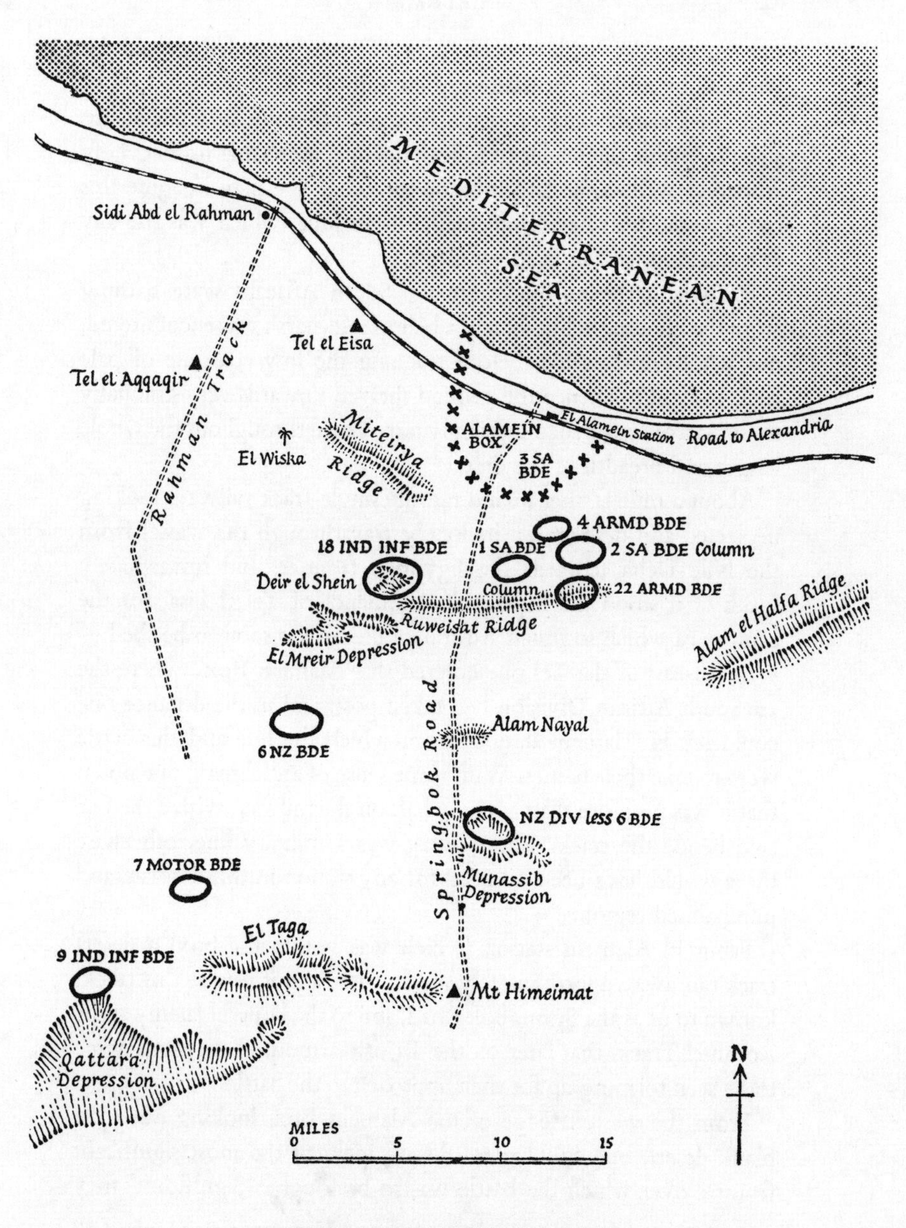

3. THE ALAMEIN LINE ON 1 JULY

one another by wide spaces, which it was intended should be watched by mobile formations or columns.[1]

A quick reconnaissance of this famous 'line' must be made at this stage to enable the reader to follow the operations that immediately ensued as well as the larger battle to come. We may imagine this reconnaissance to have been made on 30 June, which was the day before Rommell ran head-on into it.

Starting at the north, where the South Africans were bathing from the blinding white beach, a belt of salt marsh was encountered, not wholly impassable, before reaching the low coastline of pale rock and sand. Thence the ground shelved upwards very gradually to the narrow coast road – the only tarred road throughout the whole length and breadth of the desert.

About a mile farther inland ran the single-track railway, looking neglected and desolate on its lonely way through the wastes from the Nile Delta towards the Egyptian frontier, and immediately south of it stood the little rocky eminence of Tel el Eisa, for the capture of which so much Australian blood was soon to be shed.

South-east of the Tel one entered the 'Alamein Box', where the 1st South African Division had taken post, and in the distance one could see El Alamein station, from which the line and the battle were to take their names. With some sense of anticlimax, one noted that it was no more than a lonely halt on the railway, with a shed or two beside the track. The railway was a military line, otherwise there would have been no need for any station in this desolate and uninhabited region.

From El Alamein station (which was within the box) a desert track ran away approximately southwards, and it was at this track, known to us as the Springbok Road, and to the hopeful enemy as the Rommel Track, that later on the British armoured divisions were to be seen forming up for their approach to the battle.

From the western edge of the Alamein Box, looking out over blank desert, one could get a distant view of the most significant features over which the battle was to be fought. 'Significant' they

1 A 'box', when complete, was an area of ground wired and mined all round, with prepared trenches, weapon pits, etc. – an island of defence.

were only in a tactical sense, for nothing that was at all significant topographically attracted the eye in the western prospect. The shallow landscape was varied by none but the most trifling undulations. Only by a close study of the map could one make out that the line of the horizon, which was scarcely recognizable as a 'feature', was formed by a long, low ridge. This was the notorious Miteiriya Ridge and its north-westerly extension.

If, before Rommel got there, one drove over to its highest point, which was six miles away, and followed this prolongation, one arrived at a locality where the map showed a 30-metre ring contour, kidney-shaped. On the map it looked like an elevation forming the crest of the ridge and it, therefore, soon became known as Kidney Ridge. This trifling feature, less than a mile long, gave rise to an enormous amount of confusion and misdirection, for the ring contour, in fact, marked not an elevation but an indentation. The real ridge ran east and north of it and it is an exceedingly important feature to bear in mind, for here and hereabouts Rommel set some of his main defences. *See* Fig. 14.

Three miles beyond the Kidney could be discerned something rare in the desert. This was a line of telegraph poles that ran along a straight desert track that we called the Rahman Track and the enemy called the Ariete Track. At the northern end of it, gleaming in the sun, could be seen the white minaret of the small mosque of Sidi Abd el Rahman. Here Rommel shortly established his headquarters and his tank repair workshops.

All this area between the Alamein Box and the Rahman Track was to be the main battlefield. If one returned to the box and drove southwards a few miles on 30 June no troops at all were to be encountered until one arrived at a ragged, shallow depression known as the Deir el Shein. This had just been occupied by the tired 18th Indian Infantry Brigade and its supporting artillery, nearly all new troops hurried over from Northern Iraq, 1,000 miles away. This was the second 'box' of the Alamein front. Here the brigade, all alone, was somewhat anxiously awaiting Rommel's expected onslaught the next day.

Frowning immediately above the Deir el Shein was the most

pronounced feature yet encountered, running east and west across the front like a long and bony hog's back. This was Ruweisat Ridge, of evil memory. Rocky, austere, 200 ft above sea level, it became the scene of some of the bloodiest and most ill-directed fighting in the days immediately to follow, which formed the concluding phase of the Battle of Gazala.

Southward of Ruweisat, after dipping a little, the ground rose again to a large, smooth-backed swelling named Alam Nayil, which became one of the main buttresses of the British defence, and away eastward of it, at some fourteen miles' distance, could be discerned yet another prominent ridge, which one could see at a glance would be 'vital ground'. This was Alam el Halfa Ridge. It formed no part of the Alamein 'line' itself, but was a very important backstop at which Rommel, before long, was given a bloody nose.

Continuing southward from Alam Nayil, one left most of the rock behind and came to a stretch of devil's country of rough, eroded *deirs* and much soft sand, in which one's vehicle was likely to get badly stuck, so that the shovels and sandmats had often to be got out as one sweated to drive on a little farther. In the largest of these *deirs*, a deep forbidding pit, four miles long, of steep, eroded cliffs and hillocks, known as the Munassib Depression, were to be found the greater part of the New Zealand Division, who had just got back there after a hair-raising drive through the enemy lines.

Last of all, on the very edge of the great Qattara Depression, which was the end of the line, stood the most prominent of all the desert features – the steeply conical Qaret el Himeimat, or Mount Himeimat, rising suddenly like a Pyramid to nearly 700 ft. It dominated all the country northward and whoever sat on it could observe every movement for many miles around.

Westward of the line described, other boxes were at first held by scattered 'brigade groups', but all these were soon withdrawn to this general line. Other features of the Alamein position will be encountered, but those that should be most impressed upon the mind from the beginning are the dead flat terrain astride the coast road and the railway, the Miteiriya Ridge and the faint line of its extension up to the Kidney Ridge and the telegraph poles of the Rahman Track that lay beyond. In these localities we shall see the most critical fighting.

ROMMEL HALTED

Against these positions Rommel launched his tired and attenuated divisions immediately he reached them, intending to give Eighth Army no time to consolidate and to seize as soon as possible the great prize that seemed to be almost within his grasp.

His attempt to puncture the new positions was made on 1 July. Pressing with great urgency, he did not pause even for a reconnaissance – a neglect for which he was to pay a heavy price, for his appreciation of the British dispositions was very much at fault. His thrust was made astride the Miteiriya Ridge and through the gap south of the Alamein box, his intention being that one wing of his army should swing north to envelop that box, while the other wing swung south to take 13th Corps in the rear.

It was a thoroughly bad plan, badly executed, and the attack went completely awry. The left wing went astray in its desert navigation and, instead of passing through the gap south of the Alamein box, ran head-on to the box itself, was engaged by the South Africans, thrown into confusion and pinned down by fire. The 90th Light Division, formidable fighters though they were, broke astonishingly into a panic and would have fled in disorderly rout but for intervention by some senior officers. The right wing, which included fifty-five tanks of 15th and 21st Panzer Divisions, ran into the box at Deir el Shein, which they did not know was occupied.

The 18th Indian Infantry Brigade, holding this depression, was under a temporary commander and was without proper divisional control and support. With it were 97th, 121st and 124th Field Regiments, Royal Artillery, in whole or in part (without any centralised command), nine old Matilda tanks and an anti-tank company of The Buffs. Most of these were untried troops, there was a failure of communications, command of the battle was lost at the start and two of the infantry battalions and some of the guns were overrun.

General Nehring tried to induce the remainder to surrender, sending in a captured British officer in a bren-carrier under a white flag, but what was left of the garrison stood fast, the regiments fighting independently in a day of fiery heat, and 121st Field Regiment being left at the end of the day with one gun and one round of ammunition. The Germans, losing eighteen tanks, were surprisingly shaken. Six of these were knocked out at close range by the 25-pdrs of 275th Battery, under Major William Paul, and others by boldly handled 6-pdrs under Major N. Metcalf, both of 121st Field Regiment under Lieutenant-Colonel Edmund Stansfield, and by the guns of The Buffs under Major P. G. Clarke. The advance was blocked until dusk, when what was left of the garrison withdrew, having received no support from any other formation. Such was too often the fate of the lone and unsupported 'brigade group' of those patchwork days.

Although the Deir el Shein box was captured and its loss appeared at the time an unfortunate affair, it was learnt subsequently from German sources that this unexpected resistance was fatal to their hopes. Their spearhead had been blunted, their armour stopped from cutting in behind our positions at a moment when we were badly off-balance, and a precious day of opportunity lost. The actions at the Shein and Alamein boxes thus marked the turn of the tide. The day had begun for the enemy with tremendous exhilaration. He expected that before the end of it his reconnaissance elements would be on the outskirts of Alexandria itself. So slender was the margin. So thin the thread.

The day's grace enabled the British to re-establish themselves in better balance. The Royal Air Force, from their new airfields, began to belabour the enemy. The battle continued, however, with scarcely a day's intermission for almost another whole month, Rommel urgently seeking a weak spot by which to break through, Auchinleck repeatedly counter-attacking. The heat was stifling, the fighting savage and the losses heavy. Both sides were being reinforced, the British more strongly than the enemy. The 9th Australian

Division came over from Syria, took over the coastal sector and made a number of assaults, in which they captured Tel el Eisa and took Miteiriya Ridge but could not hold it.

More important were the savage battles to secure possession of Ruweisat Ridge, on whose rocky crest the shells burst with vicious detonations and in which the infantryman could find no relief from their persecution. The New Zealanders, the Indians and their British battalions stormed and won but could not hold, stormed again and won but a little. The ridge and its flanks became littered with the corpses of both sides and the feeding ground for myriads of flies.

This bitter July fighting did not constitute, as has been claimed by some, a 'First Battle of Alamein'. To take such a view is to mistake its relation to operations as a whole. It was the concluding phase of the Battle of Gazala. It was the aftermath of that rough harvest. The fighting from Gazala eastwards was continuous, with no change of plan, no new intention on Rommel's part, while Auchinleck, for his part, tried to throw him back by counter-attack.

Indeed, if the July fighting is regarded as a separate battle, it has to be recorded emphatically as a failure on Auchinleck's part, for the several offensive operations that he mounted were specified to 'destroy' or 'encircle' the enemy or to make deep penetrations and 'exploit'. In these intentions they did not succeed, nor even begin to do so. They were terribly badly laid on from the top and the courage and devotion of the regimental soldiers called upon to execute them were brought to nought by the gross faults of Auchinleck's subordinate commanders. They had meaning, however, as an 'offensive defence', for the important thing was that, although the British failed to throw the enemy back, they firmly stopped his advance. Mussolini, cheated of his triumphal entry into Cairo, after waiting three weeks, flew home to Italy in gloom.

It is not intended here to record the factual details of these fierce and often confused July battles. Their course has been briefly related in the official history. By the end of the month both sides were exhausted, having fought each other to a standstill and leaving the sandy wastes and the rocky elevations littered with smashed vehicles, black tangles of unrecognizable wreckage, broken weapons, scraps of clothing and equipment and scarred with the shapes of shattered tanks, their inner walls coated with a plaster of human flesh or their open turrets exhibiting, half-extruded, the roasted bodies of their crews.

Like heavyweight boxers retiring to their corners after a gruelling round, both sides paused to recruit and collect themselves for a new effort. It is, therefore, appropriate that we also should pause here to make a brief appraisal of the state of Eighth Army, since it closely concerns the events that were to follow and because of what has been said elsewhere.

Chapter Four

BLEMISHES AND OBSTACLES

Faults in Command – New Battle Techniques –
Life in a Tank

FAULTS IN COMMAND

It cannot be said that the direction of the enemy's offensive plans during the July fighting (as distinct from battlefield leadership) was of a very high order. Rommel had misappreciated the situation after crossing the frontier and he was now butting his head against a brick wall, only to find himself badly bruised at the end of the month. He struck in the wrong places.

Able tank leader and brilliant opportunist though he was, Rommel was lacking in certain of the qualities of all-round generalship. Robbed of the opportunity for manœuvre, inclined to see all situations in terms of tanks, and regarding his infantry (in Freyberg's words) as 'followers of the armour by day and weapon-holders by night', he was not well equipped to deal with a situation with which he was unfamiliar and which was, in fact, beyond his resources. He was to reveal the same shortcomings at the Battle of Alamein, which he stood a very good chance indeed of not losing if he had known which were the right clubs to pull out of his bag.

On the British side, however, things were even worse. We had superior numbers, but on the command levels a serious deterioration had set in. It is difficult to say anything severe enough about the conduct of the June and July battles at Army and Corps levels; and it would have been unnecessary to dwell on these matters if it had not been for the criticism and counter-criticism that has eddied around them. Military failures are by no means always due to the shortcomings of the generals; quite often the generals are let down by the troops, but in Eighth Army the troops were of a particularly high standard.

In spite of the adversities that they had suffered during this month of savage fighting and of the long withdrawal from Gazala, which would have severely strained most troops, the fighting spirit of the Eighth Army soldiers remained little impaired. Except for the newer arrivals, they were an army of young veterans and were skilled craftsmen in combat. For the greater part, they were tenacious and resilient and their understanding of the ways of the battlefield was exceptional.

Sir Oliver Leese, who came out from England a little later to take command of 30th Corps, was impressed with 'their fine morale, their high standards generally and their knowledgeable way of doing things. The standards of infantry training were excellent and the standards of gunnery very high indeed. Relations between officers and men, tested in battle, were extremely good and there was a strong sense of comradeship everywhere.'[1]

These excellences were by no means paralleled by the professional qualities of some of the senior commanders. The generals of Eighth Army, almost without exception, were men of great personal courage in battle, but it was largely by their bravery and their leadership in combat that they had risen to higher command. In Montgomery's words (to the author): 'They knew a great deal about fighting but not much about War.'

Well-tested military doctrine was being almost daily transgressed and what Montgomery called 'the stage management of battle' deplorably handled. Operations of great weight and moment were put in hand without inter-divisional conferences. Commanders went into battle with little knowledge of what was ordained on their flanks. The armour and the infantry fought separate,

1. To the author.

A Mark IV Special captured intact

An enemy self-propelled gun

German heavy artillery (8-inch) in action (*German official photo*)

German 50 mm anti-tank guns captured by the Australians at Alamein

uncoordinated battles. Different axes of advance, different objectives, different timings, inadequate reconnaissance and inadequate air photographs put the fighting soldier into battle at hazardous odds.

In 30th Corps (commanded by an officer of the most shining personal courage), there was a particularly unhappy state of affairs. Douglas Wimberley, the Highland Division Commander, on arrival in the desert from home, ahead of his division, attended some conferences at corps headquarters to learn 'the form' and was very much startled at the objections and questionings of orders by divisional commanders. These came particularly from the commanders of the Dominion divisions who, being themselves badgered by their governments with anxious questions and admonitions, would frequently counter the corps commander's proposals by the formula: 'I must consult my government about that.' Admittedly, this was not always fair play on the part of those who had a favoured position, but it showed up glaringly the lack of confidence that existed.

Leaving one of these acrimonious conferences one day, the astonished Wimberley remarked in ironic jest to his GSO 1, Roy Urquhart: 'Really! If this is the form, I shall have to consider referring any orders I don't like to the Secretary of State for Scotland!'

The misdirection of battlefield operations showed itself particularly in two serious weaknesses – the complete failure of co-operation between infantry and tanks, and the dispersal of force by the fragmentation of divisions.

The infantry-armour failure has perhaps never been summarized with more stinging emphasis than by the New Zealander, Brigadier Howard Kippenberger, one of the best fighting soldiers in the desert, when he wrote of the July battle known as 'Second Ruweisat':

> Two infantry and two armoured brigades had been employed. They had made three unrelated attacks from different directions at different times. A single small Panzer division of some twenty to thirty tanks and a fifth-rate Italian division easily dealt with all three attacks in succession and inflicted crippling losses.[1]

Before the end of July, a deep distrust of each other had grown up

1. *Infantry Brigadier* by Howard Kippenberger.

between the infantry and the armour. It became a common saying among the infantry that 'the tanks can be relied upon not to be there when you want them'. The infantry were accused in their turn of always 'screaming for tank support' on every possible occasion. 'I do not think,' admits Kippenberger, 'that we of the infantry did nearly as much as we could or should have done to ensure that we fought the battle together.'[1] Certainly most infantry commanders were as ignorant of the employment of armour as most armoured commanders were of co-operation with infantry.

The fault, however, lay on the shoulders of neither arm. It lay squarely on those of the superior commanders.

The second deadly ailment from which Auchinleck's forces had been suffering was the fragmentation and dismemberment of divisions.

The division, as we have seen, was a balanced and flexible force of considerable hitting power, having its own artillery, engineers, supply and administrative services to support an operation by any one of its brigades or even by a single battalion. Once it was broken up into small components, the hitting power was lost. This was precisely what had been happening. 'Penny pockets' were created which the enemy defeated in detail by concentrating superior forces. 'Brigade groups', 'Jock columns' and other scratch forces had become the accepted order and rule. Thirteenth Corps had almost the appearance of having disintegrated into an assortment of 'groups' and 'columns' without coherence and without any serious military value.

Auchinleck was an Indian Army officer and it was believed by many that the conditions in which training and operations there were conducted disposed him to a belief in small, mixed, mobile forces. In this he was abetted by his senior staff in the desert, Major General E. Dorman-Smith, whose brilliant intellect was highly fruitful in fanciful stratagems.

The independence enjoyed by the commanders of the Dominion divisions enabled them to resist such disintegration, not without sharp words, but the United Kingdom divisions had no such safe-

1. Op. cit.

guards. Wimberley, when he brought the Highland Division out from home, was warned by Leslie Morshead, commander of 9th Australian Division: 'The staff here are mad on breaking up divisions. They'll — you about for a dead cert.'

The integrity of a division was violated in more ways than one. Second Armoured Brigade, during the eighteen days of the most critical fighting at Gazala, were never certain whether they were under the orders of 1st or 7th Armoured Division, and so sudden and frequent were the changes that they sometimes did not even know on what wireless frequency they should be netted. Fourth Armoured Brigade, when about to attack a sitting target, were 'stolen' by a divisional commander merely because they crossed a boundary line.

There are, of course, situations in which a 'brigade group' may be justified. A brigade might also justifiably be lent temporarily to another division for a specific task, but it then became 'under command' that division, fought as part of it and was backed by all the divisional resources (a fact that a recent, much publicized critic does not seem to have understood). Montgomery often took such a step in his brilliant regroupings, but he never allowed 'brigade groups' to operate on their own.

These ailments had bitten deep into the body of Eighth Army before Alamein. Between them, they led to the severe tactical defeat of Gazala and to what came to be known as the 'nonsenses' of July. Fundamentally, they arose from transgression of the military doctrine of concentration of force. They led to very heavy casualties among some of our best troops, especially the New Zealanders. Von Mellenthin, then a lieutenant-colonel on Rommel's staff, commented on the 'complete lack of co-ordination and control' by the British, on the 'muddled' nature of Auchinleck's tactics and on the 'lack of drive' of his subordinates.[1]

Auchinleck's intentions for his July battles were well conceived, but he did not succeed in carrying them out, nor in transmitting his own impulse to lower levels. As Lord Ismay has remarked, he was internally a shy person, in spite of his commanding and impres-

1. *Panzer Battles*, 1939–45.

sive presence, in which there dwelt the soul of courage and honour.

NEW BATTLE TECHNIQUES

Besides these drawbacks inherited from earlier operations, Eighth Army found itself completely baffled during this July fighting on the Alamein positions by two relatively new and menacing weapons. These were the land mine and the anti-tank gun. Previously the Germans had not used mines in any quantity, but they now began to lay them on an increasing scale, especially anti-tank mines. They were a complete barrier to the passage of tanks, but the locations of the minefields were rarely ascertained with any accuracy and the methods of tackling them were primitive, slow and highly dangerous.

The anti-tank gun, on the other hand, was by no means new, but the Germans had developed the highly effective device of forming screens of anti-tank guns, stretching over a considerable frontage, and these guns, dug-in to ground level and almost invisible, were much more deadly than an enemy tank. It was a favourite trick of the German armour, for which we more than once fell, to entice our tanks on to the anti-tank guns, with shattering results.

The anti-tank gunner, if well-sited and strong of heart, really had the tank 'cold' nearly every time. This became all the more so with the employment by the Germans of the formidable 88-mm high-velocity gun and the similar Russian 7.62. Their numbers were continuously being increased and, in August, Flak Regiment 135 was joined by Flak Regiment 102.

So serious an obstacle had these anti-tank screens become and so shrewdly were they co-ordinated with the tactics of their own tanks that 1st Armoured Division's Operation Instruction No. 20 for the Battle of Alamein itself was to include this emphatic injunction:

> Second Armoured Brigade will start more than a match for any German armoured division. It is imperative that this strength is not dissipated against the enemy anti-tank guns, but reserved to destroy the enemy armour. The enemy will certainly try to weaken our armour with his anti-tank guns and to prevent a close

engagement between the tank until our strength has been reduced by his anti-tank screen.

The infantry who so often criticized our armour, even the most senior infantry commanders, quite failed to see, as we shall repeatedly see, that tanks, whether British or German, could no more advance in the face of resolutely manned anti-tank guns than the cavalry of their fathers' day could advance in the face of quick-firing field artillery.[1] The guns had to be eliminated first.

Alamein was to show a dramatic change in the shape of warfare. Whereas, hitherto, the tank had dominated the previous battlefields of the desert, what were to dominate the fierce struggles at Alamein were not the tank, nor the bayonet, nor the air, nor even the field artillery, but the mine and the anti-tank gun. Both required considerable guts and considerable skill to overcome. The emphasis of advantage was powerfully on the side of the defence and, against a first-class enemy, could be overcome only by great superiority in numbers.

The truth was proved again, and on both sides, of the axiom recognized after the First World War that, against strong defences, the attack could not succeed without a superiority of three to one in the zone of impact. For the defence, on the other hand, it is not numbers that matter, but fire-power: fire-power concealed within and behind physical obstacles.

LIFE IN A TANK

The warlike glamour of the tank, its intimidating aspect and its outward mien of invincibility gave to the infantry a great sense of security. Its vulnerability against modern weapons and the technical problems of maintaining it in action were less obvious.

Its frontal armour gave to the tank considerable protection but its tracks and suspension were very vulnerable to a flank shot, not only by armour-piercing ammunition but even by field artillery high explosive. Our 25-pdrs, with their swift concentrations of fire,

1. The author witnessed one such cavalry disaster at Monchy-le-Preux in April 1917.

several times stopped German armoured attacks. Indeed, a direct hit on its thick front plate by a medium or even field shell could loosen the welding and cause the front plate to drop off. A direct hit in the fuel tank was crippling, but more dangerous was the shot that, penetrating the main armour, set fire to the cartridges of the gun ammunition. In a few seconds the tank became a furnace.

It came as a surprise to many infantrymen and others that, although a tank was able to shoot with its main armament while on the move, it could at that time seldom do so very effectively. Only the most highly trained and experienced men could kill their birds on the move. Gyro stabilizers had not yet been fitted, except in the Sherman and these were imperfect. The popular notion of a tank 'charge' was likewise fallacious.

A tank could spray the enemy with its machine gun while moving (the Besa being the standard British equipment and the Browning in the Shermans and Grants); but to aim accurately with its main armament it preferred to stop. Tank battles were, therefore, largely fought out at the halt at whatever might be the killing ranges of their guns, and they would manœuvre tactically for that purpose. Whenever possible, the tank sought a 'hull-down' position – using whatever irregularity there might be in the ground to hide from the enemy all but the gun-turret. It was often said that the best man to fight a tank was an experienced poacher; they had a very successful one in 9th Lancers! In the earlier desert actions, when we had to fight with guns of inferior power, the stalking of enemy armour was an exciting and highly skilful affair.

Tanks could carry only a limited amount of fuel and ammunition and these had to be renewed in a long action. For this purpose regiments had a special echelon of unarmoured lorries ('soft skins'). When ammunition was needed they might often be required to drive right up into the heart of a battle and unload, round by round, by hand. For fuel replenishment, however, the tank had to withdraw. Except in the most critical situations, it also had to withdraw every night for mechanical maintenance tasks, for general replenishment, for food and for such rest as was possible.

Withdrawal was usually into a 'leaguer', which, in the open

desert, meant 'close leaguer', with all the tanks, soft skins, field and anti-tank artillery and infantry in a solid phalanx, defensively disposed. Withdrawal, which might involve an hour or more of cautious and difficult driving, could not be until well after dark. Maintenance by the crews and repairs by the REME detachments would go on far into the night. The crews were often too dog-tired at the end of it to bother about cooking a meal and would eat nothing but a little hard tack before bedding down where they were.

Each man then had to stand an hour's guard, so that about three hours was the maximum of sleep before the crew had to be up again and, after tea and a biscuit, drive back to their battle or patrol position. Our leaguers were always in complete darkness. The Germans, withdrawing likewise, did the opposite; they turned on arc lights for their repairs and ate a hot meal.

Life in a tank that was long in action was, therefore, physically very exhausting. It also imposed a peculiar nervous strain. The feeling of claustrophobia was but one of these strains. Crews had to be tough in both senses. To command, drive, operate its exterior wireless and man its main gun, the Crusader had a crew of only three, the Sherman, when it arrived, of five. All had to be men of intelligence as well as spirit. Upon the skill, nerve and intelligence of the driver a great deal depended. Coated in a gritty amalgam of oil and sand, he was the last man to bed down for the night and the first to get up, while it was still dark. He had to be something above the ordinary, like Brigadier Richards's stout-hearted Corporal Douglas. Upon the wireless operator, earphones clapped to his head all day and much of the night, listening to 'the babbling jargon of the air' that filled every minute and trying to evade atmospherics and enemy interference in his set, there was a considerable strain.

But it was upon the tank commander, who might be either an officer or NCO, that the greatest strain fell. He had to stand up in his open turret and maintain unceasing vigil with binoculars over the glaring desert from first light to last light. His eyes became red lozenges set in the dust that covered his face like talcum powder. He was constantly talking on the radio either to other tanks, taking or giving orders and information, or to his own crew on the separate 'intercom'. At that time cold water and hard rations were the crew's only refreshment in situations when it was unsafe to dismount and 'brew up'.

In terms of human casualties, however, the tank crews were far more fortunate than the infantry and the gunners who accompanied the infantry. The man with the rifle, the artillery FOO and the anti-tank gunner had no shield against the flying shell-splinters and the bullets. But tank wounds could be shocking. Like air crews shot down in flames, a man might be in hospital for four or five years, with one operation succeeding another, or, with bloated face and limbs and broken mind, he might wander witless in the desert.[1]

While the armour of both sides was in night leaguer, much would still be going on where they had fought their day battle. There were our own derelict tanks to recover and there were the enemy's derelicts to be destroyed by explosives. The former was the task of recovery squads provided by the Royal Electrical and Mechanical Engineers in the armoured brigade workshops. They sallied out into the night with towing and winching gear and tank transporters, like devoted shepherds, to bring home the lame and the halt. The business of 'tank busting' (and 'gun busting') of the enemy derelicts was in the good hands of the Royal Engineers. First Field Squadron RE destroyed and marked ninety enemy tanks during the Battle of Alamein.

The enemy, of course, was doing the same things. Among the prowling parties of the night, fierce little fights would take place as one side strove to recover its own injured tanks and the other to destroy them. On one occasion Brigadier Richards's intelligence officer, going to search an Italian tank for documents, came up to it at the same moment as an Italian officer arrived to recover them – and found that he was an old school friend; it was to the British lines that they both walked back.

On another occasion Major Peter Moore, Royal Engineers, out on a 'gun busting' mission one night, entered a German gun pit to find it still fully manned by its detachment. He was confronted by a

1. R. J. Crisp's *Brazen Chariots* and Cyril Joly's *Take These Men* vividly illustrated life in a fighting tank.

corporal armed with a sub-machine gun. Moore sprang at him and seized the weapon. The German threw a grenade at him, but Moore shot him with his revolver. The rest of the gun detachment fled.

Chapter Five

THE NEW COMMANDERS

Alexander – Montgomery – Horrocks and Leese – Lumsden – The Rommel Complex

ALEXANDER

In August Mr Churchill paid his historic visit to Egypt and made those changes in command that were to result in so much talk but were to have so decisive an effect.

He appointed a new C-in-C Middle East in the person of General The Hon. Sir Harold Alexander, a soldier who had proved his ability in the most adverse situations and who added to his professional excellence the highest personal qualities and gifts of character, not least of which was the 'modest stillness' of his breeding. He and 'The Auk', indeed, had a great deal in common. As his Chief of Staff, Alexander appointed Major-General Richard McCreery, a tall, lean and wiry figure of severe character who was a tank specialist but whose advice Auchinleck would not accept, as he was opposed to the splintering of armoured divisions. He was one day to command Eighth Army himself.

Though another figure was still to fill the centre of the stage in the public eye, we must at all times remember Alexander directing behind the scenes, approving or modifying the new operations that were to begin in the desert and supporting them by his able direction of the large resources at his command. Like Wavell and Auchinleck, he had other large responsibilities also as C-in-C Middle East, but his 'prime and main duty', as set out by Mr Churchill, was to destroy Rommel's forces. There were those who did not miss the significance of his name in a land that perpetuated the memory of his great namesake.

To us, however, there is a greater significance in the officer who was appointed to command Eighth Army under the overall direction of Alexander. This officer was at the time known as Lieutenant-General B. L. Montgomery. Let us take a detached look at this man who was to become so much a figure of controversy and see him as he then was.

MONTGOMERY

Montgomery, fresh from England, presented himself to the sunburnt army of the desert as a figure without any remarkable physical attributes. He had not Auchinleck's impressive presence, nor the handsome, martial bearing of Alexander, nor the rugged, bulldog features of Wavell. He was slender and wiry and not very tall. He had fair hair, faint eyebrows, a moustache clipped very close, a sharp, inquiring nose and pale blue eyes the colour of a harebell.

It was the eyes that signified. At first sight of him, one was not particularly impressed by his physical appearance, but at closer range his eyes declared much of his character. When he spoke, the absence of sonority in his voice disclosed other facets. Eyes and voice together told you that he was incisive, lucid, firm of purpose, not warm-hearted, not brooking disputation, not likely to make allowances for the fallibility of others. He was brisk and business-like. You were left in no doubt that he had decided exactly what was going to be done and that it would be done. You were at once aware that he had no use for weak instruments, nor for instruments that did not fit his hand.

A practising evangelical churchman, he was strict in his personal habits: a teetotaller, non-smoker, simple in his tastes and constantly insistent on physical fitness. Ever since Sandhurst he had been a serious and dedicated student of the soldier's trade and had made himself a complete master in the technique of that craft. He knew how to handle all its tools and understood the capabilities, limitations and tensions of his raw materials. Whether he had the quality of genius remained to be seen.

These things the observer easily saw or soon discovered in the new Army Commander, for he was an easy book to read, without obscurities or entanglements in thought or behaviour. Later, one learnt that, although quite ruthless in disposing of senior officers who did not suit him, he was far from cold-hearted and was always ready to help those who he considered deserved helping. Several of his staff stuck to him for the remainder of the war, which still had nearly three years to run.

Though severely self-disciplined, Montgomery was neither narrow-minded nor a frowning sober-sides. He laughed readily and his spirit was buoyant. He was no old-fashioned martinet and was tolerant in matters of dress and formal discipline. On his first visit to the New Zealanders, he said on arrival at General Freyberg's headquarters: 'I notice your soldiers don't salute.' Freyberg replied: 'Wave to them, sir, and they'll wave back.' Monty did so.

Thus Bernard Montgomery, though not apparently gifted by nature with those qualities that win the spontaneous affection of soldiers for a popular hero, was equipped, through his own efforts, with other qualities which stimulated immense respect, solid confidence and, before long, strong personal loyalty. He found Eighth Army something of a brotherhood and himself entered into the brotherhood. He came to command the Army and himself became its most ardent comrade and champion.

As time went on a note of genuine affection crept into all that Montgomery uttered to those under his command. Like Napoleon's *mes enfants*, his troops became 'my soldiers'. He spoke in terms of 'we' and 'us' and 'our'. At the end of the campaign he declared in glowing terms:

> My admiration for your wonderful fighting qualities. . . . I doubt if our Empire has ever possessed such a wonderful fighting machine as Eighth Army; you have made it a household word all over the world.

The way to Montgomery's heart, therefore, was to be a fighting soldier. He dearly loved a 'warrior'. Such men as Bernard Freyberg, the 'old war horse', Douglas Graham, 'that great little warrior', 'Bolo' Whistler, 'perhaps the best fighting brigadier in the British Army', John Harding, 'that little tiger', and the lion-hearted John Currie – these men won his approbation. He believed in youth, because youth can stand physical rigours, has not yet learnt caution and is willing to learn and obey. He personally appointed everyone down to lieutenant-colonel's command and some of the battalion commanders he appointed were only in their twenties. His one frailty in this sphere was that he would not have men who had independent minds and would not conform to his own.

As a commander, perhaps no one has paid a higher tribute to him than Oliver Leese, whom he summoned from England to command 30th Corps. 'Monty,' he said, speaking to the author, 'could be a most difficult and even exasperating man to anyone parallel or senior to him, but as a commander to serve under on the battlefield, it's Monty for my money any day. He made things easy for you. His orders were simple, clear and straightforward and he never asked you to do anything beyond your resources.' Wimberley, the Scot, found him 'magnificent' to serve under. The commanders of the Dominion divisions were united in paying tribute to his stimulus.

All these things were hidden, however, to the soldiers of Eighth Army when Monty arrived, with untanned knees, on 13 August. Many had heard of his name, but very few indeed knew anything about him. The sum of popular knowledge was that, when he gave lectures or held conferences in England, notices were displayed ordering 'No smoking, no coughing'. The general attitude was: Who is this fellow Monty? The old desert hands were thoroughly sceptical of all newcomers, of all who still had pink arms and knees and did not 'know the form'. They were a world and a brotherhood to themselves and a long apprenticeship was expected before a newcomer was accepted as a fellow-craftsman.

Despite what Mr Churchill said and others have repeated, it is far from true that there was any uneasiness, any 'bewilderment' among regimental officers and men before the arrival of Alexander and Montgomery. That existed only among the more senior ranks.

The morale of Eighth Army was always sound, their pride was high and they had no consciousness of fallibility either in themselves or their commander.

But they had 'flogged' up and down the same piece of desert so often that they wondered whether the process was ever likely to stop. What Montgomery did, in time, was to implant in their breasts an absolute certitude of victory and to transform an assembly of loose components into an articulated fighting machine. Even the old desert hands, who were not impressed by the arrival of a new commander from England, began before long to realize that the military machine was being properly run at last.

Almost the very first act of General Alexander on taking over GHQ was to put a stop to all talk or thought of any further withdrawal by Eighth Army. Unlike his predecessor, he appreciated that, if the Alamein position was lost, the whole Delta was *ipso facto* lost. But, as recorded in his dispatch: 'It was fairly well known that, in the last resort, the Army would retreat again, in accordance with the theory that it must be kept in being.' He, therefore, sent instructions to Montgomery to make it known to all ranks that there were to be no further withdrawals and that the Army would fight where it stood.

Montgomery lost no time in putting into effect, with all that crisp emphasis of which he was capable, a policy with which he was so much in agreement. 'We stay here alive or we stay here dead,' he said. A sigh of relief went up from the whole Army. Morshead, the Australians' commander, said: 'Thank God!'

To give emphasis to this decision, Montgomery ordered all withdrawal plans to be burnt and all non-operational vehicles to be sent away into the back areas, so that, as a New Zealand officer put it, 'We couldn't run away even if we wanted to.'[1] The new Army commander immediately toured the desert, seeing the ground and sizing up officers and men. Wherever he went he blew through the

1. It must be recorded that Alexander himself did indeed order defences to be made to cover the approaches to Cairo from the south- and south-west. They were planned by Wimberley, inspected by Alexander and actually manned by the Highland Division during the coming Battle of Alam Halfa. They were not, however, withdrawal positions for Eighth Army.

August heat of the desert a cold, sharp, stimulating breeze. Kippenberger, the New Zealander, records:

> He called, unannounced, a few days after his arrival. He talked sharply and curtly, without any soft words, asked some searching questions, met the battalion commanders and left me feeling very much stimulated.[1]

One of the correctives that Montgomery very soon applied, to the satisfaction of all commanders, was to make it clear that there was to be no more 'mucking about with divisions'. There was to be no more talk of 'battle groups' and 'Jock columns'. Though chronologically out of place, it will be convenient if we quote here a letter that he sent out and signed personally to all corps commanders on 29 September. In this he wrote:

> A cardinal point in my policy is that divisions shall retain their identities and their *esprit de corps*, and that they shall not be split up into bits and pieces which never see this parent formation. Whenever it is possible, divisions must fight as divisions and under their own commanders.
>
> There will be occasions when a Corps commander will require to resort to a special grouping within the Corps in order to deal with a particular and definite problem. Such groupings may necessitate brigades and units being detached from their own divisions and being placed under the operational command of other divisions; this detachment from the parent division will be regarded as temporary and for a definite period; when the situation which necessitated such grouping has been dealt with, the brigades and/or units will return to their own divisions.

Proceeding, he put a stop to the frequent switching of *units* from one formation to another. They were to have a permanent loyalty to one parent division. We shall see in a later chapter how, in the same letter, he reviewed the order of battle and personally decided the composition of each division.

At the desert headquarters, which he took over from Auchinleck, Montgomery was signally fortunate to find a particularly able set of staff officers, who were to serve him brilliantly. To Francis

1. Op. cit.

('Freddie') de Guingand, the BGS Eighth Army, he gave a new status as 'Chief of Staff', which was not at that time the recognized practice in the British Army, the commander being expected to do a good deal of staff and executive co-ordination himself. Under the new system Montgomery channelled everything through his Chief of Staff. It was fortunate for him that de Guingand not only knew his man already but also that he had a quick brain and a capacity for shouldering an enormous burden of work. He was also on excellent terms of understanding with Coningham's Senior Air Staff Officer, Air Commodore George Beamish.

As his chief administrative officer Montgomery retained the equally able Brian Robertson and as his Chief Engineer the brilliant F. H. Kisch. For his senior artillery officer (BRA), however, he sent home for Sidney Kirkman. Harry Arkwright was his Senior Staff Officer for armour. Bill Williams (his distinguished Intelligence Officer), Miles Graham, Charles Richardson and Hugh Mainwaring were others of this brilliant team.

Montgomery's impact was felt not only by Eighth Army, but also by the Army's great brother-in-arms, the Western Desert Air Force. They found that he brought with him 'a remarkably keen, clear and vigorous appreciation of the part that could be played by air forces in a land battle'. He immediately moved Eighth Army HQ from the middle of the desert, where it had existed in discomfort, to a position alongside Coningham's HQ by the white sea shore at Burg el Arab. Tedder wrote home: 'It was very refreshing to see at Eighth Army Advanced HQ the embryo of a real operations room copied direct from our own.' Thus began an association that was to grow ever closer and closer, making Eighth Army and the Desert Air Force one cohesive power, unmatched in comradeship and identity of purpose.

Alexander himself also set up a small tented headquarters on the sea shore alongside them and closely followed all developments.

88-mm gun in action, with the empty cartridge case seen being ejected (*German official photo*)

A dug-in 88 captured near the coast road, showing some forty empty cartridge cases and other ammunition not fired

German half-track, used for towing guns or carrying infantry into action

88-mm gun and its tractor, both destroyed by direct hits (*See* 'The Rhodesian Gunners', Ch. 16)

HORROCKS AND LEESE

Two other generals, of Montgomery's selection, were summoned from England as Corps commanders. The first of these was Lieutenant-General Brian Horrocks, who came to command the 13th. Horrocks was a man whose physical appearance very much belied his military qualities. Silver-haired, clean-shaven, classically featured, one would take him for a judge, a bishop or a don. He was, however, very much a fighting soldier. Eisenhower, when lunching with the author in Venice, said that he thought Horrocks the outstanding British general under Montgomery.

Not all his junior generals liked him, but nearly all acknowledged the extraordinary quality 'Jorrocks' had of radiating confidence wherever he went and his great gift of 'putting things over' lucidly. 'Pip' Roberts, who commanded the celebrated 22nd Armoured Brigade, testifies that merely to see Horrocks drive by gave an immediate stimulus to troops.

Some ten weeks later – only three weeks before Alamein and thus recorded here somewhat out of sequence – Lieutenant-General Sir Oliver Leese, Bt, arrived from England to take over the difficult 30th Corps command in the north. A tall and stalwart figure, he looked the traditional guardsman and was one. Energetic, inquiring and wanting to see things for himself at first hand, he was at the same time composed and relaxed, imperturbable under stress, had an easy and friendly manner, could laugh and joke with anyone and made one feel that everything was under control. He thus evoked a strong feeling of confidence in his divisional generals, to whom he was as much a leader of a team as he was a commander.

Like Horrocks, Leese had commanded an armoured division at home – the Guards' Armoured Division – and was the first infantryman to command armour. He was a familiar figure in the forward areas in his open car, which he often drove himself (very fast), in the manner of a man unburdened with cares; whereas Monty, as he sat beside John Poston (his most celebrated liaison officer), usually appeared wrapped-up and concentrated.

Leese, upon whom an exacting task was laid, was one of the great successes of Alamein. Montgomery's selection of him was a very shrewd one, for his tact, easy good manners and understanding of 'difficult' people were qualities needed in a command that included three Dominion divisions of very dissimilar characters. Without their willing co-operation, the Battle of Alamein could never have been fought, but he quickly won their confidence.

Being a fellow-guardsman, Leese already knew 'Tiny' Freyberg, commander of the New Zealanders; he had met Dan Pienaar, the South African, and well understood his Afrikaaner propensity for being 'difficult' at awkward moments. The only one unknown to him was the Australian, Leslie Morshead, but he won his allegiance at once. With the Highland Division there were no 'difficult' people and they found him 'magnificent' to serve under.

All were profoundly relieved when, from the start, Leese made it clear that their divisions would remain inviolate in the coming battle. With his arrival, there was an entirely new spirit in 30th Corps and the objections, questionings and 'bellyaching' about orders passed quietly away. 'Rickie' Richards, the able commander of 23rd Armoured Brigade and a very experienced old desert hand, said of Leese[1]: 'I always knew exactly what I had to do with Oliver. His orders were always very clear and he knew what was within my reach – a terrific contrast to what had gone before!'

Leese, like Montgomery, was fortunate in his staff. As the head of it was his BGS, George Walsh, a quiet and able gunner officer who won the confidence of the Dominion contingent; it was to him that they went with all their problems. Leese was equally fortunate in his Corps artillery commander, Brigadier M. E. Dennis, who manipulated a massive volume of artillery with an apparent ease that matched his cheerful equanimity in times of crisis.

LUMSDEN

We now come to the third of the Corps commanders in Eighth Army and a much more controversial character – Herbert Lumsden.

1. To the Author.

Soon after Montgomery's arrival in the desert, 10th Corps, a defunct formation headquarters, was resuscitated. It was initially an all-armour corps and was intended by Montgomery to act, in his own phrase, as a *corps de chasse*. Lumsden, previously commander of 1st Armoured Division, was appointed to command it.

Lumsden was a cavalryman (though originally he had been a gunner). He had first made a name for himself during the difficult withdrawal from Louvain to Dunkirk, when he had commanded the armoured cars of 12th Lancers with considerable skill. Since then he had risen rapidly, perhaps a little too rapidly. He was tall, dark and crisply good-looking. He had a fine bearing and presence and was always extremely well turned out. He was an exceptionally fine horseman and had ridden in the Grand National. He was gifted with one of the quickest of minds and had been an instructor at the Staff College. He was a strict disciplinarian, severe when conducting training, sharp in his rebukes.

In action, his severity slipped from him like a cloak. He encouraged and did not chide. He had a flair for being in the right place at the right time and his presence was a stimulus to everyone. He was quite fearless. He had considerable charm, attracted strong loyalties and to such men as Raymond Briggs was 'the very model of a born soldier'.

There are, however, those who say that Lumsden's handling of 1st Armoured Division during the withdrawal from Gazala was not all that it should have been. There are those who suggest other shortcomings. He was perhaps too strong-minded and tenacious of his own views. He was on bad terms with Alec Gatehouse, one of his own divisional commanders. He was on bad terms with Freyberg. More seriously, he was not on good terms with the Army Commander. He was outspoken in his disagreement with Montgomery's plan for the battle, believing that the armoured divisions, which he was required to command, were by that plan committed to too rash an enterprise.

His disagreement with Montgomery led to his downfall after Alamein, but he will always be remembered for his fine qualities and his able leadership in the earlier days. He was killed later in the war when serving as Mr Churchill's representative with the American forces in the Far East.

THE ROMMEL COMPLEX

Although the new generals out from England admired the spirit and quality that they found in Eighth Army, they, and a great many others also, were shocked by one dangerous germ that was then running in its veins. This was the extraordinary fact that, to the British soldier, the only general whose name was 'familiar in his mouth as household words' was that of the enemy commander and not their own. Every soldier knew of Rommel, but few knew the names of their own generals.

This, of course, was a thoroughly bad condition. A 'Rommel complex', mysterious in its origins, had been built up. In a campaign waged without fierce hates, he was regarded in much the same way as the admired captain of an opposing cricket team. He was a 'decent chap'. He played a clean game. He visited the wounded British prisoners of war. Wherever one went, whether in the forward areas or the back, Rommel was spoken of as though he were a wizard. There were some who believed, and still believe that this dangerous seed had been deliberately inseminated by German agents and fifth columnists, of whom there were plenty in Egypt, partly to create an 'inferiority complex' in Eighth Army and partly to prepare the Egyptians for Rommel's arrivel.

A British officer, dining in Cairo at just about this time, with others of the same uniform, in the house of a wealthy Coptic Egyptian, believed to be very pro-British, was horrified when the conversation turned to ardent admiration of Rommel, in which the other British officers joined. Unable to contain himself after several minutes of this, he broke out: 'This is quite ridiculous and we really ought not to be talking in this sort of way. Rommel is no more than a competent corps commander. We have beaten him once before and we shall certainly do so again.'

He had no answer but a painful and guilty silence.

Auchinleck had tried to stop this Rommel cult by the issue of an order, but it had had no effect. There was, therefore, every justification for the policy that the new commander of Eighth Army deliberately adopted. Montgomery set out to make his name and person familiar to all his troops. He adopted the Australian 'slouch' hat, covered with various cap-badges, and later exchanged it for the black beret of the Royal Tank Regiment, to which he attached their cap-badge as well as his own general officer's gold-thread badge.

There was plenty of caustic criticism in officers' messes and in the Delta, where the Army Commander's headgear was regarded as rather a cheap stunt, but this and his tank inscribed 'Monty' were externals designed to make his person prominent, and it is a fact that he very soon became a familiar figure instantly recognized by all ranks, and that there was no soldier in Eighth Army who was in any doubt who commanded it.

Von Mellenthin, the German staff officer, recorded: 'There can be no question that the fighting efficiency of the British improved vastly under the new leadership, and, for the first time, Eighth Army had a commander who really made his presence felt throughout the whole force.'[1]

1. Op. cit.

Chapter Six

PRELUDE TO ALAMEIN

Alexander's instructions to Montgomery, confirmed in writing on 19 August, were that he was 'to prepare to attack the Axis forces with a view to destroying them at the earliest possible moment', and, meanwhile, to hold the present positions.

Montgomery's appreciation of the situation, with which Alexander agreed, was that Eighth Army would not be in a position to accomplish the first and paramount task until late in October. His forces must be built up until they were sufficiently superior to overcome defences that were daily becoming stronger; he must make good many deficiencies and he must make good also the gaps in the Army's training for the particular kind of battle that he intended to impose upon the enemy.

As to the second part of Alexander's instructions, it was clear that a renewal of the enemy's offensive was likely to take place very soon and for this Montgomery prepared with every confidence immediately on his arrival. The battle that followed almost immediately – only a fortnight after Montgomery's arrival – was not only of great importance for its own sake but is also of special interest to us in showing the mistakes made by Rommel when confronted with some of the same problems that were to face the British at Alamein.

As we have noted, both sides had of late been actively recruiting their exhausted forces since the ending of the July battles. On the enemy side there arrived some complete new formations, which had been intended for the attack on Malta. The Germans had already received 164th Light Division and the tough Ramcke Parachute Brigade; the Italians sent a whole parachute division – the Folgore, spirited troops of good training and physique. Other Italian forces arrived which did not at first appear on the battlefield.

Among the new German tanks to arrive were the most powerful models yet seen on any battlefield; these were the Mark IV Specials, which, in addition to their specially hardened armour, mounted a long, high-velocity 75 mm gun, capable of killing a tank at 3,000 yards. Of these formidable weapons the German Africa Corps had twenty-seven before the end of August, as well as seventy-three or more of the only slightly less formidable Mark III Specials, which had made their first appearance at Gazala. The disparity in power, if not in numbers, between the British and the enemy tanks was thus even more pronounced than ever. Scarcely less welcome to Rommel was a new access of strength to the German and Italian air forces, which, before the end of August, approximately equalled those of the British and Allies.

Rommel was perfectly well aware, however, that a build-up of the British forces had also begun and that it was likely in time to exceed anything he could expect to reach him. He, therefore, determined to attack again as soon as his forces were sufficiently augmented, in spite of his continued shortage of petrol, large quantities of which were being spilled out on the Mediterranean as the tankers were sunk. Of the fuel cargoes sailed from Europe 41 per cent were lost during August, but by the end of the month Rommel had enough fuel for 150 miles per vehicle in the fighting echelons and he thought this would do.

He proposed now to break right through to Alexandria itself by the destruction of Eighth Army where it stood. The method and style of attack that he decided upon were typical of his previous tactics. It was to be a bold 'right hook' at the southern end of the British front, where the twelve miles of desert between the New Zealand flank on Alam Nayil and the Qattara Depression were sparsely held by 7th Armoured Division behind the minefields *January* and *February* (*See* Fig. 12).

Through this sector Rommel proposed to drive his tanks, passing to the south of the Alam Halfa ridge, and then to wheel northwards right up to the coast in the British rear, while his infantry formed a defensive flank. Twenty-first Panzer Division was then to make for Alexandria, 15th Panzer and 90th Light for Cairo.

The initial phase of this bold plan involved a deep penetration of the British front on the first night of the attack, so that at dawn the panzer divisions, having wheeled, would be facing north, ready for the round-up and the break to the coast. This meant that the tanks of the *DAK*, placed almost on the extreme right of the attack, were expected to penetrate no less than thirty miles from the start line.

It did not need any profound or astute thinking on the part of the British staff to foresee this manœuvre. It was typical Rommel, and the disposition of our forces invited such a method; indeed, deliberately so. The Alam Halfa ridge, lying at right angles to our front and with its western edge some thirteen miles behind, had been noted in the days of Auchinleck as the key to any such manœuvre and had accordingly been selected to become a 'defended locality'.

It was characteristic of the old command, however, that the defences which had been prepared there were for a 'brigade group', and that, if an action was going to be fought there, it was going to be on the old cavalry ideas of 'fluidity and mobility', 'mobile wings', 'artillery battle groups' and similar nonsenses, which had so often been disastrous before and which would have played straight into Rommel's hands. The staff appreciation written for Auchinleck by Dorman-Smith at the end of July, which embodied these suicidal notions, might almost have been written for Rommel's express benefit.

On his first tour of the desert, Montgomery saw at once the importance of Alam Halfa. He had not seen any previous staff paper. Indeed, the situation was as obvious as it must have been to any alert Staff College student. Horrocks, on arrival from England to take over command of 13th Corps, found that his staff had 'no doubt at all' what Rommel would do. Montgomery was not satisfied, however, that so important a defended locality should be a mere drawing on the map; within forty-eight hours of his arrival he occupied it, shaking the complacency of Cairo by demanding that 44th (Home Counties) Division, fresh out from England under Ivor Hughes, should be sent forward 'tomorrow'.

The brigade position was expanded to a divisional one. Orders were given that the armour was not to be 'loosed' for a gamble in the open, but to sit tight in positions of their own choosing. The exiguous defences were strengthened by 44th Division. Pits were bulldozed or blasted by the sappers for the tanks to fight in protective hull-down position. On 21 August, Horrocks, upon whose Corps the battle would fall, held a staff exercise, in the form of a 'telephone battle', that foreshadowed almost exactly the course of events that soon took place. A raid by the Australians was prepared, to be carried out on whatever date Rommel attacked. The enemy's preliminary moves were detected and closely followed in fighting reconnaissances by 208 Squadron RAF.

Virtually the only uncertainty about the expected enemy offensive was the date, but the phases of the moon pointed clearly to a night at the end of August. The method of fighting the defensive battle was determined in advance and Kippenberger, attending the conference, was struck by 'the ready, balanced feeling that we all had'.

Montgomery's orders to Horrocks were that 7th Armoured Division, if heavily pressed, were to give way slowly, harassing the enemy on the southern flank and front, and being careful to avoid 'getting mauled', while 44th Division and 10th Armoured Division awaited the main thrust of the enemy on the Alam Halfa ridge and its flanks.

The Germans and Italians attacked on the night of 30/31 August and at once met the same difficulty as the British were to experience at the Battle of Alamein. Their efforts to penetrate the *January* and *February* minefields were strongly opposed by the infantry and light tanks of 7th Armoured Division, and it took them six hours – far longer than they had calculated – to clear corridors for their tanks; so that daylight on 31 August, which should have revealed the *DAK* some twenty-two miles within the British lines, found them only just struggling clear of the mines.

Seventh Armoured Division, under Callum Renton, gave way slowly in accordance with orders and the enemy halted while Rommel made a new plan. A hot wind from the south blew a great cloud of dust before it, so that aircraft could not operate nor gunners observe with accuracy. Six hours late, the *DAK*, numbering 200 tanks in massed formation, with the Italian armoured divisions on their left, tightening the intended wheel, swung north-eastward and advanced on Alam Halfa. With the sandstorm blowing into the faces of the British, 21st Panzer Division was lured to attack Pip Roberts's 22nd Armoured Brigade (under command 10th Armoured Division), whose tanks, unknown to the enemy, were in their dug-in positions west of the ridge.

It was the first time that the British had seen the new Mark IV Specials. Their weight fell especially on the high-silhouetted Grants of 3/4th City of London Yeomanry, which could not adequately conceal themselves. The big Mark IVs sat well back and picked off the Grants one by one. The CLY were soon decimated, but Roberts, in an ably-handled action, superbly supported by the field artillery and by the stout-hearted anti-tank gunners of 1st Rifle Brigade, stood his ground, outfought the Germans' superior tanks and brought their attack decisively to a halt before darkness fell.

The next morning Rommel tried again, sending 15th Panzer Division to find the British left flank. He failed again. Fighting of great intensity went on for several more days, the brunt of it falling mainly on 10th Armoured Division under Alec Gatehouse, imperturbable under the shelling of his own headquarters. The infantry of 44th Division in the main defensive positions on the ridge itself were never engaged, and the issue had really been decided on the first day.

The enemy, encompassed on three sides, was continuously lashed by the artillery of 10th Armoured and 44th Divisions and pounded mercilessly by the Desert Air Force and No. 205 Group. Fierce air battles were fought as Kesselring exhorted the Luftwaffe pilots to support their comrades of the *Panzerarmee*. The British troops likewise experienced some sharp bombing, Kesselring having flown in an additional force of Junkers from Crete.

An attempt by the New Zealand Division to effect encirclement by a hastily mounted flank counter-attack was a failure and Rommel, unable even to hold the ground won, was allowed to withdraw without serious interference, leaving behind forty-nine tanks totally destroyed, fifty-five guns and 395 vehicles, and losing 2,910 men.

British casualties amounted to 1,750 men and sixty-seven tanks, though only half the tanks were total losses. In the air the British and Allied losses were actually much heavier than the enemy's, sixty-eight aircraft being shot down against forty-one German and Italian.

Montgomery's deliberate policy throughout was to conserve his forces for the bigger battle for which he was now planning. The enemy was left in possession of our minefields *January* and *February*, which now became his own, and, on Montgomery's express instructions, Rommel was allowed to retain the dominating height of Qaret el Himeimat in the extreme south, in order that he might have full observation over those measures that were being put in hand to deceive him of our coming intentions.

Alam Halfa was of considerable significance for the greater engagement to come. On the British side it was a model defensive battle, ably controlled and 'stage managed', in Montgomery's phrase. It had developed almost exactly as Alexander and Montgomery anticipated and Rommel, in effect, had allowed himself to be drawn into what was very like a calculated ambush. The conduct of the battle on the British side had shown very clearly the firm directing hand of a new master and presented a vivid contrast to the muddled actions of the previous twelve months. No less significant, and exemplifying a recognized maxim, was its demonstration of the advantages enjoyed by a strong defence over an attacking force that was not considerably stronger at the point of main impact.

Not the least of the results of the battle was that to all the soldiers of Eighth Army and their comrades in the air it gave a new impetus and buoyancy to their confidence in themselves and their commanders. It was the first time since 'Crusader' that the Germans and

Italians had been unequivocally defeated and seen off the field. It was the first time since its inception that Eighth Army had been handled as a closely articulated fighting machine.

In Raymond Briggs's words, the spirit changed under Montgomery's impetus from one of 'dogged defence and defiance' to one of 'knocking Rommel for six'. He recorded: 'A spirit of aggressiveness arose and was seen in the very different appearance of the soldiers themselves. . . . Only those who saw it for themselves could realize and wonder how one man had succeeded in changing the whole character of an army in three weeks.'

And Coningham wrote soon after the battle:

'In all my force there is an atmosphere of enthusiasm and expectancy at the prospect of going on to greater things as part of the Eighth Army.'

On the German side, Alam Halfa manifested some of the weaknesses that often characterized Rommel's judgement. His intelligence was very much at fault, he grossly underestimated the time needed to breach our minefields, he totally misappreciated our reactions to his attack and he failed to employ his infantry to good purpose when his panzers were brought to a halt. He did not even know that we had occupied the ridge.[1] Most significantly of all, he failed to learn from Alam Halfa that he was now up against a new ringmaster who firmly controlled all his horses as one team. What he could not help realizing, however, was that he had no further potential for another offensive as things stood, that the next blow must come from the British and that he must go over to the defensive.

Rommel took the initiative against Montgomery twice only – at Alam Halfa and four months later far away at Medenine – and on each occasion, entirely through his own misjudgements, he suffered a bloody nose. Leese, who, as a Corps commander, probably fought more battles with him than anyone else, said of him (to the author): 'I never knew Rommel to execute any exceptional manœuvre nor any that we did not anticipate.'

1. General Ritter von Thoma, Eighth Army Int. Sum. 357.

Chapter Seven

PREPARATIONS

New Weapons – New Training – The Devil's Gardens –
The Allied Air Forces Regroup – Stockpiling for Battle

With this successful defensive battle out of the way, Alexander and Montgomery began to prepare for the great offensive. Mr Churchill, with his customary drive, was pressing for it to be mounted in September, but Alexander was successful in convincing him that it could not confidently be undertaken until late in October. This was, indeed, leaving the matter dangerously late, for, apart from the obvious necessity of defeating any hostile force that might be in the field, two special considerations made it imperative that Rommel should be soundly and convincingly defeated as soon as possible.

One of these considerations was the position in Malta. So far as supplies were concerned, that position had been eased in August by the remnants of a battle-torn convoy which reached the island after a terrific fight, but the little island was still in deadly danger. If it was to survive, it was vital that the Cyrenaica airfields should be in the possession of the RAF as quickly as possible. This was a consideration that was forcefully and repeatedly represented to Alexander and Montgomery by both Tedder and Mr Robert Casey, the Minister of State in Egypt. Hitler had ordered that Malta, because of the devastation inflicted by its ships and aircraft on supplies to Rommel, must be 'paralysed'. In consequence, Kesselring began a terrific aerial assault early in October, keeping it up for ten long days before acknowledging defeat by the RAF.

The second special consideration was the forthcoming invasion of French North Africa by the British and American force under General Eisenhower, which Alexander and Montgomery knew was to take place early in November. This operation, under the code name of 'Torch', was not only a military risk but also a political one. The French territories in North Africa – Morocco, Algeria and Tunisia – were under the control of the Vichy government, theoretically neutral but in fact subservient to the Germans and certainly anti-British. Though the ground had to some extent been secretly prepared, no one in Britain or America knew for certain what sort of a reception the French forces or the French civilians would give to the Allied landings, and it was realized in London and Washington that the most promising way to swing the opinion of the hesitant Frenchman in North Africa was to achieve a resounding success in the Western Desert.

As events were to turn out, 'Torch' ran into considerable military difficulties and the Germans, who immediately rushed a strong expeditionary force to Tunisia, were not expelled from North Africa until Eighth Army, after a 2,000-mile-long chain of victories, joined hands with Eisenhower's forces in front of Tunis, into which units from Eighth Army were the first to enter. The operational commander of the combined forces was Alexander and he himself said afterwards: 'I am quite certain that the British First Army and the United States 2nd Corps could never have taken Tunis and Bizerta unaided.'

There were, of course, several other reasons – reasons of policy, of morale and obvious military reasons – why Rommel should be beaten as soon as possible, but these were particularly cogent ones. To suggest, as has been done, that there was no need to make the attempt and that Alamein was an 'unnecessary battle' is utter nonsense.

NEW WEAPONS

It was apparent to the British commanders that the coming battle, with no flanks and against deep defences, would be completely different from previous desert operations and would approximate to those of the First World War. The enemy defences had become so strong and so deep that the breeching of them would involve, as Alexander said, 'a battle on the grandest scale'. It would be a severe battle of attrition, with heavy losses to be expected and with the infantry dominant in the opening phases.

No assault could, therefore, hope to succeed unless there was a substantial superiority over the defending forces. There was no prospect of obtaining the orthodox three-to-one superiority based on First War teaching, and the British command had to be satisfied with a planned overall superiority in men and equipment of approximately two to one. The principal shortcoming was in infantry, of which there was never enough.

By the gallantry and skill of the Allied navies and merchant services, reinforcements to achieve this superiority continued to flow in during September and October. The sweating quays of Egypt were crowded with discharging cargoes by day and by night, the great base stores depots swelled and expanded across the sandy reaches of the Delta and the Canal Zone, the workshops hummed and clanged as new equipment was serviced or damaged equipment repaired, the great base hospitals received new drafts of doctors, orderlies and nurses, the reinforcement camps were filled with jostling drafts of pale-skinned soldiers and airmen experiencing their first bouts of dysentery and their first ordeal by flies, route-marching under the grilling sun by day and by compass at night, swallowing the daily tablet of mepacrine against malaria, gradually hardening themselves after the lethargy of a long sea voyage. An air of formidable preparation hung over the desert and the sultry Delta, but only the chosen few knew what was afoot. At the Gezira Club cricket and golf went on as usual and the swimming bath was as full as ever. On a hundred improvised fields the footballs bounced about in the cool of the evening. In the afternoon the staff of GHQ continued to have their long siesta.

Of all the new arrivals, the largest formed body, and one that was to bring new lustre to the desert army as well as to itself, was 51st (Highland) Division, under Douglas Wimberley. Having undergone all the trials of the newcomer and having manned the defences of the Pyramids, 'the Jocks' moved up on 8 September in rear of Alam Halfa, behind 44th Division. Here they felt at last near the battlefield and learned the ways of desert life. They accustomed themselves to the water ration, learnt how to make desert fires, underwent the experience of becoming caked with sweat and sand, discovered the enchantment of bedding down under the glittering canopy of stars and awoke to the piper's reveille of 'Hey Johnny Cope'.

Of material recruitments to the new Allied strength the most precious was the new Sherman tank, which we owed to a spontaneous act of generosity on the part of President Roosevelt and the ungrudging co-operation of General Marshall. Three hundred Shermans were sent off at once in six of America's fastest ships, and, although one of them was torpedoed and sunk next day, the loss was immediately made good. At last the British armoured regiments had a tank that could meet the best German tanks on equal terms. Mounting a 75-mm gun, the Sherman was a marriage of British and American design, based on our experience in combat. Two hundred and fifty-two were issued to units and were ready for action at the opening of the Battle of Alamein, and more were coming in. Some regiments, however, as in 9th Armoured Brigade, did not get their Shermans until the night before the battle and several of them were found to be mechanically shaky.

Another tank newcomer was the British Crusader Mark III, which mounted a 6-pdr gun instead of the little 2-pdr that all British tanks had hitherto possessed. Keenly awaited by the armoured regiments, it was soon being criticized for having most of the mechanical faults of its predecessors. About one-third of the tanks in Eighth Army were Crusaders of sorts.

Almost as welcome as the Sherman was the first of the self-propelled artillery for the support of the armour. We had improvised a model ourselves by mounting a standard 25-pdr gun in the chassis of a Valentine tank. This equipment, known as the 'Bishop' and manned by 121st Field Regiment, RA, went into action at Alamein, but it was not a satisfactory makeshift and could not compare with the

Junkers bombers setting out to attack the British (*German official photo*)

Below: Bostons of the 18 Imperturbables taking off

Bomber attack on a British battery

A Hurricane makes a low-flying attack on an enemy airfield (*German Official Photo*)

properly designed American 'Priest', which now began to arrive.

The Priest mounted a 105-mm gun, in a Grant tank chassis, with a flashless charge. It was first issued to 11th (Honourable Artillery Company) Regiment, Royal Horse Artillery, in 1st Armoured Division, was soon a success and in time became the standard equipment for all RHA regiments. It meant, however, a completely new training for the British gunners, since American artillery methods are based on those of the French, and Leggatt's officers and men had to learn a new language from American instructors of 'mils' (instead of degrees), 'panoramic telescopes', 'pro-directors' and so on.

Among the other equipment that was now flowing in was a steady increase in the numbers of the new 6-pdr anti-tank gun. By the time of Alamein most of the artillery anti-tank regiments and many of the infantry platoons had been re-equipped with this in place of the 2-pdr. In the hands of stout-hearted detachments it was to take a heavy toll of enemy tanks. A few were mounted on lightly armoured chassis to form the self-propelled guns known as 'Deacons'; they were issued to ZZ Battery of 76th Anti-tank Regiment, R.A., and gallantly handled under Major Ronald Crouch.

The 6-pdr suffered, however, from one serious defect. It was transported on an Austin lorry known horribly as a 'portee'. In contrast to the Chevrolet portee previously employed in the Middle East, its high and bulky silhouette was fearfully conspicuous and a magnet for German fire in daylight.

NEW TRAINING

Montgomery drafted his general plan for the Battle of Alamein soon after Alam Halfa and, having received Alexander's acceptance, expounded it to a conference of corps and divisional commanders by the sea-shore on 15 September (See Plate 2). He gave a comprehensive picture of his intentions and assigned each division its task. What his plan was will be seen in a later chapter. Wimberley recorded in his journal, it was to be a 'real set-piece battle of the First War type'.

Now this was a type of battle of which Eighth Army, as such, had had little experience. Their mentality was deeply engraved with the design of the outflanking movement, with the armour as the ascendant arm. Montgomery therefore ordered an intensive programme of re-training (and reorganization) to be undertaken in the brief time remaining.

The Army had now to be drilled, not for the customary desert battle of movement but for a burst-in frontally, a head-on clash, a night assault against strong fixed defences. It was to be a battle in which, in its critical first stages, the infantry were to be dominant, with the tanks geared to their movements and with massive artillery support under centralized control. All the techniques of the assault upon strong defences had therefore to be practised – the penetration of deep minefields, the infantry attack under a moving barrage, quick consolidation against counter-attack, the neutralization of enemy guns, the passage of armour through the bridgeheads won by the infantry, signal communications, administrative support and so on. Furthermore, they had to be practised under the exacting conditions of all-night attacks.

This was a formidable programme of training to be undertaken in the short time available, and the training was very tough. Whole divisions were pulled back and were worked up by stages to a point at which they conducted rehearsals of the parts to which they had been assigned, though no one but the divisional commander yet knew what that part was to be. The Highland Division rehearsed their part five times. Stretches of desert were selected that resembled the ground that the division would have to attack, incorporating the known enemy defences. Actual mines were laid and across these the infantry advanced while the sappers cleared safe lanes for the armour and fighting vehicles. Live artillery barrages were fired.

Hitherto infantry assaults behind a moving barrage had had no place in desert warfare. Barrages, indeed, had come to be considered old-fashioned and had been replaced by the artillery 'concentration', which is a characteristic of the moving battle rather than the battle of position. Indeed, many young artillery officers had not worked out a 'barrage table' since their days as cadets.

Montgomery, however, intended to employ barrages on the largest scale in a series of night attacks and the troops had therefore to be practised in walking close up behind a moving curtain of bursting shells. Oliver Leese and the divisional commanders themselves led the first waves behind the barrages to give confidence to those who were unaccustomed. There were few casualties, but in the Highland Division Major Sir Arthur Wilmot and five men of the Black Watch were killed.

By these rehearsals, sand-table exercises and other training methods the divisions cast their desert thinking into a new mould. The more the problems were examined, the more evident it became that a night attack across entirely featureless country covered with mines, barbed wire and booby traps was a difficult and complicated operation requiring careful planning in the smallest particular. How to be sure you were going in the right direction in the dark, how to recognize the imaginary line in the desert that was your objective, how to keep touch with flank units in the fog of the all-covering dust – even these primary needs were stubborn problems.

The method commonly employed in the infantry was for a navigating officer to lead the assaulting troops compass in hand and counting the paces. One need hardly say that this required a man of cool nerves. We shall see before long the stratagems employed to overcome these problems and how they sometimes failed.

In this vital training period the technique for infantry attacks was to a large extent worked out in the New Zealand Division under General Freyberg, and the other divisions in 30th Corps adopted the methods he evolved. Co-operation between infantry and armour received special attention. The Valentine tanks of 23rd Armoured Brigade thus trained with the assaulting infantry whom they were to support, and an inspired move was made when Montgomery gave 9th Armoured Brigade, a formation of fine fighting spirit, to the New Zealanders as their own armour.

In addition to this large-scale divisional training directed to the particular operation, Montgomery ordered intensive unit-retraining. The Army had suffered 102,000 casualties in the ten months from the 'Crusader' battle to Alam Halfa, and the more recent replacements had not been properly assimilated into their units. Men freshly out from home had much to learn, such as minefield operations, and a few things to unlearn, such as the slit-trench mentality and the passive attitude towards hostile aircraft. Montgomery had found on arrival that no unit training was being done.

'Officers considered', he said,[1] 'that the only training necessary was fighting. Of this the older hands had had plenty and their standards were high, but that attitude would not do. I insisted that, whether in the line or not, they should resume training, especially for the large reinforcements that had been coming in to replace casualties and for those who had been recently stepped up in rank.'

The spectacle was therefore soon to be seen, all the way along the line, except in the south, of platoons and companies marching silently out of the line in the pale mauve light after the dawn 'stand down', to carry out exercises and classes a few miles behind the front, and marching back again in the late afternoons as the sandstorms whipped up and, with an accent note characteristic of the desert theme, the empty petrol tins banged and bowled along before the dust-laden wind.

Together with this re-training, a great deal of re-organization was taking place within Eighth Army, directed by Montgomery himself. The largest and most significant was the re-formation of 10th Corps as an all-armoured corps under Herbert Lumsden. Other changes were designed, in part to shape the Army to the operations he had planned for it, and in part to establish divisional loyalties more permanently. He took a strong objection to units floating about from one division to another.

In his letter of 29 September to Corps commanders on the uses of divisions, which has been quoted earlier, he personally laid down the composition and affiliations of each division: its brigades, artillery regiments, engineer squadrons or companies, etc. These, he said, would belong 'definitely' to the divisions and 'will wear the respective divisional signs on their clothing and on their vehicles'.

Knowing that there would be some heartburning over this and that, for example, those who had worn the emblem of the 'desert rat' would hate to exchange it for another, he went on in his curt, 'typical Monty' fashion:

1. To the Author.

There may be certain individuals and units who do not like the composition of divisions as stated, and who wish for changes.

There will be no changes.

Protesting, or belly-aching, about the matter is forbidden.

A conspicuous example of these revised affiliations was the switch of 7th Motor Brigade, the famous infantry limb of 7th Armoured Division, to 1st Armoured Division. This change was made because 1st Armoured Division, which Montgomery had cast for a special role, had no infantry brigade, whereas the 7th Armoured Division, whose tanks and vehicles were mechanically in a shaky condition, was not at first intended for a principal part.

The direct order on the wearing of divisional emblems was a further fillip to the divisional spirit. The Highland Division, to whom this was a sore point, were dismayed when told on arrival in Egypt: 'Of course, you'll have to take down your flashes'. Wimberley therefore personally asked Montgomery's permission and was told: 'Of course; certainly wear your badges.'

At the end of September – the day before Montgomery's letter on divisions – his battle plan was disclosed to brigadiers and to RE commanding officers, the latter having a particularly compelling responsibility for clearing mines.

From then on operational preparations became intensive. Commanders went up the line and stared speculatively at the distant low outline of Miteiriya Ridge and its north-westerly extensions, which was to be the main objective. They reconnoitred routes, assembly areas, lying-up positions, harbours for waiting tanks and transport and forward sites for their own battle headquarters. Sapper officers went out into No Man's Land on minefield reconnaissance as best they could. Interdivisional conferences were held to arrange boundaries and to agree on the controlled speed of the infantry advance and the covering barrage. Guns were calibrated. On the edge of our own minefields advance trenches were hewn out of the rock or shovelled out of the sand, camouflaged and stocked with water and hard rations; they were small and cramped slits in which the assaulting infantry were to lie in hiding for a day before moving up to the start-line of the attack, for they had a long way to go and the start-lines were fixed as far forward as possible.

THE DEVIL'S GARDENS

Perhaps the most vital of all the preparations for the battle, however, was the technique evolved for the dangerous business of clearing enemy mines. We cannot appreciate the hazards with which the Army was faced at Alamein without an understanding of the prickly nature of those hazards and the courage of the men who had to tackle them. Official and popular accounts pass lightly over this fundamental operation, and the generals who have written their memoirs scarcely mention it.

The defensive system that Rommel had for months been building was based on mines, barbed wire, anti-tank guns and machine guns, in great depth. The Germans called these minefields 'Devil's Gardens' and the mines themselves, by a change of simile, 'Devil's Eggs'. The British, more soberly, called them 'mine marshes'. The 'garden' or 'marsh' stretched the whole length of the front and its depth in some places was as much as five miles.

The mines themselves were sown in two main frontal belts, usually a few hundred yards wide. Between these main belts, which were irregular in shape, lay an expanse of open desert, often three or four miles wide, across which, connecting the two main belts at numerous points, transverse belts had been sown, so that attacking tanks that punctured the first belt would find themselves boxed in. Reaching out from the main belts there were numerous, apparently haphazard fingers or antennae of mines and wire, designed to lure tanks of troops on to the field of fire of a concealed gun. Thus the pattern of the minefield was an irregular maze.

The front (British) edge of each belt was entirely open and the presence of mines was by day discernible only to the keen and practised eye, and by night not at all. A brisk wind might, however, blow the sand off them here and there. The enemy's own 'home' edge was usually marked by barbed wire from which hung small metal labels adorned with a skull and crossbones and the admonition

Achtung Minnen. Belts of barbed wire were also irregularly spread inside the minefield, usually to protect the 'battle outposts'.

Within these bristling devil's gardens were concealed numerous small defensive works – trenches or stone sangars (weapon emplacements with a parapet of rocks, specially favoured by the Italians) – in which were sited machine-guns, anti-tank guns, mortars and observation posts. Access to them was provided by narrow lanes through the mines. These were what Rommel called 'battle outposts'.

They were sited so that the whole of the minefield areas were covered by fire, if not by bodies; fire-power being more important in defence than numbers. The fire posts were, of course, mutually supporting. Their purpose was to delay and cripple an attacking force as it struggled through the minefields, while the main strength of the armoured and infantry divisions in the rear, having freedom of movement, disposed itself for a knock-out blow.

Here, then, was a model and formidable example of 'defence in depth'. There was nothing at all new in the technique, for it was the normal defence technique of the Germans, but its strength was in its depth. It demonstrated how a defence, with great economy of force, could hold a strong tactical advantage against an attacking force of superior numbers. The head gardener who supervised this infernal planting scheme was Colonel Hecker, Rommel's Chief Engineer, and Rommel himself watched its progress daily and had great confidence in its stopping power. The month's delay in our attack which Alexander pressed upon an impatient Mr Churchill gave Rommel the opportunity to thicken, deepen and intensify his barriers still further.

Moreover, behind these defensive minefields he began to prepare a third belt of defence, characterized by pits for dug-in tanks and anti-tank guns. This belt began just east of the mosque of Rahman and ran roughly southwards for about seven and a half miles. Eight miles from our forward positions, it was beyond the reach of a single night's penetration by infantry and it was, indeed, to prove the main obstacle to the progress of Montgomery's armour.

In the earlier and largely mobile fighting enemy mines had not had serious importance. As soon as he had been stopped in front of

Alamein, however, Rommel began minelaying on a large scale and by the third week in October had sown close on half a million of these explosive devil's eggs.

Overall, 96 per cent were anti-tank mines – German, Italian, French and the 'Egyptian' mine made by Egyptian contractors to British order and captured by the enemy. They were buried just below the soil and blew up under pressure, not necessarily destroying a tank but certainly crippling it. Wheeled vehicles were damaged beyond repair and their occupants usually killed or mutilated. The anti-tank mines were not, as a rule, set off by the weight of a man, if he walked naturally, but a man running actuated them and then there would be nothing left of him and his near neighbours.

The long Italian 'box' mine was easy enough for trained men to lift, and the corrugated, green French mine required considerable pressure to actuate it. The Egyptian mine was sensitive and tricky to handle, but the most widely used and most notorious was the German Teller. This was a round, shallow canister with a raised neck, in which the striker was seated. The Italians sowed their mines on a regular pattern – about one every five yards in each direction – which the Royal Engineers had learned to recognize, but the Germans, like the British, sowed theirs irregularly.

Even with no complicating factors, the removal of these mines was a ticklish enough job, but other devices had come in to multiply the risks. The battle of wits between the inventor of mines and the soldier who had to find and lift them at his immediate peril had just begun. The booby-trap technique had not yet reached its high-water mark of devilish ingenuity, but quite a lot of mines were trapped, ready to put a quick end to the man who tried to lift them. Thus, if one mine were lifted, a connecting device might blow up another.

More dangerous to the soldier himself, however, were various devices for killing him personally as he walked over the ground. The horrible 'shoe' mine, which blew off a man's feet (as one did Kippenberger's), had not yet made its appearance, but the S-mine used at Alamein was even more lethal. It was a small metal cylinder from the neck of which protruded three little horns. When the horns were trodden on, a ballistic charge shot the cylinder into the air about stomach-high, where it burst, discharging an all-round volley of shrapnel bullets. It was a deadly killer.

Thin trip-wires, invisible by night, might also bring sudden and violent death. The S-mine itself could be so exploded. Trip-wires were also connected to large aircraft bombs which could kill men wholesale, and did so at Alamein. Quantities of the small Italian hand grenades called 'Red Devils' lay about the minefields; themselves dangerously sensitive, if you picked one up to remove it, you might set off a mine and blow yourself and your comrades to pieces.

Such were some of the delights of Rommel's gardens. To walk among them made one's feet tingle. But in an assault the infantry of the rifle companies were expected to advance across them at walking pace without a pause, accepting casualties. It was not possible, however, to bring up their supporting weapons and vehicles – anti-tank guns, bren-gun carriers, etc. – nor any tanks, until a lane through the minefield had been 'de-loused'.

This was the particular business of the squadrons or companies of Royal Engineers in the divisions. They had, of course, plenty of specimens of all types of mine and all divisional sappers had been trained to such familiarity with them that they could disarm and dismantle them blindfold. Even in daylight and when not under fire, the business required a strict and exact drill. One had to search with the fingers below and around each mine lest a booby-trap wire was attached. One must never take a step without looking or feeling where to put one's feet. The usual method of disarming the anti-tank mine was to feel for and remove the igniter, but the S-mine was disarmed by inserting a nail into the small hole in which the safety pin had been seated before the enemy mine-layer had removed it.

All this was a dangerous enough business, which not very many men approached without some bad moments, but the first difficulty was to find the mine. Hitherto the only methods had been by visual evidence of disturbed sand, which the enemy was often very skilful in concealing, and by prodding the ground with bayonets. Besides being primitive, slow and dangerous, this could be done only by day and therefore gave the show away to the Germans as soon as it began.

This had been a contributory cause of some of the costly failures in the July fighting, as on one afternoon when, after the Royal Engineers had cleared a lane under full observance, 9th Lancers moved through, to find the enemy anti-tank guns ready waiting for them. Enemy minefields were rarely known and reconnoitred and, in the muddled methods of that period, the sappers' orders usually took the vague form of instructions to gap 'any minefield that may be found'. In the apt words of Sapper H. Flinn, of 3rd (Cheshire) Field Squadron, 'We were pitchforked unexpectedly into battles without any kind of preparation'. This was an absurd way of laying on an attack, since only too often the whole operation depended on that factor.

An analytical study issued by 1st Armoured Division recorded that 'Failures in the summer at Ruweisat Ridge had clearly shown' that sappers alone could not do the job, that co-ordination by all arms was necessary, that control of the operation must be centralized and that 'the most careful planning to the last detail' was essential.[1]

In one of these July 'nonsenses', when the anti-tank guns of 50th Division were blown up on mines and the infantry overrun by the enemy, Major Peter Moore, commanding the squadron in which Sapper Flinn served, was wounded and sent back to the Delta. Moore was an officer of the Regular service of quite exceptional qualities. To us, perhaps the most important was that he was a serious, thinking, dedicated sapper; but he was much more besides. Tall, dark, wiry, physically 'tough', used to hard living, he had already established a reputation for great personal bravery, a reputation that was to be further enhanced and to be recognized in multiple decorations. He was one of the few men who have fought with the revolver at arm's length and personally wrestled with an armed enemy. Like many officers who are successful leaders in battle, he was extremely strict in matters of training and unit discipline. In short, he was a very fine all-round soldier.

His wound healed, Moore returned to the desert in August, just after Montgomery had arrived. Almost at once he was sent for by Brigadier F. H. Kisch, Chief Engineer of Eighth Army. Kisch had

1. 1st Arm. Div.: *The Passage of Defended Minefields.*

recently held a conference of all the corps and divisional engineer commanders on the mine clearance problem and they had sent in their written recommendations. These he now handed to Moore and said: 'I am sure that there should be a *drill* for this, just as there is a drill for loading and firing field guns. Go away and come back in a week's time with your recommendations. When you have worked out a drill and I have approved it, you will form the Eighth Army School of Mine Clearance.'

This development, from which was to emerge one of the chief battle-winning techniques of Alamein, owed its origin to directions from Montgomery, who saw the clearance of mines as one of the vital tasks in the ordered and controlled 'stage management' of battle.

In due course the school was set up near Burg el Arab and Moore was given a South African and a New Zealand officer to help him. Some of the most stubborn problems that faced him right from the start were: how to devise some method of detection and clearance by night; how to locate and reconnoitre a minefield without giving the game away to the enemy; how to avoid crippling casualties that would imperil the operation. Other problems were matters of 'drill' or technique – how wide the gap should be, how it should be marked by day and night, how to keep direction, how to co-operate with infantry and tanks and so on.

By good fortune, the answer to the problem of detection by night came just at the right moment. There already existed an electronic type of detector known as the Goldak, which operated on the principle of two balanced coils, and any change in inductance caused by a metal object underground set up an oscillation that could be heard in earphones as a 'ping'. The Goldak was not sufficiently robust or reliable, but the first models of the subsequently famous Polish Mine Detector now began to come in. Operating on the same electronic principle, it had been invented by Captain J. S. Kosacki, assisted by Lieutenant Kalinowski, of the Polish Free Forces then training in Scotland, and had been accepted by the War Office in March.

This meant that at last we were not dependent on visual evidence of disturbed earth nor on primitive bayonet prodding. It meant that we could work by night. This was a tremendous step forward, but supplies of the new detector were limited and by the time of Alamein only 500 had arrived, some of which proved faulty. In the event a great deal of mine clearance had to be done by prodding. The detector looked rather like a floor polisher on a broom handle and had the objection that the operator had to stand erect while he swept from side to side a few inches above the ground; he was therefore very exposed and vulnerable and needed to be a very cool hand in an operation which was the most severe nervous and physical strain of any that had to be endured on the battlefield.

The drill for the whole operation of gapping was worked out very quickly and approved by Kisch. It owed a great deal to Lieut-Colonel Kenneth Mackay, CRE (Commander Royal Engineers) of 1st Armoured Division, under whom Moore had served, and was based on one troop (or platoon) of sappers – two officers and about forty men – per gap. For the reconnaissance, an officer and a small party moved forward, reeling out a white tape behind them; this was to become the centre line of the gap. When the reconnaissance party reached the area where air photographs or other information suggested that the minefield might be expected, they planted a blue pinpoint light showing to the rear.

They then advanced in a stooping position with arms dangling, fingers just above ground level, back of the hand to the front, feeling for trip wires and keeping a sharp lookout for S-mines. Direction had to be kept very accurately by compasses exposed to the sun the day before.

When the reconnaissance party judged that they had reached the end of the mine belt on the enemy side a second blue light was shown.

On this signal, the 'gapping party' followed and at the head of it was a pilot vehicle. Its floor was heavily sandbagged, its steering column extended for the driver's safety, and the driver himself, usually a volunteer, had to be a cool and steady hand. The purpose of the pilot was to test whether the reconnaissance party had accurately located the front edge of the minefield. In the open spaces between one minefield and another it might also discover whether there were any stray, haphazard mines. If the pilot blew up, the drill for clearing and marking a free lane began at once. There were never enough pilot vehicles, but they never lacked for drivers.

Three teams came forward, each with the task of making an 8-ft lane, the complete gap of 24 ft being calculated to allow two tanks to pass, until time permitted further widening. When the Polish detector was available, each team consisted of nine men and an NCO.

The nine were deployed in three trios. Three operated the detectors. In the second trio the two outside members, looped to each other to keep the right width, reeled out white tapes to mark the 8-ft lane. The third trio pinned the tapes down to the ground.

The team worked quickly right across the minefields, the object at this stage being to mark the lane and to clear S-mines, which was done by the NCO himself, while all hands lay flat. Having reached the far side of the minefield, they turned about and worked backwards for the actual de-lousing. For this stage, in order to minimize casualties from any mines that exploded, all hands moved at the crawl, except the detector-men.

The second trio, two of whom had previously been the tape-men, became the 'mates' or 'directors' of the detector men, keeping them going on a straight path, and putting a marker on top of each mine as its presence underground was revealed. The markers were cones cut from the flimsy whitemetal of petrol tins.

It was the third trio who actually lifted the deadly canisters. Lying prone, as they came to the silver cones gleaming in the moonlight they carefully scraped away the soil with their fingers, feeling all round and underneath and, if there was no tell-tale booby-wire attached, fitted a loop of signal wire to the mine, moved back a little way and pulled it out. If it did not go off, the 'Devil's Egg' was then disarmed by removing the igniter and stacked at the edge of the lane.

A vital feature of the drill was that the men in each trio were echeloned twelve feet back and to the left of one another and all were well spaced out. This was to avoid crippling casualties from an exploding mine or enemy fire.

Meanwhile, as this party of ten was working back to cleanse the lane, another party was working forward in the same lane. When the two parties met, the lane was clear.

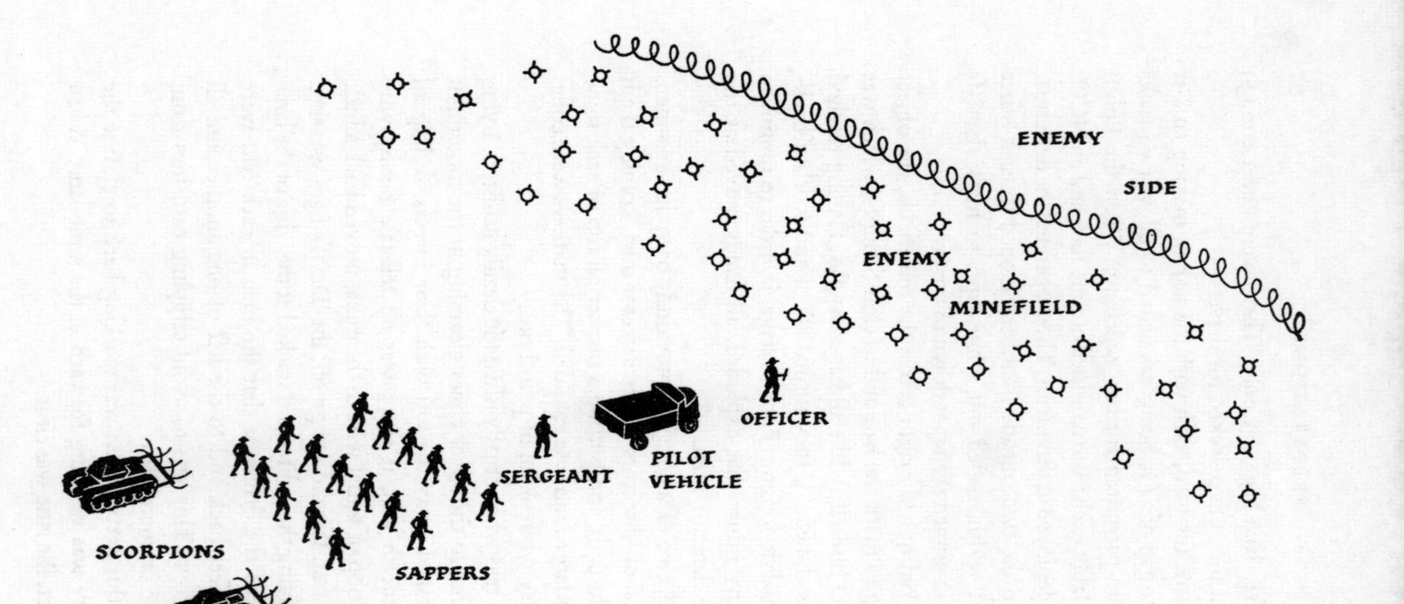

4. THE APPROACH TO THE MINEFIELD — *Diagrammatic only.*

Finally, the edges of the completed 24-ft gap were quickly fenced with a single strang of wire and planted with T-shaped posts carrying orange and green pinpoint lights, the green on the safe side.

Tanks and vehicles could now drive through the 'safe lane', while the sappers went ahead, following the reconnaissance party's white tape to the next belt of mines. Simultaneously the military police came forward with a lorryload of pickets and lamps and, with this tape as axis, marked out the route forward.

The time that this operation was expected to take, when there was no interruption by the enemy, was an hour per 200 yards, using detectors; when prodding, double that time. Needless to say, it was a very severe test of the nerve and steadiness of every man engaged.

This, in outline only, was the drill evolved. It dealt with the Royal Engineers' part of the operation. Before the great battle Moore and his squadron were posted to 10th Armoured Division and they will very soon be seen putting their own drill into practice in battle.

At the same time an entirely different and most ingenious method of mine riddance was being put to the test by means of a fearsome-looking equipment known as the Scorpion, devised by the South African engineer Du Toit. This was a Matilda tank, in front of which, thrust forward on two projecting arms, was mounted a rotating shaft, and to this shaft were attached several short lengths of heavy chain. As the shaft revolved, driven by a separate V8 engine, the whirling chains beat the ground like flails and exploded any mine that they struck. Only a limited number was ready for Alamein, manned by 42nd and 44th Battalions Royal Tank Regiment with an RE complement. They were not at first a great success, becoming very overheated after long spells of flailing and stirring up enormous clouds of dust which attracted hostile attention and which made it almost impossible to keep direction. Later, as improvements were made, the Scorpion Regiment was formed.

Clearing the mines, however, was only a part of the problem of penetrating the explosive thickets of the devil's gardens. Sappers alone, while absorbed in their sensitive task, could not fight the enemy battle outpost as well, though they were trained to do so if necessary and sometimes did. Thus it was very important to provide

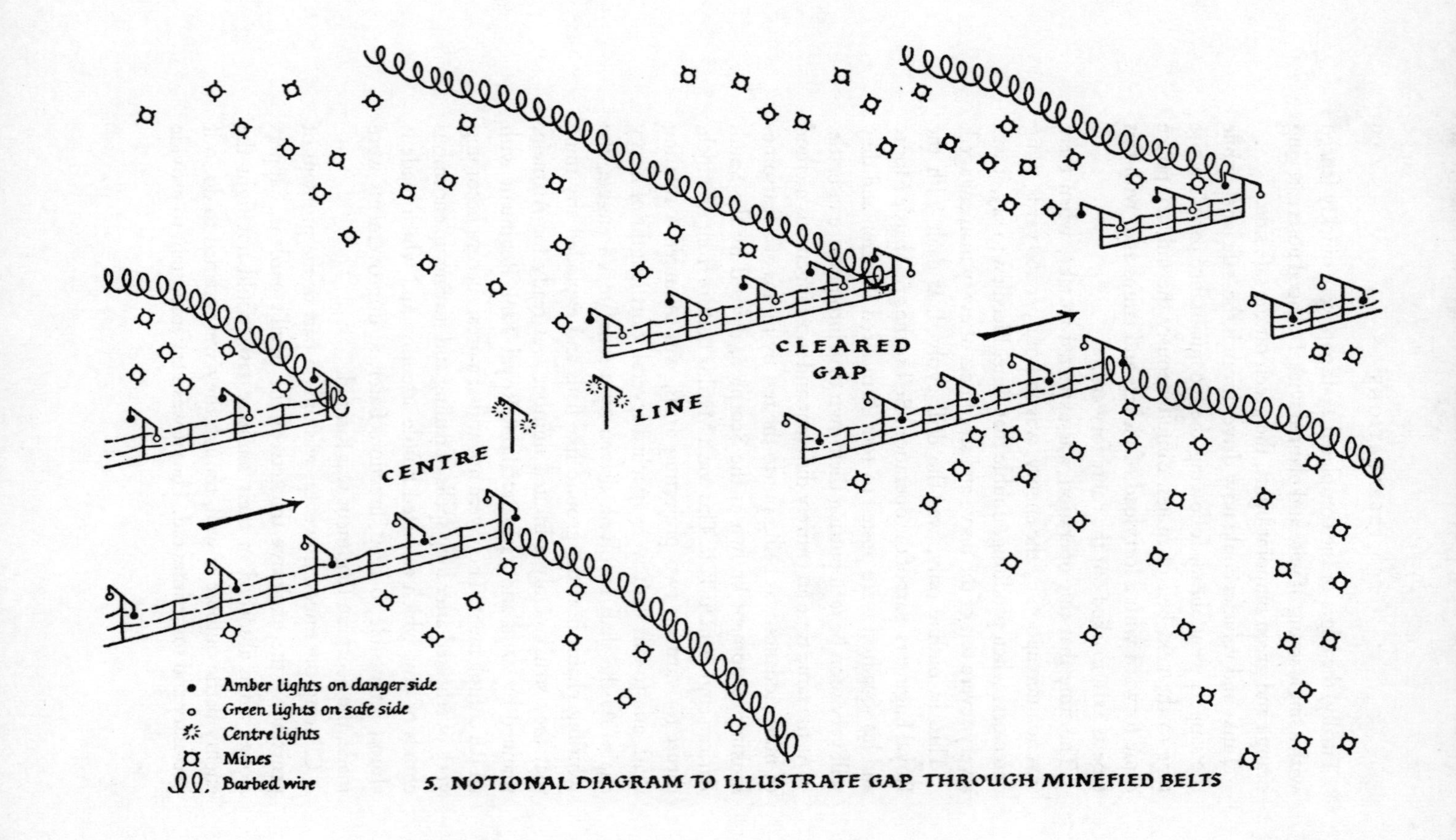

5. NOTIONAL DIAGRAM TO ILLUSTRATE GAP THROUGH MINEFIED BELTS

The Crusader; Gerald Grosvenor, CO 9th Lancers, 'up'

Crusaders moving up in the dust-fog

A 'Priest' of 11th (HAC) Regt, RHA

A 'Bishop' of 121st Field Regt, RA

them with a protective force, so that they could concentrate on their task undisturbed. Moreover, after the gap had been made, its use had to be controlled.

A great advance was made when, in time for Alamein, a composite Minefield Task Force was created in most of the divisions. Each division had its own ideas, but that evolved by 1st Armoured Division became the standard model in Eighth Army and was taught at the Haifa Staff College. In that division the force consisted, in addition to the sapper squadrons, of a battalion of infantry (2nd Battalion The Rifle Brigade), three troops of tanks, a detachment of Military Police and a detachment of Royal Signals.

The whole force was under the command of the infantry CO and he was responsible for the three gaps required for the passage of an armoured division. It was at once a mine clearance force, a fighting force, a traffic control authority, a channel of communications and a centre of information. The control of traffic in both directions was of the first importance to operations and the coolness with which the 'red caps' performed this and other duties in the minefields under fire, immaculate in their daily turn-out until they became smothered in dust, was one of the star performances of Alamein.

No less excellent was the work done under the same conditions by the Royal Corps of Signals, for good communications were vital. Thus it was the sappers, signals and military police who led the armour into battle.

A special kind of minefield task force was employed by 13th Corps down in the south. Here the main covering force for the sappers was provided by 44th Division Reconnaissance Regiment, commanded by Lieut-Colonel J. L. Corbett-Winder, the unit being completely equipped with bren-gun carriers. The 'Snail' was another ingenious device used in the south. This was a lorry dripping diesel oil, which leaves an unmistakable trail in the moonlight. Manned by 211th Field Park Company, they 'proved a lane' which the sappers found clear; it must have been the first time that a field park company, whose business was normally confined to providing stores, had led a division into battle!

Thus by the time of Alamein the clearance of safe passages through minefields had been recognized as a vital and integral part of an assault operation, requiring careful training, careful integration into the plan and an important place in the operation orders of every division.

THE ALLIED AIR FORCES REGROUP

Under Tedder's direction, reorganization and training were taking place in the air forces also. After the battle a vigorous spearhead of mobile fighter squadrons would be wanted for the pursuit and the new American squadrons had to be geared to the machine; these factors necessitated casting the Desert Air Force in a fresh mould.

A new fighter Group HQ (No.212) and a new fighter Wing (No.244) were established. An additional day-bomber Wing HQ (No.232) was brought forward from Palestine. The twenty-five British and American fighter squadrons were divided into two fighter groups, one being assembled in No. 211 Group (Group Captain G. L. Carter) and known as Force A, for follow-up after the battle, while Force B came under No. 212 Group.

The growth of the United States Air Force in the Middle East under General Brereton (later the Ninth Air Force), much of which was employed on long-range strategic bombing, made it necessary to revise plans for its control. Operational control of the American heavy bombers was placed under IX Bomber Command USAF and that of the medium day-bombers and fighter squadrons under the Desert Air Force. The day before the battle was to begin a small American Task Force HQ was set up alongside Coningham's own advanced desert HQ on the sea-shore.

Training for the coming battle was highly systematized, the emphasis being on improving radio-telephone operation and discipline, and on the difficult task of laying down smoke screens from the air, which was practised by the Bostons of 12th and 24th USAF Squadrons. The American squadrons were well trained technically, but they had not had war or desert experience. The problems of their absorption into a highly-trained mobile force were not easy, but were overcome on a human level by the co-operation of unit commanders.

We still suffered some drawbacks in our aircraft, our fighters being inferior in performance to the German Messerschmitt 109 F or G. There was a shortage of Spitfires and Kittyhawks and there were no replacements for Hurricane losses. Two Hurricane Squadrons (No. 6 and No. 7 SAAF) were equipped as 'tank busters', armed with 40-mm 'cannon' and were ready for battle after long and arduous training and high casualties.

Coningham had designed the general shape of DAF operations so that he could change their emphasis to suit conditions as they developed. In the pre-battle phases he aimed at reducing the risks of heavy enemy air attacks on our assembling troops by attacking enemy airfields by day and by night, by providing fighter cover over the Army's forward areas and constantly reconnoitring the enemy defences. As soon as Montgomery's attack began, the emphasis would change to attacking the enemy troops in the battle area as intensively as possible.

STOCKPILING FOR BATTLE

The great effort needed for the provisioning and maintenance of the troops in battle, and for the subsequent operations, testified to the soundness and strength of the administrative services of the Army and the Allied Air Forces. They were in contrast to those of the enemy, whose administrative services were unstable, badly co-ordinated and often at odds with the combatant troops. The 'Quarter-master's Battle' was won by the British before the fighting soldier rose from his trench for the assault.

For movement into the battle area from the railheads of Amiriya and Burg el Arab and other depots, the equivalent of thirty-six General Transport Companies RASC was available, with a carrying capacity of over 10,000 tons, together with six Tank Transporter Companies, which did service of the highest order in the delivery of tanks right up to the battle area. There were nine Water Tank

Companies. Three new water points were opened near Alamein and many miles of new water pipeline built.

Ten days before the battle five days' stocks of rations, ammunition and stores of every kind had been built up in the Field Maintenance Centres, the highly efficient administrative system that Eighth Army had devised for supply in the Desert. Great stocks of ammunition were accumulated, 286,000 rounds of 25-pdr shells and 20,000 of medium artillery being dumped right forward and concealed from the enemy's aerial eye; quantities were buried in the sand at pre-determined gun positions not occupied until the very eve of battle. Large reserves were at hand. In the event, the supplies available enabled the Royal Artillery regiments to fire more than a million rounds in the twelve days of fighting at Alamein – an average of 102 rounds per gun per day, while the rate for the medium artillery was higher still, reaching 157 r. p. g. per day for the 5·5's.

The establishment of the Corps of Royal Electrical and Mechanical Engineers shortly before the battle greatly improved the means of quick and efficient repairs to tanks, vehicles, guns, optical and all other equipment. Drawn from the engineering elements of the Royal Army Ordnance Corps and the RASC, with some RE, it provided workshop facilities and technicians at all command levels and co-ordination of their work from the base right up to the fighting units. The new Tank Reorganization Group created a machinery to maintain a swift and regular flow of new and repaired tanks from dockyard and base workshop right up to the front, where, complete with crews, they were fed into the armoured regiments in action by the Tank Delivery Squadrons and Troops. For the Desert Air Force a like service was carried out by the repair and replacement mechanism under Air Commodore T. W. Elmhirst, Coningham's administrative officer.

Chapter Eight

MEET THE DIVISIONS

The Dominion Divisions – The Highland Division –
The Indians – The Armour – 13th Corps Divisions

We have seen in the last chapter how Montgomery reviewed the Order of Battle, reshaped the divisions and set them to intensive training for the particular kind of battle that he had designed.

For the convenience of readers, and in order not to impede the narrative, the Order of Battle as he determined it is set out in Appendix A. Its structure is, however, an integral part of our story and a brief study of it at the present stage will repay the reader who is anxious to follow the events to come without frequent reference.

An unadorned list of units, however, will not suffice and, therefore, before considering the parts for which these divisions were ordained in the battle, we shall pay them a brief visit in their trenches, their training areas and their gun-pits and see what manner of men they were.

THE DOMINION DIVISIONS

Prominent among the infantry divisions were the three from the Dominions – as they then were – Australia, New Zealand and South Africa. Each had its own characteristics, but a factor they shared in common, as Leese testifies, was the excellence of their artillery and their medical services. Leese considered 'Steve'

Weir, the New Zealand CRA, to be the best gunner in Eighth Army. He was certainly one of the most popular – dark-haired, deeply tanned, ruggedly handsome, full of laughter and spirit, fit and alert.

There were very few Regular soldiers in these divisions, since the Dominions maintained only very small armies in times of peace. They all, however, took their military teaching from Britain and 'spoke the same language'. Their organization, drill and equipment were identical with those of Home Country units. Their staff officers went to Camberley or Quetta and many of their gunner officers to Larkhill. Many men from the Dominions and other overseas lands – particularly Rhodesians and South Africans – went to British home country units as officers. The same close identity of structure and method occurred in the various Air Forces.

The 9th Australian Division, whose emblem was a platypus surmounting a boomerang, were the people who, perhaps, had the most distinctive corporate personality. Outwardly, they had a free-and-easy form of discipline all their own. The 'democratic' image was strongly emphasized. The military character was to a large extent submerged in the civilian. The officer enjoyed small natural respect from his men by reason of his rank alone. He had to prove himself by personal example, particularly example in battle, before he was 'accepted'.

In this civilian-style army, the Regular officer was a rarity and he was generally a staff officer. The staff man held a very special place, for he was the only one who had a thorough professional training. He was regarded merely as a technical specialist. So strong was the anti-military complex in the Australian mind that the Australian Government expressly debarred any officer of the Staff Corps from being appointed to a command.[1] All commanders were citizen-soldiers, chosen for their personal qualities.

This applied even to the divisional commander, Leslie Morshead, who by profession was a shipping executive but a very fine commander indeed. He was small, swarthy, quiet-mannered, spoke

1. This is no longer so.

with a pronounced Australian accent and had an equally pronounced will. 'He gave me,' said the newly arrived Wimberley, 'a higher feeling of morale than anyone else I had met so far.' Under him the division had achieved fame in the previous year as the defenders of Tobruk (together with many British troops).

An obvious disadvantage of this system was that the senior men, though they might be fine commanders and leaders, had a limited knowledge of the mechanism and practice of military operations. This was done by the professional staff officer. The others had to learn the hard way. But the material was fine. Victor Windeyer, commanding 20th Brigade, had a good tactical brain and was cool and resolute in action; he was a Sydney lawyer and is now a judge. David Whitehead, commanding 26th Brigade, known as 'Torpy', was an angular and almost ascetic figure, who had served in the First World War. Arthur Godfrey, of 24th Brigade, was a diamond if something of a rough one, who was to be killed at Thompson's Post. He was followed by Bernard Evans, an architect, now Lord Mayor of Melbourne.

Morshead and his division of citizen-soldiers were extremely fortunate in the trained Regular Officer who was their GSO 1. This was Lieutenant-Colonel G. P. Wells, known to all as 'Bomba'. He had been to Camberley staff college and, by a fortunate circumstance, had been there with Rickie Richards, whose armoured regiments of 23rd Armoured Brigade were to give the Australians such fine tank support.

The Australians, therefore, had their own type of discipline and their own way of getting things done. To Douglas Wimberley they were 'natural born soldiers', thrustful in the attack, tenacious in defence. This excellence derived from what may be called battlefield discipline, which, in its simplest terms, means the will and desire to fight. Morshead's men were not alone in this – the Highlanders, the New Zealanders and others displayed it – nor were all Australians of the same quality, but it was certainly the distinguishing mark of 9th Division. When to battlefield discipline you add battle drill, which the Division acquired by hard and painful experience, you have a formation that knows how to win its battles.

The New Zealanders – the celebrated 'Kiwis' with the fern-lea emblem – were a rather different parcel of men. Greatly admired and regarded with affection by the whole Army, they had already proved their exceptionally fine fighting qualities on several occasions, though likewise after some hard lessons learnt. They had suffered heavy casualties in the 'Gazala Stakes' and in the July fighting, had a serious reinforcement problem, and were one brigade short at Alamein, but their spirit was as buoyant as ever and their battle technique now very high. Conspicuous among them was the Maori battalion, under their half-Maori CO, Fred Baker; they fought like tigers but needed a firm hand to control them.

Towering above them all, physically as well as figuratively, was their famous commander, Major-General Bernard Freyberg, VC. 'Tiny' Freyberg was a figure of legend throughout the Army. A man of powerful stature and bull-dog features, he had been wounded so many times, in both wars, that no one knew exactly what the count was. He was scored and creased with scars. He would frequently scratch the back of his neck, from which, after twenty-two years, small fragments of shell splinters from the wound sustained when he won his Victoria Cross kept working out through his skin. He had only just now recovered from another wound sustained at the beginning of the July fighting. He was a great friend of Mr Churchill's, who loved a warrior and who, at the victory parade in Tripoli, fell upon his neck with tears and publicly proclaimed him as 'the salamander of the British Empire'.

Freyberg was a born and natural warrior. Normally a rather deliberate thinker, not making a decision until he had weighed all the factors, on the battlefield, with the smell of powder in his nostrils, his intellect became instantly illuminated. His whole being was quickened. He had, as few other people had, the rare 'battlefield instinct', partly inborn, partly acquired from long battle experience, beginning in the Mexican Civil War of 1911. He had invisible antennae which could feel which way things were going all around him. He could sense the enemy's pulse and looked ahead to what had to be done next. His changes of plan and his forgetfulness of 'dates' could be maddening, but he was regarded with veneration and tremendous affection by everyone, for, besides being a very brave man, he was also a very kind-hearted one and always retained something of a boyish spirit. He never lost the feelings of a young platoon commander in the front line and looked at all problems from the point of view of the man with the rifle. A Grenadier Guardsman and not wholly a New Zealander, he had more than once very nearly swum the Channel, in the days when that was a very rare and considerable feat indeed.

If, as George Walsh said, Freyberg was the division and the division Freyberg, he was by no means the only remarkable figure in it. Howard Kippenberger, commander of 5th Brigade, courageous, determined, forthright, a solicitor by trade, and one of the most celebrated desert fighters; Steve Weir, the gunner already mentioned; Bill Gentry, the sturdy and equable commander of 6th Brigade; Ray Queree, the nimble-minded GSO 1, who could have done with some of his general's inches; Fred Hanson, the CRE, strong, solid, very independent-minded, who had been an infantry sergeant in the First War; Charles Upham, the phenomenal double VC – these were a few of the men who helped to win the Kiwis their renown; and when the lion-hearted John Currie, with crisp hair stolen from the sun, and his 9th Armoured Brigade were added to them, they made up a balanced fighting force that any commander from Alexander the Great onwards would have been glad to have had at hand.

This brigade was an English formation and was one of the most shining successes of Alamein. Composed of two yeomanry regiments (formerly of 1st Cavalry Division) that had not long been mechanized and a regular cavalry regiment, it had experienced very little action and Alamein was to be its first serious battle. Many of the officers were foxhunting men and two of the COs – Sir Peter Farquhar, of 3rd Hussars, and Guy Jackson, of the Warwickshire Yeomanry – were masters of hounds. Farquhar, who took over his regiment only a few weeks before the battle, was one of the few officers who had had much battle experience, but from the fine raw material that the regiments provided Currie had forged a splendid fighting machine, which, when called upon, did not hesitate to ride out upon a mission of almost total self-destruction, fore-ordained and calculated.

John Currie was himself a product of the Royal Horse Artillery. He was a vibrant personality, hard as nails, burned with offensive spirit and was charged with tremendous personal energy and drive. He had a strong sense of humour and a dash of horse-gunners *panache*. He wore a pair of old, tan-coloured canvas slacks, a khaki flannel shirt and an old, faded gunner mess cap of red, blue and gold. He suffered severely from desert sores on his hands, which he kept bound up with faded red bandana handkerchiefs.

His most astonishing characteristic, however, was his complete freedom from fear, indeed, his positive enjoyment of danger. Major Nicholas Pease, his brigade signals officer, said of him: 'He could be abominable in training or at rest, but in action he was magnificent. He became a changed man. He laughed and joked like a boy on holiday and the hotter the fire the more he enjoyed himself. He stood right up on top of his tank and took not the slightest notice of shells and bullets. If he saw anyone getting down to earth under fire, he would say, with a laugh: 'What on earth are you lying down for? Why don't you stand up?'

Like others who have been mentioned who were born leaders in action, Currie was very severe and exacting in training. When his new brigade major, young Pat Hobart, nephew of the celebrated tank general, joined the brigade in September, he recorded in his diary:

> Found that 9 Armd Bde was not a very happy party. Everybody seemed to be terrified of J.C. and there was an atmosphere of veiled distrust. J.C., experienced in battle, knew that he had to get this completely un-battle-tried brigade ready for the biggest battle yet in about six weeks' time. He was determined to do this and drove them relentlessly, which they resented.

Most of these cavalrymen had had a fairly easy, if boring, war so far and were not used to this rigorous handling, but Currie had seen what happened in battle to half-trained troops. Within a month the whole atmosphere in the brigade had changed and Hobart wrote: 'People are all starting to talk and laugh together as people should and seem to be less frightened of the Brig.' When at last they went into action together, as another officer said, 'all the hard words were forgotten and forgiven' as they followed his inspiring leadership.[1]

Currie's brigade was placed under command of the New Zealand Division and a warm comradeship ripened between them. Exclusive of headquarters' tanks, they were equipped with forty-six Crusaders, thirty-seven Grants and thirty-five of the new Shermans. They became so much a part of that division that they mounted the Kiwis' fern-leaf emblem on their tanks and came to regard it as a battle honour.

Of the South Africans, commanded by Major-General Dan Pienaar, we shall not see a great deal on this stage, as their part in the play, though important, was of short duration. Whatever they were called upon to do they did well and their armoured cars did particularly good work. With their orange flash on their shoulder-straps, the Springboks were familiar and popular figures in the desert, a constant reminder of the greatness of their leader, Jan Smuts. The division's simple badge was symbolic of the sun rising on the *veldt*.

THE HIGHLAND DIVISION

From the Dominion troops we pass to those who came from Great Britain and may look first at 51st (Highland) Division, on whom, of the British infantry, was to fall the largest part of the Alamein fighting. It was the only one at full strength. Freshly out from home in August, the 'Jocks' had learned their desert fighting technique by sending contingents into the line with the Australians, for whom they had a great admiration – a sentiment which the Aussies warmly returned.

The division came out to the desert with the memory of a tragedy to avenge, and to avenge against Rommel himself. In a last effort to stem the disasters of the Battle of France in 1940, 51st Division, led

1. Currie, having survived the whole of the desert campaign and part of the Italian, was killed by a solitary, stray shell in Normandy.

by Victor Fortune, but operating under French command, had been trapped at St-Valéry during Rommel's lightning drive through a broken country and obliged to surrender. From the ashes of the old division a new phoenix had arisen, eager to wipe out that unhappy record. The commander of the division, as already mentioned, was Douglas Wimberley, very tall and lean, tremendously energetic, a 'serious' soldier but eager and cheerful in spirit. Riding in a jeep, with his long legs tucked up under his chin, covered with desert sores and wearing the bonnet of the Camerons, he was always happiest when right in front with his troops, never bothering about food and leaving his able GSO 1, Roy Urquhart, to run divisional headquarters. His whole being was devoted to his division and, despite his English surname, he was an ardent Highlander. He was known affectionately as 'Big Tam' or 'Tartan Tam'. He believed in the outward and visible signs of corporate pride as a stimulus to the inner springs and he made sure that, wherever 51st Division went in its long trail of battle, the world should know that it had passed that way. It was a duty of his Military Police to write large the simple divisional emblem of HD all along that honourable trail.

This was something quite new to Eighth Army, who had been bred in 'security' measures and who chaffingly christened Wimberley's men 'the Sign-writers' or 'the House Decorators'; but it was a practice in keeping with Montgomery's own ideas that men should have 'a guid conceit o' themsels'. 'Security', in this matter, went overboard; as Wimberley said, Scottish troops always proclaim themselves!

Otherwise, the only outward evidence of the division's origin was in the Scotch bonnets of the infantry. Only the pipers then wore the kilt; some pipers also wore a beard. The general wear was shorts, but James Oliver, his wisdom overcoming other inclinations, required 7th Black Watch to wear trousers as a protection against desert sores. The infantry battalions were from Highland regiments and the majority of the officers and men came from Highland homes. They combined the qualities of the highlander of the glen and hillside with those of the spirited Jock of the city streets. The other units were somewhat more mixed in their origins but the Scottish element was naturally dominant.

The division's machine-gunners, however, were an exception, being a Territorial battalion of the Middlesex Regiment ('The Diehards'). They were nearly all Londoners, commanded by a spirited CO, Lieutenant-Colonel J. W. A. Stephenson, well known as a county cricketer. Between the nimble-witted Cockney 'Diehards' and the sturdy Jocks there was a warm affection. On the eve of the battle Stephenson sent a signal to his GOC, saying: *Proud to be serving under you. Scotland for ever.* And Wimberley replied: *Special message for the Diehards: For ever England.*

The quality of 51st Division was to be seen not only in their fighting record but also in the many men within its ranks who were to advance on the road to distinction: 'Nap' Murray, of 1st Gordon Highlanders, burly and prematurely bald, who was to become Commander-in-Chief of the Allied Forces in Northern Europe; Roy Urquhart, Wimberley's GSO 1, who was to achieve fame as the commander of the Airborne Division at Arnhem; Thomas Rennie, the rugby footballer, of 5th Black Watch, pipe-smoking, outwardly lackadaisical, who had been captured with the old division in France and had made a thrilling escape, who was himself to command the division and to be killed on the eve of victory in Germany; Douglas Graham, 'that great little warrior', soon to command a division, walking with a slight limp, always minimizing difficulties and given to saying 'Now here'; Lorne Campbell, the handsome VC; and yet others.

THE INDIANS

At the southern end of 30th Corps front, guarding Ruweisat Ridge, stood the veteran 4th Indian Division under its emblem of a hawk in flight. It shared honours with 7th Armoured Division as the most renowned of the old desert formations, having faced the enemy ever since O'Connor's day. It was commanded by Major-General F. I. S. Tuker, known as 'Gertie' Tuker, an intellectual soldier of the highest standing. As in other Indian divisions, nearly all the officers were British; there was a British battalion in each of the three brigades and all the artillery regiments were British. They did not have a large part at Alamein, but one brigade had a long and difficult attack to make at the very end.

THE ARMOUR

These were the five infantry divisions of 30th Corps at the start of the battle, but there was another formation in this corps of the first importance – 23rd Armoured Brigade Group. Apart from the 9th, which Montgomery had given to the New Zealanders, this hard-fighting brigade was the only armour at the disposal of Oliver Leese.

The 23rd consisted of three Territorial battalions of the Royal Tank Regiment from the Liverpool area, to which was added a Regular battalion, the 8th. They had had a bloody baptism in the grossly mishandled battle of 'Second Ruweisat' in July, but their spirit was unshaken. They were equipped with the Valentine tank, which mounted the little 2-pdr gun and was thus no match for the German tanks, but which had a low silhouette and was mechanically reliable. They were well suited, however, to the special task to which they had now been assigned – the close support of infantry. This was effected by placing one or more of its battalions *under command* each assaulting division. Appropriately, their emblem was the legendary Liver bird.

Thus 40th Battalion, who became famous as 'Monty's Foxhounds' and who had been formed from 7th Battalion The King's Regiment, supported the Australians; it was commanded by the remarkable Jim Finigan, a Liverpool business man whose diminutive figure and acute, peering short-sightedness seemed to deny the likelihood of his plucky spirit and his strong hold over his men. The 46th Battalion also supported the Australians at one stage, under the determined command of T. C. A. Clarke. The 50th Battalion served the Highland Division, led by the soldierly figure of John Cairns who later on was to die gallantly in a tight corner when going to the help of 50th Division. The 8th Battalion served initially with the South Africans. The brigade had its own artillery, engineer and other units.

It is important that the reader not familiar with these matters should bear in mind the difference in function between the armoured brigade in an armoured division, concerned most characteristically with fighting other tanks and with breaking out into enemy country, and the armoured brigade operating in close support of infantry in the assault. Given the right tank and the right training, the same brigade could do both tasks, but 23rd Armoured Brigade was used solely for infantry support.

The technique of this co-operation was by no means perfect at Alamein. That came later, but to 23rd Brigade belonged the credit for working out the problems under their gifted commander, G. P. Richards. A thinking soldier, staff trained, technically expert, 'Rickie' Richards made an analytical study of every action. After one of the disasters in the July fighting, he offered the Australians a battalion of his tanks to train with each of their infantry battalions in turn. Together they carried out day and night exercises until they had developed a common doctrine for all the problems of co-ordination, minelifting, keeping direction, consolidation under pre-arranged artillery support, preparedness for the enemy counter-attack and so on. The techniques so evolved became basic to all operations of this nature for the rest of the war.

Leaving the infantry of 30th Corps and the armour working with them, we come to the totally different 10th Corps, which GHQ had re-formed at Montgomery's special request, under the command of Herbert Lumsden. It was a formidable force. Composed, as the Order of Battle shows, of 1st and 10th Armoured Divisions, it counted altogether 434 tanks in the armoured regiments. It had been intended to include 8th Armoured Division also, under Charles Gairdner, but this division was never completed, and its headquarters, its divisional signals and other troops were employed before the battle on the important deception role.

First Armoured Division, identified by its white rhinoceros emblem, was commanded by Raymond Briggs, a Royal Tank Regiment officer, who had begun his soldiering as a private in the Liverpool Scottish in the First World War, in which he had been twice wounded. He had served in the Western Desert before the Second War and had acquired an intimate understanding of it. Lean, alert and 'black-avised', he was an able and painstaking commander, firm but tactful. His sable hair and his very deep tan earned him the name of the 'Black Prince', but in the veiled language of the radio, the simple subtleties of which seldom deceived an astute enemy, he was referred to, by association with the famous firm, as the 'Umbrella Man'. Like Monty, Horrocks, Lumsden and others, he had been an instructor at the Staff College. Briggs was not a 'Monty selection', but earned Monty's approbation. His GSO 1 was Roger Peake.

Briggs had 161 tanks in the armoured brigade of his division, of which ninety-two were Shermans. This brigade, the 2nd, consisted entirely of cavalry regiments, including, paradoxically, its motor infantry battalion, the Yorkshire Dragoons. It was commanded by Brigadier Frank Fisher, deliberate in method but with a very sound tactical sense.

The 7th Motor Brigade, which had just joined the division as its infantry element, were veteran desert fighters, composed entirely of Rifle regiments, whose tenacity and resilience in many a critical situation had won them a great name in the Desert Rats. They were commanded by Jimmy Bosvile, another of the celebrated desert 'race of dwarfs', quick in action and quick in temper. They were specialized infantry mounted wholly in small trucks and bren-carriers, with lorried supply echelons. Their strength lay in their remarkable mobility and their considerable fire power, but their weakness in numbers made them unsuitable for the assault of defended positions. Their special qualities will be seen more closely when we witness one of their battalions and their accompanying gunners in a day of Homeric fighting below Kidney Ridge.

Briggs's division was perhaps the most up-to-date of the armour. Its artillery, under 'Frizz' Fowler, included the self-propelled Priests of 11th RHA and the self-propelled Deacons of ZZ Battery in 76th Anti-Tank Regiment. It also led the way in its thinking on

Honeys kicking up a dust

The crew of a Grant brewing up at last light with 'the sun like a huge gun flash'

The 25-pounder

The 6-pounder anti-tank gun

the Minefield Task Force, largely through the influence of its able CRE (Commander Royal Engineers), Lieutenant-Colonel Kenneth MacKay. In this division, however, the Task Force was commanded not by him but by the Rifleman, Victor Turner, who will shortly be seen winning the Victoria Cross.

Tenth Armoured Division, identified by its emblem of a fox's mask, was a powerful formation of two armoured brigades, with a total of 273 tanks, and a lorried infantry brigade.

The 8th Armoured Brigade, commanded by Neville Custance, shrewd but deliberate in method and enjoying the golden opinion of his regiments, included 3rd RTR, which, led by the able 'Pete' Pyman, had suffered some hard hammerings in previous fighting, and two fine yeomanry regiments. The Staffordshire Yeomanry, led by Jim Eadie, had been largely recruited from Bass's brewery at Burton-on-Trent and they wore the Bass red triangle behind the Staffordshire Knot on their caps. The Nottinghamshire Yeomanry, more often known as the Sherwood Rangers, were commanded by an MP, the gallant E. O. Kellett, known to all, on account of his smartness of turn-out, as 'Flash' Kellett.

The other armoured brigade in the division, the 24th, was a new and untried formation not long out from England. The divisional artillery was commanded by 'Baron' Ebbels, good-looking, always well turned-out, always laughing and never, it seemed, feeling any need for sleep.

The dominant interest in this division, however, was in its commander, who was to become a figure of controversy and to have a serious row with Montgomery. We shall see for ourselves in due course the true facts behind this row, which the Field-Marshal himself represented in an unfortunate light in his *Memoirs*.

Major-General Alec Gatehouse had unquestionably been one of the outstanding tank officers of the desert fighting and he had probably had more experience of actually fighting in a tank than any other senior officer. He was a robust, four-square, John Bull Englishman, with a touch of rugged *panache* that matched his blunt independence of mind. In contrast, he had a rather high-pitched voice and a slight impediment of speech which were as familiar to the Germans as to the British. On return to the desert after an absence on one occasion the German wireless interceptor was heard to say:

'Ahllo, Alec! Zo you are back. Vell, ve are kvite ready for you!'

Gatehouse had commanded a tank company in the memorable Battle of Cambrai in 1917, and in the second war had been in battle time and again, gaining a reputation for his personal leadership and his offensive spirit against odds. Much decorated, he was a man of outstanding personal bravery, indeed, in the words of Douglas Wimberley, 'almost foolhardily brave'. At a critical point in the Battle of Alamein Wimberley found him sitting calmly before a little camp table outside his tank, studying the map, while the shells were detonating all about. Wimberley said:

'Good heavens! Why don't you get a slit trench dug?'

To which Gatehouse replied light-heartedly:

'Oh, you can't do that sort of thing in an armoured division.'

These qualities had made Alec Gatehouse one of the best-known figures in the desert. So also had his bluntness. He was outspoken to a degree and did not give a damn for anyone. He was on bad terms with Lumsden, whose orders he interrupted and questioned almost to insubordination. On occasions Lumsden would remark icily:

'I am giving orders.'

Upon which Gatehouse would say loudly to his GSO 1, Bill Liardet:

'Take down the Corps Commander's orders in writing.'

The hostility derived, no doubt, from a simple clash of personalities as between the rugged and the polished, the RTR officer and the cavalryman. Gatehouse did not take kindly to the intellectual type of soldier that Lumsden was. He would speak somewhat scornfully of 'the Staff' and 'Staff College types', yet was on the warmest terms with his own staff, who immensely admired him. So also did the rank and file, for Gatehouse was a soldier's soldier.

It need not surprise us in the least, therefore, that Montgomery, who did not care for independent subordinates, and Gatehouse, who was subservient to no man, should before long strike sparks from the flint of each other's will.

13TH CORPS DIVISIONS

These two corps – 30th and 10th – are to fill the major part of our narrative, but down in the hot south, under 13th Corps, were other formations which had also some hard fighting to do and which were afterwards to take the lead in the battles of the pursuit.

South of the Ruweisat Ridge and on the left flank of the Indians, 50th (Northumbrian) Division sat astride Alam Nayil and stretched away southward to the harsh features of the Munassib Depression. They wore the distinguished TT emblem (for 'Tyne and Tees'). The 50th, like the 51st and the 7th Armoured, was another of the great fighting divisions that Montgomery afterwards took with him wherever he went, using them in one major assault after another through Africa, Sicily, Normandy and onwards.

Their commander at Alamein was the spectacled, tough and much decorated 'Crasher' Nichols, who at Eton had fought a record struggle with Oliver Leese in the wall game. His infantry came mainly from Durham and Yorkshire, and his Durham Brigade and his Rhodesian anti-tank gunners were shortly to be sent north to help the New Zealanders and Australians. To replace his third brigade, decimated in the early fighting, Colonel Katsotas's Greek Brigade, ardent patrollers and collectors of Italian ears, had been temporarily included in his command.

Southward again of 50th Division, holding a long front in rough ground and much soft sand, stood the division that had the hardest luck of any. This was the 44th, which had formerly been commanded by Brian Horrocks and was now by Ivor Hughes. Drawn mainly from Kent, Surrey and Sussex, and not long out from England, it suffered heavy casualties before and during Alamein and two of its brigades were taken away to provide lorried infantry for 7th and 10th Armoured Divisions. Thus dismembered, the division was broken up soon after Alamein.

This division worked in close association at Alamein with the already famous 7th Armoured Division, who, wearing their 'desert rat' emblem, stood behind the 44th in and about the soft sand of the Ragil Depression. They were commanded now by John Harding, that little tiger whose unhidden fire kept every man on his toes and who was one day to become Chief of the Imperial General Staff.

The division had no infantry brigade at this time. Mechanically, it was in a run-down condition; its tanks had seen long and hard service and its wheeled vehicles were maintained only with difficulty – a factor that was to condition its employment. It had no Shermans. Its main strength lay in 22nd Armoured Brigade, which had 126 tanks of various kinds and which had done so well at Alam Halfa under the able 'Pip' Roberts, yet another man of small stature with a remarkable battlefield flair.

In 4th Light Brigade there were only eighty-one tanks, but the division had a phenomenal array of about 170 armoured cars, many of which were employed in patrolling the enormous No Man's Land, five miles wide, which stretched between the opposing minefields.

Last of all, away down under the shadows of Mount Himeimat, in difficult ground, the Free French stood on guard under the distinguished command of General Koenig, the hero of Bir Hachim. They were a mixed force of French and French-Colonial troops and were under command of 7th Armoured Division.

Chapter Nine

THE PLAN

Considerations – A Battle of Attrition –
The Red Herring – The Enemy's Difficulties

CONSIDERATIONS

While training and reorganization were going on Montgomery was maturing his plans. The problem before him was that his divisions were confronted by thirty-eight miles of deep and intricate defences, having no flanks or other opportunity for manœuvre. The scope for surprise was small.

There was no cover to give natural concealment from the enemy to the large preparations necessary before the offensive – the movements and assembly of whole divisions, the positioning of tanks, guns and operational vehicles, the accumulation in the forward areas of very large stocks of ammunition and stores of all sorts, the preparation and marking of tracks for the forward movement of a great mass of vehicles to the vital sectors.

Nor were the forward areas alone concerned. The multitudinous activities in the rear – the great stocks of petrol, rations and the construction of water supply points in particular – might be equally revealing of intention to the eyes of the enemy cameras from the air.

Equally serious were the indications that might be given by the registration shoots necessary for the artillery to confirm their precise positions, the nature and volume of the mass wireless traffic that filled the atmosphere (to which the enemy systematically listened, as we did to his) and the pattern of the activities of our air forces.

Reviewing the relative strengths, Montgomery had cause for satisfaction that by the middle of October he would have a superiority of more than two-to-one in tanks, with more still on the way, that his artillery was of an exceptionally high standard of training and provided with enormous stocks of ammunition, that the Desert Air Force was sufficiently strong and well served to achieve air superiority and that his infantry would be adequate in numbers to force their way through the defences. He knew well, however, that the enemy's potent weapons were nearly half-a-million mines and the tank-killing guns which he handled with such remarkable boldness and skill.

Two large questions Montgomery had, therefore, to decide initially were the nature of the battle that he would impose upon the enemy and the point of his main effort. His first intention, communicated to the corps and divisional commanders only at the conference on 15 September, was to attack in two sectors simultaneously, with the main effort in the north.

He designed to 'trap' the enemy in the positions in which they stood and destroy them there. Thirtieth Corps was to breach the northern defences and 10th Corps was to pour through with its armoured divisions and position itself 'on ground of its own choosing astride the enemy supply routes'. The enemy armour would thus be obliged to attack our armour in this chosen position and would be destroyed. The enemy infantry would then be rounded up.

Simultaneously, there was to be another attack in the south by 13th Corps, which would be of a secondary nature and designed primarily to prevent the enemy from sending 21st Panzer and the Ariete Divisions to reinforce the northern sector.

This was the broad conception on which was based all the reorganization, disposition and training of Eighth Army that took place during the five weeks before the battle, the formidable supply, repair and technical preparations to support it, and Coningham's dispositions in the air. In its general conception the plan conformed to the now traditional desert pattern of destroying the enemy

Relative Strengths

By 23 October the Allied and enemy forces stood at the following strengths (computed from British and enemy field returns on comparable bases by the Historical Branch of the War Office, except for the last two items):

	Allied	*Enemy*
Men	220,476[1] ('fighting state')	108,000[2] (53,736 Germans)
Tanks (fit for action)	939 (in forward area)	548[3] (249 German)
Guns, field and medium (in action)	892	552
Guns, Anti-tank	1,451	1,063
Mines	—	460,000
Aircraft (serviceable)	530	350[4]

1. Includes about 20,000 non-effectives.
2. 18,000 German reinforcements landed just before and during the battle. A further 77,000 Italians were in rear areas.
3. Rommel gives 537 on 24 October.
4. Exclusive of long-range bombers in Greece, Crete and Sicily.

armour first and then mopping up the unprotected infantry; it departed from the usual pattern only in putting the main emphasis on a northern drive instead of the usual swinging movement up from the south.

As the weeks passed, however, Montgomery began to be troubled with doubts about some aspects of the plan. He was satisfied with the standards of leadership and the fighting qualities of officers and men but was apprehensive that some of them had not had the right kind of training for the sort of battle that he proposed to fight. He thought, he tells us, that he might be asking too much of them.

On 6 October, accordingly, he decided, while adhering to the main lines of the plan, to shift the emphasis.

A BATTLE OF ATTRITION

That emphasis should now be, not to destroy the enemy's armour first, but his infantry. The aim would not be to 'trap and destroy' but to destroy by attrition. He would rely mainly on the close-quarter fighting qualities of his regiments, which he knew to be of a high standard, on the flexibility and tactical skill of the artillery and on the powerful backing of Tedder's air forces.

Under massive artillery support, our infantry and their supporting tanks would breach the minefield defences and then proceed to wear down the enemy infantry by a process of attrition that he called 'crumbling'. Tenth Corps' armoured mass would pass through, form a protective front, and place themselves to receive and break the attempt that he knew the enemy's armour would make to come to the assistance of their infantry. The enemy was to be repeatedly hammered and methodically destroyed piecemeal. He would be made 'to dance to our tune' by the constant pressure of our initiative.

'Having thus eaten the guts out of the enemy,' Montgomery said, 'he will have no troops with which to hold a front. His Panzer army may attempt to interfere with our tactics and may launch counter-attacks; this would be just what we want. . . . The eventual fate of the Panzer army is certain – it would not be able to avoid destruction.

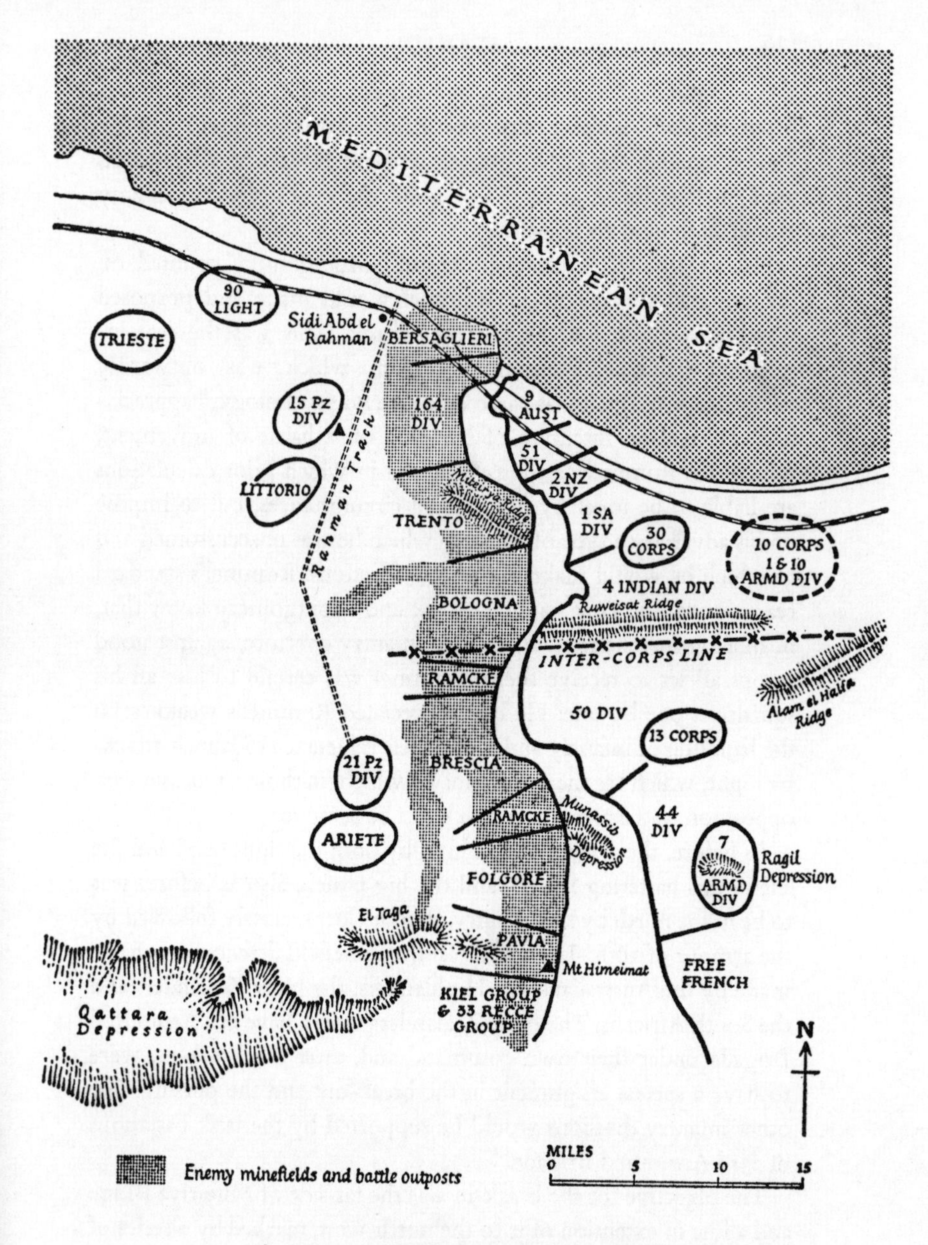

6. THE ALAMEIN LINE ON 23 OCTOBER

It is significant to note that in both editions of this plan it was Montgomery's purpose that the British armour should not be 'loosed' against the *DAK*, but, as at Alam Halfa, should position itself on favourable ground and await the attack that the enemy would be bound to launch.

Having studied Rommel's methods, Montgomery counted on the mistakes that he knew Rommel would make and proposed thereby to invite him to destroy himself. This was the real inspiration behind Montgomery's plan, which was outwardly pedestrian but which was based on a shrewd psychological appreciation. He had no intention of bringing on a battle of movement, which was Rommel's strong point and in which prior calculations are liable to be upset by unexpected circumstances, but to impose on his adversary a type of battle to which he was unaccustomed and to which he would make the wrong reactions. Rommel's standard reaction was the tank counter-attack and Montgomery knew that, in making such attacks without an infantry overture, against good troops all set to receive them, Rommel was certain to lose all his squadrons one by one. He had appreciated Rommel's weakness in the handling of infantry and knew their reluctance to launch attacks by night, which are the one means by which, in those circumstances, opposition to the armoured attack can be removed.

As before, there were to be blows by both the right hand and the left in this battering match, and the big punch, also as before, was to be in the north by the infantry of 30th Corps, closely followed by the armour of 10th. The assault on the minefield defences was to be made by the Australians, the Highlanders, the New Zealanders and the South Africans. The New Zealanders would have 9th Armoured Brigade under their own command and, after the break-in, were to have a special assignment in the break-out and the pursuit. The other infantry divisions would be supported by the tank battalions of 23rd Armoured Brigade.

The objective for the break-in was the far side of Miteiriya Ridge and a line in extension of it to the north-west, marked by a series of small features and together forming, in effect, a continuous low ridge, merging into what became known as Kidney Ridge. This

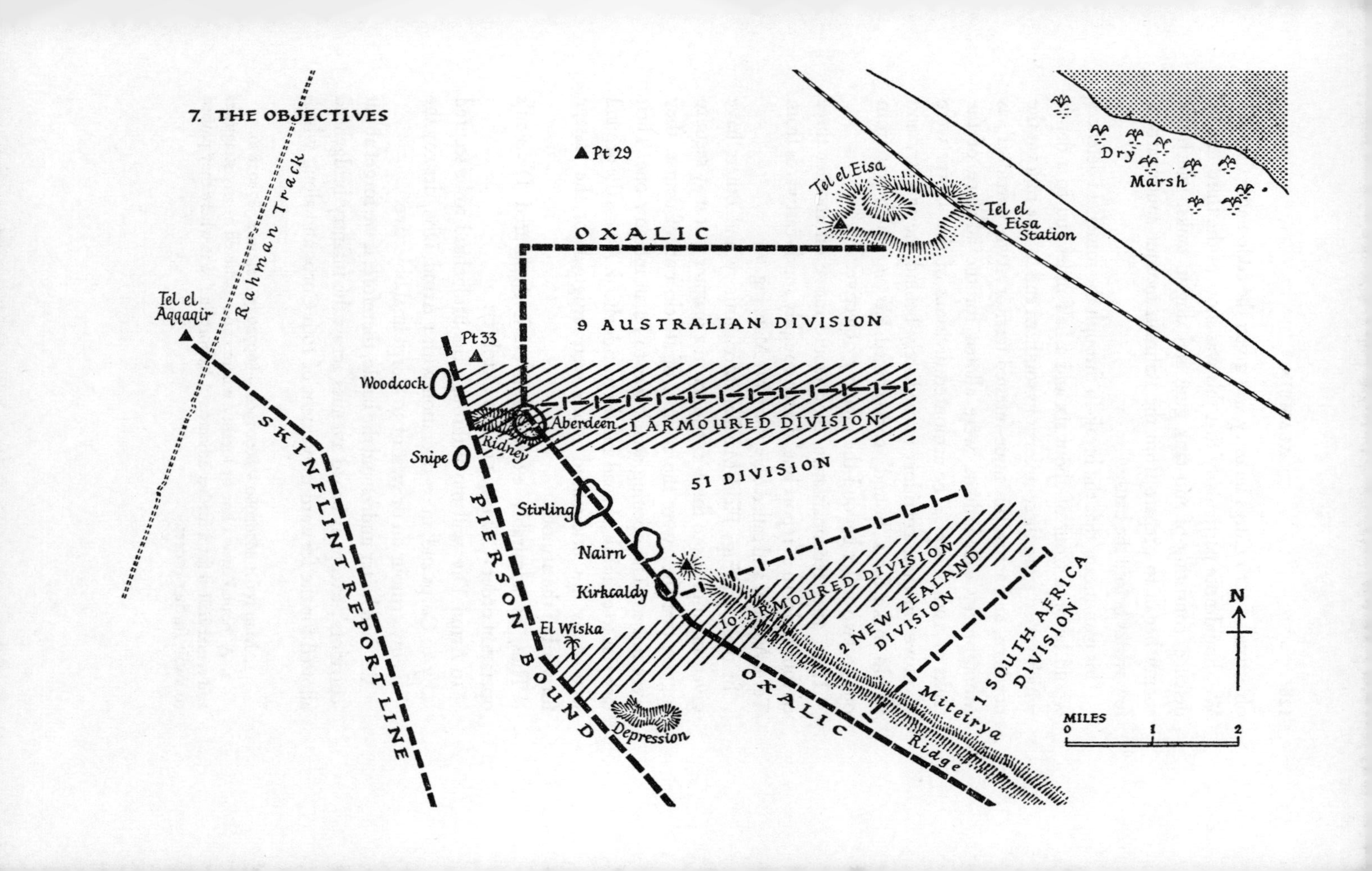
7. THE OBJECTIVES
Rahman Track
Tel el Aqqaqir
SKINFLINT REPORT LINE
Pt 29
Pt 33
Woodcock
Snipe
Kidney
Aberdeen
PIERSON BOUND
OXALIC
9 AUSTRALIAN DIVISION
1 ARMOURED DIVISION
51 DIVISION
Stirling
Nairn
Kirkcaldy
El Wiska
Depression
10 ARMOURED DIVISION
2 NEW ZEALAND DIVISION
1 SOUTH AFRICA DIVISION
OXALIC
Miteirya Ridge
Tel el Eisa
Tel el Eisa Station
Dry Marsh
N
MILES
0
1
2

objective of 30th Corps infantry was given the code-name *Oxalic.*[1] We should note particularly that this was short of the third line of defence, consisting of anti-tank guns and dug-in tanks, which the enemy began to prepare from the Rahman mosque southwards a few weeks before the battle.

This plan meant that the break-in through the minefield defences would be on a front of about six and a half miles and to a depth which varied from three miles at its southern end to five miles at the northern, and across this mine-infested territory two 'corridors', as Montgomery called them, were alloted for the advance of the tanks of 10th Corps. The armoured divisions of that Corps were to move up these corridors immediately behind the infantry and would make for a 'bound', code-named *Pierson*, which was from one to two miles beyond the infantry objective.

Then, after reconnaissance, they would move on another three or four miles to a 'report line' drawn roughly south-eastwards from Tel el Aqqaqir and called *Skinflint.*[2] (*See* Map, Fig. 7.)

In their writings Field-Marshal Montgomery and others have given an emphasis to these 'corridors' in a manner that may seem to suggest that they were the avenues of attack, but, of course, they were not so. The opening attack was to be an infantry one. Their task was to establish a broad and deep bridgehead. Across the ground secured by this bridgehead routes were assigned for the passage forward of the armour.

Thus, as admirably expressed in 10th Armoured Division's operation order (OO No. 11 of 19 October):

> 10 Armd. Div. will move through the bridgehead to be secured by 30 Corps and, in co-operation with 1 Armd. Div., destroy the enemy armour on or west of 30 Corps final objective.

We shall better understand the battle, therefore, if we forget about 'corridors', except as broad avenues across the infantry bridgehead allotted for the forward movement of 10th Corps and along which

1. Map refs.: 86702980 – 86702960 – 86972923 – approx. 87802870.

2. A 'bound' was a line or locality where tanks gathered in any stragglers and remarshalled for a further advance. A 'report line' was where they paused to await further orders.

they would clear their own minefield gaps. The infantry divisions would clear their own lanes for their fighting vehicles to move forward. In fact, across the whole bridgehead, eighteen or more lanes were designed to be swept on the first night by the sappers of all the divisions.

For the left-hand punch by 13th Corps in the south, there was no material change of plan. The French were to capture the dominating height of Himeimat and Hunter's Plateau to the west. To the south of the Munassib Depression 7th Armoured and 44th Divisions would blow a hole in the minefields and, if conditions were favourable, exploit success by a swing to the north.

The low mechanical condition of 7th Armoured, however, was a controlling factor in these calculations. The main purpose of the southern operations was to keep the enemy guessing about our main intention and to oblige him accordingly to keep 21st Panzer Division and the Ariete Armoured Divisions down in the south. The enemy must be led to believe, for as long as possible, that we intended to follow the usual tactics of an enveloping attack from the south.

If there was not a quick success, and penetration seemed likely to be made only at great cost, 13th Corps attack was to be called off, in order to keep 7th Armoured Division intact for future operations.

The tasks that Montgomery accordingly assigned to each Corps Commander were these:

30th Corps: To secure a bridgehead (*Oxalic*) beyond the enemy defence zone before dawn and assist the passage of 10th Corps.

10th Corps: To pass through *Oxalic* and bring on an armoured battle on ground of its own choosing; if there was no opportunity of this, operate to prevent enemy armour from interfering with 30th Corps' crumbling operations. Corps first bound – *Pierson*; advance subsequently to *Skinflint* to challenge attack.

13th Corps: To penetrate enemy defences south of Munassib for the passage of 7th Armoured Division, but not to allow that division to become mauled; and to secure Qaret el Himeimat.

Such was the plan in outline. The code name chosen for the

operation was *Lightfoot* – significant enough for those who would have to walk over those miles of minefields. Other things being ready, the date for the operation was determined by the moon, for 'artificial moonlight' had not yet been invented. The maximum period of natural moonlight was necessary for the troops, especially the minelifting parties, to see what they were doing. And, as Montgomery calculated that the battle would last ten days or more, a waxing moon was the thing.

The date accordingly chosen was 23 October.

Zero hour, the time at which the infantry were to go into the assault, was to be 10 p.m.

Another of Montgomery's leading principles was to take his troops into his confidence and explain to them the plan of battle. It was not sufficient merely to order them to assault at a certain place and time. He wanted them to feel that they were trusted comrades in 'an enterprise of great pith and moment'. So began a practice that was to become almost a normal routine before every large battle.

The junior ranks could, obviously, not be told until almost the last minute, but, having training and other considerations in mind, Montgomery ordered that the news should be broken progressively by ranks, beginning himself with the corps and divisional commanders at Burg el Arab on 15 September. Brigadiers and COs of RE units were taken into confidence on 10 October, the sappers having a special responsibility for preparation.

By a series of directives Montgomery told all senior officers what sort of battle they must train for – a 'real rough house', a long 'buffeting' of many days 'under the continuous strain of hard battle fighting', one which would demand that men's physical condition should be 'really tough and hard' and in which 'determined leadership will be vital.' This insistence upon hard unit fighting was, no doubt, increasingly influenced by the information that began to come in of the third defensive belt that the enemy was preparing beyond the reach of a one-night attack, but of which we probably had only partial evidence.

Among the generals, whose comments Montgomery invited, the

plan was not without its critics. Lumsden and Gatehouse were apprehensive on the part of the armour. They foresaw that, as the tanks emerged singly at the ends of the corridors and attempted to fan out right and left, they were likely to be picked off one by one by the anti-tank guns that would be immediately concentrated upon them. And if the infantry should be unable to get right through to the 30th Corps objective, the tanks would be caught in exposed positions in daylight in the minefield, unable to manœuvre.

Gatehouse thought it impossible for the sappers to clear mines to such a depth in a single night. (In fact, the time between Zero hour and next morning's first light left only half an hour more than the theoretical best possible.) Both foresaw confusion and congestion in the narrow gaps through the minefields as the great mass of tanks, guns and vehicles strove to get forward, and these gaps would soon be 'taped' by the enemy artillery.

To all these objections Montgomery firmly replied, 'Nonsense'.

De Guingand and Walsh, the chiefs of staff of Montgomery and Leese, attending Lumsden's corps conference for the battle, were both disturbed to find that Lumsden seemed to have little faith in the plan. The two staff officers reported accordingly to their chiefs. There were those among the infantry also, particularly the Dominion infantry, who, remembering the July fighting, declared: 'The tanks won't go through'. Freyberg said so frankly.

Monty reacted immediately. The armoured attacks, he said, 'must and shall' go through. Moreover, if the areas of their corridors were not completely cleared by daylight on 24 October, the armoured divisions must fight their own way through into open country beyond. He had plenty of tanks and did not mind how many were lost if the result were achieved.

These doubters – whose doubts were by no means invalid – were, however, but a very small handful and were to be counted among the senior officers only. Among the regiments and the battalions no such clouds disturbed the horizon. Nor did those who were unhappy about the plan give any sign of their disquiet. Major Jack Perrott, of 2nd (Cheshire) Field Squadron, recorded that Gatehouse was an inspiration to 10th Armoured Division during training and that when the time came for the plan to be announced he was 'inspired by Alec Gatehouse's enthusiasm'. Lumsden and Gatehouse, being obliged to accept the plan, did not lack the loyalty to carry it out as best they could.

THE RED HERRING

Though the plans were at first disclosed only to the most senior officers, all men of perception could see that something was brewing. To everyone the almanac of things to come was always the moon. In the Warwickshire Yeomanry John Lakin and Clive Stoddart, watching the old moon wane and the sickle of the new rise and swell, were reminded of Winston Churchill's dramatic words when he had talked to them one sweltering day in August. 'Gentlemen,' he had said, 'you will strike an unforgettable blow against the enemy. The corn will be ripe for the sickle and you will be the reapers.'

We have seen that this offensive plan involved the movement of multitudes of troops, tanks, guns and vehicles, together with the piling up of great stocks of ammunition and stores, and that the total lack of cover made it impossible to conceal these activities from the cameras of the enemy. In the absence of any opportunity of surprise by manœuvre, it was vital to the success of the plan that some means should be devised of surprise by deception.

How, then, could we deceive the enemy? How present a picture which, looked at through his wideawake eyes, would convince him that it was not a fake? The answer resolved upon was that, since the main evidence could not be concealed, it should be falsified.

The enemy must somehow be led to believe that our main effort was to be in the south. As far as possible he must also be left guessing about the timing of our attack, but it was appreciated that the phases of the moon would give him some indication.

The co-ordinating brain behind the ingenious plan now evolved was that of Charles Richardson, an officer on Montgomery's planning staff. It was on such a grand scale that it was given its own code name of Operation *Bertram*. It involved planning in minute detail,

The dangerous hour: a Crusader and a Vickers machine gun silhouetted against the grey-and-crimson streamers of 'first light'

A tank problem: extricating a wounded man

Military police extricating a corpse, headless and charred, from an enemy tank

the employment of a large labour force, quantities of transport and the mocking-up of very large numbers of dummies made from wooden battens, hessian canvas, cut-up petrol tins and suchlike material. The exact position to be taken up in the zones of attack of every tank, gun and vehicle was fixed several weeks in advance and then *Bertram* began to operate.

What then did the enemy see? In the north he saw a fairly heavy concentration of lorries and light vehicles of various sorts and, although at first he wondered what this might mean, he ceased to concern himself when he saw little change in the pattern as the weeks went by. Likewise he saw advanced slit trenches dug well in front of the forward infantry positions, but he got used to these also.

Farther back and farther inland, in the Staging Areas, he saw quantities of tanks, armoured cars, guns and their attendant trucks – real ones, these – sitting astride the system of tracks leading to the southern front, and he calculated that, as long as they stayed there, he would have two days' notice before they could be in battle positions. He saw a concentration of artillery near the Munassib Depression. He saw a water pipeline, complete with pumping stations and water-storage towers, being methodically laid in a trench that pointed directly to the south and he calculated that the rate of progression was such that it would be completed soon after 1 November. He saw dumps of stores and ammunition accumulating in the same quarter. He saw 10th Armoured Division move up openly and almost ostentatiously to positions on 13th Corps front. His listening sets heard the busy wireless traffic of a tank formation preparing for operations.

He did not, however, know that this wireless traffic consisted of prepared signals sent out by the inoperative skeleton of 8th Armoured Division, he did not see that the pipeline being laid by 578th Army Troops Company, RE, was made of pieces of petrol tin, he did not see 10th Armoured Division move silently out of their southern position and leave dummies behind them. He did not see, on the northern front, the flimsy shapes of the sham lorries cast aside as the tanks, guns and scout cars and real lorries moved into their places.

He did not see beneath the vast and convincing camouflage nets the huge stocks of warlike stores assembled at El Alamein station, and he did not recognize in the innumerable lorry-like objects up and down the front the deliberately shaped stacks of ammunition and rations.

Nor, twenty-four hours before the battle, did he see the attacking infantry move quietly up to the advanced trenches, empty and camouflaged, that they had previously dug close to the start line of their assault.

THE ENEMY'S DIFFICULTIES

To what conclusions, then, did the enemy come from these and many other evidences, and from his assessment of the probable factors, and what was his condition of meeting the threatened attack?

Rommel flew home on leave to Germany on 23 September. His health was poor and he required treatment. His place was taken temporarily by General Georg Stumme, a leading exponent of armoured warfare, who had been engaged in the hitherto victorious campaign in Russia and who, no doubt, was not sorry to exchange that bleak theatre of war for the sun of Africa. He took over from Rommel on 22 September.

He found that the Axis atmosphere was not a happy one. Divided authority had led to mutual recriminations, and prescriptions for remedying the several ills remained unexecuted. The rear administrative system was infirm and shaky and presented a striking contrast to our own well-articulated and ably-directed system. Relations between ground and air were also bad. Rommel, a few days before he flew home, had sent in a long list of his requirements and a pessimistic report on the prospects.

What concerns us more nearly is that he had given orders to increase the depth and strength of his defence. The front face of each minefield box was to be lightly held by battle outposts, guarding the outer minefield and disposed in depth. The front line of the main defensive zone was drawn back behind the second minefield belt and from here the zone extended for a depth of up to two miles. The third line of defence, from Sidi Abd el Rahman southwards, including anti-tank guns and dug-in tanks, was begun. It was this line, manned by the guns and tanks of 15th Panzer and the Littorio Armoured Divisions, which in the event was to trouble us most.

As the map in Figure 6 shows, these two enemy armoured divisions were located in this area, with 21st Panzer and the Ariete Divisions in the south. It has often been said that this arrangement must have been Stumme's, as it was unlike Rommel to divide his armour. In fact, the dispositions were Rommel's own, his intention being to be able to plug quickly any breach in the defences that we might make on any part of the front.

Another feature of his dispositions, which he had been employing for some time, was to stiffen the Italian infantry, in whom he had little faith, with German detachments. Thus, in the south, squads of the Ramcke Parachute Brigade were posted at key points among the Folgore Division (though the Folgore did not need this corseting), and of 164th Light Division among the Trento in the north.

Stumme and his staff watched the British preparations with care. They noted the active patrolling by our infantry in the south. They followed from day to day the move forward of our supply dumps and, from the height of Mount Himeimat, watched the daily methodical progress of the dummy pipe-line. They observed the pre-battle attacks on their fighter airfields at Daba and Fuka by the Desert Air Force. But the accumulation of evidence led them to no definite conclusion. They could not be certain what was genuine and what was fake.

On 20 October Stumme issued a directive which said that a British attack might come at any time and any place. The probabilities were examined on each section of the front, but, on balance, he considered that our main effort was most likely to be made on 'the northern part of the southern front', which meant somewhere about Munassib.

The day before, Stumme had made a depressing report on his administrative posture. The water supply in the forward areas had partially failed, the troops were undernourished and the sickness rate was rising. The shortage of petrol was a constant anxiety and there was a lack of spares for mechanical transport.

However, we must be in no doubt but that, in spite of these uncertainties and these deficits, the morale of the German troops, if not of the Italians, was very high and their fighting spirit as strong as ever. They were tenacious and resourceful, swift in their reactions, ably and courageously led at all levels, experienced in battle. They could, on occasions, fight like tigers.

While these intensive preparations were being made on both sides, there had been some fighting to be done, apart from the day-to-day business. In particular, an attack was launched on the night of 30 September by the Queen's Brigade of 44th Division against the formidable defences of the Munassib Depression, held by the Folgore Division and the Ramcke Parachute Brigade. The objects were to secure better concealed areas for the deployment of artillery and to lend added colour to the picture of an impending offensive in the south.

In this attack the 6th and 7th Battalions of the Queen's won their objectives, but in the 5th Battalion two whole companies were wiped out and a third decimated. The brigade commander proposed to renew the attack the next night, but Horrocks called it off. The brigade had suffered 392 casualties, but the ground won on the north and east sides of the Depression was consolidated. A memorable incident in the operation was the advance and deployment under fire of 57th Field Regiment, RA.

LIGHTFOOT

Chapter Ten

D DAY

Mastery in the Air – The Plan Proclaimed –
'On Your Marks!' – The Barrage

MASTERY IN THE AIR

D Day approached. The waiting tanks and guns prepared to move into their secret positions. Maintained at an even flow, the transport companies continued daily to augment the mounting piles of shells, cartridges, bombs, hand grenades and all the other stores of war. The artificers and mechanics tested and serviced the guns, tanks, aircraft, armoured cars and small arms under their care. As it was before Agincourt,

> The armourers, accomplishing the knights,
> With busy hammers closing rivets up,
> Give dreadful note of preparation.

Staff officers worked far into the night at plans, maps, air photographs, intelligence reports, administrative instructions, operation orders and march tables.

Yet none but a few knew what lay ahead. In the forward localities the infantry and the artillery observation officers gazed out over the sere and shadowless wastes ahead, seemingly devoid of life but dotted with the shapes of burnt-out tanks, of wrecked vehicles and of scattered remnants of equipment, 'where black death keeps record of his trophies'. Nightly, the infantry patrols continued silently to range the wide expanses of No Man's Land, seeking information of the enemy. Daily the squadrons of the air, 'with strong wings scaling the upward sky', bent their bright courses. The nights grew colder; men wore their battledress blouses in the evening and the early morning, and their greatcoats by night. But the middle hours of the day were very hot still.

The first blows were struck from the air. They were aimed at securing superiority over the enemy air forces from D Day onwards, so that there would be the minimum interference with our ground operations and so that the Desert Air Force and their co-operating squadrons from that day onwards could concentrate on attacking the enemy's forward troops.

Coningham began, accordingly, with heavy bombing attacks on the enemy airfields. On 19 October the German fighter airfields at El Daba were attacked by Baltimores of 55th and 223rd Squadrons, fighter-bombers of 2nd and 4th Squadrons South African Air Force and by the Royal Australian Air Force. Night attacks followed by Bostons, their targets illuminated by the Albacores of the Fleet Air Arm.

Next day the Italian airfields at Fuka were bombed and another punishing visit paid to El Daba. On the 21st the Wellingtons joined in. Blow followed blow. By day and by night the attacks were kept up until the 23rd without intermission. By the 23rd, at a cost of only thirteen British aircraft and one American, our fighter patrols roamed over the enemy's forward airfields continuously without challenge, complete masters of the air. In readiness for the next phase of close engagement and pursuit, Coningham moved two fighter wings forward to advanced airfields at El Hammam.

THE PLAN PROCLAIMED

The time drew near for all men to be taken into the Army Commander's trust.

On 19 and 20 October Montgomery made his memorable expositions at the Amariya Cinema to all officers down to the rank of lieutenant-colonel of how the battle was to be fought, how it would develop and how long it would last. It was an occasion not likely to be forgotten by those who attended. To many it was a day of revelation. It was the day that Montgomery finally and firmly impressed upon the Army not only his professional personality but also the inevitability of victory. In a rapt silence the gatherings of officers – sunburnt, experienced, not easily impressionable, most of them already proved leaders, many of them bearing upon their persons or their clothing the scars and emblems of hard service – listened to that incisive, rather metallic, completely matter-of-fact voice telling them in professional form exactly what was going to happen. It was no mere pep-talk, no homily on heroics.

He told them of his original plan and of how he had changed it. He reviewed the enemy's situation and our own, emphasizing our superiority in all departments. He told them that his plan for what he called a 'crumbling' operation to destroy the enemy first would require a hard, slogging 'dog fight'. We must destroy the enemy methodically and piecemeal, without ever relaxing pressure. We must maintain offensive eagerness. The whole affair, he calculated, would last twelve days and they must not expect spectacular results too soon. The enemy could not last out a long battle; we could, and, if we gave him no rest and stuck to the proper battle techniques, victory was certain.

The old desert hands, with 'sand between their toes', who clung to the old loyalties and who had greeted with scepticism the arrival of the new men from home, went to the gatherings with no very high expectations. They were case-hardened. They came out of the cinema, however, utterly convinced. They experienced, for the first time, a complete assurance that unequivocal victory was at last to be their reward and that never again would they need 'to flog up and down the same piece of desert'. Even so seasoned a hand as Victor Turner, professional soldier and disciple of the old regime, declared that it was 'absolutely thrilling'.

For most of those who listened, Alexandria and Cairo lay for ever behind them as they came out of the cinema. Never again would they savour their flesh-pots and their squalors, or feel the bed-bugs bite them in Kasr-el-Nil barracks and Abassiyah, or enjoy the English relaxations of Gezira and the Turf Club, or be cheated in the Kasbah, or gaze appraisingly upon the pyramids and the sphinx.

On 21 October, on Montgomery's orders, the COs themselves broke the news to all their own junior officers and men, sitting silent and absorbed in semi-circles on the sand, with diagrams of the coming battle before them and with the sun blazing down on their bronzed limbs. From that briefing no man was excluded except only those who were then in the foremost positions, lest they should be raided by the enemy, and those who were to go out on patrol.

On that day all leave was quietly stopped without any official announcement. Thenceforward Eighth Army was safely locked up without bars in the great immensity of the desert. On the same day Montgomery paid a final visit to the assaulting divisions to see if they were all 'well and comfortable'. He found the Army's morale, he declared, 'on the top line'.

Few men who were in the desert at that hour will ever lose the memory of the heartening breath that swept across the sandy wastes and rocky desolations, that blew invigoration into the cramped trenches, the sweating gun pits, the close-battened tanks and the expectant squadrons of the air. It was tremendously exciting, tremendously challenging. An Army whose pride and spirit was always high became infused with a new buoyancy of spirit and a new conviction of their power to win. Lieutenant-Colonel Bob Turner, addressing his Second-13th Australian Battalion and feeling the inspiration of Montgomery's address, gave them his own text from *Macbeth* to take into battle: 'Be bloody, bold and resolute'.

Major Jack Perrott, addressing his sappers of 2nd Cheshire Field Squadron and striving to pass on to them the enthusiasm he had caught when Gatehouse addressed the officers of 10th Armoured Division, declared that 'the battle was won before it had started'. Sapper Flinn, of the companion 3rd Cheshire Field Squadron, felt an exhilaration never experienced on the eve of any other battle. 'The dynamic little man in the funny hat', he said, 'convinced us entirely that we were going to win and that the shambles of the past were over.'

Harding, the new commander of 7th Armoured Division, recorded that 'the atmosphere of well-designed, objective preparations, lively expectancy and quiet confidence pervaded the division and indeed the whole Army'. McCreery, Alexander's Chief of Staff, severe, matter-of-fact and emphatically no 'Monty man', declared that the morale of the infantry was 'sky-high'. Briggs observed that there was 'a lighter spring in men's steps', a confidence in their bearing, a new ring in their voices, and a positive direction in their thinking.

Kippenberger, breaking the news to 23rd New Zealand Battalion, whom he had selected for the first violent burst into the enemy lines, told them that this was the greatest moment of their lives. Theirs was the duty and the honour of breaking in. 'I expect you to do it', he said, 'whatever the cost.'

Romans, the battalion's ardent CO, a man who in battle burned with fires of exaltation, called the men to their feet and led them in 'three fierce, and thundering cheers.'[1]

The evening sandstorms blew up, the empty petrol tins bowled along before the wind, banging like fire-crackers, the flies swarmed under a torrid sun, the screaming Stukas dive-bombed occasionally from the brazen sky, the shells and machine-guns crackled, as of old, but a new stimulus and a new purposefulness were clearly abroad in that far desert.

Extraordinary measures were taken, under the *Bertram* plan, to conceal from the enemy the last moves forward. On the night of 20 October, First and Tenth Armoured Divisions began to move up by stages to their assembly areas behind 30th Corps front. The main bodies immediately sank into wireless silence, but small detachments selected from men with 'recognizable voices', whom the enemy would already have heard talking on the air, were left behind in the training areas to maintain a simulation of normal wireless activity. Gatehouse himself, together with Bill Liardet, his GSO 1, had to journey back so that their well-known voices could be heard.

On reaching the assembly areas, tanks, guns and vehicles slipped secretly into the positions occupied by the dummies of the *Bertram* plan. From then on no movement of men or vehicles was allowed

1. Kippenberger, op. cit.

by day except what was unavoidable. No smoke from fires, no lights, no washing, no airing of beds, no digging. Tracks made by the tanks moving in were obliterated by dragging wire trailers along them.

The utmost care was demanded to ensure that, on the featureless ground and in the dark, the assaulting infantry of 30th Corps should start on the right line in relation to the artillery barrage and keep its ordered direction. On 51st Division's front, Lieutenant-Colonel J. C. Stirling, of the 5th Seaforth Highlanders, virtually lived for four days and nights in No Man's Land, identifying and marking exactly the 2,500 yards of start-line, and clearing and marking the nine lanes leading up to it through our own minefields. The start-line was to be a few hundred yards out in No Man's Land. To find the exact pin-points of each terminal, he employed officers converging from various directions, marching by compass and counting their paces. These lines were required to be marked with nine miles of white tape, but, in order that they should not be observed from the air or by an enemy patrol, he laid them out first with telephone wire, ready to be quickly replaced by tape on the night of the 23rd itself.

'ON YOUR MARKS!'

On the night of 22 October the assaulting infantry of 30th Corps, the heavily-laden machine gunners, the artillery Forward Observation Officers and the engineers of the mine-clearing teams, lit by an early moon, moved quietly forward to the shallow slit trenches that had previously been dug, camouflaged and provisioned, on the home edge of our own minefield, steel-helmeted, equipped and ready for the great test.

The next morning, which was a Friday, Montgomery himself moved forward to a small tactical headquarters, alongside those of Leese, Lumsden and Coningham, their vehicles all dug-in.

All that day the waiting soldiers in front remained motionless in their cramped trenches, forbidden to move for any purpose whatever, roasted and blistered by a blazing sun and preyed upon by clouds of flies. They spoke a little to one another and tried to get some sleep, but for the most part each man was occupied with his private thoughts. It was an extremely trying day, the physical discomfort aggravated by the high tension of expectancy. Peter Moore and his minefield sappers of 10th Armoured Division felt 'all very keyed up and a bit frightened, but determined that the thing was going to work this time. for we had so often seen it go wrong before'.

The long, burning day dragged on. The waiting soldiers felt as though cut off from the world. Before them stretched a country seemingly as empty and barren as it had been for thousands of years, shadowless and motionless, except for the 'Devil's Waters', the dancing mirages of the afternoon, but, as well they knew, impregnated with the buried engines of death and peopled with the unseen outposts of the distant enemy. As the day wore on, every man began that small and meaningful gesture which he was to repeat with increasing frequency in every hour to come – looking at his watch.

The sun began to sink in a crimson bed behind the enemy lines. The charged air gave up its burden of heat and the cool evening breeze mercifully flowed in, expelling the hateful flies. A meditative colonel closed his sketch-book with a sigh and put away his pencil. The twilight phantasms dissolved. Suddenly it was dark. The myriad stars began their nightly watch. The chill of evening made men shiver a little.

The soldiers got up from their cramped trenches, their accoutrements creaking as they stretched, moved about and relieved themselves. Hot meals came up from the battalion lines in the rear. Officers and NCOs went up and down, checking equipment and ammunition and ensuring the utmost quiet. Water-bottles were inspected. A tin of bully beef and a packet of ration biscuits was issued to each man.

Out in front of 51st Division, Stirling and his men of 5th Seaforth Highlanders, spectral shadows working against time, quickly ran out the white tapes of the start-line in No Man's Land and lit the pinpoint lamps that showed each battalion its way ahead through our own minefield. At the Regimental Aid Posts, the Medical Officers, among the very bravest of all men on the battlefield, with their orderlies and their stoical stretcher-bearers, prepared to be about their business, and there, also, were likely to be found the battalion padres.

The main tracks from the rear built by 30th Corps on the northern front – Sun, Moon, Star, Bottle, Boat and Hat – were likewise lit with their distinguishing signs. The anti-tank guns, bren-carriers and other operational vehicles of the infantry moved up and parked, to await their chance to traverse the minefields. The divisional commanders and brigadiers drove forward to their tactical battle headquarters in the vicinity of the front line. The Valentines of 23rd Armoured Brigade, having, like chrysalids, cast off the canvas skins of their dummies, emerged in their fighting aspect and crawled forward to mate with the infantry whom they were to accompany – Finigan's and Clarke's to the Australians, Cairns's to the Highlanders, Winberg's to the South Africans. John Currie, bubbling with laughter at the prospect of action, brought up his more powerful tanks to the New Zealand sector, the formidable shapes of the new Shermans silhouetted against the background of the stars; it was the first time that the American tank had been summoned into battle and in the mustering squadrons all ranks braced themselves for the challenge to its baptism of fire. Pat Hobart, Currie's brigade major, wrote in his diary: 'My mind stopped revolving over and over, checking over every detail of plans, orders and preparations. If anything had been forgotten, it was too late now to do anything about it. Felt rather tense but somehow fatalistic.'

Montgomery's battle message was read out to the troops, in which he declared his confidence that if every officer and man entered upon this battle with the determination to fight and kill and win, 'we will hit the enemy for "six" right out of North Africa'. Then he went on:

> Let every officer and man enter the battle with a stout heart, and with the determination to do his duty so long as he has breath in his body.
>
> And let no man surrender so long as he is unwounded and can fight.
>
> Let us all pray that 'the Lord Mighty in battle' will give us the victory.

Men looked again at their watches.

The infantry started to fall in by platoons and to move forward throughout our own minefield to the white tapes of the start-line in No Man's Land. In the New Zealand Division Reg Romans, eager and ardent, his shirt sleeves rolled up, led his battalion forward with sections in single file, fifty yards apart. To Lieutenant John Van Grutten and Sapper Flinn, both of 3rd Cheshire Field Squadron, the scene looked for all the world like the start of some great and stern athletics contest.

In 51st Division every man was wearing a white St Andrew's cross on his back as a recognition signal in the dark and in 1st Gordon Highlanders every officer was carrying a rifle like his men. The machine gunners of the Middlesex Regiment, one platoon to each battalion of Highland infantry, took up their heavy loads – seven men to a gun, carrying gun, tripod, water and ammunition for their 6,000 yards carry. Wimberley, the knees of his long legs drawn up to his chin, drove up in his jeep to his battle headquarters in the front line. He looked at the gaps in our own minefield and saw that they were properly lit for the move forward to the start-line.

'As we drove about', he records in his journal, 'everything was deathly silent. I remembered First Cambrai, in 1917, how quiet it was before Zero. It seemed a good omen. Then I stood at one of the minefield gaps and watched my Jocks filing silently through, heavily laden with picks, shovels and sandbags, as well as their weapons and accoutrements. At the head of each battalion was its CO, his piper at his side. It was only possible now for me to pray. I went back to my battle headquarters and had a little food.' The generals had now handed over to the regimental soldiers.

At the start-line the infantry, the minefield sappers and the machine gunners spread out in their correct order in the spacing at which they were to advance. At a quiet order the infantry fixed bayonets. The navigating officers, compass in hand, took station in the centre of each battalion and company. The taping squads fell in immediately behind them, ready to reel out the white line of the battalion axis.

Dead silence lay over the whole desert. The swelling moon rode high, large, serene, illuminating the spectral scene with blue light.

By its bright light men peered again at their watches, waiting for the mighty roar which they knew would burst out behind them at twenty minutes to ten.

Every man in Eighth Army and the Desert Air Force now had his eye on his watch, counting the minutes. Behind the infantry, where the hidden armoured divisions lay, the flimsy structures of the dummy lorries were cast aside, to reveal to the inscrutable moon the naked features of guns and tanks. On the Springbok Road, just south of El Alamein Station, 1st and 10th Armoured Divisions, after a difficult and skilfully planned approach march, refreshed and took such rest as they could until their turn to go forward at 2 a.m. In the Warwickshire Yeomanry a radio set picked up the air of 'The White Cliffs of Dover' on the BBC.

Robert Wright, commanding 76th Anti-tank Regiment in 1st Armoured Division, wrote in his journal: 'I could not help having a feeling of pride and confidence; proud to be taking part in a battle likely to prove decisive, confident that the leadership, the men, the tanks, the guns and the aircraft were now enough to deliver a real punch. Except for one or two vehicles moving on the coast road, everything was very still. The scene reminded me of the marshalling of the performers before entry into the arena at the Aldershot Tattoo. Even now our eyes were focused on Tripoli, 1,300 miles away!'

On the airfields away in the rear the bomb racks had been charged and the air crews briefed for the night's tasks. They were to illuminate the enemy country by flares, bomb gun positions, attack concentrations of troops with low-flying aircraft, jam the enemy's radio by specially-equipped Wellingtons, lay clouds of smoke to create confusion and drop dummy parachutists.

The Royal Navy also had their part to play and a small force had put out to sea. Their task, with RAF co-operation, was to make a feint landing in the enemy's rear at Ras el Kenayis, a promontory near Fuka, with the intention of creating confusion and nervousness and of occupying the enemy's reserves.

That evening Stumme radioed his routine evening report to Hitler's headquarters in Germany:

Enemy situation unchanged.

The new training: RE mine-clearance teams await the signal from the reconnaissance officer

Terence Cuneo's fine painting of mine-clearancc at Alamein (note the white tape)

The barrage: a gunner officer watches the last few seconds . . .

and gives the order: *Fire*

THE BARRAGE

Meanwhile, a little way behind the infantry were the men who were counting first the minutes and then the seconds perhaps more precisely than anyone else – the artillery.

At the appointed second, 882 field and medium guns were to open fire, in Montgomery's words to the author, 'like one battery'. For this second the gunners had been preparing all day and the gunnery staffs for much longer. The fire plan prepared by Kirkman for the whole thirty-eight miles from the sea to Himeimat had been allotted and sub-allotted from Army to Corps, Corps to division, division to regiment and regiment to battery. The gunners' maps were covered with transparent traces on which were marked with precise care the parallel lines by which a curtain of shells would move forward by leaps of 100 yards for the whole depth of the infantry's advance.

But it was not to be a 'barrage' in the true sense; there were not enough guns for that. On the New Zealand front, as an example, there would be only one shell every forty-five yards. It was to be mainly a series of moving concentrations of shell fire on known or suspected points of enemy resistance. The first fifteen minutes, however, were to be devoted to concentrations on the enemy's own gun positions, plotted from air photographs and by other means, in order to reduce the volume of fire that would break on our infantry.

At the little headquarters of each battery – usually a hole dug out of the sand and rock – the Command Post Officer and his assistants, working with artillery board, range table and slide rule, had patiently calculated the line and range for each of the eight guns of their battery for every step in the long ladder of fire. The arithmetical corrections had been applied for the barometric pressure, the temperatures of the air and the cartridge, the direction and force of the wind, the difference in height above sea level between each gun and its target. Still further corrections had to be made for each gun individually, as also for each batch of shells and cartridges if they differed from the normal.

The Command Post of each battery was quite close to the two Troops of four guns and before long the completed gun programmes, which were foolscap forms covered with a mass of figures, went out to the Gun Position Officer of each Troop, who was a subaltern. The GPO, through his Tannoy loud-speaker set, or by other means, then summoned his four Nos. 1, who commanded each gun and who were nearly all sergeants, and explained his task to each. There was a start of astonishment when he told them that they would have to fire 600 rounds per gun that night.

Back in each gun pit, under its dun camouflage net, the No. 1 went through the barrage programme with his gun-layer, explained the task to his detachment and prepared his ammunition, which for days had been gradually accumulating and had lain buried in the sand. He saw that water was at hand for sponging out the gun when it became over-hot, ensured that all moving parts were working smoothly and tested his sights. An artificer came round to test the gun's recoil apparatus.

Every man in the detachment now knew the nature of the tremendous call that was to be made on him. It was to be the most massive artillery onslaught ever seen in the continent of Africa and the biggest of the British Army anywhere since 1918. Except for ten minutes' rest each hour to cool the gun, they would be required to maintain a high rate of fire for five and a half hours continuously, and if they came under fire themselves from the enemy must not pause or take cover. When all was prepared, the sweating detachment bedded down in the sand for what rest they could get.

The quick desert twilight fell and all down the long line Eighth Army awoke to sudden activity. The gunners saw a flood of traffic crawling forward – tanks, scout cars, carriers, lorries – and great clouds of dust were kicked up, neutralizing the moonlight. In the rear of the gun position, the pin-point lamp had been lit on the night picket, on which the layer would centre the vertical cross wires of his dial sight to put his gun on the right line.

The men had a hot evening meal and looked at their watches, as everyone throughout the Army was doing. Through the camouflage net overhead the moon glinted wanly on the polished parts of the gun.

The GPO went quietly round the Troop to see that all was well. The men began to break open the green metal ammunition boxes. Though the night air was chill, they stripped to the waist, for soon they would be dripping with sweat.

At about 9.30 the GPO, from his position in the centre rear of the Troop, ordered crisply:

'Take post!'

The faint moon-shadows were agitated into sudden life as the gun detachment sprang to their places – No. 2 on the right ready to operate the breech mechanism, the layer on the left at his dial sight, with the elevating and traversing wheels at his hand, the other numbers at the trail or by the stacked ammunition. The No. 1 ordered:

'HE, 117, Charge 3, load.'

The layer set his driftscale plate and range reader to the Charge 3 settings, No. 4 stepped forward with the 25-lb high-explosive shell, armed with its instantaneous 117 fuse, and slipped it into the open breech of the gun. No. 1 himself, with a short, truncheon-like rammer, rammed the shell home and as the copper driving-band engaged with the rifling of the barrel there was a deep, bell-like ring. No. 4 half-turned, took the long, brass cartridge case from No. 5, showed it to No. 1 to prove that it contained the full three charges of propellant, and pushed it into the breech with his closed fist. No. 2 slammed home the breech-block with a metallic clang.

The sergeant ordered: 'Zero One Five Degrees.'

By the light of a hand torch the layer set the scale on his dial sight to the figure which would bring his gun pointing towards its target and, by means of hand signals, directed the trail to be swung over until he found the light on the night-aiming-point in the prisms of his sight.

'Angle of Sight 5 minutes Elevation.'

The enemy battery was a little higher above sea level than his gun and the layer made the correct setting on his sight clinometer.

'10,800.'

The layer, repeating '10,800', quickly set the range to the enemy battery on his range-scale plate. The muzzle of the gun lifted up and up as he turned the elevating handwheel for approximate elevation first. He cross-levelled his sight till it was vertical, then, with his eye glued to the rubber eyepiece, laid accurately on the night aiming-point and finally levelled his sight clinometer bubble for exact elevation. Then he reported:

'Ready.'

The gun was ready to be fired, the detachment alert and tensed, but there were still some minutes to go. The GPO ordered:

'Troop, rest.'

The detachment relaxed, but stayed at their posts. Someone cracked a little joke and there was a subdued laugh. The sergeant was looking at his watch continuously and presently he said: 'A minute to go'. The last long seconds dragged by till at last there was a crisp command, from the GPO:

'Take post!'

Alert and keyed once more, like runners poised for the starting pistol, the detachment, at their action positions, awaited the ultimate order. There was a tingling silence over all the desert as the moon and the multitudinous stars looked down on an army waiting to spring.

At forty seconds before Zero, when the first shell was due to burst on its target, came at last the order:

'B Troop, fire!'

The Battle of El Alamein had begun.

The storm of fire that burst was an experience never to be forgotten by those who heard it. The trumpeting of the 'Alamein barrage' echoes still within every man's memory. It had not the volcanic violence of the great barrages of the First World War, such as those of Arras and Amiens, when the staccato barking of the serried ranks of field guns was fortified by the deep-throated roar of the heavy howitzers and the sharp cracks of the 60-pdrs, yet there was a quality in the clamorous roar that was peculiarly memorable. It had a tremendous and imperious assurance. It rang with confidence. It proclaimed itself irresistible. It told men that at last a firm hand was now directing the great orchestra with professional mastery.

Everywhere men who were not engaged stood and watched entranced at the long line of leaping gun flashes ripping open the night sky for thirty-eight miles and listened to the urgent and compelling roar, drowning the sound of the aircraft passing overhead. The oldest hands felt the spell of the moment. Freyberg, veteran though he was, stood 'fascinated and awed', muttering to himself about the greatness of the cause for which they fought. At Kippenberger's armoured command vehicle 'the maddening incessant clamour of the guns became deafening. A whole field regiment was firing directly over our heads from a few hundred yards back. The waiting group of officers and orderlies stood on the lee side to get some shelter from the uproar and the concussion'.[1]

Commanders of divisions and brigades found it difficult to go back to their headquarters and wait for news. Their hearts and thoughts were with the gallant battalions and the mine-lifting teams now on tip-toe. In the Highland Division the thoughts of one officer flew to Macaulay's lines on the Angel of Death, as the steel shards, with a sound as of a multitude of wings, swept unseen overhead.

In the air, unheard in the general din by their comrades on the ground, forty-eight Wellingtons were dropping 125 tons of bombs on the enemy gun positions. The bombing, the tremendous storm of shelling and the successful jamming of the enemy's radio by the specially-equipped aircraft, completely disrupted his signal system. It was a long time before Stumme's headquarters knew what was happening and, so little did he appreciate the impact of the occasion, that his uppermost thought was merely to conserve his stocks of ammunition.

Thus for fifteen minutes all the guns of 30th Corps, supported by the Desert Air Force, pounded the enemy guns with no reply. The artillery plan then began to vary with each division's needs. The gunner regiments prepared for their long programmes of mixed concentration and barrage in support of the infantry assault. They knew that the infantry were already walking forward, bayonets fixed. In the Troop that we have just been watching the GPO ordered:

1. Op. cit. An 'armoured command vehicle' (ACV) was a lightly armoured lorry fitted up as a mobile operations room.

'Serial B.'

The sergeant, omitting all unnecessary repetitions of previous orders, gave in succession the new ones:

'Charge 2.'

'Zero Three Degrees Two-o minutes.'

'4,800.'

'Fire by order, 5 rounds gunfire.'

The gun was now laid on the enemy's forward defences. The GPO, his eye on the second-hand of his watch, waited until it was seventeen seconds short of 10 p.m. and then called out:

'B Troop, fire!'

Up in front the infantry walked forward to the attack.

Chapter Eleven

THE FIRST NIGHT

The Infantry – The Sappers – The Armour –
The Guns – Attack in the South

THE INFANTRY

To reach their objective on the *Oxalic* line the South Africans were required to advance some three miles from their own forward defences, and the Highlanders and Australians distances up to five miles. The sheer physical effort, under the strains imposed and after a night and a day of discomfort, was considerable, especially for those most heavily laden, such as the machine-gunners, each of whom had to carry the equivalent of three-quarters of a sack of coal, and the wireless operators of the artillery FOO, while the nervous stamina of the mine-lifting sappers would be stretched to the uttermost.

These distances had been somewhat reduced by the advancement of the start-line into No Man's Land, but there still remained the dark miles of minefield honeycombed with unseen enemy cells. Because the penetration demanded was very deep on most of 30th Corps front, intermediate objective lines had been laid down, at which the attacking soldiers could pause to reorganize and correct those losses of direction and cohesion that are almost inevitable in a long night attack, or at which new units, advancing from a new start-line, could leap-frog the first waves.

These intermediate objectives varied in each division according to the distance and to the siting and strength of the enemy defences. Thus on the Highland and Australian fronts there were three intermediate lines and, on the New Zealand front, one, this line being co-ordinated with their neighbours' and constituting the 'first objective' of 30th Corps.

In every one of the battles that was to be fought within this battle, the overshadowing element of the *mise en scéne* and the one that distinguished it from fighting on any other terrain, was the enormous clouds of dust that enveloped the field. The artillery barrage that preceded every attack was the prime instigator of these artificial dust storms, adding to them the drifting smoke from its own shell-bursts. The obscuration was further thickened when the tanks growled up, churning the sand into powdery dust. Night, when nearly all the attacks were made, darkened again the spectral gloom, so that most of the battles were fought in swirling, fog-like clouds.

In these circumstances it was extremely difficult to locate any enemy post contesting the way, whereas the enemy could discern the moving silhouettes advancing towards him. Such, of course, is nearly always one of the advantages of the defence and explains why a few can so often bar the way to many.

The infantryman's problems of keeping direction and of recognizing, when he reached it, an objective which was completely unidentifiable were resolved in part by the help of the artillery. Though the desert maps were unreliable and of small scale, the gunners' facilities for fixing their own positions on a 'grid' by methods of survey enabled them to discharge a projectile in almost exactly the required direction and, with very little error, to the right distance. Indeed, in nearly all the actions of the battle now begun it was the curtain of shell-bursts in a barrage that showed the infantry the general direction and the distance they had to go.

On a broad frontage, however, there was still the danger that a particular unit might stray off-course into the section of its neighbour. Against this an ingenious and simple device was employed. The bofors guns of the Light Anti-Aircraft batteries were brought into the plan. Their part was to fire bursts of coloured tracer shells along the boundaries between each brigade and division; it was a device that proved most effective through the dust and smoke.

These expedients, however, were not sufficiently exact for individual battalions and companies. They were accordingly led by a navigating officer whose exacting task it was in the din and dust to walk forward with his eyes glued to a hand compass, counting the paces as he went. In the 7th Battalion The Black Watch six navigating officers fell killed or wounded on this first night. Behind the navigating officers white tape was reeled out to mark the battalion's centre-line for those coming up later. Another party in the rear set up a line of masked hurricane lamps along the tape.

The prime duty of the leading companies in each battalion was to 'lean on the barrage' as closely as the shell bursts allowed, so that they could pounce on any living enemy before they recovered their wits and manned their weapons. Let us remind ourselves, however, that, although heavy concentrations of artillery fire were aimed at known or suspected enemy strongpoints, the 'curtain of fire' in front of the advancing infantry was a very thin one, but, for want of a more convenient expression, we must continue to use the term 'barrage'. When the barrage ceased to move forward and became a standing barrage, the infantry knew that an objective had been reached, and this fact was emphasized with smoke-shell fired right across the front by the field artillery as part of their barrage programmes.

Another device for helping the infantry to identify their objectives was to illuminate the sky immediately above by the crossed beams of searchlights, but this did not prove very satisfactory.

Thus everything possible was done to help forward the leading rifle companies and those who went with them. The rest was up to their skill in battle and their courage. Their prime duty was to reach their objective, not to stop and fight enemy posts between the thin-spread sections, unless obliged. These were the quarry of the mopping-up troops that followed. Once the leading companies fell behind the barrage, they would have to fight the rest of the way with their own weapons against enemies concealed at ground level.

How exacting was the task laid on them may be imagined from the fact that, of the 17,000 men in an infantry division of three brigades, even when at full paper strength, scarcely 4,000 were available to assault with rifle and bayonet, and in practice the number was always very much less. The leading line of a battalion, when attacking 'two-up', seldom exceeded 200 men.

These few had to overcome resistance, seize a position and hold it until gaps had been cleared through the minefields for the tanks and their own anti-tank guns to come forward. If daylight came before support could reach them, their position would become highly sensitive.

For all this, the time provided by one night was exceedingly short. A little less than eight and a half hours of darkness remained after Zero hour. For the sappers, this allowed scarcely more than half an hour beyond the theoretical best-possible. Could the infantry reach their final goal on time and could the mines be lifted fast enough? This was the crucial thing.

While the British guns were bombarding those of the enemy, the waiting rifle companies crossed their taped start-lines and quietly moved forward under cover of the din, counting their paces and timing their progress, to positions a little short of the enemy's forward defences. There they lay down and waited again for a minute or two, listening, and stirred by those little quiverings and tremors which all but the most stolid experience at the moment before going into action.

Then came to their expectant ears that pause in the bombardment which told them that their gunners were preparing for the new target, the infantry target. It was a pause more charged with immediacy than any other moment, for it told them that their own hour was about to strike. 'Their duty and their honour' lay immediately ahead; so also did their peril. They peered again, and for the last time, at their watches.

On the stroke of ten o'clock they heard above them a sudden swish, increasing in pitch, as of hundreds of great birds coming in to alight. A second later the barrage burst in front of them like one instantaneous salvo. 'It fairly caught my breath', recorded Humphrey Wigan, the Middlesex machine-gunner. 'It stunned even our own troops,' wrote Major H. Gillan in the Australian Division, 'and the ground vibrated under our feet like the skin of a kettle-drum'. The darts of red bofors tracer shot along their flanks and the beams of the directional searchlights shone out. For the rest of the night, that swish and crash and continuous trumpeting of the guns behind were to be the harmonic of all the minutes.

With rifles at the high port and with long bayonets gleaming wanly in the moonlight, the infantry stepped out towards the curtain of smoke and dust. What would they meet beyond it? Above the smother of the barrage the enemy's rockets shot up into the sky all along the thirty-eight mile of front, calling for the help of their artillery; but none came. Every three minutes the barrage jumped forward a hundred yards and the moving line of men closed up on it. It was, said Kippenberger, too slow a pace for his eager soldiers. It was too slow also for the ardent Highlanders, in action for the first time. Some of the leading companies were up to the barrage so quickly that they had to halt and wait, and then, as it jumped forward again, they were quickly in among the enemy.

The roar of the barrage filled and overshadowed all thought and feeling. Humphrey Wigan kept repeating: 'By God, this is wonderful!' Sapper Flinn, of the 3rd Cheshire Field Squadron, ready to drive forward his truck of mine-lifting stores, experienced a sudden leap of his feelings from the pit of his stomach to his racing heart and said: 'Now nothing can stop us!' The generals watched, listened and some of them prayed. The brigadiers, awaiting their time to go forward, fidgeted beside their wireless sets, anxious for the first news from ahead. 'Our hearts,' wrote Kippenberger, 'were with the gallant rifle companies.' Montgomery glanced at the text from *Henry V* in his caravan: 'Oh God of battles, steel my soldiers' hearts' and went quietly to an early bed.

In 51st Division, the kilted pipers, erect and proud beside their battalion and company commanders, broke into their wild-sweet music, heard shrill and high above the crash of shells, carrying the melodies of loch and glen across the foreign desolation. On their flanks the Australians and the New Zealanders, too, heard the heartening strains and knew thereby that, though the Jocks had vanished into the dust and the darkness, they were there.

'All my thoughts', said Robert Weir, of the Cameron Highlanders, 'were pleasant thoughts; and when our piper played *The Road to the Isles* I asked myself: "I wonder if it is".' For he knew that 'the Isles' were the celestial islands of the Blest. Piper Duncan McIntyre, in Blair-Imrie's company of 5th Black Watch, nineteen years old, hit quickly twice, continued to play, but a third hit brought him to the ground. Dying, he still continued to play and, when his body was found, the bag was still in his oxter and his fingers still upon the chanter.

The counteraction of the enemy, dazed by the violence and suddenness of the bombardment in depth, was slower than usual. The bombardment of the enemy batteries had been completely successful. For a long time very few of their guns spoke, so that our infantry got away to a clean start. When the enemy artillery did respond to the SOS rockets, their fire fell not on the foremost waves of our infantry but on those coming up behind. Not until after the first hour or so did the counterbarrage become serious. What was more damaging in the early stages, and indeed throughout, were the trench mortars; a high proportion of the wounds sustained by the British troops that night was from mortar fire.

After the first shock the mortars and machine guns that had not been eliminated by direct hits from our artillery burst into life after the barrage had passed over, firing on fixed lines or on shadowy shapes moving up towards them in the dusty moonlight. Many stuck to their posts, fighting back tenaciously. Others of the enemy posts, as we have seen, had been inaccurately plotted on our maps or not located at all, due to the difficulty of interpreting desert air photographs.

Such posts as lay directly in the path of the infantry were, for the greater part, quickly overcome. Those in the gaps between the thin-spread sections were passed by. The first trickles of prisoners began to file in, many of them stunned by what Rommel called 'the terrible

British artillery', covered in dust and half-dressed; an Italian officer came in wearing red pyjamas.

Thus 30th Corps' first objective beyond the first minefield, and halfway to the final *Oxalic* line, was won without serious difficulty or heavy casualties all along the line. The forward companies saw the barrage stand still, the white clouds from the smoke-shell, as they burst overhead, drift across the front to mark the pause, and the searchlights cross their beams somewhere overhead. The first waves halted and dug themselves in, while the second waves came up, put out tapes for their own start-line, disposed and oriented themselves to go through to further objectives.

On the front of 5th New Zealand Brigade, however, the exalted Romans, having taken his objective, three-quarters of a mile within enemy territory, with unexpected ease and finding no enemy there, was not satisfied to stop, as his orders prescribed. He said to his adjutant, Angus Ross: 'We can't stop here; we haven't fought yet.'

Filled with what Kippenberger described as 'ferocious ardour', he swept on, through the shell and smoke of our own standing barrage, fought his way without artillery support for nearly another mile right to the foot of Miteiriya Ridge, far ahead of anyone else and far ahead of the barrage also. There he stopped, endured the storm of the creeping barrage as it caught him up again and passed over, and held his ground until the astonished 21st and 22nd Battalions came up in due time. Then, dishevelled but full of fight, he fell back to the line where he should have stopped.

Everywhere along the front, however, enemy resistance stiffened violently after the first objectives had been gained and the final assault began. Beyond lay the second main minefield belt. Yet other minefields lay there also, at present undisclosed, unexpected and far more troublesome than the first. The enemy's battle outposts became stronger and thicker. Defences unrevealed by air photography sprang to life. His artillery awoke to the situation and began to shorten range. The battlefield was wrapped yet more thickly in a veil of smoke and dust from the bursting shells and the exploding mines.

The barrage began to outrun the leading companies as they were forced to stop and fight the enemy in their way.

Here and there the infantry triumphantly won their objectives, but here and there their attacks began to be held. The deeper they penetrated the thinner became their ranks and the stronger became the enemy's defences. It is time, therefore, that, as the final objective is approached, we should stop to record, all too briefly though it must be, the separate fortunes of the battalions. We shall begin, in traditional manner, at the right of the line, where 9th Australian Division was posted.

The Australians

Right up on the sea coast, where 24th Australian Brigade lay under Arthur Godfrey, nothing more was attempted than a feint attack, as one of the measures to keep the enemy guessing. It was made between the sea and Tel el Eisa. The brigade was supported, from positions in front of the infantry, by the new 4·2-inch rifled mortars of 66th Chemical Warfare Company, RE, who on this one night shot off the complete stocks of their high explosive in the Middle East.[1]

South of Tel el Eisa, however, the Australians made their genuine attack. It was entrusted to Whitehead's 26th Brigade on the right and to 20th (temporarily commanded by Hugh Wrigley) on the left. They had a long way to go, the *Oxalic* line being four miles ahead.

Whitehead's attack, very deep but on a narrow front, was a complete success. His was the vital mission of providing right flank protection to the whole Army on the now exposed open shoulder of the attack. This dangerous flank stretched for 7,000 yards, of which 3,000 yards had formerly been No Man's Land. His bayonets were too few for all his tasks. With some facing west on the newly won objective, the remainder, as they turned to face north, could cover only 4,000 yards of the flank. He therefore plugged the 3,000 yards gap with a special mixed force, under Lieutenant-Colonel Ted

1. The original *raison d'être* of these companies was to fire poison gas, if used by the enemy first. This was the first time that the rifled 4·2-inch mortar was used in action.

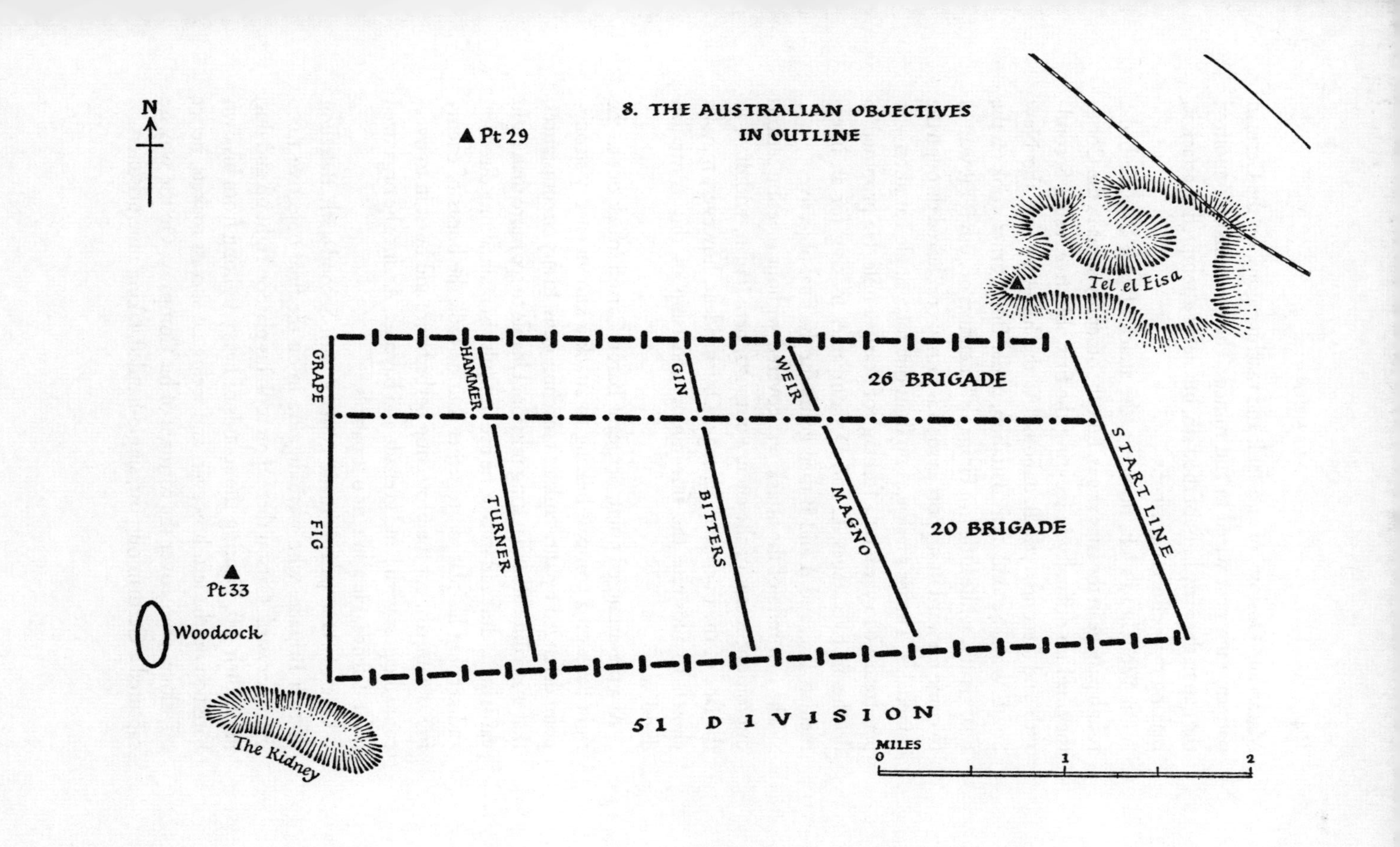
8. THE AUSTRALIAN OBJECTIVES
IN OUTLINE
N
Pt 29
Tel el Eisa
GRAPE
FIG
HAMMER
TURNER
GIN
BITTERS
WEIR
MAGNO
26 BRIGADE
20 BRIGADE
START LINE
Pt 33
Woodcock
The Kidney
51 DIVISION
MILES
0
1
2

Macarthur-Onslow, of anti-tank and machine guns, on the German pattern, each post wired in and mined. The Germans reconnoitred the gap in the early light of the 24th, but never attempted to attack it, making their efforts elsewhere.

On Whitehead's left, however, the attack of 20th Brigade had a rough passage in the later stages. Like the other divisions in the Corps, they had no difficulty in securing the first objective, using Second-15th and Second-17th Battalions. At the half-way line the New South Wales Second-13th Battalion, under Bob Turner, took on the final assault, while little Jim Finigan's Valentines of 40th RTR waited to come forward in support as soon as paths were cleared through the minefields. Turner's task was no light one for a single battalion – to penetrate 2,600 yards on a frontage of nearly a mile. He proposed to do this in two stages, C and D Companies making for an intermediate line, and A and B then going for the final objective.

The first mile of the attack was covered without meeting serious opposition; many of the enemy outposts, here Italian, withdrew in the face of the oncoming barrage. One incident, however, may be chosen to illustrate the fine junior leadership of this Australian division.

At a pre-arranged point, Sergeant Baron Carson struck out to the right flank on a compass bearing to attack a known enemy strong-point defended by anti-tank and machine guns. In any circumstances, that was a difficult and testing mission. Unable to see more than eight yards in the dust and smoke, he had difficulty in maintaining direction and keeping his platoon together, but he took the bursts of enemy fire as compass, cut the protecting barbed wire and burst in to overcome the post with hand grenade and bayonet. At once he organized it for defence. He also sent out patrols.

One of these patrols made contact with Second-48th Battalion of 26th Brigade, who were digging in on the final objective 1,000 yards forward. Carson thereupon took his platoon right up and dug in on their left. Hearing the sounds of heavy fighting from his own battalion on the left, however, and seeing no success rockets, he set off, alone, to discover the fortunes of his Company. On the way he captured a German outpost, single-handed, taking nine prisoners.

The barrage

Waiting sapper teams silhouetted against the light of the barrage

They get down to their job

Meanwhile, on reaching the battalion's intermediate line, A and B companies had leap-frogged C and D and begun their attack upon the final objective. Almost immediately they became heavily embroiled. Barbed wire, S-mines and trip-wires entangled their feet and mutilated their ranks. In spite of this, the two companies fought their way with the greatest determination right to the front edge of the final positions. The division had adopted a standard battle drill by which attacks had to be completed by an hour which permitted full consolidation before daylight – defences dug, anti-tank guns sited, posts wired and mined. Turner therefore halted his attack at extremely close range, with the objective almost in his hands.

Captain R. G. Sanderson, commanding A Company, seeing a party of enemy approaching and supposing them to be surrendering, ordered his men to cease fire. He stood up to take them and was immediately shot down. Lieutenant E. F. Norrie, already seriously wounded, took command and ordered the advance to continue, when he himself was killed. Lieutenant C. A. O'Connor, also wounded, and in action for the first time, came forward to lead the Company, led an assault against a German outpost, captured it after a bloody hand-to-hand struggle, and was mortally wounded. Only one officer was left in the company.

B Company, falling to the command of Lieutenant F. S. Treweeke, fared little better after overcoming one strong position, where they 'carpeted the ground with German dead', and took twenty-three prisoners. Their positions untenable, the companies were obliged to give ground and quickly dug themselves into 'doovers' about 1,000 yards from their goal.

Finigan's tanks, free at last from the minefields, came forward at first light, looking to Turner 'like battleships in line ahead', squatted on the new FDLs and suppressed in the most convincing manner the many targets that were presented to their guns.

The Highlanders

On the Highland Division's front, Wimberley's battalions everywhere made good progress, though unable to capture all their objectives on the first night. There was stiff opposition after the

9. THE HIGHLAND DIVISION OBJECTIVES *Code names given in part only.*

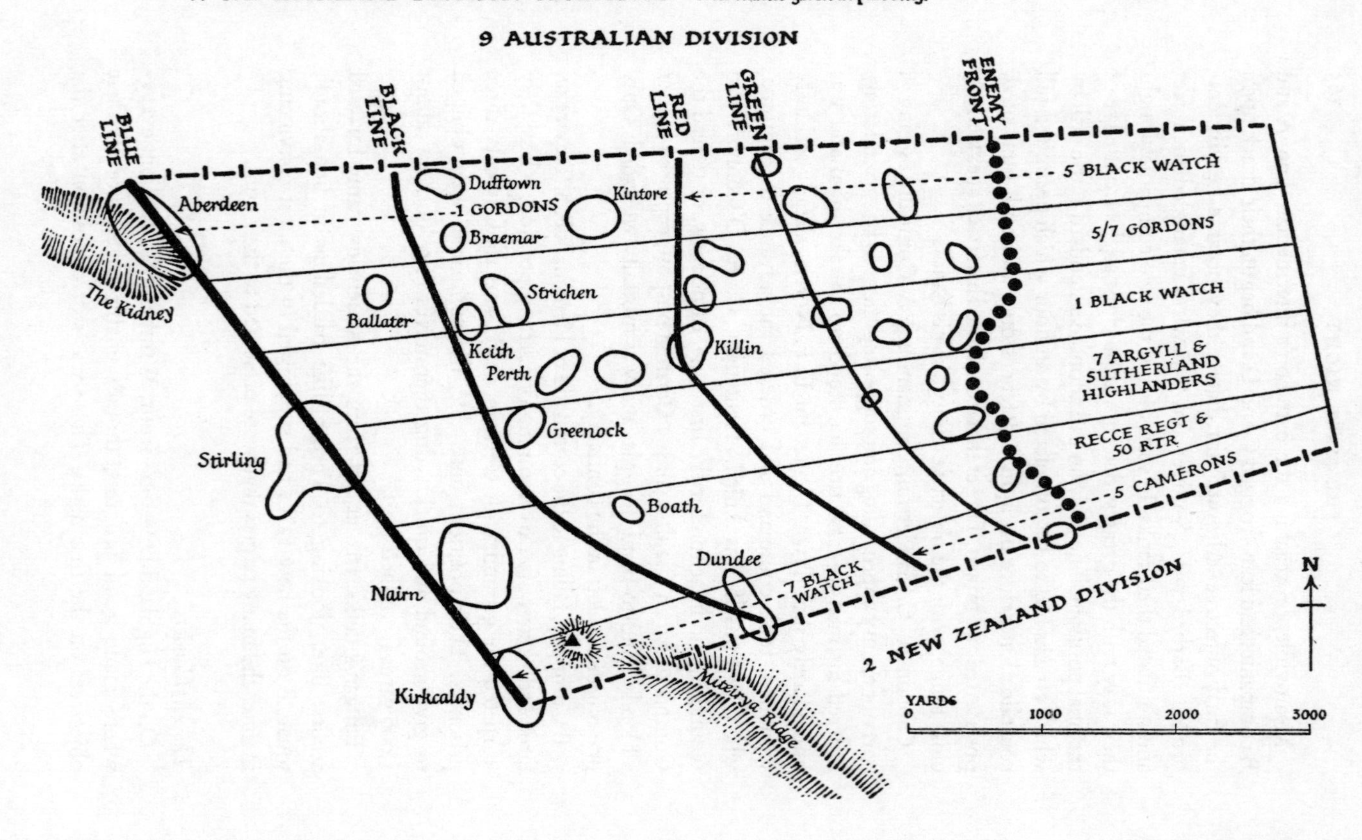

halfway line, with grievous casualties. The minefields on their front were found to be much more numerous than had been expected. Under the added strain and under the fire of by-passed battle outposts that had to be fought off the mine-lifting sappers were delayed. In consequence, the Valentines of 50th RTR, under John Cairns, were delayed also.

In this division, the Corps *Oxalic* objective was known as the Blue Line, with three intermediate lines on which to pause for reorganization (*See* Fig. 9). On the Blue Line lay four of the enemy's strongest defences, which in divisional orders were named *Aberdeen*, *Stirling*, *Nairn* and *Kirkcaldy*, the last being the culminating point of Miteiriya Ridge at its north-western end. One squadron of Valentines, carrying two platoons of infantry on their backs, was allotted to help 1st Gordon Highlanders capture *Aberdeen*, another in like manner to help the Argylls on to *Stirling*, and the remainder, under Cairns himself, for the capture of *Nairn* with the divisional Reconnaissance Regiment.

On the division's extreme right, next to the Australians, 5th Black Watch, led by Thomas Rennie, secured the halfway Red Line with smooth precision. There 1st Gordon Highlanders, commanded by the burly Horatio Murray and accompanied by their Middlesex machine gunners, leap-frogged them at the halfway line and made off with two companies in the dusty moonlight for *Aberdeen*. This was a defended locality on the long, low feature to become notorious in the ensuing armoured battle as 'Kidney Ridge'.

As the leading companies of 1st Gordons were preparing to advance, a solid wall of shell fire confronted them and remained stationary. Wigan, leading 12 Platoon of the Middlesex, recorded that 'the ground shook and reverberated, the air seemed to be solid with metal'. For some reason, he thought of the parting of the Red Sea waters. Major Michael du Boulay, watching from the start-line before it was the turn of his company to go forward, recorded that 'I personally never saw in the whole war anything to compare with the barrage A and C Companies had to go through. As a spectator, it seemed to me impossible that anyone could survive.'

It was at first thought that this could not be the enemy's counter-barrage but our own, in which there had been some error of timing. The companies were told, however: 'You have got to go through.'

Go through they did; the two leading companies led with great dash by Hubert Skivington and James McNeil, but suffering fearful casualties. Emerging from it, they were brought up short by two or more German Spandaus some sixty yards ahead. Skivington, accompanied by Harry Gordon and Bruce Rae and about a platoon of men, attempted to charge but he and about half the platoon were killed.

Enraged by the death of his friends, Lieutenant Ewan Fraser, one of those men who feel exhilarated in battle, having ordered covering fire by bren guns, went out alone, got in behind the enemy machine guns and wiped them all out with grenades. The two companies had won their objective, which was the intermediate Black Line.

Skivington's company, which had gone into action with five officers and 102 men, was by 2 a.m. reduced to one officer (Lieutenant Harry Gordon) and eighteen men. McNeil's company had suffered similarly. McNeil, a big, stalwart man, of whom it was said that it would take more than one shell to knock him down, merely coughed when he was first hit in the chest, but a second shell wounded him mortally. Thus, sorely bruised but unshaken, and commanded by junior officers, the little handful dug in and hung on, a lonely outpost in the wild night. Yet Bruce Rae, another of those men who positively enjoyed battle, when asked by Gordon how he felt, replied: 'Oh, I feel as though I had had a couple of bottles of champagne.'[1]

The Gordens' two rear companies, with their troop-carrying Valentines, meanwhile waited anxiously on their start-line. They were intended, on receipt of a success signal from the forward companies, to follow through, leap-frog them and assault *Aberdeen*. No news came, however, and the shelling was very bad. Murray properly decided that 'the situation did not permit the forward movement of infantry on tanks', and he accordingly released the

1. For several weeks afterwards C Company received no officer reinforcements and the platoons, in Gordon's words, were 'superbly commanded' by sergeants.

Valentines. In the early hours of the morning, still without news of what had happened ahead, he led forward his other two companies.

After going about 500 yards, however, as the result of a hazardous reconnaissance by Captain Charles Barker with a section of carriers, Murray decided to dig in where he was and await daylight. Du Boulay, meeting Murray at this juncture, observed feelingly:

'I say, sir, this is absolute hell!'

'Nothing to be frightened of, Mike,' replied Murray.

'Good God, sir!' exclaimed du Boulay with even more feeling, 'aren't you?'

There we shall leave 1st Gordons for the time being and shall resume the story of their trials and ultimate triumph in the next chapter.

The second of the most troublesome objectives on the Highlanders' front was *Stirling*. It was a particularly strong position, defended by numerous machine guns and nine field and anti-tank guns, of which at least two were 88s. It was the target of 7th Argyll and Sutherland Highlanders, under Lorne Campbell, a tall and slender London Scot. On his avenue of approach to *Stirling* there were not a great many enemy outposts, but, being largely dead ground, it was heavily impregnated with mines of all sorts, including large aircraft bombs – a factor that applied equally to the whole of the southern half of the Highland Division sector.

In common with other battalions, Campbell's problem was to conserve sufficient strength, after a four-miles attack, to assault the tough nut at the end of his avenue. To do this, he proposed to push right through to the Black Line with only two companies, and then to put in his B Company and A Company coming forward on Valentines of 50th RTR.

Thus, almost from the start-line, the Argylls and their Middlesex machine gunners incurred heavy casualties from the enemy's counter-barrage and from mines. D Company lost all its officers. A big aircraft bomb wiped out a whole platoon. The Middlesex suffered sharply also. Nevertheless, the strong outpost *Greenock* was stormed with gusto and the Black Line secured. The Valentines and their accompanying infantry, however, impeded by the mines, could not be got through in time and Campbell, too weak now to attempt the assault on *Stirling*, halted and dug in.

It was on their extreme left that the Highlanders had their most shining success of this night. There, next to the New Zealanders, 7th Black Watch advanced under their able and gallant young CO, James Oliver, a slight, alert figure, quick-thinking, cheerful and good-looking.

Leap-frogging 5th Cameron Highlanders at the halfway line, 7th Black Watch directed their attack on *Kirkcaldy*, that part of the Corps final objective which lay beyond Miteiriya Ridge, at its north-western extremity. Here the ridge culminated in a sharply ascendant feature shown on the map as Point 33[1]. Between it and the line where the Black Watch took over from the Camerons was the intermediate Black Line, which lay at the foot of the ridge.

From the moment they leapfrogged the Camerons, the battalion began to come under heavy and damaging shelling, which continued throughout the remainder of the attack. Casualties mounted rapidly. All the six officers who were detailed in turn to act as navigation officer were killed or wounded.

Few enemy were bodily encountered at first, but as the Black Line was approached the crumps of trench mortars were added to the shelling and an unexpected minefield was struck. It was thick with S-mines, Italian Red Devils and murderous 250-lb aerial bombs on trip-wires. From one of these aerial bombs, although the Jocks were moving at five yards' interval between men, a whole platoon of about thirty men was wiped out as it went up with a terrific roar. The S-mines, jumping stomach-high, killed or gravely wounded more. The Red Devils crackled under foot.

These ravaging casualties, however, did not deter Oliver's Black Watch. They walked forward steadily to the music of the piper. When the smoke shells from their artillery told them that they had reached the Black Line, the strength of the four rifle companies had been reduced by more than half.

Here, in accordance with the divisional plan, there was a halt for

1. Map ref.: 87002927.

fifteen minutes before making the final advance to the Blue Line, still another mile ahead, beyond the Miteiriya Ridge, which now faced them. Oliver quickly reorganized his stricken but unbowed battalion, forming them into two composite companies. One of these he put under the command of Charles Cathcart of Pitcairlie, and ordered him to continue the advance.

This Cathcart did with great daring and determination. With less than a hundred men, with the barrage now lost, but with his piper still playing, he stormed up Miteiriya Ridge, passed through yet another minefield beyond the ridge, pushed over barbed wire obstacles and triumphantly gained his Blue Line objective.

He got there with about forty men. They were the remnants of two companies which had begun more than 200 strong. All the five officers who fought through with his little force were killed or wounded, Cathcart himself being one of the wounded.

He set to work at once to organize his 500 yards' front, drawing back a little and to the left when he calculated that he had overshot his mark, and made contact with 21st NZ Battalion. There he remained with his handful of men, the wounded and the able, exposed and without relief, for the remainder of that night and all next day.

The action this night by 7th Black Watch was thus a shining example of leadership, initiative and guts at all levels in a battalion inspired by the fighting spirit. Their casualties on this night and the further seven nights and days that they held their position numbered 261 killed and wounded, including nineteen officers and two sergeant-majors. Nearly all were incurred on the first night.

Elsewhere on the front of 51st Division the assaulting battalions designated to go right through to the *Oxalic* line had equally hard fighting. Under Hugh Saunders, 5/7th Gordon Highlanders, advancing on the left of their 1st Battalion, made excellent progress until reaching the enemy outpost *Strichen*, when, like their fellow-Gordons, they were met by a wall of fire. One company was nearly wiped out. With no strength to press the assault, Saunders halted his companies. It was a critical moment for untried young soldiers. They looked at their CO in the hurricane of fire and saw him quietly light a cigarette. They stood fast and dug in and took *Strichen* next day. On their immediate left, 1st Black Watch, under Neil Roper-Caldbeck, overcoming all opposition, went right through to the Black Line, which was their objective, in excellent order. Indeed, Captain Gerald Osborne seized a battery 1,000 yards ahead before being recalled.

The New Zealanders

On the left of 51st Division, the New Zealanders, attacking Miteiriya Ridge, stormed over the crest and won nearly all their objectives in the face of very heavy casualties. So thoroughly did they crush the opposition that both their own 9th Armoured Brigade and Gatehouse's 8th Armoured Brigade got clean through, in a manner that we shall see presently.

Freyberg – and he was not alone – had been concerned that the timings of *Lightfoot* left very little margin for clearing passages through the minefields and pushing up the supporting weapons and the armour. At his final divisional conference Gentry, commanding 6th Brigade, remarked: 'Even if it goes like an exercise, the mine-lifting is virtually impossible in the time.'

The division advanced to the attack with Howard Kippenberger's 5th Brigade on the right and Gentry's brigade on the left. They used only one battalion each for the first objective, but had the Maori Battalion following to mop up, a task at which they were extremely competent. Behind them, as the New Zealand Sappers cleared their gaps in the minefield, John Currie's tanks waited their chance to go forward, with the Royal Wiltshire Yoemanry on the right under Peter Sykes, the Warwickshire Yeomanry (Guy Jackson) on the left and 3rd Hussars (Sir Peter Farquhar) following up.

For some hours Freyberg and his brigadiers fretted at their tactical headquarters with little news of the fortunes of the battalions ahead. On 5th Brigade's sector we have seen how Romans, leading 23rd Battalion in exalted mood, swept on beyond the first objective. But of this Kippenberger knew nothing. The sappers, however, were making good progress on the minefield gaps and at 11.30 p.m. Kippenberger, feeling that he could wait no longer, ordered up

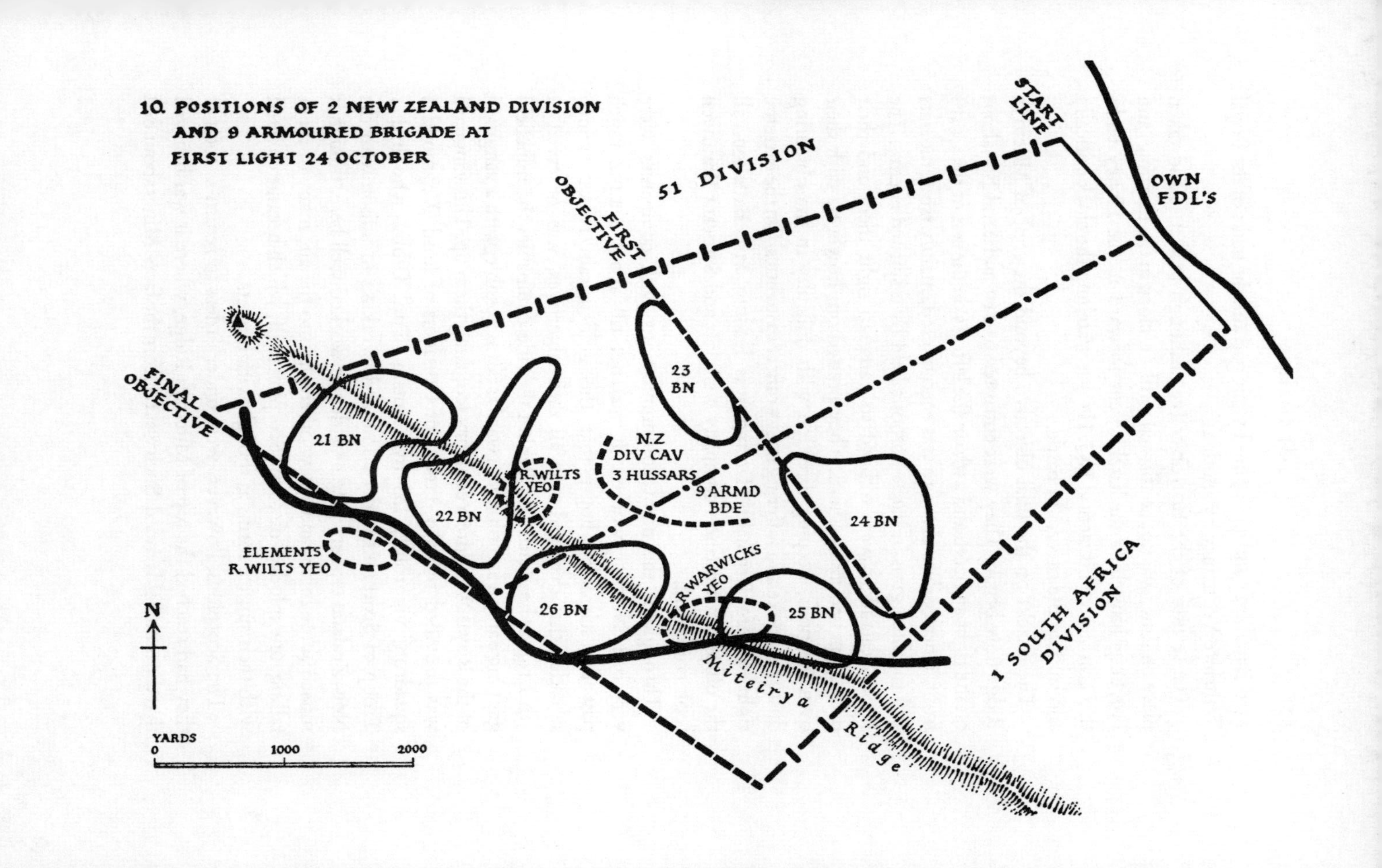

10. POSITIONS OF 2 NEW ZEALAND DIVISION AND 9 ARMOURED BRIGADE AT FIRST LIGHT 24 OCTOBER

23rd Battalion's anti-tank guns by one gap and the tanks of the Royal Wiltshire Yeomanry by another.

The seizure of the first objective, although in fact it had taken place on time, was not confirmed until 3 o'clock in the morning, and Freyberg himself immediately went forward in the Honey tanks that constituted his tactical HQ. He was watching the clock critically and sniffing the breezes of battle.

The attacks on the final objective beyond the crest of Miteiriya Ridge now began. They were entrusted to 21st and 22nd Battalions on the right and 26th and 25th on the left. As on the rest of the Corps front, a heavy defensive fire was encountered, mainly from mortars and machine guns in battle outposts held by a spirited enemy. The New Zealanders were obliged to pause to fight them and their barrage passed away ahead. They pressed on, however, with their own weapons, keeping direction with difficulty in the obscuring dust and smoke and suffering heavy officer casualities. On the extreme right, where Reginald Harding was leading 21st Battalion, all the officers in Butland's company were lost and Sergeant Bramwell took command.

Throughout the night communications with companies were very bad. Nothing worked. It was not till about 4 a.m., much past the scheduled hour, that the golden rain rocket, which signalled that they had won all their objectives, was observed at 5th Brigade headquarters. Behind the rifle companies the minefield gapping party was pushing forward as fast as possible, with a vanguard of the Royal Wiltshire Yeomanry scotching them up. This vanguard was provided by two Troops of Crusaders of Lord Weymouth's squadron, vigorously led by Captain 'Tim' Gibbs, who had a Troop of Scorpions under command, working in unison with the New Zealand sappers. The new device worked well here, though it missed some mines and threw others up into the air, many of them falling, unexploded, on to the Scorpion itself, which became covered with their sinister forms as though with limpets.

The Scorpions, however, were under orders to return as soon as they had reached the top of Miteiriya Ridge, where it was believed that the minefields ended. Such was far from the facts. Mines abounded beyond the ridge. It was getting dangerously late. If the tanks could not get through before first light they would have small chance against the enemy guns.

The Wiltshires accordingly pressed forward under the impetus of Peter Sykes, while the New Zealand sappers bent afresh to the infested ground. The heavy squadrons advanced. They went up on mines one after the other, but continued to press forward, passing ahead of the infantry, The crews of the wrecked tanks stuck to their guns and, as soon as it was light enough, began to engage the enemy where they stood; but they were now sitting targets and were all knocked out, most of them being shot up in flames. They were just that little bit too late. Sykes was very badly wounded and, for a brief hour Lord Weymouth took command until the arrival of Alistair Gibb.

At about the same time as the Wiltshires went ahead, the tanks of the Sherwood Rangers, under 'Flash' Kellett, in 10th Armoured Division, emerged likewise in the centre of the divisional front, and we shall see in the next section the vivid and stirring events that occurred.

Meanwhile, Gentry's brigade on the left had been pressing forward after a rough passage. On its right 26th Battalion, under Den Fountaine, had fought through to the final objective and, indeed, advanced beyond it. On the left, however, 25th Battalion, led by Ian Bonifant, a young man whom Gentry described as 'full of fire and guts', had gained the crest of the ridge, but could get no further, the 2nd South African Brigade on his left flank having been brought to a halt.

At about 4 a.m. Gentry himself went forward on his new brigade front in a tank of the Warwickshire Yeomanry, who were his supporting armour. It was, he recorded later,[1] a strange journey. Though the undefinable odours of the battlefield hung over all the moonlit scene, the 'ordinary noises of battle' had moved on and a strange quiet for a while possessed the captured ground east of Miteiriya Ridge. The little coloured lights marking the new minefield gap along which he travelled stretched ahead, it occurred to him, 'like some sort of fairyland and it was almost impossible to think of it as

1. To the Author.

a battlefield, strewn with death and destruction beneath the blanket of night. So thorough had been the counter-battery fire of our gunners.'

As Gentry breasted the ridge, however, the impression changed and the streams of tracer from several machine guns on his left, firing along the length of the ridge, showed him that Poole, his South African neighbour, had been checked. He therefore ordered Bonifant (who had been slightly wounded) to swing back the left flank of 25th Battalion.

At the same time he saw with satisfaction the tanks of the Warwickshires, under the stalwart Guy Jackson, coming forward and going up just at first light to engage the enemy in the gloom ahead. Gentry knew that it was now too late for the armour to go through to its ultimate mission, but he felt content that the situation was secure. It was the first time that the infantry had ever seen the tanks right up in forward battle positions at first light. Virtually the whole of Miteiriya was in our hands, though not quite all the ground beyond it.

The South Africans

The cause of the halt imposed on 2nd South African Brigade was a strong German outpost which had escaped detection in the air photographs and in which the Germans were fresh and unshaken. The Field Force Battalion suffered devastating casualties, which imposed a restraint on the whole brigade. On their left, however, 3rd South African Brigade successfully burst right through to their final objective in a model attack; they did not need to summon the help of 8th RTR, who were on call but who lost a few of their Valentines on mines.

On the extreme left wing of 30th Corps front the 4th Indian Division carried out a vigorous raid.

Thus, as Oliver Leese looked at his map early on the morning of 24 October, he had every reason to be satisfied with the achievements of his infantry divisions. On the right and left extremities the objectives had been gained. There were some indentations on each divisional front, but overall, the assaulting soldiers of the Corps had in one

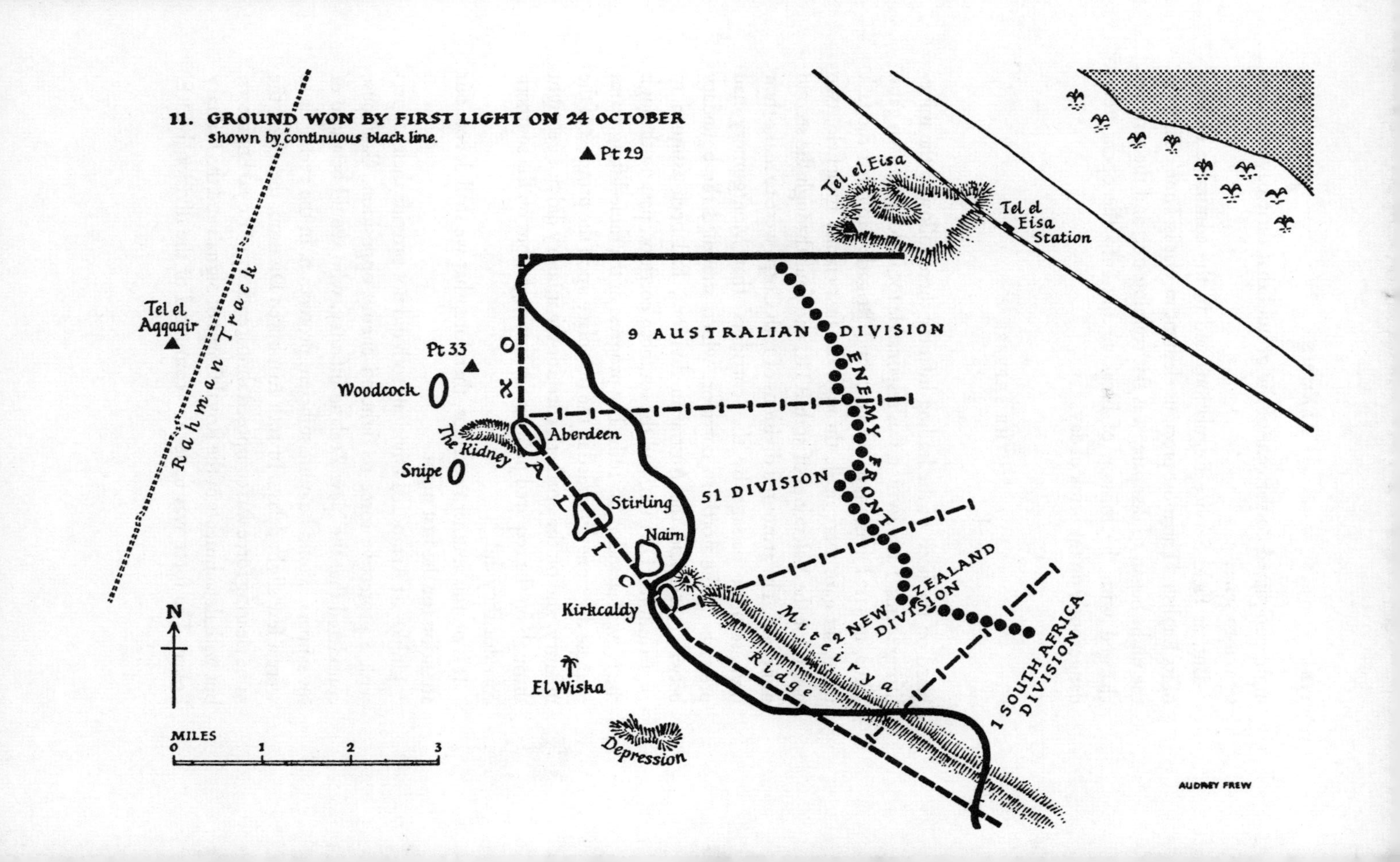

11. GROUND WON BY FIRST LIGHT ON 24 OCTOBER
shown by continuous black line.

night conquered 80 per cent of the ground that their bayonets had set out to seize.

But, as Field Service Regulations said in the admirable lucidity of its English, 'The most precious element in war is Time'. Time, as the night began to dissipate, was fast running out, and the armour, charged with the mission of breaking out into the open, stood dangerously on the brink of day.

THE SAPPERS

Hard on the heels of the leading infantry there followed the mine-lifting teams. Each division was responsible for making its own gaps. Thus, in 51st Division, in which 152nd Brigade provided the task force, six gaps were made through the first enemy minefield, two being for the Valentines of 50th RTR, and four through the second minefield. The armoured divisions of 10th Corps were to make their own separate passage by the 'corridors' that Montgomery had prescribed; the northern corridor, which straddled the boundary between 51st and the Australian divisions, had been assigned to 1st Armoured Division, and the southern corridor, passing through the New Zealanders, to 10th. The progress of the mine-lifting teams of these divisions depended in the first place upon the progress of the infantry, and on the northern corridor the infantry did not get right through on the required path on the first night, but on the southern corridor they did.

It is on this southern corridor, therefore, that we shall devote our attention for the first night.

Unlike 1st Armoured Division, 10th did not provide their sappers with a protective force to fight off enemy opposition. Gatehouse considered that the New Zealand infantry, who would be ahead of his sappers, would be quite sufficient protection. In the event, there were a few slight delays. In 10th Armoured Division, therefore, the mine clearing force was composed almost entirely of Royal Engineers, but with detachments of the Royal Corps of Signals and the Military Police. The force was under the command of the divisional CRE,

Lieutenant-Colonel Gilbert McMeekan, a tall, strongly-built officer of fine presence and vigorous personality.

He was very fortunate in the sappers under his command. Those on the strength of the division were 2nd and 3rd Field Squadrons and 141st Field Park Squadron. They were Cheshire units and a large number of the original recruits had come from the New Brighton Rugby Football Club. In 2nd Squadron Major Jack Perrott had as his second-in-command Captain J. C. Rigby, a Cheshire County cap. We shall see more of this squadron on the second night.

Third Field Squadron was commanded by Major Peter Moore, the fighting sapper who had run the Eighth Army School of Mine Clearance and devised the new drill. That drill was now to be subjected to the severest of trials. The squadron already had a fine record, having fought in the brief, turbulent campaign in Greece as well as up and down the Western Desert. They had had a rough time in the July fighting, having been pitchforked into mine clearance tasks in ill-planned battles. Moore had a good lot of officers, with the tall, thin David Edwards as his second-in-command, and some fine NCOs, including Sergeant Bill Stanton, the stalwart glassblower from St Helens, strict in discipline, courageous leader in action, old enough to be called 'Dad'; Corporal Hardwick, who had already won the Military Medal; Corporal Herring, a courageous junior leader; and Corporal Ronald Delve, the singing carpenter from Neath.

These Cheshire squadrons were quite insufficient for the big mine-clearing job that McMeekan had to do and he was lent additional units for the night. These were 571st Army Field Company from Devon and Cornwall (Major Yeates) and 573rd Army Field Company (Major Brinsmead). A further unit, 6th Field Squadron (Major Collins), was directly under command 24th Armoured Brigade at first. Perrott's 2nd Field Squadron was also not employed on the first night, taking station with 8th Armoured Brigade in the great mustering of tanks on the Springbok Road. The three Scorpions allotted to the division were lent for the first night to the New Zealanders, but achieved little.

There remained, therefore, three units for the first night's attack.

They were required to clear four 16-yard gaps, which were a continuation of 30th Corps' 'Bottle', 'Boat' and 'Hat' routes, and a spare route named 'Ink'. Brinsmead took Bottle on the right, Moore took Ink and Boat in the centre and Yeates took Hat. The routes had to be carried right the way through to the final infantry object beyond Miteiriya Ridge. A reserve, mainly from 141st Field Park Squadron, was under Major Carr.

The barrage crashed down, the New Zealand infantry closed up to it and the sapper reconnaissance parties, immediately on their heels, stepped out on a compass bearing according to the drill. McMeekan was on Boat route, immediately behind Moore's squadron; he was perhaps the only man to follow that barrage in a staff car and he sat right out on the roof of it 'in order to see the troops'. This was the route designated for the tanks of the Sherwood Rangers and for Gatehouse's own divisional headquarters. That route we also shall follow first.

There was a No Man's Land of about a mile before the first enemy minefield, the location of which was well enough known. The gapping parties of 3rd Field Squadron walked forward to within 500 yards of it, with their sandbagged pilot vehicle driven by Sapper Shaw, their mine detectors, their large reels of white tape, their tin mine-markers, their pickets and lamps.

They waited expectantly for the blue light from the reconnaissance officer, while the guns trumpeted behind them and the barrage roared ahead. McMeekan found it 'soothing'. The moonlight, not yet obscured by dust, wanly illuminated an other-worldly scene in which the few score sappers seemed to be alone in a realm of noise. 'We felt rather lonely and naked', recorded Moore, 'without any escort of infantry or tanks.' But this was his only concern. His men had been trained to a hair for what they had to do and each man, as he waited, went through his own part in his mind.

The blue light showed ahead and they were off. The machine guns began to crackle like electric drills and their tracers flicked along the line. A few shells began to fall. The pilot vehicle, creeping towards the blue light, blew up and burst into flames. Enemy machine

9th Lancers, waiting to go forward on Moon Route (marked by the cairn), watch the gun flashes ahead

Shermans of C Squadron, 9th Lancers, after forcing the passage of the last minefield, 24 October

The counter-barrage

Australian troops with a wounded German after the capture of an outpost

guns and mortars turned on it at once, like steel filings drawn to a magnet. Moore, Driver Shaw and one or two others leapt for fire extinguishers and in about ten minutes put out the signal flames.

Thus there was a trying delay right at the very start. McMeekan looked at his watch. It was 11.20. Twenty minutes late, and time was already the most precious factor. He moved right up and sent runners out laterally across the minefield for news of the other routes. Signals arrived to lay telephone cable, but the shelling increased, the wires were cut and telephone communications were never of any value. Wireless, as we shall find, was little better and throughout the night communications were the one shortcoming that bedevilled him.

Moore's sappers got down to work at once in their echeloned teams, sweeping with their detectors, feeling with their fingers, marking and pulling out the mines and taping the sides of the lane. This was the real thing at last after weeks of training. Knowing that time was precious, they worked as fast as their delicate and dangerous task allowed, moving forward yard by yard, eyes to the ground, ears turned to the detector's alarm, trying to ignore the distracting sounds of battle all around, trying to be cold-blooded in the heat and emotion of conflict. Tellers, Italian mines, a few S-mines and mines of other sorts were lifted from the soil of the Devil's Garden and made harmless. It was not very difficult work at first, for, the wind having blown away the sand in many places, the mines there lay clearly exposed.

At first they worked without serious interference from the enemy, but before long a German heavy machine-gun came to life very close on their left hand. Moore dispatched Lieutenant John Van Grutten, the casual young Cambridge undergraduate, to attack it with rifles and hand grenades, and the gun was silenced. The squadron pushed on, got right through the first minefield, lit the little orange and green lamps and sent word back to the Sherwood Rangers that the gap was through. The squadron prepared to move on to tackle the next minefield.

Moore, however, was anxious. A detachment of Military Police should by now have come forward in lorries with a load of pickets to mark the route forward between the two minefields. There was no sign of them; what could have gone wrong? He looked at his watch. Time was terribly important.

Then in the dusty moonlight he saw a small figure moving slowly towards him. As the figure came nearer he saw that it was staggering under an enormous load of pickets; by the broad red band round the man's helmet, he saw also that he was a Provost corporal. He spoke sharply to him:

'Good God, what are you going here? Where's your lorry?'

The little corporal answered with unconcern: 'Sorry to be late, sir. Afraid the lorries got shot up. A lot of casualties, sir. So I've carried up as many pickets myself as I could. I'll be right back for some more, sir.'

What had happened was that the two Military Police lorries, 100 yards back, had both been hit by shellfire. All the redcaps, including the sergeant-major, had been killed or wounded except for the little lance-corporal. McMeekan arrived on the scene, provided some of his reserve sappers to replace the Provost and looked after their wounded, but the lance-corporal meantime went ahead alone. McMeekan did not see him again, but the route was marked and lit all the way before dawn.

Third Squadron hurried forward to the next main enemy minefield. They were in the thick of the battle now. The din increased as the enemy weapons replied to our own more vigorously. German and New Zealand dead lay in greater numbers, and many wounded waited anxiously for help to come. The second minefield was found to be much more thickly sown than the first. Trip-wires and the booby-trapped Italian Red Devils became more plentiful. The S-mines were encountered wherever there was dead ground and Moore, crawling to a flank to find a deviation, was saved only by the eye of an alert subaltern beside him from putting his hand down upon the deadly horns.

As his teams topped Miteiriya Ridge, the enemy's fire increased in intensity and the sappers' casualties grew. All their expertness and all their coolness were called for as they handled the infernal machines in the dark, following the precise drill that they had been taught and trying to make themselves insensitive to the devil's carnival around them. It needed guts to stand up and stay standing up when everyone else was either lying down or running, for they were now right up with the leading infantry beyond the crest of the ridge. In the left of the squadron's two gaps, two of the detector operators were hit one after the other, but on both occasions the stalwart Sergeant Stanton took his place.

It was in this second minefield that Moore most felt the need for protective troops to fight off enemy posts interfering with his work. Several enemy machine-guns were now firing at his team from both flanks and although most of the bullets were whistling overhead, a German heavy machine-gun opened accurate fire from only seventy yards away on the right. It became difficult to make progress, for any movement brought immediate fire. Moore was about to send back for his reserve Troop to attack the position, when a New Zealand officer, seeing their difficulty, attacked the position with two of his men with tremendous dash and, amid an eruption of bursting grenades, killed or captured every man in the post.

While 3rd Squadron was sweeping its way through the second minefield, McMeekan prepared to go forward again, when Moore's sergeant-major unexpectedly appeared out of the gloom on foot. He had been sent back in a Dingo (Daimler scout car) to report progress, but on the way back between the two minefields the Dingo had been blown up by a stray mine. That meant that there were one or more 'indiscriminate' mine sowings between the two main belts, and McMeekan employed his last reserves as teams to clear them.

About the same time Moore's reconnaissance officer[1] came back to report that he had been right through to the objective beyond the ridge, ahead of the infantry. McMeekan therefore, his staff car having been knocked out, went forward in his Humber armoured car, with the reconnaissance officer and sergeant-major clinging to the outside. His Intelligence Officer, Lieutenant Alesworth, followed in a sandbagged jeep, with Driver Crump at the wheel. On the way McMeekan picked up a corporal who was moving Moore's wounded out of the path of the tanks and passed the wreck of the sergeant-

1. Either James Hague or Bernard Jarvis.

major's Dingo. They began to approach Miteiriya Ridge, with McMeekan standing up in the turret of the car and the other three clinging to the outside of it.

Half a mile from the crest of the ridge an air-burst shell from an 88 detonated within a few feet of them. The corporal was badly wounded and McMeekan was shattered by concussion. His right ear was bleeding and the ear-drum broken. A tremendous roaring filled his head, which felt about to burst. There was a small wound in his right arm.

Some New Zealand infantry came up and applied shell dressings to both men. McMeekan sat on the ground, put his head between his knees and in a minute or two felt better. He remounted his armoured car, which was undamaged, and drove on over the half-mile of the rough gradient to the crest of the ridge.

The shelling was now considerable and many dead lay strewn over the rocky slope. He found that a bank ran along the crest of the ridge and that Moore's few vehicles were tucked in under it. Moore himself arrived very soon and reported that both his gaps, Boat and Ink, were making good progress, not much behind time and that his teams were, in fact, in front of the infantry. It was 3.30 in the morning and 8th Armoured Brigade was due to start through in half an hour. The urgency of the situation pressed hard upon the two officers. A report came from Brinsmead that Bottle gap was through on the right, but no news could be got from 571st Field Company on Hat. So McMeekan set out to discover for himself, transferring from the armoured car to his jeep.

Almost quite deaf, he took the wheel himself with Driver Crump beside him, but he had to change places with him when he failed to hear a Maori's challenge to stop him and a bayonet flashed menacingly against the side of the jeep. A hundred yards on another party of Maoris roared at them and Crump said: 'They say we've run into a minefield, sir.' McMeekan dismounted and found a trip wire wrapped round the back axle.

It was a near squeak, but as the two men bent to remove the wire, McMeekan saw to his delight a German skull-and-cross-bones sign with the warning *Achtung Minen*. He had stumbled on the Germans' own gap through their minefield.

Close by he found also the reconnaissance party of 571st Field Company. McMeekan learnt from the sergeant in charge that, led with great daring by Lieutenant Herbert Darville, they had been right through to their objective beyond the ridge, had put up their guiding light and were waiting for the gapping party to work up to them.

By now McMeekan realized that there were no infantry in front of him, that 6th NZ Brigade had been unable to gain their objective on this front, and that he and his sappers were the foremost troops. He was not deterred. There was still just time to make a path for the armour if the German gap was a safe one. He decided to test it.

The reconnaissance party had a detector mounted on bicycle wheels, which they called a 'pram'. Conscripting Crump into the reconnaissance team, McMeekan made off over the crest to the German lines. Two men operated the pram, with McMeekan and three others lined out on either side, looking for any fresh marks in the sand which might show that the enemy had closed the gap at the last hour: six men ahead of the whole army, strolling slowly along, eyes glued to the moonlit ground.

The enemy, himself uncertain of the position, was maintaining a curtain of desultory shell and machine-gun fire along his side of the ridge. Impelled by the urgency of the hour, the little sapper party paid no heed to the fire, but McMeekan was careful to keep a man glued to his less deaf ear.

The luck could not last long. About 150 yards beyond the crest, two machine guns opened up close on their left, the tracers flicking just over their heads, narrowly missing. They dropped to the ground and McMeekan made a rapid appreciation. He contemplated completing the reconnaissance by crawl, but his watch showed him that it was already 4.30. No time. With three gaps swept and a fourth clear for at least halfway, he thought he would be justified in calling the armour forward. The roaring in his head forgotten, he felt all Africa within his grasp if the tanks could be shepherded through within an hour. He crawled back with his little team as fast as he could.

He hurried back to Boat gap, where his armoured car still was, to call on the armour by wireless. But both the wireless set and the operator had been badly shaken when, at the moment of his having been blasted by the air burst, he had fallen on top of them. He wished ardently that he had had his own Signalman McKay with him.

It was maddening to him that the whole plan might fail because of a single faulty wireless. He jumped into his jeep again and drove as fast as he dared back down the Boat gap and found that 8th Armoured Brigade was already rumbling up. He shouted to the first squadron leader that the way was clear, and close behind he found Neville Custance, the brigade commander, himself. Custance told him that the column on the Hat route was well up but, as was to be expected, did not know what was in front. McMeekan replied: 'Very well, sir, I will go over and guide them.'

He made his way across with the greatest difficulty, obstructed by wire, trenches and gun-pits, found to his disgust that the column on Hat had received orders to halt and doubled back again to Boat, bent on urging the armour to hasten forward before first light. He found a gunner officer and asked for the use of his wireless to speak to brigade headquarters. The gunner demanded to see his identity card and McMeekan produced it, fretting at the delay. A few seconds later another gunner asked for it, and the card fell from McMeekan's hand, which was quivering with rage and impatience. Then Douglas Packard, commanding 1st RHA, whose guns were coming into action under shell-fire just behind, turned up and took the irate, determined and almost stone-deaf CRE to see Custance personally.

But it was too late. Half an hour too late. The tanks of Flash Kellett's Sherwood Rangers ahead had been brought to a halt by the enemy.

While McMeekan had been trying to get the Hat route opened up, the sappers of 3rd Field Squadron had been 'working like demons' to complete Boat. Moore, like his CRE, was getting more and more anxious about time. A hard driver in training, in action, like other good leaders, he encouraged and guided and was always on the spot when he was most wanted. Before long, like Brinsmead on Bottle, he was ahead of the New Zealand infantry, but his men were as steady as rocks under the continuous fire as they crept forward, sweeping, marking, lifting, taping.

It was getting on towards six o'clock and the sky was beginning to change from black to grey and the stars to fade as he watched his men work through to the very end and saw a sapper put up the last marker. Then he turned and raced back as fast as he could through the gap that had been made. At the end of it, in the expanse between the two minefields, he saw the tanks of the Sherwood Rangers lined up, nose to tail, waiting for the word to go forward. He jumped on to the leading tank and shouted to the officer in the turret:

'For God's sake, get up as quickly as you can, or you'll run into trouble.'

The tanks moved immediately, and Moore himself led them forward. They climbed up the rocky slope and came up on the crest. Moore could see the stalwart Sergeant 'Stan' standing at the head of the gap in the half-dark, boldly waving them on. They answered his signal and as they debouched from the head of the gap their black shapes became silhouetted in the dull grey light before dawn.

A few hundred yards ahead a screen of dug-in anti-tank guns in the enemy's main battle position was waiting for them. There was a terrible 'clang' as the tank that Moore was leading was hit by a solid shot. He at once ran back to the next tank in the line and guided it round in front of the first. Within a few feet of him it suffered the same fate. He ran back for a third, with a like result.

In the first five minutes six were hit and burning. In a very short time the Rangers had lost sixteen tanks. The markers put up by the sappers were knocked down by shell fire, so that other tanks, trying to open out to a flank, went into the minefield.

Faced with this situation, Flash Kellett tried to call forward the machine gunners of The Buffs, who formed part of his Sherwood Rangers regimental group, to suppress the enemy anti-tank guns. He could get no answer from them on the radio. He therefore summoned his field gunner, Major David Egerton, commanding

B Battery, 1st RHA, whose OP tank, a Honey, was next to his own in the column. Could he, Kellett asked, do anything about those chaps in front?

Egerton, a young Regular officer, looked through his spectacles into the pre-dawn, which was still too dark for discerning anything at a distance but solid, black objects. The intimidating streams of red tracers from the German 50-mm wove their patterns all around, and the flames of burning tanks glowed on either hand. But all that he could see ahead were the flashes from the enemy's guns, dug in on the reverse slope of a slight fold in the ground, a few hundred yards away. He said:

'I don't think I can do any good, sir, but I'll have a try.'

He called his battery into action. They were still in the long column in the Boat minefield lane, between the second and the third squadrons of the Rangers' tanks. In the confines of the minefield gap it was impossible for the guns to deploy. Captain Peter Jackson, commanding the 'gun group', without hesitation decided that the only direction to go was forward.

Pulling the eight 25-pdrs of the two Troops out of line, he led them through the din and deployed them in a 'crash action' in the open, some 300 yards beyond the minefield, Downham Troop on the right, Sahagon Troop on the left. It had all the atmosphere of a horse-artillery action in the old tradition, in front of the whole army. So close were they to the enemy that a German 50-mm gun was attacked and silenced by Lieutenant Pat Grant with hand grenades.

The two Troops opened fire immediately over open sights, but the only targets they could engage were momentary flashes in the night from unseen weapons. These, as Egerton knew, were poor targets for a gun and fall of shot could not be observed. The shapes of his own guns, however, were dimly silhouetted and began to be more clearly revealed as the sky grew paler. They came at once under heavy fire, from anti-tank artillery, machine guns and rifles, but resolutely continued to engage.

Egerton's own tank, 200 yards ahead, was hit. Deprived of mobility and communications, he walked back to his battery through the hubbub. He found both Troops to be suffering heavy casualties, men dropping at the guns every minute. They continued to engage, and here and there the flashes began to diminish.

The approaching dawn, however, brought an end to the gallant little action. Seeing the Rangers' tanks themselves beginning to withdraw to the cover of the ridge, Egerton gave the order: 'Cease firing; prepare to withdraw.'

The hump-backed 'quads' drove up in the dissolving gloom, led by the Troop-sergeants with the steadiness of a drill-order. Their distinctive shapes, familiar to the enemy in many a lively action, brought a new access of fire. The quads drove on, wheeled right and left of their Troops, hooked on to their guns and drove back, very fortunate that only one of them was knocked out.

Some twenty wounded still lay out on the ground to be picked up and evacuated. David Mann, leader of Downham Troop, began to do so but was himself mortally wounded. Jack Tirrell, leader of Sahagon, an ex-ranker officer who already wore the ribbons of the MC and DCM, had better luck and got his wounded out piled high on his Honey. It was almost full daylight and, as the crimson radiation of the approaching sun glowed behind the rocky crest of Miteiriya, the funeral plumes of the smoking tanks were dyed blood-red.

When everyone else had vacated the position, Egerton himself and such other officers as remained walked quietly away in the morning light and, as they did so, Jackson was wounded by a 50-mm shell that burst between him and Egerton.[1]

Meanwhile, Moore and his sappers were manning some German trenches, prepared to help the infantry against an enemy counter-attack. To Driver Flinn, who was perhaps the first man to drive a vehicle beyond the ridge, this was the worst part of the night, but he drew comfort from the nonchalance and dry humour of Corporal Delve. A Stuka attack passed almost unnoticed, for, as Flinn said, 'a couple of dozen bombs in the middle of that lot meant nothing'.

The order came from McMeekan for the sappers to withdraw, their task completed. Flinn drove some of them back in his Chev. to the area ordered a mile or so back. He then made two further trips

1. Egerton later lost a leg while serving under the Author's command in 13th Anti-Tank Regiment in Italy.

up to collect wounded, bringing back New Zealanders, sappers and several badly burned men, in great pain, from the Rangers' tanks. The minefield gaps, now revealed to the enemy, were under observed fire and a long-range duel between the tanks had begun.

Dirty, tired, thirsty, 3rd squadron withdrew full of pride that they had done their job. So excellent had been their training that they had not suffered a single casualty from mines; nor, indeed, had any other RE unit in the division. They relaxed and began to brew up for breakfast. Sergeant 'Stan' took off his steel helmet. A shell burst about seventy yards away and a splinter from it embedded itself in his skull.

The other sapper units in 10th Armoured Division had maintained the renown of their Corps with no less spirit. 'The mad bastards are way ahead,' a New Zealander had said when Flinn, driving up his stores lorry, stopped to ask where they were. In 573rd Company, on Bottle route, Second Lieutenant Eric Smith was leading the sweeping party ahead of the infantry beyond Miteiriya Ridge. Various enemy machine guns were traversing the area in their methodical fashion. Smith, already himself wounded, carefully observed the arcs of each gun as revealed by their tracers. As each in turn swivelled towards him, he dropped his team to the ground, resuming between the lulls.

In the 571st Company Lance-Corporal Harold Greatrex was driver of the pilot vehicle. It was blown up and he was wounded. Refusing medical aid, he unloaded his stores and carried them forward to the sweeping party 300 yards ahead, making four journeys through the enemy's counter-barrage.

All along the 30th Corps front, as well as in the sector north of Himeimat, where 13th Corps were attacking, the dust-clouded moon looked down on similar exploits. Only on Miteiriya Ridge, however, did the sappers succeed in making a way for the armour right through to the final goal, for in the other tank corridors the infantry themselves were brought to a halt.

Thus the mine was the weapon that most seriously obstructed the break-out of Eighth Army's armour. On Miteiriya Ridge an extra half-hour of darkness would have done the trick, though whether, even so, the armour could have got through is a question that the next night's operations were to answer. By any test, however, the achievements of the New Zealand infantry and of 10th Armoured Division on this night stand out as exploits of the highest order.

THE ARMOUR

While the actions precedent to their own were taking place, the two armoured divisions of 10th Corps were awaiting their turn to go forward in a 'regulating area' on the Springbok Road south of El Alamein station.

This they had reached after an intricate approach march brilliantly planned by the staff. They were a formidable and impressive force, numbering more than 5,000 tanks, guns and vehicles of various sorts. Their minefield task forces, however, had gone ahead with the infantry, as we have seen on 10th Armoured Division's corridor, and their field guns, other than those in close support of the armoured brigades, had previously taken post to join in Eighth Army's fire plan.

At the Springbok Road, still maintaining wireless silence, they refuelled, removed muzzle-covers from the guns, fed belts of ammunition into the Besa and Browning machine guns and were strictly marshalled in their order of progress. The enemy positions lay six miles ahead of them on the south and nine on the north. They were not to move until 2 a.m. when 1st Armoured Division, using the Sun, Moon and Star routes, was to make its way up to the northern corridor, and 10th Armoured by Bottle, Boat and Hat to the southern.

Lumsden's orders to Briggs and Gatehouse were that their divisions, having cleared their own minefield gaps through the territory won by the infantry, were to deploy on the *Pierson* bound, approximately a mile ahead of the infantry on the north and two miles on the south, putting out anti-tank screens with their infantry brigades on their open flanks. From this bound it was intended, after reconnaissance, to move on another three or four miles to the *Skinflint* report line running south-eastward from Tel el Aqqaqir, with the hope of bringing the enemy armour to battle there.

Briggs, on the northern corridor astride the boundary between the

Australians and the Highlanders, intended accordingly to deploy 2nd Armoured Brigade on a line just west of that insignificant kidney-shaped ring contour which has already been briefly mentioned and which gave its name to the ridge in which it was a depression, with 7th Motor Brigade forming a flank on the right.

Gatehouse, having two armoured brigades in his division on the southern corridor, placed 24th Brigade on the right and 8th on the left, with 133rd Lorried Infantry Brigade following to form a defensive flank to the south.

At the Springbok Road the waiting divisions saw ahead of them the long, continuous flickering of the gun flashes stretching away into the night as far as the eye could reach and heard their insistent clamour. In a tank of the Warwickshire Yeomanry Clive Stoddart, watching the moon, thought of moonlight steeplechases and of the pictures in the dining room at home. It was bitterly cold and as the men of the armour shivered in the moonlight the first flush of excitement at the magical opening of the barrage began to flag a little. Their own entry into the stormy waters ahead was not to be so dramatic as the infantry's – no hidden start-line, no Zero Hour, no barrage. They would crawl slowly into battle, their fortunes in part dependent on those of the soldiers ahead of them. All were keenly looking forward to the performance of the Sherman in its first battle. They prayed above all that they would be able to get through the last minefield and out into the open among the enemy before daylight. As they waited, a lone German aircraft dropped a single bomb on 2nd Armoured Brigade.

Since we have already seen 10th Armoured Division going up into action in the southern corridor, it is 1st Armoured, and particularly its 2nd Armoured Brigade, that we shall follow as they begin to drive across the Springbok Road at 2 a.m. They crept forward in line ahead at the prescribed speed of three miles in the hour, following the long line of masked lamps that lit the three Corps routes. It was a difficult and tiring speed for the wheeled vehicles.

Almost nose-to-tail, the brigade advanced in the accepted desert manner in three regimental groups, the Bays (Lieutenant-Colonel Alex Barclay) on Sun route on the right, 9th Lancers (Lieutenant-

Colonel Gerald Grosvenor) on Moon in the centre and 10th Hussars (Lieutenant-Colonel Jack Archer-Shee) on Star. In each regimental group the Reconnaissance Troop led in scout cars, followed by two squadrons of tanks, regimental headquarters, the third squadron, the affiliated battery of 11th RHA in their new Priests, a squadron of the Yorkshire Dragoons as motor infantry, a battery of 76th Anti-Tank Regiment, the bofors guns of 42nd Light-Anti-Aircraft Regiment and finally the echelons of supply lorries carrying ammunition, petrol and water for the tanks. Briggs, Fisher and Bosvile were on Moon route with their small tactical headquarters.

As the columns progressed, great clouds of fine white dust, churned up by the tank tracks, obscured everything. Very often even the tank or vehicle in front could not be seen and the march became a nightmare for the choked and blinded drivers. Reaching what had been our own front line, they passed through gaps in our minefield that had previously been cleared by 275th Field Company, RE, and emerged into No Man's Land, where the crumps of bursting shells ahead and the rattling of machine guns began to challenge the trumpeting of the guns behind.

The leading squadrons reached the captured enemy forward localities ahead of time at 4 a.m., found the gaps that had been cleared by the sappers of the Minefield Task Force under Victor Turner and followed their tiny coloured lights forward. At the second minefield, however, they were brought to an exasperating halt, for Turner's force was having to fight its way through against the battle outposts left by the infantry. The Companies of 2nd Rifle Brigade and the troops of tanks were now being engaged on all three routes and in the centre the opposition had been strong enough to require a company of the Yorkshire Dragoons to be called forward from the rear of the regimental column. Thus it was not until well after first light that the second belt was cleared and the armour able to go through. Turner's Force then encountered further minefields which had not been known to exist.

As dawn approached and the leading tanks were still barely half-way to their *Pierson* bound, the COs of the armoured regiments, still in close column and hemmed in by mines, found themselves faced with the kind of predicament that Lumsden and Gatehouse had foreseen. They had three courses open to them: to push on ahead of the infantry regardless of mines and anti-tank guns; to remain in their lanes nose-to-tail; or to risk deployment where they stood. The first and boldest course was to invite either glory or disaster, the second would be to present a golden target to enemy guns and aircraft and the third would risk losses from mines.

Archer-Shee was about to give orders to 10th Hussars to push on, when orders came from Fisher to deploy where they were. The regiments did so and appear to have suffered no losses from mines at this stage.

As the sky lightened, the regiments were able to see where they were. Ahead the ground rose gently for about 3,000 yards to the skyline formed by the ridge of elevated ground that came to be known as Kidney Ridge, and on this higher ground, as the leading squadrons very soon discovered, the enemy guns were posted. The Bays were very soon in action with them in the north and were in contact with the Australians on their right and 1st Gordons on their left. In the centre the two leading squadrons of 9th Lancers were moving slowly forward to the crest and on Star route 10th Hussars were also in action, watching the left flank. Thus the brigade as a whole reached an area about three miles short of the *Pierson* bound.

The hold-up at the head of the long, single-file train of tanks and vehicles crawling up through the dust-enveloped lanes inevitably delayed all those in the rear; so that by the time the armoured brigade was brought to a halt, Bosvile, ardent and fuming, had not been able to lead his Motor Brigade from its night halt on the Springbok Road.

In the southern corridor somewhat better fortune attended 10th Armoured Division. As we have seen, both 8th and 9th Armoured Brigades had been able to top the Miteiriya Ridge, but 24th Brigade, following 8th by the same routes, did not leave the Springbok Road until 4.30 a.m. and by sunrise had got no further than the old enemy front line. The lorried infantry brigade, like their opposite numbers in 1st Armoured Division, had still not yet even made a start.

THE GUNS

Thus ended a long night of exceedingly hard fighting by the troops of 30th and 10th Corps. The gates of the enemy stronghold had been broken open and a firm foothold had been secured within his bailey from which to renew the momentum of the attack. In the assault upon those gates, the way had been shown by the guns and now, in hundreds of gunpits, the exhausted gunners lay asleep where they had fallen as soon as the last series of their long night tasks was over. The hardest labour had fallen on the medium gunners, with their larger weapons and their heavier shells. Deafened, red-eyed, coated with dust raised by the blasts of more than 600 rounds, the gunners were oblivious to the cold dawn wind. Outside the pits stood the great mounds of brass cartridge cases and the stacks of green ammunition boxes that they had emptied that night. The guns themselves, sponged-out, clean and cool at last, lay in their carriages loaded and ready to be fired at an instant's notice in response to a call from the infantry or the tanks ahead. Beside each gun, muffled in his greatcoat, a red-eyed sentry stood.

Not all the gunners, however, were able to take this temporary rest. Many of the batteries, as soon as their last series was fired, were required to limber up and go forward to new positions, joining the long, slow queues in the clouds of dust, meeting the guarded files of dreary prisoners walking in and the sand-dimmed shapes of ambulances jolting down the tracks with their grievous loads, passing at the track side the still, blanketed figures for whom dawn brought no reveille, observing the coolness of the Military Police as they directed traffic under shell-fire in the swirling minefields, deploying at length in their new position. There they quickly laid out their lines of fire from the GPO's instruments and fired a few rounds to register their new positions at the orders of the FOO in the infantry and tank positions ahead.

In 1st Armoured Division, the new Priests of 11th RHA were very soon given their baptism as A Battery escorted the Bays, B the 10th Hussars and E the 9th Lancers. The gleam of early daylight gave both sides plenty of targets and within a few minutes all the regiment's OPs were calling for fire as the FOOs ordered *Troop target!* on their wireless sets. Without hesitation, the guns swung out from the columns of tanks in the cleared gaps, drove into the enemy minefields and from there opened fire. The whole area of last night's operation was being smartly shelled by the enemy and the next day's battle had begun.

ATTACK IN THE SOUTH

While this big punch was being delivered with the Army's right hand, another punch, equal in vigour but much smaller in size, was being delivered by the left.

Horrocks's plan for 13th Corps was broadly similar to the northern plans, but in the zone of impact selected – Himeimat and the rough desert to the north of it – the forces he had available consisted only of 7th Armoured Division (having no Shermans and no infantry brigade), part of 44th Division, which was covering a wide front, and the Free French, but 50th Division was available for supporting operations. The main effort was to be by 7th Armoured and 44th Divisions and there were thus not nearly enough infantry for a really hard punch.

The outline plan was for the infantry of 44th Division, in the Army Commander's phrase, 'to blow a hole' through our old minefields *January* and *February*, of which we had allowed the enemy to retain possession after the battle of Alam Halfa, and form a bridgehead beyond. Seventh Armoured Division were then to pass through. At the same time the Free French, under command 7th Armoured, were to attack the commanding Himeimat feature, which dominated the main battlefield and the terrain westward of it known as Hunter's Plateau. The distances were considerable, especially for men on foot. Between our new minefields, *Nuts* and *May*, there was a space of four and a half miles. Between *Nuts* and *January* there was a No Man's Land of six miles. After the penetration of *January* there was nearly another two miles before reaching *February*, which was a formidable belt, 1,000 yards deep.

Captured battle outposts

An Advanced Dressing Station of the Highland Division on D plus 1

Highland troops occupying an enemy trench

The difficulty confronting Horrocks, and John Harding, commanding 7th Armoured, in particular, was to reconcile two apparently conflicting tasks. On the one hand, they had to attack with sufficient determination to oblige the enemy to keep 21st Panzer and Ariete Armoured Divisions down in the south, and, indeed, to make a break-through if all went well; but, on the other hand, they must not incur casualties that would cripple 7th Armoured for any future operations for which it might be required. The prospects of an easy success, however, were not high. The mechanical condition of the armour and wheeled vehicles was poor, the defences were strong and deep, the enemy (mainly the Folgore and the Ramcke) of high quality, the country ahead rough and broken or quilted with soft sand, and the attack must necessarily be on a narrow front that would expose open flanks requiring protection against counter-attack. These, however, were not considerations to deter such a tiger as Harding.

The attack of the British divisions was directed on a point in *January* three and a half miles north of Himeimat.[1] Immediately after dusk 131st Brigade, consisting of three battalions of the Queen's Royal Regiment from West Surrey, who were under command 7th Armoured for the operation, moved up to a forward assembly area. They were in high fettle. The attack over *January* was to be made by 1/7th Battalion under a barrage, and as Zero hour approached they walked up through the gaps in our own minefields and so over the long expanse of No Man's Land in the bright moonlight to their start-line.

Close on their heels came a strong minefield task force commanded by Lieutenant-Colonel Lyon Corbet-Winder, which consisted of 4th and part of 21st Field Squadrons RE, six Scorpions under Major Foster, two companies of 1st Rifle Brigade, a squadron of armoured cars under Major John Lawson, 11th Hussars, and 44th Division Reconnaissance Regiment, the special unit equipped entirely with bren-gun carriers. Behind this minefield task force 22nd Armoured Brigade and 4th Light Armoured Brigade, each with its battalion of motor infantry, awaited their opportunity to go forward.

1. Map ref.: 88102565 and a point 500 yards farther south.

Unlike their comrades in 30th Corps, the attacking infantry were under fire from the beginning. The 1/7th Queens were being shelled before they left the start-line and machine-guns and mortars soon added their stings. The second-in-command, Major E. W. D. Stilwell, and two other officers were killed at the outset. In spite of this, *January* was overrun and it seems that small numbers even reached the final objective. There, however, they were isolated in rough and broken country and many taken prisoner. The CO, Lieutenant-Colonel R. M. Burton, was shot trying to escape, but others succeeded. The survivors withdrew successfully to a wadi just west of *January* at 3 a.m., reformed under Captain P. R. H. Kealy, and took up protective positions at the head of the minefield gaps soon after they were made.

The minefield force similarly had to fight its way through. Required to make four gaps, they found themselves impeded by soft sand, and harassed from the start by damaging enemy fire. The flailing Scorpions, crawling forward in huge clouds of dust and shattering noise, were most resolutely handled by Foster, but one by one they became eliminated by casualties or breakdowns, and the sappers had then to have recourse to lifting the mines by hand. This they did with the usual steady nerve and sangfroid of their kind, but it was not until 2.30 a.m. that the two southern gaps had been cleared, and only then after several enemy posts had been attacked and subdued by 1st Rifle Brigade and after several carriers of the Reconnaissance Regiment had been left blazing in the lanes. By 4 a.m. 5th RTR, the Royal Scots Greys and the two Rifle Brigade companies were through.

One of the gaps was being enfiladed with damaging effect by an Italian gun, the flash of which was stabbing the night from about 2,000 yards ahead. Lieutenant-Colonel Freddie Stephens, commanding 1st Rifle Brigade, thought he could make out the emplacement in the moonlight and ordered up a machine gun platoon under Sergeant Buxton. The four guns, mounted on trucks, came into action very quickly. The effect, in Stephens's words, was 'quite instantaneous' and later in the night all the detachment were found dead – a remarkable piece of night shooting. The gun was then

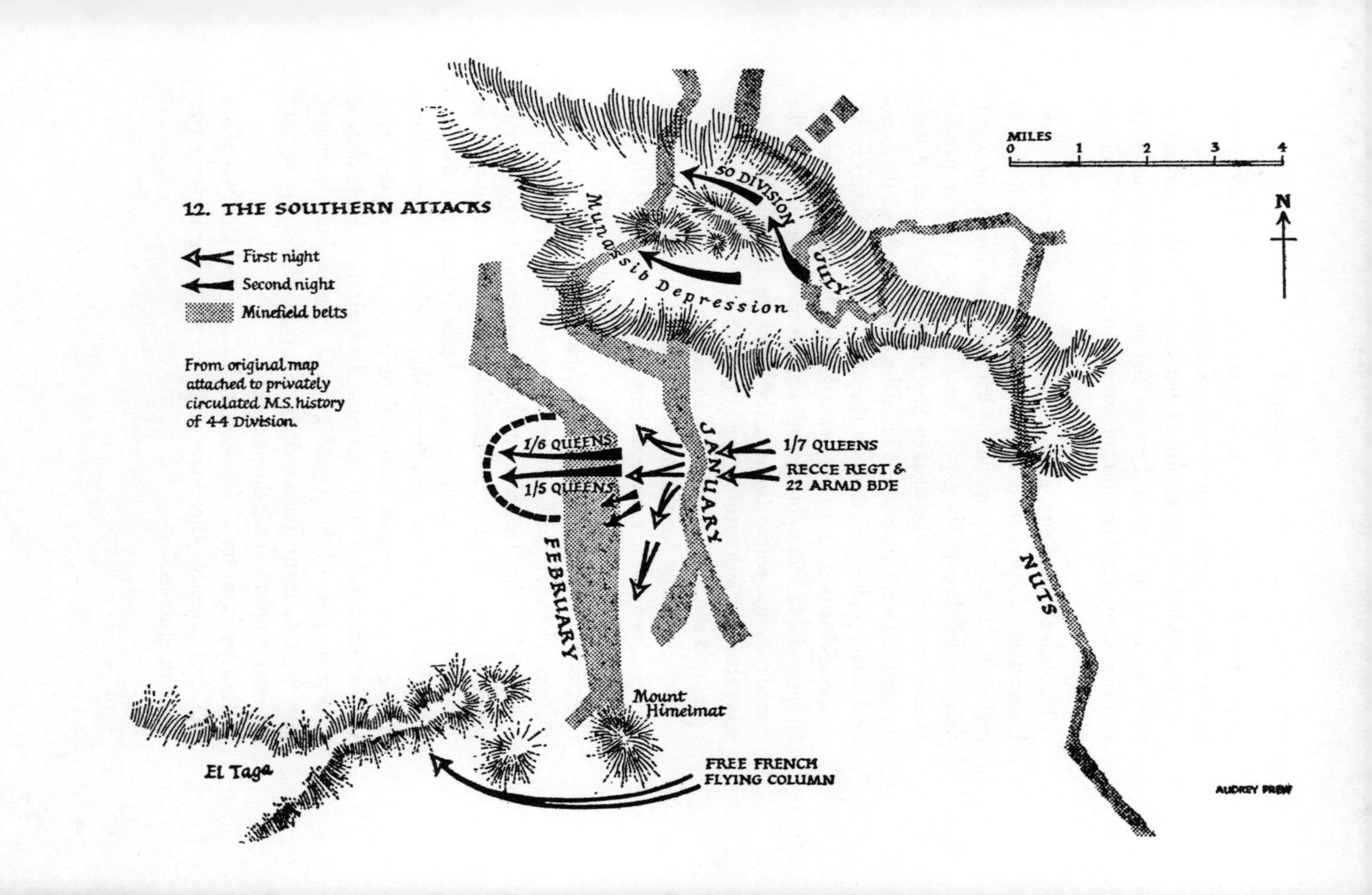

12. THE SOUTHERN ATTACKS
First night
Second night
Minefield belts
From original map attached to privately circulated M.S. history of 44 Division.
MILES
0
1
2
3
4
N
50 DIVISION
JULY
Munassib Depression
1/7 QUEENS
RECCE REGT & 22 ARMD BDE
JANUARY
1/6 QUEENS
1/5 QUEENS
FEBRUARY
NUTS
Mount Himeimat
FREE FRENCH FLYING COLUMN
El Taga
AUDREY FREW

turned round and its entire stock of ammunition fired off against another enemy battle outpost with great effect.

Corbet-Winder's force, bruised but unshaken, then set out to cross the long open space between the two minefields to tackle *February*, accompanied by most of Lawson's armoured cars. Time was getting on.

Through the gaps now made in *January* came the armour of the Desert Rats, accompanied by the anti-tank guns of their Rifle regiments. With the Greys on the left and 5th RTR on the right, they crawled through the gaps in clouds of dust and smoke, past the blazing carriers and the stricken Scorpions. By 4 a.m. they were through and were organizing a bridgehead. An hour later, the minefield force, pushing on through the night with diminished ranks, reached *February* and began to breach that also; but the night was now far spent and further fighting made it impossible to get through the second minefield before daylight. The *January* bridgehead, however, was extended southwards by bold offensive action against fighting opposition almost to the slopes of Himeimat.

Horrocks having decided to hold the ground gained and to resume the offensive next night, the assaulting troops withdrew to the open ground between the two minefields. There, sitting under direct observation, particularly from the height of Himeimat, tanks and infantry alike had a gruelling time from the incessant enemy shelling.

Meanwhile, the Free French in the rugged ground in the extreme south had also faced great difficulties. Attacking against strong opposition, they successfully conquered much of the ground before them, but the sand was so soft that they could by no means drag through their anti-tank guns and, being counter-attacked by a German armoured column known as the Kiel Group, were obliged to give up most of the ground won. The pyramid-like mount of Himeimat therefore remained in enemy hands, for his artillery observers to plague us in the plain below.

Thus by dawn on 24 October, 13th Corps had achieved about half their objective after some very heavy fighting between two determined forces.

Chapter Twelve

D PLUS ONE

(Day 24 October and Night 24/25)

The Brittle Morning – Fighting in the North –
Aberdeen – Attack by 10th Armoured Division –
The Southern Battle Renewed

THE BRITTLE MORNING

Soon after daylight on 24 October, which was a Saturday, the generals were up in front, seeing the situation for themselves, holding quick conferences and considering the next steps. Gatehouse roared up the Boat route to Miteiriya Ridge with tremendous *panache*, sitting on top of his command tank in a white *poshteen* and black beret, looking larger than ever and intentionally conspicuous. With his instinct for the feelings of the soldier in the more trying hours of battle, he drove right up on to the ridge, accompanied by Ebbels, his genial CRA, and toured about, grimly noting the burning tanks of the Sherwood Rangers and the Staffordshire Yeomanry at the minefield exits ahead, as he had feared they might be. Likewise John Currie, wearing his red, blue and gold cap, walked the whole length of the New Zealand front to visit his regiments of 9th Armoured Brigade, shot at by every kind of weapon but returning unscathed.

Montgomery, Leese and Lumsden likewise came up, to talk to Freyberg and Gatehouse. The newly-broken battlefield over which they passed was one of the strangest that any of them had yet seen.

Across the stark sandscape, already scarred with the wreckage of the night's destruction, huge packed columns of tanks, guns and vehicles of all sorts slowly lurched and jolted amid billowing clouds of dust up the demarcated routes across and between the Devil's Gardens. Everywhere the engineers were widening the minefield gaps, along which signallers were laying telephone lines and constantly repairing them as they were broken up by shell fire, ambulances were going up and down, salvage parties were recovering damaged tanks and vehicles. Sudden squalls of fire from German and Italian artillery burst along the lanes as soon as they had been photographed from the air, setting light to vehicles here and there and thickening the man-made dust-storm, amid which the white-sleeved Military Police, as though on a race day, dispassionately directed the thronging traffic.

In the spaces between the main belts of mines, and sometimes right in among the mines also, all sorts of units were seeking to deploy in their forward moves, competing with each other for patches of favourable ground in the all-enveloping dust. Field artillery regiments, fretting, like impatient motorists, to get on, swung off the routes, unlimbered and came swiftly into action, often under fire, all men moving at the double to answer the calls that were already beginning to come in from the FOOs ahead. In the urgency of operations the guns respected no one, their muzzles often but a few yards from some post or vehicle, until its blasted occupants absconded in distraction.

On the rocky slope of Miteiriya, where the greater part of two armoured brigades was assembled, and a third was about to crowd in, the congestion was astonishing. So thick upon the ground were the tanks, guns, vehicles and men that it seemed impossible for any shell to pitch without hitting something. So fog-like was the suspended pall of dust that no aircraft could be discerned overhead.

Along the bank which so conveniently ran just beneath the crest of the ridge for part of its way, the British tanks, hull-down, were exchanging shot for shot with the enemy. The ridge and its forward slope were very hot spots. The shells cracked viciously on the rocky surface and merely to show one's head was a draw a waspish burst of fire from half a dozen Spandaus. Both sides hit each other hard. In spite of these angry exchanges, the New Zealand sappers on the sector of 5th Brigade, when they saw the tanks of the Royal Wiltshire Yeomanry immobilized in the forward minefield, as recorded in the last chapter, set to work in broad daylight and under direct observation to clear lanes to them. Prodding with bayonets, they followed the set drill as though on a demonstration. Displaying superb battlefield discipline, they made no 'heat of battle' haste. As each man was killed or wounded, another stepped quietly in to take his place.

Large stretches of the new ground were under direct observation from the enemy to a considerable depth. The most dangerous thing to do, now and for the next few days, was to move about. Wimberley's jeep went up from a burst right under the wheels which killed Colin Cruickshank (his driver) and Lance-Corporal Anderson, very gravely wounded Lieutenant Crosbie and flung Wimberley out unconscious and battered. In the south, the Chaplain of 1st Rifle Brigade was himself killed while conducting a burial service. John Harding, in full view, was driving away from a conference with his brigadiers of 7th Armoured Division when a shell burst beside the jeep and killed his ADC, Captain H. Cosgrave.

In the most forward positions the front-line soldiers sat tight in the ground newly conquered, under sudden bursts of violence. Tired out after their all-night struggle, they waited for the expected counter-attack. The sand began to drift over the innumerable dead bodies of friend and enemy. As the sun rose in its strength, the wounded of both armies, waiting to be found, lay blistering in its breath, tormented by flies and with no relief from the continuing fire.

But the spirit of all men in Eighth Army, in spite of the brittle nature of the situation that always arises on the morning of an assault, was still very much in the ascendant. Stephenson, the Middlesex CO, jolting up a Highland gap in a jeep to inspect his machine-gun positions, saw a dying Cameron in a minefield. He stopped, dismounted and went across to offer help. The soldier, thinking only of his battalion and not of himself, replied steadfastly:

'We're quite all right, sir.'

Then, mistily recognizing the CO of the Diehards, he added with touching gallantry: 'The Diehards are there, you see, sir.'

To reinforce the front-line soldier, his comrades of the air made a special effort that day. All through the 24th the day bombers and the fighter-bombers shuttled to and fro in that impressive good order which comes from polished flying and which always gives comfort to the heart of the infantryman squatting in his hole in the ground. The 'eighteen imperturbables' – the RAF Baltimores and the South African Bostons – became a familiar and encouraging spectacle of the air. In the north the main effort was made against those enemy forces from which the counter-attack was to be expected – 15th Panzer and the Littorio Armoured Divisions – but in that effort eight bombers were shot down and twenty-seven damaged by gunfire. In the south the cannon Hurricanes put out of action a German unit equipped with captured British tanks. That day the Desert Air Force flew 1,000 sorties and the United States Air Force 147.

The enemy, after the first surprised shock, had reacted well. The German Panzer Grenadiers had fought as one always expected them to do and, of the Italians, the Folgore in the south and the Trento in the north had also resisted stubbornly enough until the close approach of the bayonet. But in the enemy headquarters behind there was an uneasy atmosphere. The ravaged communications, disrupted by the RAF or torn by shellfire, gave only the scantiest and most uncertain information of what was happening. Accordingly, Stumme drove out in his car early in the morning to see for himself the state of affairs, accompanied by Colonel Buechting and driven by Corporal Wolf. He ran into a storm of fire. Buechting was killed. Wolf swung the car round and Stumme appears to have jumped out of it and to have fallen dead from a heart seizure.

Command of the *Panzerarmee* was taken over by General Ritter von Thoma, a tall, lean old warrior scarred with many wounds, who had until then been commanding the *DAK*. He did not take a very serious view of the situation, decided that no major readjustment of his forces was necessary and that the British penetration was such as could be sealed off by local counter-attacks. He still kept

21st Panzer and the Ariete Divisions in the south and he still kept 90th Light Division in reserve. His forces were in good order; the British had not yet got right through his main defences; the batteries of anti-tank guns, dug in to the ground level and invisible, still barred the way and there were still plenty more mines.

Yet his reconnaissance aircraft must have told him that some 700 British tanks were now deploying or advancing on 30th Corps front.

Montgomery, as he assessed the situation early that morning, had good cause for restrained satisfaction. In the south, 13th Corps were doing what he wanted of them. In the north, the infantry of 30th Corps had bitten deep into the enemy position and had taken most of their objectives. The armour had very nearly got out on Miteiriya Ridge. Another half-hour of darkness might have done the trick. But north of Miteiriya Ridge the multiple minefields encountered and the by-passed battle outposts had so delayed 1st Armoured Division that, at first light, they were still more than two miles short of their destination.

At the conference which he held with Leese, Lumsden and Freyberg, in the forward area, Montgomery gave order for the attack to be resumed that night where it had left off, with the original objectives. The particular import of this was that, while the infantry of 30th Corps had only minor operations to perform, the armour of 10th Corps must reach and deploy on the *Pierson* bound. The prime need was to get the armour out into the open before the enemy front stiffened. The Army Commander impressed upon Lumsden that he was prepared to accept large tank losses to achieve this end. First Armoured Division must fight its way forward with its own resources as quickly as possible and 10th Armoured must renew operations that night to enable the New Zealand Division to exploit southward into the open according to the plan.

FIGHTING IN THE NORTH

North of Miteiriya Ridge, the immediate needs on the morning of the 24th were for 1st Armoured Division to push on and for the

Highlanders to improve their positions. The armour was much delayed. As we have seen, Turner's Minefield Task Force, encountering battle outposts left behind by the infantry, had had to fight for a path for the sappers. When the night dissolved into dawn, they found themselves completely overlooked by Kidney Ridge and again came under damaging fire, this time observed fire. Very fine work was done by the sappers of 7th Field Squadron and by the Rifle Brigade carrier platoons of B and C Companies under Peter Innes and Dick Flower, who got through in the face of direct fire from 88s on the crest. Innes had both legs broken by shell fire. The second minefield was fully gapped by 7 a.m. but then a third was encountered, and, ultimately, no fewer than six belts in all had to be penetrated.

What had seemed in the planning stage to be a reasonable possibility of clearing two main minefield belts in one night turned out in the event to be the impossible one of clearing multiple ones. Sun route was the first to be cleared, enabling the Queen's Bays to get well forward on the Australian sector by the afternoon of D plus 1, but Moon was not right through for 9th Lancers until later and Star (the route for 10th Hussars) not until next day, by which time the sappers and Turner's Minefield Task Force were physically and emotionally exhausted.

The regiments of 2nd Armoured Brigade did not, of course, wait for the completion of these lanes, but pushed up as far as they could. Archer-Shee, CO of 10th Hussars, was twice blown up on mines in the attempt to press forward. The armour became dispersed among the Highland infantry in circumstances that were to become irksome to both. Long-range fighting between tanks began early.

Soon after sunrise, with the shadows long and crisp on the desert floor, a force of long-gunned Mark IVs and IIIs of 15 PZ Division appeared in the distance and began to bear down on the front of the Highland Division and 2nd Armoured Brigade. They were engaged at 2,000 yards by Fisher's tanks and, apparently surprised by this long-range performance of the Sherman, which they now met for the first time, turned away northwards, leaving some of their tanks in flames. Firing high explosive for the first time, the Shermans began to take toll of the enemy anti-tank guns also much more effectively than had been possible with solid shot of pre-Alamein tanks.

The new Priests of 11th RHA likewise had their baptism of fire. Supporting the Queen's Bay on the Australian sector, A Battery engaged some probing enemy tanks over open sights and saw them off. For the first time, they used 'airburst' and 'bouncing' HE against infantry in trenches and against targets beyond a crest betrayed by dust clouds. Working right forward, all the batteries of the regiment sustained direct hits on their Priests from the enemy's guns, but the day's actions were distinguished by the fine behaviour of the detachments, particularly the humble ammunition numbers, who fed the guns and whose duty required them to be out in the open on the ground.

The enemy's anti-tank guns were terribly difficult to locate, but when a squadron of Bostons swept out of the sky and began accurate bombing just ahead of 10th Hussars, the long barrels of the 88s were seen to swing upwards to engage them. Thus disclosed against the early morning sky, they at once drew the eager fire of 10th Hussars and the guns of B Battery HAC. Here the Tenth got their first 88. This nice example of 'ground support for the air' was repeated at each sortie of our aircraft and became the regular practice of our armour. The business of our armour, however, was not to engage in long-range duels, but to get forward to ground where they could bring on a battle with the enemy tanks. Raymond Briggs, returning from the forward squadrons with Fisher, was visited about midday at his Tac HQ by Lumsden, fresh from Montgomery's battle conference. Lumsden told him that the Army Commander was 'not satisfied' with the progress made and that the armour, if delayed by the incompletion of the infantry task, must fight its own way through regardless of losses, and that immediate action to do this must be taken. This order Briggs passed to Fisher by radio, saying he must push ahead at all costs. Fisher enquired: 'Do you mean "at all costs" literally?' To which Briggs replied: 'Yes, I do; at all costs.'

The results were immediate. In 9th Lancers Lieutenant Otto Thwaites leapt out of his tank and guided his Troop forward on foot, searching for mines. In Lieutenant B.S. Agate's Troop the sappers of 1st Field Squadron advanced under close enemy fire, rifle in hand. Both Troops, crammed closely together, pushed through and made for the high ground ahead. Agate's tank was hit at once in an oil tank and began to burn. He and his crew, however sat fast and continued to engage the enemy until expressly ordered by Major George Meyrick to bale out. Ninth Lancers and 10th Hussars both wheeled towards Sun route as soon as it was through.

A spirited attack in the afternoon by 2nd Seaforth Highlanders, under Kenneth McKessack, enabled 9th Lancers to push ahead and gave a fresh impetus to operations.

McKessack had probably been intended to go right through to the stronghold named *Stirling* on the ridge ahead, which was 51st Division's ultimate objective in this sector, but Wimberley, when he gave his orders, was still dazed from the blowing-up of his jeep and had just had a tiff with Fisher, and he ordered McKessack to 'attack due west through 1st Black Watch 1,500 yards beyond the the minefield' – which was, in fact, a little short of *Stirling*. The main purpose, however, was to facilitate the advance of 9th Lancers.

The Seaforths attacked across the mines at 3 o'clock with only three companies. It was a gallant affair in glaring daylight in the face of heavy mortar and machine-gun fire. B Company lost all their officers and their sergeant-major, and command was taken by the company clerk. Led by Major Gilmour, the remnants of the two leading companies reached their objective successfully and dug in.

The minefield was then gapped and Gerald Grosvenor passed through with 9th Lancers. Not long afterwards Grosvenor's regiment, attacking frontally, overran *Stirling* itself, thanks to a bold diversionary attack by 50th RTR to draw fire from the 88s in the stronghold, in an operation in which Cairns's battalion lost nine tanks on mines.[1]

By soon after 4 o'clock all three regiments of Fisher's brigade had forced ways through the minefields by Sun route and were beginning to stretch out in front of what they soon began to call Kidney Ridge, but still east of the enemy's main gun line.

1. 23rd Armd Bde *Report on Operations.*

The enemy then did exactly what Montgomery wanted. As Fisher's tanks, emerging from the gaps, spread out to deploy in front of the infantry, high clouds of dust behind the enemy lines in the Kidney sector gave notice of some large activity. Von Thoma's tanks were mustering. It was their favourite hour of attack, with the sun declining behind them and dazzling their enemy. About half an hour later they launched their counter-attack, a counter-attack made by instinct and as a matter of course, not of judgement. Thus began the first of many tank battles that were gradually to wear down the German armour, as Montgomery intended. He counted on their automatic habit of counter-attack and he knew that by this means he could destroy them.

The attack was made by 15th Panzer and the Littorio Armoured Divisions. In the usual enemy manner, it was made at slow speed under the cover of anti-tank guns, on to which the enemy sought to entice our armour. Fisher's regiments, however, stood fast where they were. Very soon more than a hundred tanks on each side were engaged and a battle of considerable moment and intensity developed. Vigorous artillery fire accompanied the cannonade of tank versus tank. Part of the enemy attack fell unavailingly on the London Rifle Brigade on the Australian flank, as will presently be recorded. The weight of the enemy's fire fell not least on the British infantry; the Yorkshire Dragoons suffered severe casualties in their exposed positions and so also did the Highland battalions, on whose terrain most of the British tanks took station.

The action went on until darkness began to obscure the field, when the enemy withdrew, leaving twenty-six of his tanks burning or totally wrecked. His counter-attack had been a complete failure and the destruction of his armour had begun. The British regiments lost no less but could afford to do so. What was more important was that in this, the first of the considerable tank engagements of Alamein, they had demonstrated their prowess and held the field.

They leaguered where they were, with a minefield behind them and scattered mines all round. Enemy machine-guns and snipers, creeping close up, bothered them all night and the Allied air forces, preceded by flare-dropping aircraft, laid their bombs very close to the safety limits. About midnight the maintenance echelons drove up and the tank crews got down to their mechanical tasks, to refuelling and to replenishing the ammunition bins. The fitters, who had been working all day under shell fire on the tanks damaged in the minefields in the early morning, came forward with their tools and began the new sessions of the night.

That same night (24/25 October) 20th Australian Brigade, in a fine minor exploit, completed the seizure of their ultimate goal. During the afternoon, just as the first tank battle was about to begin, Bob Turner, CO of Second-13th Battalion, was mortally wounded, and his adjutant, Ronald Leach, killed while talking to Jim Finigan, CO of 40th RTR, and the battalion was now almost officerless. George Colvin, however, came up from reserve to assume command and, abandoning the plan for a formal assault behind a barrage, made a plan with Simpson, commanding Second-17th on the right, for a combined silent attack. Surprising the enemy outposts, the two battalions captured the final *Oxalic* objective with few casualties, hacked out their 'doovers' in the iron-hard ground, brought up their anti-tank guns and, with 40th RTR in close support, were ready to meet the enemy's counter-attack by dawn. It was a model operation.

'ABERDEEN'

On the left of the Australians, 1st Gordon Highlanders also pressed on towards their final goal, not with immediate success, in circumstances of great difficulty and vexation.

We have seen in the previous chapter how, on the first night, A and C Companies of the Gordons, penetrating a murderous barrage, secured the Black Line, which was their target and which was three-quarters of the way to the battalion's final Blue Line objective, known as *Aberdeen;* and we have left the other two companies and the CO of the battalion, 'Nap' Murray, halted about a mile behind them. The two forward companies were cut off, Murray had no news of them, the shelling was heavy and continuous and the situation was brittle and precarious.

Twice Lieutenant Harry Gordon, now commanding the remnant of C Company, had sent runners back to acquaint Murray of the situation. He had seen both of them killed. Finally, he sent Sergeant-Major Thompson, telling him, 'You have got to get through.' This Thompson did, bringing heartening news to the anxious Murray. Accompanied by Thompson, Murray went forward himself, found the companies decimated and slightly off-course, but sitting securely on the ground they had won. On a second visit in the afternoon to plan a resumption of the attack, he was wounded in the violent exchange of fire as 10th Hussars, in 2nd Armoured Brigade, having pushed through, began the tank battle that has already been recorded. He was evacuated from the field and command of the battalion fell to Major James Hay, who that night led up the rear companies and reunited the battalion.[1]

In order to present a consecutive narrative, we shall follow the remainder of the operations of 1st Gordons against *Aberdeen* out of their chronological order, since the sequence of events typifies the situation battalions often had to face and since there has hitherto been no little confusion about the operations on this important sector. The confusion was also only too evident on the ground itself at the time, for, on top of the inherent problems of desert fighting, the forces of two different army corps were fighting on the same soil for different objectives, neither having much knowledge of what the other was doing. We shall see more of this problem.

On the night of 24/25 October, therefore, 1st Gordons, or what was left of them, reunited under James Hay, stood on the Black Line, a short mile from their final goal. D Company, under the dour South of England Kenneth Paton, was then ordered to advance. Apparently it was intended that they should secure *Aberdeen* itself, which, we may remind ourselves, lay on the north-eastern rim of the scarcely distinguishable Kidney feature which was so difficult to identify on the ground.

With Paton and D Company went 12th Platoon of the Middlesex

1. 10th H. history mistakes the Black Line for the Gordons' final objective.

Regiment, under Humphrey Wigan, with their Vickers heavy machine guns. Summoned hastily to accompany the Gordons, Wigan was led to understand that the operation was only a patrol. Patrolling was scarcely an operation on which machine gunners were ever liable to be included, but Wigan, not questioning, at once assembled his platoon in the dark and, in order to lighten their heavy loads, told his men that water, rations and small packs would not be necessary. It was the typical small mistake of one not yet experienced.

D Company of the Gordons and 12th Platoon of the Diehards advanced, traversing yet another minefield. There was some light, indiscriminate shelling and flares rose frequently from the enemy lines, causing the advancing soldiers to 'freeze' in their steps every few minutes. As they negotiated some barbed wire, they heard the rumble of a tracked vehicle ahead and dropped to the ground. The vehicle stopped short of the wire barely fifty yards ahead and a voice shouted out in German, asking what unit they were. There being no reply, the vehicle swung sharply about and disappeared into the night. They had been spotted.

When they had cleared the wire about ten minutes later, it was accordingly no surprise that mortar and small-arms fire began to develop and the enemy's flares began to shoot up into the sky every few seconds, illuminating the scene almost continuously. There then took place a totally unexpected encounter, illustrating what was perhaps the first of several unforeseen incidents when two formations are operating on the same ground. In the light of one of the flares, there stood revealed several British motor vehicles, apparently abandoned. Since the enemy employed a good many captured British vehicles, this occasioned no great surprise, but caution was clearly necessary and, while the Highlanders halted, a voice ahead called out loudly: 'Does anyone here speak English?'

The ring of the voice was authentic and, after a little while, Paton, joined by Wigan, went forward and to their astonishment met an officer of the London Rifle Brigade (7th RB), from 1st Armoured Division. They had advanced by Sun Route through the Australian sector and had orders to deploy in support of 2nd Armoured Brigade. In deploying, their vehicles had been blown

Tanks of the Staffordshire Yeomanry burning in front of El Wishka, dawn 25 October

Grants and Sherman C Squadron, Warwickshire Yeomanry, on the left flank of Miteiriya Ridge, p.m. 24 October

Maoris of 2nd New Zealand Division

The 'devil's fairyland': a complex of tracers photographed on the night 24/25 October, very probably Miteiriya Ridge

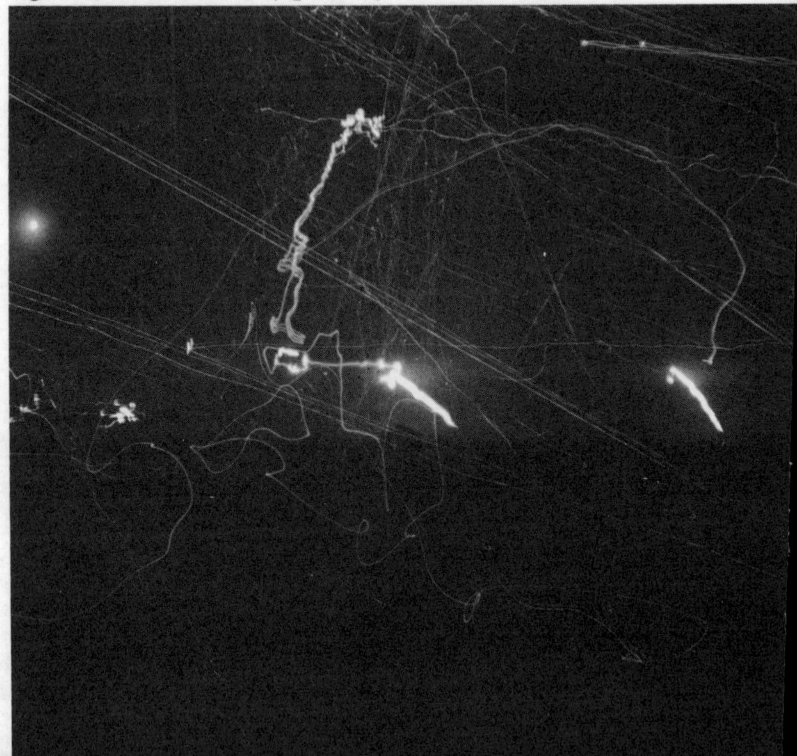

up by mines and they had been brought to a halt by small-arms fire from positions in front of *Aberdeen*, with many casualties.

In view of the uncertain situation and of the need to be dug-in before dawn, Paton decided to halt his small force likewise, deploying the Middlesex machine guns on his left. Thus the Jocks had Cockneys to right and to left of them and not the least of the sparse comforts of the situation was the Riflemen's possession of some anti-tank guns.

The ground was solid rock and by first light on the 25th few of the trenches were more than a foot deep. The sounds of the picks must have been clearly audible to the enemy. Wigan's Vickers guns and the Vickers and 6-pdrs of the LRB were virtually on open ground. Daylight on the 25th found them in full view from the enemy and their positions were soon being 'plastered' by shells, mortar bombs and streams of machine-gun bullets. They could see little of the enemy in his dug-in positions, but vigorously engaged any target offered, though thereby further revealing their positions. Two machine-gun detachments of the Riflemen were picked off man by man, one of whom had his head taken off by an anti-tank shot. The Middlesex suffered also, one gun being knocked out.

The wounded of all units endured severe trials of fortitude, lying in shallow slits in the rock under the blazing sun, scourged by flies, the Middlesex wounded being without water or food. Operational vehicles of the LRB which had not been withdrawn and which could not disperse in the minefield drew particularly heavy fire on the Australian boundary. The watching Aussies of Second-13th Battalion recorded that 'the carnage was terrible to watch' and their Regimental Aid Post was swamped by wounded Riflemen, who were treated by Captain Philip Goode and a captured German doctor.

But they stayed put, stuck to their weapons and in the afternoon the Riflemen away on the right had their rich revenge as the enemy made his counter-attack of that day. A mixed force of German and Italian tanks appeared from behind the ridge. Advancing characteristically at very slow speed, with dust blown ahead of them like a rising storm, they bore down on the Riflemen near the Australian boundary, intending to drive our infantry from their newly-won positions.

The 6-pdrs held their fire until the enemy tanks had closed to about 800 yards, the layer of each gun holding a tank in his sights as it crept on. At that killing range they opened fire and a violent action burst out in 'stupendous noise'. One after another the tanks were hit and several were quickly engulfed in flames and smoke, but the remainder still came on 'like an irresistible steam roller'. They were supported by field artillery fire which was poured in disconcertingly from German positions to the north of the Australian flank, thus appearing to the Riflemen to have come from 'almost behind us'. The Londoners, however, held their ground with great resolution and the enemy was brought to a halt by the guns of Lieutenant Jack Salt and Sergeant Allen at 250 yards. Obliged to withdraw, the enemy, in addition to other losses, left behind fourteen smoking and blazing wrecks.

This was the first infantry *versus* armour action of Alamein and the first of several manifestations that were to follow (exemplified on both sides) of the helplessness of tanks in the face of stoutly manned anti-tank guns. It was a fine and highly significant little action that has hitherto remained in obscurity to nearly all but those who took part in it.

Meanwhile, back at 1st Gordons' battalion headquarters on the Black Line, James Hay had been preparing to reinforce Paton's little force, cut off in their precarious scrapes in the rock in front of *Aberdeen*, that night. He set out on a reconnaissance in a bren-carrier, accompanied by Major J. E. G. Hay (known as 'Scrappy' Hay) and Major Michael du Boulay, commanding B Company. In the belt that separated them from Paton the carrier struck a mine. James Hay took the full brunt of the detonation, being severely wounded in both legs. Scrappy Hay, though himself shaken, then took command – the third CO of the Battalion in thirty-six hours. An attempt to unite with Paton was made that night with B Company under Du Boulay; though the distance was not more than

400 yards, the attempt failed. Du Boulay was given a fallacious bearing, which brought him head-on to *Aberdeen* itself and on to the machine-guns posted in the derelict tanks. Outlined in the moonlight against strong machine-gun positions, his companies were brought to a halt. Unprepared for such opposition and unsupported by artillery fire, du Boulay, himself wounded, very properly ordered a withdrawal.

Unaware of these misadventures, Paton's small force hung on expectantly. As the second night came on, they rose with relief from their cramped slits, did what little they could for the wounded, improved their diggings and serviced their weapons. The men in the worst case were the Middlesex, without water or food after a day of fierce heat. Wigan sent out a party to search the wrecked vehicles of the LRB, but several of them were still burning and any movement near them was observed and at once drew fire. A sergeant, however, was able to draw off some water from one or two radiators that had not been damaged and this liquid, foul though it was, averted for the while the most pressing danger. The outer casings of the machine-guns themselves, which had lost water during the day's shooting, were replenished in the traditional emergency manner.

When no relief or reinforcement came, the Jocks and the Cockneys accepted the situation with stoic cheerfulness. The idea of withdrawing entered no one's head; in his captured German diary Wigan recorded simply: 'As we couldn't go forward, we stayed where we were.' Lieutenant W. M. MacFarlane and six men managed to get through to them with some tins of water, but there was still no relief for the machine-gunners.

The second day, the 26th, dawned and at once both sides were in action again. Another of Wigan's guns was knocked out. The wounded of both units were grievously in need of evacuation and his own men faint from lack of water and food. Towards noon he decided that some action would have to be taken if his men were to survive. He discussed the situation with Paton in his nearby scrape and they decided that someone must attempt to get back to the battalion.

Having apparently overheard this conversation, Lance-Corporal H. Sleeth, one of Wigan's section orderlies, at once volunteered. Wigan hesitated. It was a mission of great danger and Sleeth had already been hit twice – once in the back and the second time in the arm. The young officer looked at him hard, weighing him up; Sleeth was a quiet, rather reserved man, a trifle older than the average, steady and sensible. Wigan reflected that, having been hit twice without being killed, he probably had a charmed life and, if anyone could get through, he would.

He briefed the NCO as best he could. Waiting for a lull in the shelling, he sent him off. He watched him cover the first 200 yards when, entering the minefield which they had traversed two nights before, he was lost to view over the intervening swell of ground.

Entering the minefield, Sleeth was free of observation, but he was careful not to hurry, in case, by treading heavily, he set off a mine. He was tired and his mouth was very dry. The desert shimmered in the heat of the afternoon mirage and he felt dizzy. He had not gone far when the shelling opened up again. A mine, possibly actuated by a shell splinter, blew up within a yard or two of him and flung him violently to the ground. Dazed and shaken, he got to his feet again and somehow made his way to his company headquarters, where he collapsed at the feet of Captain Michael Pearson.

A few hours later, as soon as it was dark, refusing to be evacuated, he led Pearson up to his platoon in a bren-carrier, bringing water, food, ammunition and reinforcements.

A little afterwards, Brigadier Graham and Hay having gone up to see the position for themselves, the remainder of 1st Gordons moved up, but were spared the necessity of assaulting *Aberdeen*, for its garrison, having been severely shot up at dawn on the 27th by the 6-pdr Deacons of ZZ Battery (76th Anti-Tank Regiment) and having been given a hot time by everyone else, surrendered and the Gordons occupied. Major H. A. F. Fausset-Farquhar, fourth CO within a week, took command.

The key-points of Kidney Ridge were all now in our hands, but it remained a very hot horizon and anyone who showed his nose above it was immediately shot up.[1]

ATTACK BY 10TH ARMOURED DIVISION

While 1st Armoured Division was slowly forcing its way forward on 24 October in the Kidney sector and while the other divisions of Eighth Army were planning to resume operations that night, preparations of special interest and promise were being made on Miteiriya Ridge.

We have seen how, following as closely as possible on the heels of the New Zealand infantry and the sappers, the armour had been brought to a halt on the ridge by the approach of daylight, just when they seemed to be on the brink of achieving their break-out. We have seen also the extraordinary congestion of warlike traffic immediately behind the ridge and in the dust-blown approaches to it, with one division overlaid upon another. All the factors of a 'grand military mix-up' were present if there had not been a high standard of control by commanders and staff officers and spontaneous discipline by the intermingled units.

Later in the morning Montgomery gave to Lumsden those orders that we have outlined for the continued advance of the armour. It was clear, however, that, on the Miteiriya sector, the bridgehead won the previous night could not be exploited in daylight and, accordingly, preparation was made for the break-out of the armour that night.

The operations of 10th Armoured Division that ensued became the occasion of the unfortunate row between Montgomery and Gatehouse, but no adequate account of those operations has yet been made public. On this score there is something that has to be put right historically and the operations are, therefore, of particular concern to us; they are also inherently of tactical consequence and

1 The accounts of the operations in front of *Aberdeen* in this and the previous chapter are compiled mainly from the personal narratives of Major-General Wimberley, General Sir Horatio Murray, Lieutenant-Colonel Du Boulay, Major Harry Gordon, Major Wigan, Lieutenant-Colonel Barker, with other informants on points of detail.

of the liveliest interest as a battle chronicle. We shall, therefore, watch them as closely as we can, with the help of the records and of personal narratives.

Lumsden's orders (given, consequent upon the Army Commander's conference, in 10th Corps Operation Instruction No. 3) were that 10th Corps should continue its advance to First Bound *Pierson*. The method of doing so would be for 10th Armoured Division and 9th Armoured Brigade to 'deploy clear of the enemy minefields, and, linking up with 1st Armoured Division on their right, be prepared to meet an attack by enemy tanks'. The interpolated phrase is important.

Alec Gatehouse's division was by nightfall massed behind Miteiriya Ridge to the number of some 250 tanks. It was a formidable display of Shermans, Grants and Crusaders, their intimidating shapes clearly lit by the bright moon now riding at its full. They lined up in the minefield lanes together with their 'soft-skinned' vehicles in regimental groups, each armoured regiment, in its own allotted lane, being accompanied by artillery, engineer and infantry sub-units (an open-desert grouping that disabled the CRA from giving full artillery support). Far behind them the Wellingtons of 205 Group were preparing to pass over their heads to bomb the enemy armour.

On the right of the division, at the northern end of the ridge, was Kenchington's new 24th Armoured Brigade Group, consisting of 41st, 45th and 47th RTR, equipped with a preponderance of Shermans, 5th RHA, commanded by Rawden Hoare, 11th King's Royal Rifle Corps and 6th Field Squadron RE.

On the left was Neville Custance's 8th Armoured Brigade Group, made up of the Sherwood Rangers under the dashing 'Flash' Kellett, the Staffordshire Yeomanry under James Eadie, wearing the Bass red triangle, 3rd RTR under 'Pete' Pyman, 1st RHA under the brilliant Douglas Packard, 1st Buffs under the courageous Smith-Dorrien and 2nd (Cheshire) Field Squadron RE.

The Sussex brigade of lorried infantry had orders to occupy the ridge as a 'pivot of manœuvre', in the desert phrase that had now become of dubious validity. Their field gunners were 104th RHA (Essex Yeomanry) under R. S. G. Hobbs, familiarly known as

'Pooh' Hobbs. Each brigade was also accompanied by light anti-aircraft batteries and 6-pdr batteries from 84th Anti-Tank Regiment and a battery of 73rd was with Kenchington.

To these brigades of 10th Armoured's own were added Currie's 9th Armoured Brigade, who were to operate on the left and shape their course towards the south. They had been withdrawn from the ridge early in the evening and the Royal Wiltshire Yeomanry, who had sustained heavy losses, were left out of the coming battle.

Such, in outline, was the composition of the powerful force that, as the dusty day drew on, gradually assembled, the greater part of it behind the rocky ridge. Forward of the ridge the desert sloped down almost imperceptibly for some ten feet in a distance of a mile, pock-marked with innumerable gun-pits, and then it rose again hesitantly for fifteen feet to another long, slight undulation known for convenience as the Wishka Ridge, where stood a lone palm tree. As traced in the map, the *Pierson* Bound was a little short of the ridge on 10th Division's front. Between the Miteiriya and Wishka features there was thus a broad, shallow, depressed zone in which any formation brought to a halt would be liable to methodical destruction. To reach the *Pierson* Bound, as may be seen in Fig. 13, Kenchington had to advance an average distance of about two miles and Custance a trifle more.

Zero hour was 10 p.m. and the attack was to be supported by a bombardment from nearly 300 guns under a fire plan quickly made by 'Baron' Ebbels.

Before the tanks could get on, it was realized, there was still more to be done in the tricky business of mine lifting. It was likely to be even more tricky tonight. There was a special difficulty for 24th Armoured Brigade, as the axis of advance now ordered for them started diagonally across the routes already cleared and marked. This change of direction arose from Montgomery's requirement that morning that Gatehouse's division should link-up with Briggs's, thus obliging Kenchington to veer nearly due west, instead of pursuing the south-westerly bearing of the original 'corridor'.

The clearing of the lanes for this brigade would be the duty of 6th Field Squadron, under Major Collins, and McMeekan (still almost completely deaf from the previous night's shattering) felt distinctly apprehensive about their ability to carry out this tough assignment, for it was their first battle. The field squadrons of both brigades this night were under command their armoured brigades and, therefore, not under McMeekan's operational orders.

For 8th Brigade the duty fell on 2nd (Cheshire) Field Squadron. We have noted in Chapter Eleven that it was commanded by Major Jack Perrott. Senior sister unit of 3rd Squadron, who had done such fine work the night before, it was a squadron with a high morale and offensive eagerness. Attending the Order Group of 8th Armoured Brigade, Perrott learned from Custance that he was required to provide three gaps, one for each armoured regiment, each to be in prolongation of Bottle, Boat and Hat routes. He was to begin at last light, which was at 7.30, and finish by 10 o'clock, when the armour would pass through.

This was a straightforward enough task, but a very dangerous one, for the enemy now knew the direction that each of these lanes would take if prolonged, while Hat was his own approach gap, which would quite certainly be specially watched, re-sown with mines at the enemy's end and covered by fire.

Nonetheless, Perrott felt tremendously elated and buoyant after the brigade 'O Group'. For this his squadron had been ardently preparing day and night for several weeks under what he described as the inspiration with which Alec Gatehouse had imbued the whole division, and the knowledge that this was the 'big moment' for his squadron filled him with ardour. This enthusiasm he did not fail to communicate to his own little O group immediately afterwards, when he apportioned their tasks to the Troop leaders. Bottle route he assigned to Andrew Ramsay and Geoffrey Kneale, Boat to F. G. Caldwell (a young Regular officer who, though not yet 21, had already won the MC and Bar) and Philip Holborn, and the dangerous Hat to Captain Peter Hattersley and Leslie Sage. The squadron had been assigned a company of infantry (from another formation) for their protection, but we may dismiss them from our story, for they arrived very late with no platoon officers, with no training for this special work, and were of no value at all.

Darkness fell and, before the moon rose, the three Troops of 2nd Squadron set out filled with confidence and offensive eagerness. The first task on each route was a reconnaissance. Perrott himself was on Boat route with Griff Caldwell and together they walked over the top of Miteiriya Ridge, down the forward slope and on ahead of the infantry, unescorted, unarmed and wearing soft caps. The moon had risen.

Quite suddenly some ten figures got up from a lying position a little distance ahead and stood facing them, rifles in hand. Perrott said quietly: 'Take it quietly, Griff. They must be Jerries. Turn round and walk back casually.'

Together they did so, expecting at any moment a fusillade of bullets in their backs. But none came and they strolled quietly back to their own lines.

On Hat route on the left, however, Hattersley was not so fortunate. He set out on his reconnaissance with Sapper Heath and when out in front they were confronted by a group of Germans who rose up from the ground in exactly the same manner, thirty yards ahead.

Hattersley, a crack shot with the new weapon, instantly seized the Tommy gun that Heath was carrying and, dropping to the knee, opened fire on the enemy. His fire was returned and he was almost instantly shot in the head. He died in the arms of Sapper Heath, who was then taken prisoner. Angry rather than dismayed, Heath protested violently that a doctor should be fetched at once to attend to his Troop Commander, but his plea was unavailing, and he was taken back to the German lines and held in a covered defence post with some Germans and one Italian who, from time to time during the night, entertained the party with a piano accordion.[1]

When Hattersley and Heath failed to return, Lieutenant Sage or Sergeant Groves attempted to make a second reconnaissance, but by this time the route was firmly closed by the enemy, who, as was to be expected, had sited an enfilading 88-mm, which opened up as the reconnaissance party advanced. This was the route assigned

1. Early next morning, seeing a bren-carrier cruising about in the confused situation, Heath dashed out to it, secured the capture of his captors and bore away the piano accordion.

to 3rd RTR, under Pyman. It would have been folly to persist with it and Pyman agreed that it should be abandoned.

Meanwhile, Caldwell's Troop was making excellent progress on the centre route, where only Teller mines were encountered. So also was Ramsay's Troop in Bottle route on the right. Perrott, inspecting both routes, found them already filling up with the great press of traffic as the regimental groups mustered in their ordained sequences. He reflected that the deep growl of the tanks, which at night projects its drum-roll so far upon the waves of sound, must be clearly audible to the enemy. He returned to his wireless truck, which was on Boat route. The place was not only being shelled but also machine-gunned. A New Zealand sergeant and four men were trying to get some sleep close to the truck, but were kept awake by the waspish bursts of the Spandau. The sergeant, getting up from from his trench as Perrott was about to speak on the radio, said to him: 'That gun's bothering you, Major; we'll settle the bastards.'

He roused his four men and all disappeared into the night. After twenty minutes, the Spandau ceased to chatter and a little later the sergeant came back and said simply to Perrott: '*That* won't worry you any more, Major.'

He and his men, having suffered no casualties, then slumped down once more on to their rocky bed. The episode, so typical of the fine fighting spirit of the Kiwis, made a tremendous impression on Perrott and his sappers.

At ten o'clock the barrage roared out and the tanks began to crawl forward in line ahead between the little green lights. The Staffordshire Yeomanry were on Bottle route, the Sherwood Rangers, Custance's brigade headquarters and 3rd RTR on Boat. But tonight the enemy was not to be caught unawares. The advance of the armoured brigades across the ridge had scarcely begun when to the moon's radiance was suddenly added the fiercer light of parachute flares as the enemy aircraft came over to discover what was going on. The desert was lit up as though by floodlights and the long columns of the British armour, with their artillery, their lorries, and the carriers of their infantry, were glaringly revealed.

In a moment the roar of the barrage was drowned by a more shattering eruption as the bombs cascaded upon the creeping columns. They fell first upon the lorries of the Sherwood Rangers loaded with petrol, oil and ammunition, and upon the battalion headquarters and A Company (under Major B. M. Horley) of The Buffs, on the centre Boat route immediately behind Perrott. These burst into flames and explosions and in an instant Boat route became, in Perrott's recorded words, 'the most enormous crackling furnace, which lit the desert up for a radius of two miles all round. The gap was illuminated like a street with modern lighting and everything in it was silhouetted to the enemy'.

The flames, thus clearly revealing the British intention, attracted yet more bombs, incendiary and HE, and to these were quickly added the shell fire of the enemy's artillery. His infantry, getting up from their trenches, poured in small-arms fire. The attacks spread quickly to other units. The leaping gun flashes on both sides, the blazing vehicles and the brilliant radiance of the moon made union with the trumpeting of the artillery and the crash of shell and bomb to create an inferno of light and uproar. Custance's own headquarters, immediately behind the Rangers, was caught in the angry chaos, the first stick of incendiary bombs falling six yards from his tank. All the vehicles of The Buffs' headquarters were destroyed. Some twenty-two petrol and ammunition lorries were on fire. Farquhar, before leading up 3rd Hussars later, saw the charred bodies of their drivers and mates still upright in their cabs, as they had been at the moment when the attack fell on them. The brigade dispersed as well as the cramping mines permitted but could not avoid the spread of the conflagration. The barrage passed ahead and was lost as the brigade strove to prevent disorganization. Through all this stormy disturbance, however, Captain Geoffrey Brooks, the Rangers' medical officer, his Aid Post demolished by a direct hit, went quietly about the field, accompanied by the chaplain, George Hales, tending the wounded with the absorbed devotion of their kind.

In front of these fierce conflagrations, silhouetted against it to the enemy, peppered by bursting ammunition from the burning lorries close by, stood Perrott's wireless truck. At the tail of it, sheltering as best he could, Perrott himself was operating the radio set to brigade headquarters. He had ordered his men to disperse, but his greatest fear was to be called by brigade and not be on the air to receive them. Caldwell, ignoring orders, refused to leave him. Boat route, blocked by wrecked and burning vehicles and still under bombardment, was clearly out of use for the time being, as well as Hat, and Perrott, listening to the chatter of the brigade net, wondered anxiously what was to be done. Static electricity and enemy jamming made wireless communication very bad all that night, but Perrott, after a long vigil, deduced that orders were being given to halt the advance. There was a sustained and critical conversation, conducted in the most difficult conditions, between Gatehouse and Custance. Custance was convinced that the operation now had no chance of success, but Gatehouse at first would not agree to any calling-off. Meanwhile, the bombardment by air and by artillery continued and did not stop, apparently, for more than three hours.

Later in the night, having had leave to withdraw and having just lain down to sleep beside his radio truck, Perrott was summoned to go up immediately to 8th Brigade headquarters again. There he saw Ian Spence, Custance's brigade major, who told him that 3rd RTR, followed by the Sherwood Rangers, were now to go through the one viable gap and he was asked if he would lead them into it. Making way over to Bottle on foot, he did so, walking to the head of it with Pyman. He saw that all the little lamps were lit and led through Pyman's regiment, accompanied by B Company of The Buffs (Major J. P. N. Samuelson) and a battery of 1st RHA. He watched their spectral shapes begin to fan out beyond the lane. He wished them luck and felt elated that the attack was 'on' again.

Meanwhile, the least affected by the bombing, the Staffordshire Yeomanry, had been making good progress by Bottle route under the determined leadership of Jim Eadie, partnered by C Company of The Buffs under Captain J. B. Worts. Pressing steadily forward, after losing two tanks on mines and overcoming some enemy opposition, they saw at length the dim form of the Wishka Ridge outlined against the curtain of stars. Eadie then made a personal reconnaissance with a few Crusaders and the carriers of The Buffs. Finding no opposition on the ground, he led his regiment forward and occupied the slopes of the ridge. He had successfully reached the *Pierson* Bound. It was a fine performance and one of the oustanding successes of the battle.

While these mixed fortunes were being experienced, Gatehouse himself was on Boat route immediately in rear of 8th Armoured Brigade. He was in the correct position for the commander of an armoured division in action, though Liardet, his square and stocky GSO 1, considered it was too far forward for good staff work.

He had a small tactical headquarters of two tanks, which were under occasional shell fire. Besides Bill Liardet, he had with him his ADC, James Hanbury. Against the chill of the night Gatehouse was wearing his usual *poshteen* and beret. Ebbels, also in the right place for a CRA, was alongside him in another tank. Gatehouse had resisted Custance's suggestion that the attack should be called off and was trying to push his regiments on. He was angry with 24th Brigade who, he thought, should have been able to overcome some opposition they had met and were making very slow progress. As the night wore on, the position did not improve and his difficulties were increased by the bad wireless conditions. It was with difficulty that he could make out what was going on and he could not exchange any conversation with his divisional Main headquarters, which was near the Springbok Road, about eight miles away.

In the early hours of the 25th a Signals officer from 10th Armoured Division Main HQ came up to Gatehouse's Tac HQ on Miteiriya Ridge and told him that, wireless speech being impossible, Lumsden wanted to talk to him on the telephone. Gatehouse, therefore, mounted a jeep, accompanied by Hanbury and driven by Trooper Cadogan, and jolted back to his Main HQ. There ensued a long conversation on the telephone; according to the divisional log, it lasted for more than an hour, but this, of course, we must accept with reserve, there being only one circumstance in which it is likely.

Gatehouse (whose regiments had in fact begun to make progress) now wanted authority to withdraw behind the ridge. Like Custance, he foresaw that, as the result of the delays, his brigades would be revealed at daylight in dangerously exposed ground, off balance and an easy prey for the enemy's waiting guns. Lumsden, who was inclined to agree, reported in turn to Eighth Army.

At Montgomery's forward headquarters, de Guingand, his BGS, who had already been troubled by what he had heard from the J Service[1] and Lumsden's reports, walked over to the headquarters of 30th Corps, which was a few yards away, and asked Oliver Leese for his advice. He knew his chief's objection to being disturbed unnecessarily at night, but the situation now was critical. Leese advised him to wake Montgomery and to call an immediate conference.

De Guingand did so and, at the uncomfortable hour of 3.30 in the morning, with bombs falling nearby and amid the clamour of anti-aircraft fire, there took place, in the Army Commander's map lorry, that meeting of himself, Lumsden and Leese, followed by Montgomery's personal telephone conversation with Gatehouse, which the Field-Marshal and General De Guingand have themselves related.[2]

In spite of the hour and the situation, Montgomery was in a cheerful and confident mood. He heard reports from Leese and Lumsden on the situation. Lumsden told him that Gatehouse wanted to withdraw all his regiments to the ridge, because of the dangerous situation to which they would be exposed in daylight, and that he himself shared that view. Lumsden knew that Gatehouse was available on the telephone at his Main headquarters and it may be inferred that he had asked him to stay there in view of the conference now being held. Had Gatehouse returned to his Tactical HQ on the ridge, no one could have spoken to him.

Montgomery wished Lumsden to telephone to Gatehouse and tell him that the attack must be continued, but Lumsden asked the Army Commander if he would do so himself.[3] Montgomery spoke

1. A system devised by Eighth Army for analysing the wireless traffic of units in combat.

2. *Memoirs* and *Operation Victory*.

3. Field-Marshal Montgomery to the Author.

to Gatehouse accordingly and, in his own words in his *Memoirs*, 'discovered to my horror that he himself was some 16,000 yards (nearly ten miles) behind his leading armoured brigades. I spoke to him in no uncertain voice, and ordered him to go forward at once and take charge of his battle; he was to fight his way out, and lead his division from the front and not from the rear.'

This imputation, one feels sure, would never have been made if Montgomery had been fully apprised of Gatehouse's movements. Whatever shortcomings Gatehouse might have had as a divisional commander, he was never the man to be found at the back of a battle. The outcome was that Montgomery ordered that there should be no departure from the general plan, but he accepted the modification that the advance of 8th Brigade should be limited to the one regiment already forward (the Staffordshire Yeomanry), the remainder to be retained on the ridge.[1]

The orders issued in pursuance of this decision were recorded in 10th Corps log at 4.30 a.m. and in Eighth Army log at 4.45 a.m. as follows:

10 *Armd Div* (G 1)
10 Armd Div plan:
(i) 24 Armd Bde to advance to 86682936–86782900.
(ii) One regt of 8 Armd Bde to move SE to assist 9 Armd Bde, to be there by daylight.
(iii) Remainder 8 Armd Bde remain on Miteiriya Ridge and improve gaps.

While the generals had been conferring with some asperity, the men of 10th Armoured Division had, in fact, been making better progress. Sixth Field Squadron, RE, had doggedly been cutting a double swathe through the mines for Kenchington's two forward regiments, 41st and 47th RTR. Conditions had been extremely difficult. The rate of progress was that of a sapper on his hands and knees, listening, peering, feeling with his fingers, straining to keep

1. In detail, it might be said, this is not precisely the same as the more general 'my orders were unchanged; there would be no departure from the plan'.

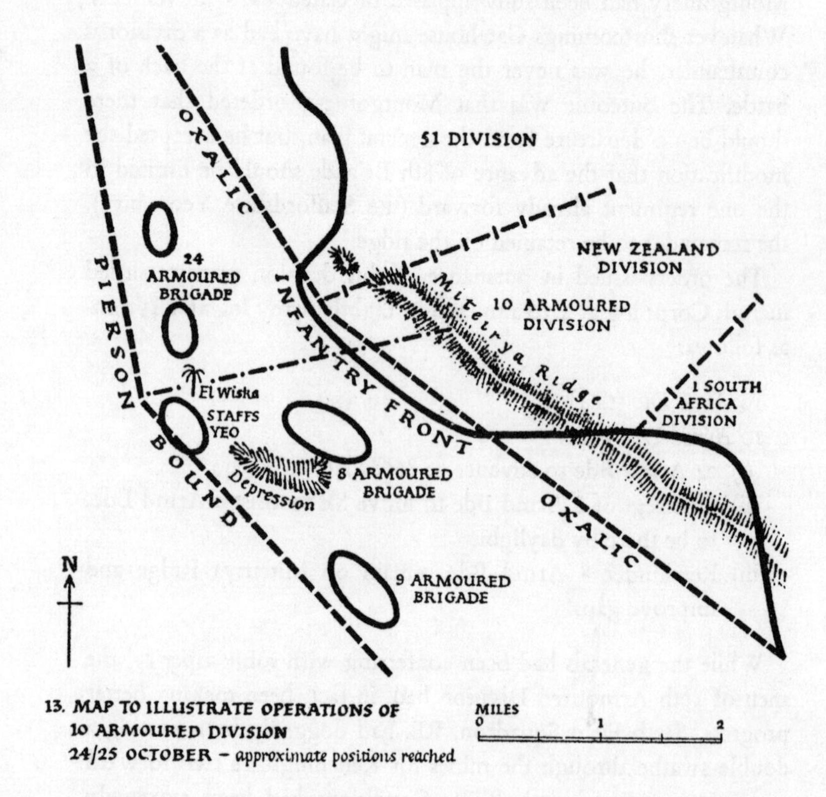

13. MAP TO ILLUSTRATE OPERATIONS OF
10 ARMOURED DIVISION
24/25 OCTOBER – *approximate positions reached*

Terence Cuneo's painting of the action at *Snipe*. *L* to *R*: Turner, Francis, Toms, Calistan, Barnett

Some RB survivors of *Snipe*. *L* to *R*: Ayris, Miles, Irwin, Bird, Holt-Wilson, Hine, Calistan, Chard

The 6-pounder of 239th Battery that was safely brought out, photographed next day; it was Sergeant Wood's

Some 239th Battery survivors of *Snipe*. Identities uncertain

his nerve amid the uproar, the streaking tracers and the flying projectiles.

The lanes completed, Kenchington's squadrons rallied, formed line ahead and went through slowly, disposing of some slight opposition from enemy guns. On receipt of the new orders, which for them were but the old orders sharply repeated, the two regiments pressed forward quickly and at 6.15 on Sunday morning Kenchington reported that they had arrived on the *Pierson* Bound. The third regiment, 45th RTR, remained in reserve on the ridge to give covering fire.

It is, however, highly doubtful whether the 41st and 47th did actually get as far, and the brigade major, going forward in two tanks to verify the positions, received direct hits on both tanks at close range after covering 2,000 yards. However, the occupation of a precise ground objective in the desert war had less significance than elsewhere; 24th Brigade got far enough forward, as events turned out, and in due course made contact with 1st Armoured Division and began fighting enemy tanks.

In 8th Armoured Brigade there is a different story to record. Before the orders to retain two regiments on the ridge had been received, the Sherwood Rangers and 3rd RTR, debouching at last by the Bottle route, had been making good progress after the bombing attack. By 5 o'clock in the morning, groping their way across the pock-marked lunar landscape, they had advanced for perhaps about a mile. Some hundreds of prisoners had surrendered to them, to be gathered in by the 1st Buffs, whose carriers marched between the tanks. At that hour they sighted the dim shapes of the Staffordshire Yeomanry ahead of the slope on Wishka Ridge, while away on the left were to be discerned those of 9th Armoured Brigade. The original orders to reach the *Pierson* Bound had thus been very nearly fulfilled.

About half an hour later, as the stars began to fade before the advance of another day and the chill dawn wind swept icily over the grey scene, the Staffordshire Yeomanry came under devastating fire from 88s that they could not see, and from dug-in tanks. John Lakin, of the Warwickshire Yeomanry, watching from the ground won by 9th Armoured Brigade on the left, saw the Staffordshire's tanks 'go up in sheets of flames one by one, just as if someone had lit the candles on a birthday cake. It was a scene I shall never forget.' It was from here that Lakin took the photograph in Plate XXV.

The Wishka ridge was in fact strongly defended by the enemy, being part of the anti-tank screen that ran up behind the Kidney feature to *Woodcock*, of which we shall hear a great deal more. The Staffordshire Yeomanry quickly lost ten tanks and Eadie ordered them back a little to save further loss.

The two other regiments then, according to the new orders, withdrew right back to Miteiriya Ridge.

A little later Eadie himself drove back to the ridge, where he saw Gatehouse. Eadie was weeping. Some of his dearest friends had just been killed before his eyes, their bodies roasted or broken in pieces. He had lost virtually a whole squadron. Two nights of fighting had cost him thirteen out of his fifteen Crusaders, fourteen out of his twenty-eight heavies. He was certain to lose more if he stayed out in the open and he asked Gatehouse's permission to withdraw.

Gatehouse had been in an angry mood; the events of the night had given him ample cause. But the quality of the man inside the general now appeared to the little group of spectators. Eadie's distress touched him deeply. His own grievance was instantly annulled. His anger melted and he became, in the words of Ian Spence, who was standing by, 'the soul of charm'. He spoke very gently to Eadie and, accepting a responsibility that was in keeping with his judgement and his conscience, if not with his orders, gave him the permission that he wanted.

Thus by soon after sunrise all three regiments of 8th Armoured Brigade, after having very nearly reached their goal, were back on the ridge from which they had started.

There are many obvious questions that one may ask about this much-debated night's operation. There are also some less obvious ones. Why was not an infantry attack put in ahead of the armour? Why was the Lorried Infantry Brigade not sent forward to secure Wishka Ridge? Was too much armour being used? Why were the regiments of 8th Armoured Brigade recalled from an objective nearly reached?

These and others are valid questions and there are answers to them that may also be valid. At least two courses that might have produced better results clearly suggest themselves. It is not, however, our purpose to speculate wisely after the event, nor to suggest any apportionment of blame. Hindsight on military operations is a game much overplayed by authors, especially those who have never been in battle. It was the bombing attack that bedevilled the operation from the very start and, in the face of the unpredictable, criticism is of little validity. On the brigade level, Custance, faced with a situation of exceptional difficulty, had directed affairs with calmness. On the broader level, the men of 10th Armoured Division had proved Montgomery's belief that, with their own resources, they could fight their way through to an objective, but the enemy guns had shown that they could not stay there by daylight alone.

Field-Marshal Montgomery has recorded that 'by 8 a.m. all my armour was out in the open', by which he meant beyond the minefields. However, the 8th Armoured Brigade, though they had reached 'the open' in this sense, were no longer there by that hour, though 24th were and so, as will be presently recorded, were 9th. General De Guingand is mistaken in saying that the New Zealanders and 8th Brigade were, by 8 a.m., clear and 'advancing southwestwards'. Fundamentally, it may be said that the inability to 'break out into the open' was due to the fact (aggravated by the bombing) that 'the open', as more generally understood, had yet to be reached.

Freyberg records that, at a conference held about this time, Lumsden observed (with a regrettable mixture of metaphors): 'Playing with armour is like playing with fire. You have got to go carefully. It is like a duel. If you don't take your time, you will be run through the guts.' However, on the Army front as a whole, the objective of the operations was being successfully, if slowly, maintained, for 1st Armoured Division, soon linked with 24th Brigade, had begun their long battle of attrition with Von Thoma's tanks and guns as Montgomery required that they should.

For us, what is most important is that the operations so far, and for several more days still to come, demonstrated again that the arms which dominated the battlefield were the mine and the anti-tank gun, giving to the defence an advantage that completely neutralized any superiority in numbers possessed by the offence. Until the mine and the gun were disposed of, tanks could not fulfil an offensive function. To the mine a slow and painful answer had been found, but few people seemed yet to appreciate that to the dug-in, almost invisible anti-tank gun the best answer was infantry and field artillery. When the tanks of either side attempted to assault the guns, the result was slaughter, as these pages will show. In spite of modern inventions, the infantry remained the Queen of Battles. Quite likely, they will always remain so.[1]

Meanwhile, away on the left of 8th Armoured Brigade, striking southwards, 9th Armoured Brigade, accompanied by the Honeys of the New Zealand Divisional Cavalry, had also nearly reached the *Pierson* Bound, after having badly beaten up some enemy infantry on the way with their machine-guns. Platoons of the Foresters, moving up coolly between the tanks in carriers or on foot, had taken a good bag of prisoners. Currie was there, of course, and Freyberg drove out over the fire-swept saucer in his Honey to see him in the morning. It was intended that the New Zealand infantry should follow them later for the break-out drive.

Third Hussars had led the attack. Surprisingly enough, they had gone up by the stricken Boat route, passing the burning wrecks of the Sherwood Rangers. Emerging from the minefield, they fanned out, the Foresters among them and the Crusader screen, under Major C. M. Clark, doing tremendous execution with the 'scything

1. Apart from the meagre entries in the divisional log and war diary, the account of Gatehouse's personal movements before his talk with Montgomery is based mainly on the evidence of Major-General Liardet, Colonel James Hanbury, Captain George Thompson and Brigadier Ebbels. The breakdown in health which General Gatehouse himself has most unhappily suffered has prevented his personal narrative from being taken, but I have had the benefit of assistance from his son, Mr Robert Gatehouse.

sweeps' of their Besas machine guns before Clark himself was killed. The Warwickshire Yeomanry were up on their left.

Daylight found the brigade in an uncomfortable position, though not so vulnerable as that of the Staffordshire Yeomanry. Sitting in a saucer between Miteiriya and Wishka Ridges, they were very soon under fire by well-sited guns and tanks at a range of 1,000 yards or more. Currie eagerly awaited an attack by the enemy armour. When none matured, he proposed, believing that there was not much in front of him, to go forward and attack, but he needed first to withdraw to refuel. Freyberg, however, fearing Lumsden would not let him come back, would not allow him to do so.[1]

There, partially protected by smoke put down by the NZ gunners, they stayed, being shelled all day, losing several tanks, but knocking out thirteen of the enemy's and ten guns and taking 300 prisoners. Three of these tanks were knocked out by John Lakin, of the Warwickshire Yeomanry, when, cut off from the rest of his regiment, he carried out a sortie alone.

Currie, the eternal subaltern, could not sit still. If restrained from attacking, he could not be stopped from reconnoitring. This he did, going far out alone, in his Crusader. His tank was hit and lost a track. Pat Hobart, his brigade-major (whose own tank had been hit the day before), went out in another Crusader to pick him up, but found his indomitable brigadier lying on his back, hands (wrapped in red handkerchiefs to cover the desert sores that plagued him) clasped behind his lion-coloured hair, laughing heartily.

On his return, Currie climbed up on to Lakin's tank and ordered him to collect two others, saying: 'We are going up to sort out those. . . .' Lakin turned a man out of his tank, took the gunner's seat himself and handed over the tank to Currie. They sallied out over the crest to within some 800 yards of a battery of four German 55 mms.

There ensued a duel in which the shooting on both sides seems to have been very bad. Lakin fired about fifty rounds of shot without scoring a direct hit, but they had the satisfaction of seeing the Germans abandon their positions. Currie then drove over to his

1. F-M Montgomery and Brigadier Queree to the Author.

own disabled tank and recovered his maps and papers, while Lakin tried to keep the enemy quiet.

Just before dusk, in accordance with the new orders given on the 25th, which we shall notice in the next chapter, his brigade withdrew to Miteiriya Ridge. True to his training, Currie withdrew last. His tank would not start, but Hobart, just in time, ran across to 3rd Hussars and got Alan Dawes to drive over in his Grant, hitch a tow rope on to Currie's tank and tow it out, while the enemy shelled them hard and Currie laughed and Hobart got left behind, so that he had to run alongside the Grant and beat upon the sponson door before they pulled him in.

Such are the unreasonable instincts of man that they respond to the calls of the dead no less than to those of the living. As 3rd Hussars withdrew through the minefield gap on the slopes of Miteiriya, Captain Hector Chadwick's tank was hit. He and his whole crew were killed. Two days later his brother Tom went out in a scout car to look for his body. As soon as he crossed the ridge a direct hit killed him also.

Similarly, in 2nd Field Squadron, RE, Lieutenant Leslie Sage went out to look for the body of Peter Hattersley on the morning of the 25th. Pyman provided him with a tank, which moved up to a hull-down position to enable him to search the ground with his field glasses. But this would not do for Sage. He crawled out into the open, past the infantry front, searching the Hat route. He was sniped from an enemy trench and shot in the leg. He turned about and wormed his way back on his belly, while the tank gave him covering fire with its machine gun. Three months later Sage returned to the ridge, searched the ravaged battlefield and found the grave, dug by the enemy, of his well-loved squadron leader.

THE SOUTHERN BATTLE RENEWED

In the south, directly under the eager binoculars of the enemy on Himeimat, the troops of 7th Armoured and 44th Divisions, though under continuous fire which plagued them all day on the 24th in their narrow, congested bridgehead and which raked the new-cut lanes through the mines, held firmly to the bare ground that they had won between *January* and *February*. The armour edged up to the outskirts of *February*. Later in the day thirty German tanks bore down on the northern flank but they remained at a distance, hull-down, watching.

John Harding came up and held a conference with his brigadiers in the lee of a tank, with the shells dropping uncomfortably close. He heard their reports and gave his orders for resuming the offensive. As the sun rose higher, the desert shimmered in the heat haze and the salient continued to be swept by fire, so that very little reconnaissance of any value could be done and it was impossible to locate the enemy post with accuracy.

The attack on *February* was, nevertheless, resumed that night. Without elaborate re-arrangements, the 1/5th and 1/6th battalions of the Queen's formed up simply on the line of the foremost tanks and moved forward under a barrage. They had 2,500 yards to go. Keeping well up to the barrage, they thrust right through *February* and began to consolidate half a mile beyond it, very exposed and under close fire from the open flanks, and there they anxiously awaited the arrival of the armour.

Behind them, in extremely trying conditions, the sappers of the minefield force succeeded in sweeping two lanes through the thickest of mines, accomplished almost entirely by bayonet prodding. It was one of the stoutest of efforts, made with great determination and at heavy cost; but infantry and engineers seem to have advanced on different axes and to have lost touch, so that, when 22nd Armoured Brigade moved up through the lanes with the City of London Yeomanry and 1st RTR, they found themselves under close fire from anti-tank guns that had escaped assault by the infantry. The exits from *February* became completely blocked by knocked-out tanks and by other tanks which, seeking a way round, went up on scattered mines. Thirty-one tanks were quickly disabled and no headway was possible without incurring further loss.

The Queen's, however, hung tenaciously on to their exposed bridgehead salient, galled by fire on their long flanks from dug-in enemy posts that were as close as a hundred yards, enduring what their historians calls 'a terrible experience' and their wounded in acute distress. The whole area on this sector for miles around was under direct enemy observation.

The remainder of the effort on the southern front is soon told, though a trifle out of due chronological order. On the evening of this day, which was Sunday, 25 October, in accordance with the policy of avoiding serious tank losses, the armour was withdrawn. Had the forces been available and had it been in accordance with the Army Commander's plan, there is no doubt that a little more pressure would have secured a break-out here and the enemy's tanks would have been brought to battle.

The Queen's battalions, having stuck to their hard-won bridgehead beyond *February* all day, withdrew later in the night, still under fire and with more casualties, to a position east of *February*, after a gallant exploit that has been given no place in any major account of the battle. They had done all that had been required of them. They were relieved by the Kent brigade (132nd) under the celebrated fighting brigadier 'Bolo' Whistler. The relief was carried out under heavy shell fire, the enemy having guessed what was up, but the Kent regiments took the most resolute action and were dug-in by 4 a.m.

The same night (25/26 October) an attack immediately to the north was put in by 50th Division on the rugged Munassib Depression. This had originally been intended as an operation in support of the main actions by 7th Armoured and 44th, and it was put in, quite properly, despite the changed situation. The main attack was made by 69th Brigade, a fine brigade of Yorkshiremen under the able leadership of Brigadier Cooke-Collis, a tall and imperturbable young commander who consoled himself for his slight deafness because 'it prevents me from hearing the shells burst'.[1]

Their task was to attack the formidable feature frontally from the east and north. This they did and 6th Green Howards, under Lieutenant-Colonel G. C. P. Lance, secured nearly all their objectives with great dash, but 5th East Yorkshires got entangled in wire and the terribly lethal S-mines and suffered 150 casualties. An attempt

1. To the Author at that time.

was made by 50th Division to renew the attack next night, but General Nichols called it off.

Indeed, the whole of the southern operations were now halted on Montgomery's orders. They had served their main purpose, which was to contain the two enemy armoured divisions in the south as long as possible. They had been expensive in infantry, 1st Rifle Brigade, for example, having lost nineteen officers and many of their best NCOs in the sticky minefield operations. The bulk of 7th Armoured was withdrawn, leaving elements of 44th Division, the Free French and a few other units, to form a very exiguous defensive front. A loud-speaker unit was installed to simulate the sounds of tank movement at night.

The enemy still sat on top of Himeimat, watching everything that was being done in the sandy plain below, like an eagle in its eyrie.

Chapter Thirteen

THE CHANGE OF TUNE

(Day 25 October and Night 25/26)

Maintaining the Initiative – Tank Battles – Highland and Australian Attacks – Rommel Returns

MAINTAINING THE INITIATIVE

Henceforth our narrative is concerned exclusively with events in the north, and thither we return on the morning of 25 October, which was D Plus Two.

As the sun rose on that Sunday and breathed sudden warmth into chilled and tired limbs, it disclosed a widened battlefield drifting with clouds of dust and smoke, scarred with the wrecked and burning hulks of tanks, vehicles and guns, littered with bodies in all the sad postures of death and scattered with the debris and desolation of combat. Westward of Miteiriya Ridge the two armies glared at each other across the minefields. On Boat route, where the bombing had taken place the night before, the scenes of human and material destruction were, in the words of David Egerton, the gunner, 'pretty horrible'. Behind the ridge the British tanks, their crews dog-tired, sat hull-down, watching and engaging. There was another sharp attack by German dive-bombers. On the eastern lee of the ridge was a congested mass of tanks, vehicles, guns, carriers and men of two divisions, stationary for the greater part or moving warily among the mines. Everyone not too tired to think was wondering what the next move would be.

As the sun waxed and commanders took stock of the situation, it became apparent that it had not improved, to any significant degree, in the past twenty-four hours. The front was firmer, 1st Armoured Division had progressed and were at grips with the enemy, 24th Brigade had got out and were joining hands with them, but no vital new development had occurred to transform the prospect. There was a danger of a premature stalemate.

Soon after 9 o'clock Freyberg met Oliver Leese and emphasized that the infantry and the armour had no common front, that the enemy were reinforcing and would be stronger the next day. It would be impossible to exploit south with infantry as intended, the element of surprise having been lost. He urged that an attack should now be directed westward from the bulge now showing prominently on the map, with another timed bombardment, to a depth of 4,000 yards.

'We all knew', he recorded, 'that the first attack had just failed to push the enemy off his gun line and this further attack would, I considered, take us beyond his minefield and gun line into an area where the tanks would have room to manœuvre.'[1] He was certainly right in his proposition that what was needed was another assault by infantry, had they been available, not tanks. The main minefields having now been penetrated, the most serious obstacle to progress was the anti-tank gun, and no means were so effective for overcoming it as infantry and field artillery.

The Army Commander held a conference with Leese, Lumsden and Freyberg at noon. It was clear to him that no dividends were likely to accrue from any further attempt to break out south-westward from Miteiriya Ridge at that time. Many commanders would have doggedly persisted and perhaps succeeded at heavy cost, but among the military precepts that Montgomery taught was to avoid 'reinforcing failure'. The Miteiriya operations could not, of course, by any means be called entirely a failure, having achieved results very important to his plans, but they gave no immediate promise of the break-out south-westward which he intended and which he at length did achieve from a little farther north.

1. *The New Zealand Division in Egypt and Libya.*

He now demonstrated this precept by firmly turning his back upon Miteiriya Ridge. At the same moment, looking in an entirely different direction, he began to demonstrate a second characteristic precept: retain the initiative and 'make the enemy dance to your tune'. This he acted upon by beginning a series of blows at unexpected points which kept the enemy guessing and forced them to react as he wished them to do, in pursuance of his 'crumbling' policy.

He ordered accordingly that 10th Armoured Division should be withdrawn that night, except for 24th Brigade, which was to pass to the command of 1st Armoured Division in the northern 'corridor' (a term no longer valid). Ninth Armoured Brigade was also to draw back, taking station behind Miteiriya Ridge with the Kiwis. The latter were to organize for defence and to husband their infantry. In the South, 13th Corps was to break off its operations.

The new point of attack chosen by the Army Commander was without any doubt an inspiration. Instead of continuing to drive west and south-west, he suddenly turned his face to the north. He resolved that, from the top of the new bulge in our line, where the Australians kept watch upon our flank, he would make a surprise attack towards the sea.

This would not only be of great value in the 'crumbling' process, but it would also quite certainly make the enemy dance very quickly indeed to the new tune. A northward thrust, threatening to trap strong forces of 164th Light Division and the Italian Bersaglieri and to throw open the main road *behind* the mined areas, was one to which the enemy must be extremely sensitive and it would divert his attention to a new danger area. The attack by 50th Division on Munassib the same night would add to his uncertainties.

Foreseeing how events might shape themselves, Montgomery had already warned Morshead the day before to be ready for this new thrust with his Australians. He now ordered the attack to take place tonight. Meantime, 1st Armoured Division, with Kenchington's brigade under command, was to press forward in the Kidney sector; Montgomery hoped that there might be an opportunity for the armour to reach the Rahman Track at the northern end of the *Skinflint* report line. Here it would not only disrupt the enemy's main lateral supply roads to the south, but from here also it might be able to strike northwards to get in behind the northern salient.

The emphasis of the whole battle was thus to be shifted overnight. In support of this new thrust, Montgomery asked for maximum air support for the Australians. Throughout the day the enemy air forces were very subdued. Our fighters patrolled over their airfields without interference and even the obsolescent Hurricanes flew without escort. The splendid efforts of Tedder's pilots could not, of course, entirely annul those of the enemy and throughout the battle there were frequent Stuka attacks, short and sharp, and little night bombing. Unlike the sustained bombing on the night of the 24/25 October, which completely upset Gatehouse's attack, these swoops had no influence on operations.

TANK BATTLES

The day of 25 October was signalized by the sustained hammering of 1st Armoured Division to break the barriers in the Kidney sector, provoking Von Thoma to a violent reaction later in the day.

Since first light the division had been disposed approximately on the *Oxalic* line or a little short of it. In 2nd Armoured Brigade, Fisher still had the Bays on the right, 9th Lancers in the centre and 10th Hussars on the left. Southward, and in touch, was 24th Armoured Brigade. North of the Bays, Bosvile brought up 7th Motor Brigade, who threw out a carrier screen to make contact with the Australians on the right and who made their surprise encounter with Paton's company of the Gordons on the left.

Soon after first light, 2nd Armoured Brigade, now almost clear of the entangling minefields, began feeling forward towards *Pierson*, but were barred by a zareba of anti-tank and field guns deployed approximately on that line. The Kidney sector became very hot. The *Aberdeen* position on the ridge had not yet been seized by 1st Gordons and we begin to encounter other defences of which we shall hear much as the battle progresses – Point 33 opposite the Australians, *Snipe* of heroic memory and *Woodcock*. These defended localities were part of Rommel's main defences, behind the minefield 'battle outposts', where he hoped to destroy whatever elements of an attacking force succeeded in penetrating his Devil's Gardens. He very soon attempted to do so.

In the dawn twilight the Bays renewed their overnight attempt on Point 33, but were met by point-blank fire from heavy anti-tank guns that had been brought up during the night and concealed among the derelict tanks that the Bays themselves and their supporting artillery had knocked out the day before. Six leading Shermans were lost in five minutes and the regiment withdrew. Until the enemy anti-tank guns could be shot out of the way progress was impossible, but the difficulty was to locate them. Only puffs of dust from their blast gave some vague evidence.

Later in the morning Von Thoma's attempt to throw us back began to develop. Nearly the whole sector of 1st Armoured Division, including the positions of the Australian infantry, was subjected to heavy shelling, and it was in this shelling that the Australians witnessed the 'terrible carnage' of 7th Rifle Brigade. Through the smoke and dust, fleeting glimpses were caught of distant tanks and trucks manœuvring and all the forewarnings of an impending counter-attack in the typical German manner disclosed themselves step by step.

The bombardment increased as the mirage began its shimmering dance about noon. The enemy command tanks felt their way forward cautiously to make a reconnaissance and then retired to give their orders for battle. A little later a smoke-screen was laid down on the front of Second-13th Australian Battalion. The whole frontage of the Kidney sector was prickly with expectation as the sun reached his most savage hour. The British forces – infantry, armour and artillery – bathed in perspiration and powdered with dust, braced themselves with complete confidence.

A whole series of counter-attacks was then thrown against the British, with an ineptitude which showed that the enemy commanders wholly failed to appreciate the very nature of the situation and the potential of the forces opposing them. The attacks were made with the enemy's usual skill in minor tactics and with his usual forcefulness of purpose; but they were made piecemeal, at different places and different times. Mounted by 15th Panzer and the Littorio Divisions, accompanied by infantry and supported by concentrations of fire from field and anti-tank artillery, they were directed in turn against the Riflemen of 7th Motor Brigade (with the results that we saw in the last chapter), against Second-13th and Second-17th Australian Battalions (separately), against 24th Armoured Brigade farther to the south and against 2nd Armoured Brigade. All failed and at considerable loss.

Second-13th, still partly equipped with the little 2-pdrs, sat motionless when the attack on them developed until the enemy was within 100 yards and then opened fire as though at a single word of command. The whole line of tanks 'shuddered to a standstill', the foremost within forty yards of the little guns. Not a single tank in the enemy's leading squadron escaped.

The last and heaviest attack, mounted with fifty-five tanks, fell upon 9th Lancers and the Bays. Although the Bays now had only three Shermans left, the attack was repulsed decisively and the enemy, having lost eighteen tanks very quickly, left the field.

These were the first of many sharp reverses that the enemy armour was to suffer in this sector. Although 1st Armoured Division lost twenty-four tanks that hot and dusty day, they claimed in their diary to have knocked out fifty-three. In all, in two days' fighting since first light on the 24th, not fewer than seventy-seven German tanks had been destroyed or effectively disabled on the northern front and probably half as many Italians. It was an impressive achievement, with which Monty, so far, was 'well content'. The steady destruction of the enemy tanks, begun on a small scale the day before, swelled to a fuller measure. This was exactly what Montgomery wanted. This was what he had counted upon. The enemy was playing straight into his suit.

On the other hand, in the face of the enemy's own well-integrated barriers of anti-tank guns, Briggs's regiments could make no progress on the ground, which was also important to the Army Commander's plan. The task assigned to them to thrust west and north-west by that evening was not yet achieved. Making one more attempt on the troublesome Point 33, Fisher sent in 10th Hussars with artillery support at a late hour, but they met a fate similar to that of the Bays. Major George Errington, calling for the supporting artillery barrage to be stopped because its smoke and dust prevented him from seeing the enemy, found himself encompassed by heavy guns at close range.

Three Shermans were quickly knocked out. Their escaping crews were just saved from capture by the redoubtable Sergeant Maile, who attacked the Germans coming out to take them with his bren gun.

During this day there developed a good deal of friction between the armour and the infantry, more particularly the Highland Division. The tanks, still held at bay, were fighting their battles in or near the infantry FDLs. They were drawing heavy fire, adding to the infantry casualties. They were 'milling about' a great deal and their movements, as well as those of their wheeled vehicles, were dangerous to the infantry soldier in his trench, especially at night. A Scottish colonel, trying to get some sleep, said to a squadron leader: 'I wish you'd go away.'

The presence of the tanks was a valuable protection against an enemy attack, but the infantry did not yet understand armoured action and expected the tanks to 'waltz through'. What the man on foot did not realize – because nobody told him – was that our armour were methodically knocking out enemy tanks in the way that they should and were thus beginning to win the battle. Both arms were a little to blame for lack of understanding.

About the same time there also developed that serious difference over the reading of the desert's expressionless face, which we have already noted. The oldest hands, who had 'swanned' about the desert for two years and prided themselves on their map-reading, were nonplussed at identifying the little folds and dips and swellings which looked so anonymous in the Kidney sector and which did not seem to relate themselves to the contour lines on the map. There was particular confusion over the recognition of the Kidney 'ridge' and *Aberdeen*. The 30-metre ring-contour, shaped like a kidney, seemed on the map to be an elevation, but in fact it was a shallow depression; the real ridge did not run along the terrain enclosed by the ring-contour, but to the east and north of it, with a spur to the west, as

The Hammering of the Panzers. *Top*, a Mark III Special. *Bottom*, a Crusader passing a burning Mark IV

The Hammering of the Panzers

may be seen in Figure 14. A hummock crowned with a rocky pimple was at first assumed by 10th Hussars to be *Aberdeen*.

These differences of opinion were to have considerable bearing on some of the operations to follow and caused anxious arguments before attacks were mounted. It was agreed afterwards that the Scots, though newcomers to the desert, were on this occasion more nearly correct than the experienced 1st Armoured.

HIGHLAND AND AUSTRALIAN ATTACKS

While the armour was thus eating into the enemy's tank strength during the day, the Highland and Australian infantry were preparing offensive operations for the night.

Three battalion operations were set on foot in 51st Division. The first of these we have seen brought to a temporary halt on 1st Gordons' sector immediately in front of *Aberdeen*. A second was launched by 7th Argyll and Sutherland Highlanders, under Lorne Campbell, against *Nairn*, which had originally been the target of the Divisional Reconnaissance Regiment and 50th RTR, but which they had been unable to reach on the first night.

The Argylls attacked south-westwards from their *Greenock* position with three weak companies in bright moonlight at 11 p.m., without benefit of artillery. *Nairn* was a formidable position, which was divided into three separate objectives. The attack was made with great determination at considerable cost. There was a fierce and bloody close-quarters fight right in the German trenches. One by one their positions were overcome at push of bayonet. Sixty Germans were killed in their weapon pits, but the Argylls suffered severely also. A Company lost all its officers and Company Sergeant-Major F. Young took command with the competence of a natural leader. Before the end of the operation Captain J. C. Meiklejohn was the only officer left alive and unwounded in the three companies.

Next morning Meiklejohn found that the Germans had closed in behind him and that he was cut off, but he hung on alone for three days. Unavailing attempts were made to get through to him with water, ammunition and supplies, yet Captain Aymer Wilson, the doctor, and his stretcher-bearers, 'quartering the ground like questing spaniels', in Lorne Campbell's words, somehow managed to get away all the wounded. Brigadier Houldsworth himself was one of the first to get through and found Meiklejohn's gallant band 'in excellent spirits.'

The third of the Highlanders' operations on the night of the 25th went easily. This was against *Stirling*, originally the final objective of the Argylls.

We have seen already that 2nd Seaforth Highlanders had secured a line not far from it on the day before and that afterwards this powerful strong point had been overrun by the armour. It was believed to have been reoccupied by the enemy, and 5th Black Watch, under Thomas Rennie, were now ordered to attack it, with a squadron of 46th RTR following up for support if required. Like the Argylls' attack on *Nairn*, it was timed for 11 p.m. and without artillery support.

Two companies were put in, led by George Dunn and Charles McGregor. The battalion walked silently towards the ridge in bright moonlight in extended order. Not a shot met them and when at length they topped the flat-headed ridge, expecting trouble, the moon revealed nothing to them but the dark shapes of the shattered 88s and the sprawling forms of some 30 dead Germans of 164th Light Division.

To the surprised view of the Jocks, a solid, black shape, long and low, was seen approaching, resolving itself as it drew near into the form of a German armoured car. The Scots lay low and allowed it to come right up to them, when an officer took a pot shot at it with his revolver. The bullet flooked through the driver's slot in the armour and killed him. The stalled vehicle was carrying two other Germans, who jumped out and surrendered. In the car was found a hot meal intended for one of the outpost garrisons and it now became the Jocks'.

Dawn, however, brought a disagreeable surprise. In the hard rock, the Black Watch had been able to hack out only a few shallow scrapes for their protection, but, as the darkness dissipated, a force of Germans was revealed entrenched not more than fifty yards ahead. Sniping and mortaring began at once. Lieutenant Jock Cordiner, his platoon bothered by the snipers, ran out, accompanied by two or three men, with grenades in their hands to suppress them. The Germans allowed them to approach within ten yards and then riddled them with bullets. The enemy's fire became increasingly damaging to the exposed Scots; McGregor was killed and Dunn wounded.

Meanwhile, Rennie observed what was going on from his battalion headquarters about a hundred yards back. He came up himself in his apparently lackadaisical manner and swiftly organized a classic platoon attack under cover of smoke from their own little 2-inch mortars. It was a model illustration of a text-book manœuvre often laid on for demonstrations of tactics at home but too rarely employed in live battle. It was a complete success and the German force surrendered to a man. Such minor incidents as these illustrate the unexpectedness of the desert situations and the resourcefulness they demanded.

With the exception of *Aberdeen*, which fell to 1st Gordons within twenty-four hours, all 51st Division's objectives were now secured. It was a fine performance for a virtually new division in their first action. The losses had been heavy – probably heavier than those of any other division so far. Before the end of the battle the Camerons had lost twenty-five officers; of ten subalterns who came to them on this day to replace casualties, all but one were themselves casualties in the next few days. The Argylls lost 275 (13 officers), 7th Black Watch 261 (19 officers). But the division had proved the value of their training and the inspiration of their tradition. The tenacity and resource of their infantry – territorial heirs of regimental names lustrous in history – the superb support of their hard-driven artillery,[1] the devotion of their Royal Engineers, backed by their units of the administrative services, were collectively the hall-marks of a fine and well-integrated fighting machine.

The most important of the operations of the night of the 25th, however, was the northward attack which Montgomery had called

1. Two gunner COs in the Division were killed early in the battle: J. H. B. Evatt, 61st Anti-tank Regt., on the 27th, and R. A. L. Fraser-MacKenzie, 40th Light AA Regt., on the 26th.

upon the Australians to launch. It was the first bar in that change of tune which was to alter the whole orchestration of the battle and to provoke the enemy to the most furious and fateful of dances.

Morshead's assignment was by no means an easy one. From an open flank he had to drive a narrow salient into the enemy position, and from this salient, which would certainly become a very hot one, he would have to turn east. The whole operation was to become one of three phases, and for this night his plan was a bold one with a limited objective. This objective was the elevation known as Point 29[1] and an enemy strongpoint[2] on the relatively high ground north-east of it.

Point 29 – about twenty feet higher than the surrounding desert – lay about a mile and a quarter to the north of the far end of the bulge. It was a very important artillery observation post and was strongly held by 125th Panzer Grenadier Regiment (see Figs. 8 and 16). Morshead's patrols had reported that few mines were to be found in the immediate path to this locality and that same evening another patrol had a very lucky bag: they captured two senior officers of 125th PZ Grenadiers who had marked maps of the area and who talked surprisingly freely.

The attack was made at midnight by 26th Australian Brigade, with 'Monty's Foxhounds' of 40th RTR standing by, and supported by seven regiments of field and medium artillery, while Wellingtons of the RAF dropped 115 tons of bombs in the battle area. The assault was remarkable not only for its swift and convincing success but also for the manner in which it was carried out. It was begun by Second-48th Battalion, who advanced on Point 29, and forty minutes later Second-24th, forming up behind the position captured by the right forward company of their comrades, attacked separately to the north-east. The action went like a model demonstration, both units seizing their objectives at once, with a bag of 240 prisoners. What was most remarkable, however, was the manner of the capture of Point 29.

The CO of Second-48th, Dick Hammer, was a very remarkable character. 'Hard as nails' was the motto that he had impressed upon his

1. Map square 868300.
2. Map. ref. 87053008.

battalion, who called him 'Tack' and who found that they were the nails to his hammer. Formerly a cavalry man, he had commanded a mechanized machine-gun unit and had a feeling for cavalry action. Having learnt that there was only one minefield on the path to his objective, and that not a difficult one, he resolved on a daring and imaginative manœuvre. His two leading companies advanced some 900 yards on foot in the conventional method and seized the minefield. The sappers cleared gaps. Then the battalion's third rifle company, mounted entirely in bren carriers, moved up through the gap, advanced four abreast across the remaining 1,000 yards to Point 29 itself, under cover of a sharp artillery concentration, charged and surprised the German garrison. The Australians leapt from their carriers and there followed what was the bloodiest hand-to-hand fighting of the battle, the Germans resisting with plenty of spirit until overcome.

Point 29 was a key position on the Alamein battlefield. When Rommel shortly returned from Germany, he at once showed that he was peculiarly sensitive at this spot. It was, in fact, this sector, and not Kidney Ridge, as stated by other writers, which was to him 'Hill 28'. Fighting was to rage violently all round the captured ground for the next week as the enemy strove to recover Point 29, but they strove in vain against the tenacious grip of the Aussies.

During this fine action Private P. E. Gratwick won a posthumous Victoria Cross for great individual heroism which materially assisted the operation. His platoon commander and sergeant were both killed and the platoon reduced to a strength of seven men, but he restored the momentum by single-handed leadership of the most inspiring degree. He charged alone against the enemy strongpoint that had halted them and completely destroyed it with grenades, wiping out a mortar crew and a machine gun detachment. He then proceeded to attack another enemy post and inflicted casualties in that also before he was himself killed.

His was one of two Victoria Crosses won at Alamein by Second-48th, who had already been awarded one at Tel el Eisa in July (Private Gurney) and were to win yet a fourth in New Guinea Sergeant Thomas Derrick).

ROMMEL RETURNS

That evening, at Hitler's desire, Rommel arrived back at his desert headquarters. He had been keeping in touch with the situation and on his flight from Germany had made a short halt at Rome, where he had taken the opportunity, yet once more, of pressing the urgency of the need for more petrol and ammunition and he had demanded that every available Italian submarine and warship should immediately be put to use to make good the shortages.

On arrival in the desert, he took over affairs forthwith from Von Thoma. The lean old warrior, cool and detached, did not seem to be seriously disturbed by the situation. He appeared to regard it in terms of ground lost or won, which was of minor importance in the desert, and the character of the battle as one of attrition was not yet evident. But Rommel's report to Germany that night was full of disquiet. He noted that the Trento Division had already lost half its infantry and most of its guns, and that 164th Light Division had lost two battalions and some artillery; that the fuel situation was an anxious one; and that the British had great superiority in guns and armour.

'Fifteenth Panzer Division', he recorded later in *The Rommel Papers*,[1] 'had counter-attacked several times on 24 and 25 October but has suffered frightful losses in the terrible British artillery fire and non-stop RAF bombing attacks. By the evening of the 25th, only 31 of their 119 tanks remained serviceable.'

In point of fact, his losses in personnel up to that moment did not exceed 3,700 (very much less than the British losses), of whom 2,100 had been taken prisoner. The tank resources remaining to 15th PZ Division appear to be slightly understated and no mention was made of the tanks of Littorio, which were used freely against our infantry and which still numbered at least eighty. We may note also that Rommel's ammunition situation was nothing like as bad as he from time to time represented, as the British knew to their cost, for the shelling was incessant and heavy for long periods.

'Our own air force', he continued, 'was still unable to prevent

1. Ed. B. H. Liddell Hart.

the British bombing attacks, or to shoot down any major number of British aircraft. . . .

'Our aim for the next few days was to throw the enemy out of our defence line at all costs and to re-occupy our old positions.'

Once again, therefore, Rommel had resolved upon the wrong tactics. Instead of husbanding his straitened resources and forming a new defensive front, he put everything to the hazard by wasting his strength against a superior force which, as Alam Halfa should have taught him, was not to be shaken by the methods of earlier days. By deciding to counter-attack in force, and continuing repeatedly to do so with tanks instead of infantry, he did exactly what Montgomery wanted him to do and so laid the faggots for his own cremation. Had he copied Montgomery's tactics at Alam Halfa, he might well have brought his adversaries to a point of frustration. The follies of 'over-extension' were to become rapidly more apparent.

Against the enormous weight of evidence, he clearly did not at first properly appreciate the situation. He still kept 21st Panzer and the Ariete Divisions down in the south and the only action he took on the morning after his arrival was to dance smartly to Montgomery's tune.

Chapter Fourteen

THE DAY OF CRISIS

(26 October)

Counter-attack – Reappraisal – The Last of Miteiriya –
The Critical Conference – Rommel's Counter-Plan

COUNTER-ATTACK

The success of the Australian exploit against Point 29, small though it was in extent, but occurring on the very night of Rommel's return to the desert, touched him on the raw. He reacted violently, just as Montgomery wanted him to do.

Apprehending that our purpose, apart from cutting off the Axis forces in the coastal sector, was to drive in behind the main minefields, and expecting us to make a farther thrust northwards to the coast road, Rommel resolved to restore the situation in that sector immediately and to regain Point 29. To do so, he ordered a massive counter-attack, employing 164th Light Division, the Italian 20th Corps and everything that was left of 15 PZ Division. To support this powerful blow against a small sector, he added a strong force of aircraft, comprised of fighter-bombers, Stuka dive-bombers and protective fighters.

The hit-back was a complete failure. Our own watchful eyes in the air soon spotted the great assembly of tanks, guns, infantry and vehicles marshalling itself for the onslaught, with their protective fighters circling overhead. The Allied air squadrons and the soldiers on the ground made immediate counter-preparations and as the enemy strove to move forward he was met by a storm of shelling and by a violent bombardment from the waves of Baltimores and Mitchells that flew eagerly in upon so spectacular a target.

There followed a great battle of air and ground, with roars of bombs that shook the desert floor, their tremors felt beneath the feet of our own troops, and with great clouds of smoke and dust obscuring friend and foe alike. Fierce conflagrations from stricken tanks and aircraft added to the scene and the sky became reticulated with a pattern of darting tracers. The German and Italian fighters fought hard to protect their own troops, and their Stukas and fighter-bombers launched attack after attack on our soldiers on the ground, but in the face of the dash and vigour of our own fighters they were unable to press home their assaults.

Rommel himself watched the attempt against what was to him Hill 28, recording afterwards, with that somewhat plaintive exaggeration that marks his *Papers*, how 'rivers of blood' were 'poured out', how 'tremendous British artillery fire pounded the area' and how the bofors fire directed against his aircraft, the densest he had ever seen in Africa, was such that 'the air became an inferno of fire'.

Thus Rommel's first big counter-attack was broken up in ruins as soon as it began. He had failed to appreciate the situation with which he was confronted. He was opposed now not only by superior numbers but also by an army better equipped, better trained, better led than of old and one that fought as an integrated machine under a very firm control from the top. The relatively easy successes he had had against the ill-co-ordinated British forces in June and July were over. He and Von Thoma between them, now, by bad tactics, lost far more tanks than they could afford.

REAPPRAISAL

In consequence of Rommel's counter-attack on Point 29 there were no German tanks facing 1st Armoured Division in the Kidney sector that day, though they were seen in the distance moving away to take part in that operation. Our own tanks, however, whenever trying to move forward, were immediately destroyed by anti-tank guns that could only rarely be located.

Thus on 26 October the advance of Eighth Army towards its purpose appeared to have come to a dead stop. The armour could no more break through the barrier of unseen guns than the enemy armour could break in against ours. Eager enough to join battle with each other, the tanks were as helpless against the anti-tank gun as the horsed cavalry of their fathers' days had been against machine guns and field artillery.

Our own tank losses, of course, much exceeded the enemy's. They amounted so far to about 300, but many had not been destroyed and were being recovered and repaired. We had some 800 more. Rommel still had some 400, still a formidable force if properly employed. In officers and men we had lost 6,140, of which one-third were in 51st Division.

Thus in tanks our battle casualties were, as far as we can judge, rather more than twice as many as the enemy's and in officers and men nearly twice as many. This was approximately the ratio to be expected in an assault against prepared defences, though the casualties in personnel on both sides were unexpectedly light in a battle of this ferocity, because of the wide dispersion that the spaces of the desert permitted. The tally was to be very different before the end.

An appraisal of losses at that time, however, meant little. The tactical prospects were what mattered and they were not promising to the British outlook. We had not yet punctured the enemy's hide, not yet broken into the inner bailey of his fortress. We had won a marked tactical success, but not a decisive one. Montgomery, who had been 'well content' the day before, was anything but content today. Indeed on that Monday, in the words of Oliver Leese, we were 'within an ace of losing our grip of the battle'. Likewise Freyberg: 'Although the Battle of Alamein never looked like failing, it had its critical moments.'

Montgomery went forward to see Freyberg and found the old warrior still convinced that one more strong infantry attack on a broad front with a powerful artillery barrage would succeed in breaking through the hard crust of the enemy's front. He did not like attacks on a narrow front and was always, right up to the end of the war, a firm believer in the creeping barrage. Speaking to Leese, Freyberg again pressed for an 'attack on a three-division front without being tied to a firm base, for which we did not have the troops'.[1]

However, though eager to attack again, Freyberg had serious misgivings about the physical ability of his own infantry to carry out any further 'major attack'. His rifle companies had already been reduced to half-strength or less (50 to 60 men) and no further New Zealand reinforcements were to be had. One more assault would so cripple his infantry that they would not have the numerical strength to take part in the exploitation and pursuit for which the Army Commander intended them. This situation Freyberg put into writing in a letter to Leese that day.

For the time being, while he considered the situation, Montgomery's orders to Leese were that 30th Corps should secure their front against counter-attack, patrol actively and withdraw from the line any troops that could be spared, in preparation for a new major attack, to which he now set his mind.

Throughout that day, anxious though it was, Montgomery was assessing the position dispassionately as he visited the divisions. He was a realistic but always positive thinker, and he did not himself entertain the slightest anxiety, nor concern himself with any fear of a possible breakdown of his plan. Such things never entered his head. His way of thinking was directed only towards resolving the best course for driving his purpose forward. He was the soul of confidence. He had won the battle of the break-in; what now remained was simply to determine the best method of winning the break-out. No 'new plan' was necessary; the plan resolved upon stood. Wimberley recalls how, standing up in his tank, Montgomery called at the 'elephant' shelter[2] dug into the sand which was Highland Division's headquarters, as he often did, and how he 'radiated complete confidence'.

1. Op. cit.
2. Made from curved sheets of heavy corrugated iron.

Sitting afterwards in his caravan on the dazzling white beach, Montgomery spent much of the day balancing the courses open to him. Two factors that he had to provide for were the lack of New Zealand and South African replacements and the fatigue of those divisions of 30th and 10th Corps that had been doing most of the fighting. He was impressed by the success of the Australians, however, and was now thinking in terms of diverting his main thrust along the axis of the coast road, instead of from the present bulge – just as Rommel thought he was doing. What was first intended as a diversion took shape in his mind as a new avenue to the main break-out. That design assumed precedence in his mind for the next three days.[1]

By the evening of that day he had made up his mind.

THE LAST OF MITEIRIYA

Before his new thoughts had been disclosed, however, other operations in pursuit of the basic plan had been loosed. The larger of these, by 1st Armoured Division in the Kidney sector, was to be ennobled by one of the battle's most golden exploits and on that account deserves a chapter to itself. The other was a night attack by Gentry's 6th New Zealand Brigade and the South Africans to complete their conquest of the middle and southerly parts of Miteiriya Ridge.

An advance of about 1,000 yards was involved and the fight was a sharp one. The enemy was, of course, well prepared. Notwithstanding a violent defensive fire, the rifle companies of both brigades thrust through to their final objectives on the far slope of the ridge, the New Zealanders taking ninety prisoners. The newly-won objective then came under severe fire from the enemy and the gaps through the mines were enfiladed by heavy machine guns so acutely that it was impossible to push forward the supporting weapons. New gaps had therefore to be made by the sappers and before daylight the situation was firm.

The fiery ridge, strewn with the blackened hulks of burnt-out tanks, the remnants of shattered vehicles and all the detritus of a fierce battle, its rocky surface littered with the bodies of the still unburied

1. *Memoirs*, pp. 131–132.

dead, vanishes now from our story, as Montgomery prepared a new blow.

THE CRITICAL CONFERENCE

While the attacks of the New Zealanders and South Africans were in full career, the infantry divisional commanders themselves were summoned to a 30th Corps conference and thither they made their way in the moonlight – Freyberg, Wimberley, Morshead, Tuker and Pienaar. It was held in a small elephant shelter down by the sea under the fizzing glare of a Tilly lamp. They found Oliver Leese, who had recently come from a conference with Montgomery, in a serious mood.

In Leese's own words afterwards,[1] 'the atmosphere among this group of dynamic men in the tiny corrugated-iron hut was tense, almost electric'. Looking round in the harsh light at the little group of generals, mostly commanders of Dominion troops, Leese apprehended the difficulty of the task before him. He could not command their unquestioning obedience as he could those of the British army. He had to secure their co-operation by conviction. In what he had to put before them there was no room for compromise. Each of them, he knew, had had victory snatched from him at the last moment in the previous desert fighting, and he had to secure their trust that they would not now be exposed to the likelihood of a similar fate again.

He began by telling them that the situation was now critical and that the offensive would collapse unless its momentum could be maintained and the initiative continually pursued. The threatened stalemate must be broken. He repeated to them what Montgomery had been saying to him an hour or two earlier: 'As long as you can make a German commander dance to your tune, you have nothing to fear; but once you allow the initiative to pass into his hands you are liable to have plenty of trouble.'

Therefore, Leese told his generals, the Army Commander had decided to follow up the Australians' initial success by a further thrust to the north, where Rommel had already betrayed his sensitiveness.

1. To the Author.

The Australians must 'draw everything they could on to themselves for a few days, by the twin threats of cutting off the enemy troops in the coastal pocket and of opening up the coast road behind the minefields.

He glanced at Morshead and saw no flicker of hesitancy disturb that swarthy face.

While the Australians were thus drawing fire upon themselves, Leese continued, the divisions of 30th and 10th Corps were to be regrouped at once in order to form a fresh surprise striking force for a break-out to the Rahman Track. This striking force, as originally intended, would consist of the armour of 10th Corps and the New Zealanders, accompanied by 9th Armoured Brigade.[1] These formations were now to be withdrawn into reserve to reform and recruit their strength for the new endeavour. The headquarters of the New Zealand division, however, together with their artillery, would remain in the line in charge of a sector and would be given the temporary loan of 151st Brigade (the Durham Brigade) from 50th Division.

Meantime – and here Leese knew that he was coming to what was perhaps the trickiest point for one of his audience – there would be a redistribution of 30th Corps divisions. This was necessary to fill the gap made by the withdrawal of the New Zealand infantry and to assist the Australians by abbreviating their frontage. The Highland Division was therefore to take over the sector of 20th Australian Brigade and there was to be a consequential side-step all along the bulge; the attenuated New Zealand division would shift into the Highland sector, the South Africans would take over from the New Zealanders on the northern part of Miteiriya Ridge and 4th Indian Division would move into the South African sector and would pass to the command of 13th Corps. The movements were to be complete by dawn on the 28th and the Australian attack was to be mounted that night.

1. 7th Armoured Division was not included, as erroneously supposed by some. Harding's division, still located in the south, was in Army Reserve and was still shown as such in Montgomery's directive of 30 October (not 20 October, as dated in the *Memoirs*).

This reshuffle, Leese was well aware, was quite a difficult tactical operation in the best of circumstances, and doubly difficult to carry out in forty-eight hours. But he was conscious that what was likely to provoke even more uneasiness, especially on the part of Pienaar, was the withdrawal of the armour into reserve. The South Africans were touchy and had to be handled with care. Like other infantry divisions, they were very 'over-run conscious', that is to say, apprehensive of being over-run by tanks, and the surrender of their 2nd Division at Tobruk was still for them a fresh and poignant memory. Leese was therefore careful to emphasize that as long as the enemy was kept on the defensive, by being hit hard on one sector or another, there was no fear of anyone being overrun. The great thing was to reorganize the front as quickly as possible and get the right people out and the right people in.

His uneasiness about the reaction of the South Africans, whose front would be extended somewhat, was not unwarranted, for at this juncture Pienaar made an interjection. He did not think, he said, that he would be in a position to do what was wanted, for he had not enough transport for the move.

This was exceedingly awkward, for it would have vitiated the whole operation. Freyberg, however, knew his man and his racial foible. In an undertone, he ascertained from Ray Queree, his GSO 1, what his own transport position was and said to him: 'Good! Then I'll spike his guns; he doesn't like accepting help.'

Aloud to Pienaar, Freyberg said:

'Is it only transport that's worrying you, Dan? No other difficulty?'

'No, just not enough transport.'

'Can we help you, then? I'll give you any transport you need.'

Pienaar's objection at once vanished at this shrewd and gentle challenge; he did not need help. He would manage somehow. Thereafter, as Leese knew he would, he played up splendidly. Indeed, all began to vie with each other to make the plan a complete and memorable success.

Such, in brief, were Montgomery's intentions for the renewed pursuit of his plan. There were those in high office, both in England

and in Africa, who, when they heard that the armour was to be 'withdrawn into reserve', were startled into the gloomiest reactions, apprehending that this meant that the attack had been a failure and was being called off. There was considerable uneasiness in the Cabinet at home. It was, however, a typical Monty manœuvre and he has said that whenever a commander is seen to withdraw troops at a critical moment in a battle one may surmise that he is about to win a victory.

However that may be, it is certain that, like the first decision to swing the attack to the north, this reorientation of forces at a critical moment was a brilliant conception. But on the already strained staff officers of Corps and divisions the task imposed yet more anxious hours and sleepless nights. Thus through the rolling clouds of dust, lashed by the occasional burst of shell fire, some 60,000 men, with fleets of vehicles, guns and tanks, jolted and crawled into their new positions in the next thirty-six hours, guided by the steadfast and devoted Military Police. The scenery was being shifted ready for the next dramatic act.

ROMMEL'S COUNTER-PLAN

Rommel also was making plans. In pursuance of his resolve to drive the British back whence they had started, all along the bulge, he was preparing to mount a major onslaught with all the force he could assemble. Curiously, it was to be directed at two points – against the Australians at Point 29 again, and against 1st Armoured Division in the Kidney sector. The attack was to be made the next afternoon (the 27th) and to take part in it he brought forward from reserve his most seasoned infantry, 90th Light Division, replacing them with the Trieste Division from Fuka and, after a great deal of hesitation, he at last ordered up 21st Panzer Division from the southern front, together with 50 per cent of the artillery that was in that sector.

This formidable blow was, therefore, to be struck by 21st and the remains of 15th PZ Divisions, the Littorio Armoured Division, 90th Light and 164th Light, the Bersaglieri and elements of the Trento Division. Thus the whole of Rommel's German divisions (but not

German Mark IV tank dug-in near the Rahman Track

Briggs's tank knocked out in the hour of victory. *R* to *L*, standing: Briggs, Roger Peake (his GSO 1) and Fowler (his CRA). Seated and still keeping radio contact, is probably Corporal Mullen. Tanks of 10th Hussars in background, some burning

Von Thoma dismounting from Singer's scout car

Montgomery and Von Thoma at 8th Army HQ; the third officer is probably Captain Robin Gray, Cameron Highlanders

the Ramcke Brigade) were to be thrown in and, as before, the attack was to be supported by the full weight of the Axis air forces. On the face of it, it was a tremendously serious challenge.

That night 21st PZ Division and the artillery reinforcements moved north in accordance with orders and were heartily bombed on the way.

Chapter Fifteen

THE RIFLEMEN AND THE GUNNERS

(Night 26/27th and Day 27th)

Attempts to Push On – The Great Stand at *Snipe* – Repulse of the Counter-attack – The *Woodcock* Affair

ATTEMPTS TO PUSH ON

First Armoured Division was not among those who were to be withdrawn into reserve immediately. In the next two days they were plunged into some of the stiffest fighting of the battle and, for one of their infantry regiments and the anti-tank gunners who accompanied them, the most glorious. The operation upon which they embarked on the night of D plus 3, 26 October, ran head-on to Rommel's massive counter-attack the next day, and the division, in repelling it, administered to the enemy tanks the same astringent medicine that our own tanks had so far been compelled to swallow. They proved again that the stoutly manned anti-tank gun on the ground could see off the enemy armour with heavy loss; they proved it, moreover, in a hastily occupied position devoid of natural advantage.

General Briggs's intention was to maintain his attempt to drive right through to the *Skinflint* report line on the Rahman Track, which, as we have seen, was the enemy's main lateral supply route. There, from positions of his own choosing, he hoped to invite attack from the German armour and destroy it.

Though the enemy was constantly laying fresh minefields, it was now mainly the anti-tank gun that was arresting the armour. The ground westward of the *Oxalic* ridge was extremely exposed and was securely covered by these guns. Briggs, therefore, resolved to attack two of the enemy's fortified localities by night with his motor infantry and to use these localities as firm bases from which his armoured brigades – the 24th still being under his command as well as his own 2nd – could thrust westward to *Skinflint*.

One of these fortified localities, disclosed by air photographs to be heavily gunned and wired, and known by the code-name of *Woodcock*,[1] lay on the north-west of Kidney Ridge, and the other known as *Snipe*,[2] and less heavily defended, about a mile to the south.

It had been Briggs's intention to attack *Woodcock* only on the night of the 25th, using both 2nd Battalion King's Royal Rifle Corps (the '60th Rifles', William Heathcoat-Amory) and 2nd Battalion The Rifle Brigade (Victor Turner). We shall go back a day to record in outline what happened then, as it formed the prelude to the larger work to follow and because it shows the problems of the desert war in startling form.

Turner's battalion had by midday on the 25th only just completed their exacting mine-clearance task, when he and Heathcoat-Amory were hurriedly summoned to the headquarters of 7th Motor Brigade to receive orders for the operation from Bosvile. Briggs himself was there. Bosvile was using as his HQ one of the new Churchill tanks which 1st Armoured Division had received for running and maintenance trials (not for operations) and its stout armour gave valuable protection against the shell fire under which the armoured formations' conferences were so often held.

Having received their orders, the two COs set out to reconnoitre a start-line, jolting forward by jeep along Star Route in the stifling hour of the mirage. At the end of this route were two stone cairns, which they agreed would serve them excellently. They then went farther forward to make contact with Roper-Caldbeck commanding

1. Map ref.: 86552966.
2. Map ref.: 86582948.

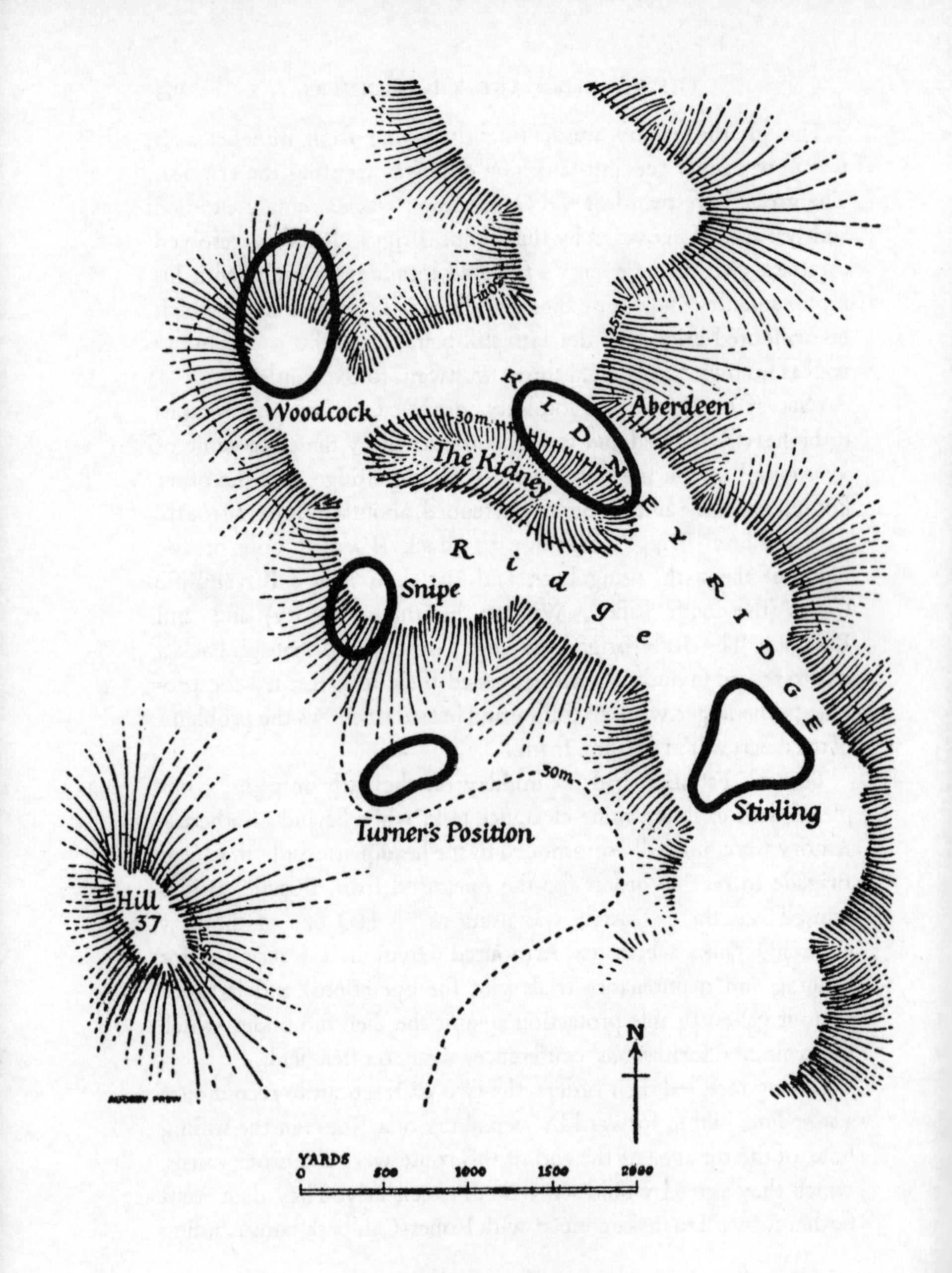

14. KIDNEY RIDGE

1st Black Watch, on the Highland Division's Black Line, through whose terrain they would have to pass in their attack.

The meeting took place under some high-velocity shellfire and a carrier of the Black Watch was hit and 'brewed up' within twenty yards of the three COs as they talked. To their astonishment, the riflemen were told that the faint ridge they could see ahead, which they would have to cross, was still held by the enemy and that 5th Black Watch, under Thomas Rennie, was actually to attack the outpost pointed out to them as *Stirling* that very night, with the same Zero hour as their own.[1] This took the riflemen aback, for Roper-Caldbeck's location of *Stirling* revealed a difference in map reading, between 1st Armoured Division and 51st Division, of 1,000 yards.

Turner and Heathcoat-Amory returned to their brigade headquarters in what Turner described as 'considerable doubt and confusion' and their proposed attack for that night was, naturally, cancelled. Rennie's operation against *Stirling*, as we have seen, was carried out successfully, as well as Campbell's against *Nairn*.

At 4 p.m. next day, the 26th, however, Turner and Heathcoat-Amory were again urgently summoned to Bosvile's headquarters. Briggs, who was again there himself, had now decided to attack *Woodcock* with 60th Rifles only and to launch 2nd Rifle Brigade on *Snipe*. The twin operations were to have top priority and to be supported by all the available artillery in 10th and 30th Corps. At first light on the 27th, 2nd Armoured Brigade was to move forward to *Woodcock* and 24th Brigade to *Snipe*, as their 'pivots of manœuvre'. It was thus what is popularly termed a 'two-pronged attack'.

Time was exceedingly short. Zero hour was 11 p.m. and only a couple of hours or so of daylight remained. Turner, assured of his own division's confidence in their map reading, hurried off through the dust and the intermittent shells to collect his scattered companies, and he sent Lieutenant Dick Flower to arrange a start-line that would not inconvenience the Black Watch. He then collected his officers and gave out his orders from Roper-Caldbeck's command post.

He had only just finished doing so when Flower returned to say

1. See Fig. 9. Early narratives confused the two Black Watch battalions.

that he had fixed a start-line, but that Roper-Caldbeck was still convinced that Highland Division's map locations were right and the armoured division's wrong. This gave Turner 'a bad fright', as he worked out that, if this were so, the artillery plan to support his attack would catch the flank of 5th Black Watch in their new position.

Very concerned at this danger, he broke away from his Order Group and made such speed as he could through the darkness to the headquarters of 7th Motor Brigade yet once more, leaving his second-in-command, Major Tom Pearson, to collect the battalion and their accompanying gunners and sappers and dispose them on the start-line.

At Bosvile's headquarters he ran, unexpectedly, into a formidable gathering of the 'top brass' – Lumsden, Briggs, Wimberley and 'Frizz' Fowler (Briggs's CRA), besides Bosvile. Turner put the urgent problem to them, whereupon Briggs observed with apparent decisiveness:

'My CRE has surveyed in Star Route and he tells me that it is not more than 200 yards out at any point throughout the whole length of its six miles.'

Wimberley countered, however, by saying with equal emphasis: 'I am quite sure we are right, as we have *walked* every damned yard of the seven miles from our home minefield to where we are now, and we can't be wrong. So we can't be far off the mark.'

Lumsden chimed in with one of his light-hearted racing analogies and said:

'Come, gentlemen, I think we might make a book on this.'

'You seem to forget, sir,' Wimberley said, 'that I am a canny Scot, and, what's more, I've an idea that you are, too.'

'Oh,' Lumsden replied with a laugh, 'I think we might risk a bawbee or two!'

Fowler brought the discussion back to a more practical note. 'As far as this attack is concerned,' he said, 'there is no real cause for alarm, as my fire plan will be over-safe for the Black Watch.'

It was now the turn of the man most concerned in the controversy.

'In that case, sir,' Turner broke in, 'it will be no bloody good to me at all.'

'I'm afraid it is too late to alter anything now,' Fowler said.

'Very well. I shall just have to form up as if the Armoured Division's interpretation is correct and if it isn't, I shall just march on the flank of the falling shells.'

With this very unsatisfactory conclusion, Turner hurried off into the night to his battalion, already waiting on the start-line.

The attack on *Woodcock* by 60th Rifles is best related first. Accompanied by some guns of 76th Anti-Tank Regiment, the battalion began its advance in clouds of dust raised by the barrage and by its own bren-gun carriers, which, in the motor battalion method, preceded the soldiers on foot and caused them great difficulty in keeping direction. Overcoming a little opposition, they followed, as best they could, the shadowy clouds and the noise, and when the noise stopped they stopped also and put themselves in a posture of defence.

First light, however, showed Heathcoat-Amory that he was south of *Woodcock* and in an exposed position that would be wholly untenable by day. He, therefore, moved at once to a more secure position. The arrow had missed its mark in the murk of desert war.

THE GREAT STAND AT 'SNIPE'

A little farther south, the small mixed force that Victor Turner was to lead in the attack on *Snipe* had been hurriedly assembling in the dark, moving gingerly through the mines. We shall associate ourselves with this exploit as intimately as possible, for it was in every sense remarkable. Not only was it to show the British soldier in one of his finest hours, not only was it unexpectedly to deal one of the most telling blows against the German counter-attack that matured next afternoon, but also it was to illustrate in the most vivid fashion how the mischances, misunderstandings and dark uncertainties that beset the soldier in a vague and confused situation can be overcome by his own self-reliance and battle discipline.

Let us first look at some of the men who were to give these valiant proofs.

The force allotted to Turner for this exploit consisted of his own battalion of the Rifle Brigade, the residual part (after casualties) of a battery of 76th Anti-Tank Regiment, Royal Artillery, and sixteen sappers of 7th Field Squadron, Royal Engineers, under a 'damned good' subaltern, as Turner called him, Lieutenant N. Graham.

The riflemen and sappers had been through a very trying time on the Minefield Task Force. After three days and two nights continuously on a mission that taxed their nerve and their stamina, they had been able to snatch only a few hours' sleep. Indeed, Tim Marten, the Rifle Brigade adjutant, had not slept for five days. The riflemen had been operating in separate and dispersed companies on different minefield lanes, and they had now to be hurriedly collected together and launched into an operation for which a motor battalion was not intended and for which it was not properly equipped.

For, as noted briefly in Chapter Eight, a motor battalion was very strong in fire power but very weak in numbers. It was trained as a highly mobile, semi-independent unit for ranging far and wide in the open desert. Its strength lay in the thirty-three bren-carriers of its Scout platoons, its anti-tank company newly equipped with sixteen 6-pdrs, its machine-gun platoons equipped with the Vickers gun and its platoon of 3-inch mortars. Unlike the majority of conventional infantry units, it was highly efficient in radio telephony.

In addition, 2nd RB quite unlawfully possessed a number of machine-guns which they had 'salvaged' from wrecked British aircraft and installed in their carriers and with which they had delighted during the desert war in sallying out at night like moss-troopers to 'beat-up' the enemy leaguers.

Thus the only men armed with the rifle, bayonet and grenade of the assault soldier were the men in the three 'motor companies', who numbered only some ninety in all, unless the machine-gunners discarded their Vickers. Casualties in the mine-clearing had reduced this number to seventy-six and the bren-carriers were down to twenty-two. Indeed, the whole combined force of riflemen, gunners and sappers in the epic battle now to be fought numbered less than 300.

Victor Turner himself was a Regular soldier of moderate but solid build, prematurely bald, very energetic and lively, with fifteen months' experience of desert warfare. Some of his officers and men had had more. In his battalion there was a dash of Irish, but, otherwise, the rank and file were nearly all Londoners and very largely from the East End; the coming action, indeed, was to prove once more that in a tight corner there is no better fighter than your Cockney. It was characteristic of a Rifle battalion that most of the men, and several of the officers also, such as Turner himself and Tom Bird, were of small stature.

Except for some recent reinforcements, they were young desert veterans who, like the other Rifle regiments, had been accustomed to serving as handmaids to the armour, playing the less spectacular rôle on many a turbulent stage. They were not afraid of tanks, which they had faced many times, and were accustomed to living hard, to getting a move on and to fending for themselves in the most trying situations. Many of them were Regular soldiers and several had already been decorated.

Prominent among the men were: the swarthy and handsome East-ender, Sergeant Charles Caliston, formerly a champion boy boxer, very strong, finely co-ordinated in physique and highly thought of by his officers; the strongly-built, four-square Regular, Sergeant J. E. Swann; the smart Sergeant J. A. Hine from Acton, another Regular already wearing the Military Medal; Sergeant Ayris, from Limehouse; the puckish Sergeant Miles, from Southwark; Corporal A. Francis, 'magnificent Cockney' and a modern edition of the 1914 'Old Bill', tremendously reliable and always seeking where he could help; Sergeant G. H. Brown, who was reputed once to have stolen a railway engine, but who had won a very fine DCM; Company Sergeant-Major Jack Atkins from Skegness, slender and intelligent; the squat, tough Sergeant Dolling and the equally tough Rifleman D. A. Chard, often in trouble when not fighting. All these and others we shall see standing up without the blink of an eye to the repeated assaults of the German and Italian tanks.

The companies were commanded by David Bassett (A company),

Michael Mosley (B), Charles Liddell (C) and Tom Bird (Anti-Tank Company), who had already won the Military Cross and Bar; 'Tim' Marten, highly intelligent and fortunate in having a sense of humour, has been noted as Turner's adjutant.

The anti-tank platoons were commanded with a fire and spirit at times little short of the spectacular by Lieutenants J. E. B. Naumann, J. E. B. Toms, J. B. D. Irwin and A. B. Holt-Wilson; all but the last-named were to be hit and knocked out during the coming fight.

Allotted to the battalion for this exploit were eleven gun detachments and other details of 239th Anti-Tank Battery, from 76th Anti-Tank Regiment, Royal Artillery. Five of these guns, however, did not succeed in arriving at the rendezvous and the remaining one and a half Troops were led by Lieutenant Alan Baer, very tall, very lean and angular, an Oxford undergraduate, who commanded G Troop. He was a keen musician, an interest he shared with Alex Barclay, CO of The Bays, who was a friend of Cole Porter's and who kept a jazz band recruited from Joe Loss's dance orchestra.

With Baer was another Troop commander, Second Lieutenant Fred Willmore, an athletic young man, recently commissioned and wearing the ribbon of the Military Medal. He brought only two guns of his Troop (Sergeants Wood and Hillyer), his other two having been blown up on mines during the Division's struggle to get forward on the first day.

The regiment had originated from North Wales, having, before conversion, been a Territorial battalion of the Royal Welch Fusiliers. There was fine material in these detachments: the thick-set, hefty Sergeant Bob Smith, a steelworker from Sheffield, very strong in body, stalwart in morale and a fine inspiration in battle: Sergeant Cullen, a quiet, well-educated and exemplary Scot; the steady, well-turned-out Sergeant Ronald Wood, and others whom we shall notice.

These gunners of 76th Anti-Tank Regiment were more experienced with the 6-pdr than the riflemen, who had had little practice with it so far. As befitted those whose task was to await, while under close fire, the menacing onset of tanks, their great quality was their steadiness. Before leaving to join Turner, Baer had been warned prophetically by Major R. A. Wyrley-Birch, the Rhodesian, second-in-command of the regiment and one of the most experienced desert fighters: 'From all the signs, I should think it highly probable that you are in for a death-or-glory affair.'

Turner likewise gave the warning to his Order Group that this would be a 'last man, last round' assignment, and Baer, as he listened, experienced that mixture of excitement and self-doubt which is the experience of most men at the challenge of the ultimate test. The men, for their part, listened quietly and gravely.

One other small group was added to Turner's force – Captain Noyes, 2nd RHA, who, with his signallers, came as FOO.

Such in outline was the composition of the little force hastily assembled in the lines of 1st Black Watch for the attack on *Snipe*.

The moon was getting later now. The ground, beyond the *Oxalic* line of ridges, changed suddenly from hard rock to treacherous soft sand and a scattering of low camelthorn scrub. It became almost entirely featureless and extremely exposed, except for the usual small, anonymous folds in the desert and except for an oval mound about three-quarters of a mile in length, seen on the map as a 35-metre ring contour[1] and rising to 37 metres, which we shall accordingly call Hill 37, for it is important to our story. The exposed nature of this terrain was, indeed, one of the chief reasons why 1st Armoured Division had so far been unable to get on beyond *Oxalic*.

In short terms, what Turner was called upon to do with this force was to make a night dash through enemy-held country, to establish an island of resistance until the arrival of 24th Armoured Brigade next morning and to continue holding it while the tanks operated forward.

The orders that Turner had given a few hours before to his mixed force required that the advance should be on a bearing of 233 degrees, 'unless the barrage comes down on a different bearing, in which case you follow the barrage'. Zero hour was 11 p.m. The advance was to be led by two bren-carrier platoons in the usual motor

1. Map squares 864293 and 864292.

battalion method, followed by A Company on the right and C Company on the left on foot, with B Company following up.

All the guns, however, were to remain on the start-line under his second-in-command, Major Tom Pearson, together with the third Scout platoon, the wireless sets, the doctor (Captain Arthur Picton) and his ambulances and the Section trucks, carrying water, rations and ammunition, until the 'success signal' was given by the attacking companies.

As for consolidation tasks on capture of the objective, all that Turner could do was to give each company a sector of the compass, A Company having a sector of 140 degrees facing north-west to north-east, B Company about the same facing south-east to south-west, and C Company completing the circle round to the north-west again. The anti-tank guns were apportioned to these sectors for all-round defence.

On his arrival at the start-line only a few minutes before the barrage was due, Turner, in no little anxiety of mind, found that his command had also got there only twenty minutes before. The moon not yet being up, the night was very dark and cold and the move forward of the sub-units out of the minefield lanes, now 18 inches deep in fine dust, had been made in conditions similar to those of a dense night fog. Two of the anti-tank portees had collided and, together with their guns, could go no farther. The start-line was under intermittent shellfire, but the force just had time to dispose itself in the order of attack before the barrage, which was due to begin at Z minus 5. They began to move up at once and at 11 o'clock the barrage was in full blast.

It was then observed that the barrage was on a bearing not of 233 degrees, but of about 270 degrees. The companies immediately wheeled to the west, but it took ten minutes to change front, and it was not until ten past eleven, with the barrage already well ahead, that the carriers advanced, followed by the infantry and sappers. The moon was now up, its large face tinted yellow by the dust particles that filled the atmosphere.

Turner, wearing corduroy trousers and a leathern jacket, was riding in a wireless jeep, driven by Tom Bird, who, like several officers, was wearing the old desert hand's *poshteen*. Almost immediately the jeep drove straight into an empty enemy weapon pit. It was extricated with difficulty, but, otherwise, for the first thousand yards all went well; there was a little fire, but no opposition on the ground.

Some barbed wire was then encountered and the carriers were delayed for five minutes while Graham's sappers went in to test for mines. None was found and the advance continued. Parties of enemy were observed, running away, and the carriers opened fire on them. The going became exceedingly bad, with much soft sand. More scattered groups of the enemy were seen running away and twenty German prisoners were captured without resistance; they were engineers.

Tim Marten was following Turner in one of the 15-cwt wireless trucks known as a 'gin palace' and he was measuring progress by the vehicle's speedometer, reporting from time to time by air to Captain Charles Wood, GSO 3 at 7th Motor Brigade headquarters. Thus: 'We have just done the Cambridgeshire distance.' Then: 'Getting on for the Cesarewitch now.' And finally: 'Just running up to the winning post.'

The barrage, however, went on and on. The 2,000 yards' advance that Turner had counted upon was passed and when some 3,000 yards had been traversed Turner, his mind nagged all the time by the doubts about map locations, became anxious. He, therefore, asked Noyes, the FOO, to call for a round of smoke from 2nd RHA on the objective. As this landed within 300 yards of him, he thought it good enough and halted the advance.

In fact, the force never reached the correct map reference of *Snipe* at all, and finished up 900 yards approximately SSE of it.[1]

The success signal was given both by wireless and by Verey light at a quarter past midnight. This was what Pearson, with the anti-tank guns and supply trucks, had been waiting for back on the start-line. He had been under brisk shellfire for about an hour and at about 11.30 a lone enemy aircraft, after releasing a parachute flare, had dropped a stick of bombs which set two vehicles on fire

1. At 86622939.

and caused a few casualties. Picton, the stout-hearted medical officer, went to their assistance and was treating the wounded when the success signal went up. Pearson started forward at once with his guns and vehicles, leaving the doctor and his ambulances behind. Events were to prevent Picton from reaching a gallant company of men who sorely needed him. Mercifully, however, his devoted medical orderly, Rifleman S. H. Burnhope, very small, not very significant, coupling his medical duties with those of company barber, but stout of heart, was among those who went forward.

Pearson and his party had a rough ride. One after another his vehicles sank into the soft sand and there was a long delay while sand-mats, shovels and tow-ropes were got out. The 6-pdrs were in the worst case. Those of 239th Battery were seriously handicapped by the fact that some of the vehicles were not equipped with four-wheel drive. Alan Baer himself, however, was fortunately riding in one of the new American half-tracked vehicles of which there had been a small issue – the White Scout Car – driven by Lance-Bombardier Voce. Accompanied by Willmore and Sergeant Norrie, he picked his way forward by compass under the yellow moon, escaped contact with any roaming enemy, reached the supposed *Snipe* position, made a reconnaissance and drove back. Making three or four journeys, he towed his guns up one by one with their detachments and a little ammunition. His remaining guns got up on their portees. All six of the Royal Artillery guns that had set out thus got forward.

Pearson, also making two or three trips, got forward thirteen of the Rifle Brigade guns, making, together with the RA guns, nineteen 6-pdrs in all. Water, rations and machine-gun ammunition arrived in sufficient quantities in trucks, but, as the unexpected events were to prove, there was far too little ammunition for the 6-pdrs. Off-loading was completed by 3.45 a.m.

Meanwhile, the motor companies, very thin on the ground, had taken up their allotted sectors and had dug-in. The sand was excessively loose and would not hold to the shape of a trench or weapon pit, but slid back as it was dug. The place turned out to be a German engineer-stores depot and it fortunately provided Turner with a dug-out, which he took as his headquarters and in which he posted Marten and the wireless set, manned by Signalman 'Busty' Francis and another. A few other small dug-outs were also found in the area occupied. Telephone lines were run out from Turner's command-post to each of the companies. The ground was foul with excreta and the bodies of some dead Germans lay about. The sand being now undisturbed by vehicles or shells, the moon shone clearly over a wide distance. Turner was able to see that the position was in a slight depression, which, when daylight came, turned out to be in the shape of a shallow oval, about 900 yards long and 400 wide.

While the motor companies were consolidating, the carriers of the Scout platoons, as was their wont in motor battalions, drove outwards to reconnoitre and cover the consolidation. Those of A Company went out north-westward without incident. Those of C Company, under Dick Flower, however, had a spirited brush with the enemy. Having gone 250 yards, they encountered barbed wire, which suggested another minefield. Resolved to investigate, Flower found a gap and went through it for fully a mile in the moonlight. Some sixty enemy appeared and began to run away. The carriers engaged them and took fourteen prisoners.

About 200 yards away in the moonlight Flower then made out the shapes of some thirty-five tanks together with a number of soft-skinned vehicles. Most people would have been satisfied with obtaining this useful information and would have withdrawn in the presence of tanks, but Flower brazenly opened fire with his bren-guns and set fire to three vehicles. At this contumacious behaviour, the enemy tanks moved out and opened fire. They hit an old derelict vehicle a few yards from one of Flower's carriers. The derelict burst into flames, the carriers were illuminated and one of them was hit by a shot from the tanks. The prisoners made a dash to escape but were mown down by both friend and enemy. The tanks advanced menacingly against the carriers, firing both their guns and machine-guns, and Flower, returning their fire, by mere instinct, withdrew before them. Thus did Turner's small force begin its exploit in the offensive spirit that was to inspire it throughout.

What Flower had stumbled upon was in fact a night leaguer of a mixed force of tanks, self-propelled guns and vehicles, part German and part Italian, under the command of the German, Colonel Teege, and known as the Stiffelmayer Battle Group. It was located on the long mound to the south-west which we have called Hill 37 and beyond the brow of which Flower had penetrated. It was soon evident to Turner, in fact, that the desert around him was, except to his rear, alive with enemy. All to the westward numerous camp fires were to be seen at no great distance. The moon and their lights enabled him to discover another tank leaguer about 1,000 yards to the northward, which was, in fact, a leaguer of 15th Panzer Division. Numbers of enemy vehicles could also be seen.

By now the anti-tank guns had arrived and had been sited as well as was possible by night. The Vickers and bren-guns had been posted. Digging-in had been barely completed when, at about 3.45, the deep-throated rumble of tanks in motion was heard from the direction of Teege's leaguer. Very soon their sombre shapes could be seen advancing in two bodies. One was obviously shaping course to join the northern leaguer of 15th PZ Division, but the other made straight for Turner's position, moving in line-head.

The guns were immediately manned and loaded. Fire was withheld until there was a certainty of a kill with the first shot, for the 6-pdr's poor sights made night-shooting very chancy. As the leading tank of the more southerly column drew near, it was seen to be a big Mark IV, with its menacing long gun. It was permitted to penetrate right into C Company's terrain and hit at a range of thirty yards by Sergeant Brown. The shot glowed red-hot as it sunk into the armour-plate and the tank burst into flames. At the same time a Russian 7·62 cm self-propelled gun was likewise knocked out and 'brewed up' on A Company's sector on the west by the broad-shouldered Sergeant Swann, who, determined that his position as platoon sergeant should not deny him a shoot, took control of Corporal Cope's gun.

The remainder of the enemy force immediately altered course and made away, but a number, as was to appear at first light, halted and took cover in small, scrub-smudged folds in the ground only a few hundred yards to the west.

Only one of the crew of the big Mark IV escaped. Leaping out, he ran to a trench a little way off, whence, with commendable aggression, he sniped at the British positions for the remainder of the night until a rifleman, locating him at first light, crept out and finished him off with a grenade.

These two kills with the new guns caused immense jubilation. The riflemen had heard with delight of the exploit of the London Rifle Brigade two days before on the edge of the Australian front and were eager to emulate their brother Green Jackets. From this moment the garrison was fired to a most astonishing degree with an eager and offensive confidence. As events disclosed themselves, this spirit swelled into something even more impressive – the exultant spirit of the happy warrior.

Shortly after this the garrison unaccountably sustained a serious loss in the disappearance of 2nd RHA's FOO. For some reason, never explained, Noyes left Turner's dug-out at about 4 a.m., possibly to find a good position for observation, lost his way, ended up miles away in the lines of the London Rifle Brigade, whence he was never able to return. His signallers remained, but the lack of a FOO was to be sorely felt.

At 5.45 a.m. Pearson returned to the Highland Division lines with the non-fighting transport, taking the prisoners with him. He also was never able to get back to the position, urgent though its needs became, for at the approach of daylight the pace of events began to quicken. Sergeant Swann and CSM Atkins should have gone back with him, but asked permission to stay.

Half an hour later, as the sky began to change to the colour of pewter and the bitter pre-dawn wind whipped across the desert, Turner was able to assess more clearly the nature of his footing in the inhospitable landscape. The almost flat scene, stretching for a mile and a half all round, shadowed by the faint anonymous folds and ripples of the desert, was overlooked by the slight elevations that formed the horizon on all sides except the south. Patches of low, scrubby camel's thorn stippled and darkened the desert canvas

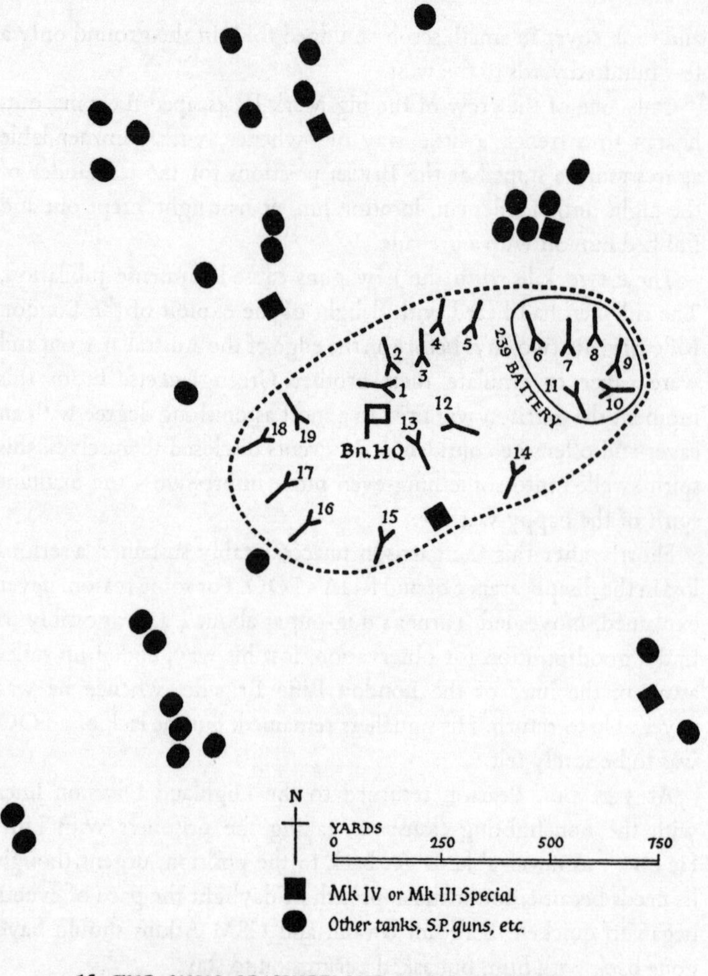

15. THE GUNS OF 'SNIPE' AND THEIR VICTIMS

From the original in the report of 1 Armoured Division Committee of Investigation, showing the position of the 6-pdrs, after re-deployment of some, and the wrecks still found at the inquiry a month later

1 HINE
2 MILES
3 SAUNDERS
4 BRETT
5 NEWMAN
6 HILLYER
7 CULLEN
8 BINKS
9 WOOD
10 NORRY
11 SMITH
12 SAVILL
13 KEHOE
14 AYRIS
15 PEARSON
16 CALISTAN
17 DOLLING
18 BROWN
19 COPE

here and there, affording some exiguous cover for those who knew how to use it.

This scrub extended into the shallow oval in which the garrison had taken station and they had been quick to take advantage of it as they sited their weapon pits and trenches, knowing well, however, that full daylight would show the need to alter their dispositions. The excellence of their concealment and digging, indeed, saved them from a great many casualties in what Turner called the 'deluge of fire poured down on us for the rest of that day'. The gun-pits were never really pin-pointed by the enemy. Turner noted, however, that the faint undulations and the scrub provided some strips and zones of dead ground which an equally experienced enemy could put to advantage in any attack upon him.

It was in this grey dawn twilight that the enemy tank leaguers both to the north and to the south-west were to be seen starting into motion. For some such activity Turner had been watching, for he knew that at the approach of light all tanks would break leaguer and move out to whatever was their mission for the day. Contrary to his expectation, they moved westward.

To the surprise of the garrison, a number of the German panzers which had halted in dead ground after their attempted move in the night suddenly broke cover at ranges of from 600 to 800 yards. They thus offered highly tempting rear and flank targets at killing ranges to the riflemen's gun detachment as they peered out in the biting wind.

In such circumstances, it was perhaps not in accord either with doctrine or with their mission for the garrison to disclose their positions and engage. But they did not feel in a calculating spirit that day and could not resist the temptation to attack. The dawn was shattered as eight or nine guns barked with the 6-pdr's sharp, high-velocity crack. The results were spectacular. Eight tanks and self-propelled guns were destroyed to the north (all being found derelict on the battlefield subsequently) and a further eight were claimed from Teege's battle group to the south-west, of which three were still derelict on the ground a month later. Upon the unfortunate crews who attempted to escape the machine-guns poured their streams of bullets.

Bursts of unrestrained cheers ran through the garrison at the thrill of this dramatic success. A ripple of exaltation seized all ranks. From that moment they felt themselves to be on top of the enemy. Sixteen birds for breakfast was a very good start to the day's shooting.

This display of aggression, however, was answered by the inevitable counter-action. Their position disclosed, the garrison was heavily shelled. Sergeant Saunders was killed and his gun knocked out by a direct hit and two other guns were damaged beyond immediate use.

The sky changed from pewter to pearl and the crimson streamers that preceded the approach of the desert sun spread out along the eastern horizon. It became evident that some of the gun positions must be altered. Thus, Alan Baer found one of 239th Battery gun's field of fire obscured by a hump a cricket pitch away. Moreover, some guns had dug themselves into the soft sand in the last shoot – as was to recur frequently during the day – and had to be pulled out and resited. To alter positions in daylight was a dangerous and difficult task. The bren-carriers had to be called upon to shift the guns and the movement immediately attracted enemy fire. Captain Hugo Salmon, Bird's second-in-command, was gravely wounded and lingered for some six hours before he died, devotedly tended to the last by Rifleman Burnhope, the medical orderly.

At about the same time a single German soldier, who had been lying concealed in the very centre of the position, was seen to leap up and run at full speed westward. He was unarmed. Quixotically, the riflemen let him go. Not a shot was fired. 'We all instinctively felt,' said Bird afterwards, 'that he was not fair game.'

Full daylight revealed to Turner only too clearly the nakedness of his position. To the north, scarcely to be recognized as elevations, he thought he could make out Kidney Ridge and *Woodcock*. Much more obviously and more threateningly, the mound of Hill 37 appeared to south-west, the point of observation of much of the fire directed against the garrison. To north, west and south enemy movement and activity of all sorts was to be seen. Marten, coming up from the dug-out where he had been reporting events by wireless to 7th Motor Brigade, looked round the morning scene, where the shadows were beginning to sharpen under the rising sun, and asked:

'Have we come to the right place, sir?'

Turner answered: 'God knows. But here we are and here we damned well stay.'

He expected 24th Armoured Brigade to appear on the scene very soon but, meanwhile, long used to work in close association with gunners, he was fretting at the loss of his FOO. The picture around him was alive with targets and he would need gunner support if attacked by infantry. On his orders, Marten reported the loss of Noyes to brigade headquarters and asked urgently for a replacement. One was promised, but never arrived, for from now onwards the British lines to the east and the approaches to them were so scourged by enemy shellfire that nothing could get forward.

The anticipated appearance of 24th Armoured Brigade was not long delayed, but it was of a totally unexpected nature. At 7.30 a.m., as the huge crimson globe of the sun began to climb out of the British lines, great clouds of dust heralded their approach. The Shermans and Grants breasted the slight crest of the *Oxalic* line and halted to search the exposed ground ahead with their field-glasses. Two thousand yards ahead they saw a strongpoint of guns and weapon pits among the camel's thorn, with a sprinkling of burnt-out German tanks hard by. Not recognizing what was intended to be their own 'pivot of manœuvre', they promptly opened fire on it with high explosive. Much of the fire fell on 239th Battery, who lay nearest to them.

This was galling. In an attempt to stop it, Turner sent out his intelligence Officer, Jack Wintour, on the dangerous mission of making his way to our tanks in a bren-carrier. This Wintour accomplished. He succeeded in abating the fire of the leading squadron, but the remainder of the brigade continued to bombard their friends. The irrepressible Wintour then calmly returned.

At 8 o'clock, 24th Brigade began to move forward towards Turner's position. Immediately they did so Turner observed about twenty-five German tanks, nearly all of which were the latest and most powerful long-gunned 'Specials', taking up hull-down positions behind Hill 37 to oppose them. In doing so, they presented themselves as targets to Turner's guns. In spite of the long range, the 6-pdrs at once engaged the big tanks and brewed up three of them at 1,100 yards. As their crews baled out they were shot down by machine-guns from the advancing Shermans. The armoured brigade now knew who were their friends.

Half-an-hour later the Shermans joined hands with the garrison. Instead of bringing the relief that it promised, however, their arrival brought on a fight of violence and confusion. Drawn as by a magnet, the enemy attacked our exposed and halted tanks with every weapon that they could bring to bear – from their hull-down tanks, from the anti-tank guns of 115th Panzer Grenadiers and 33rd Panzerjagers and from the heavy shells of their medium artillery.

In this onslaught our tanks got very much the worst of things. Both sides laid down smoke screens and the whole area became an inferno of smoke, bursting high explosive, dust and darting tracers. The German armour employed the highly effective tactics of putting down a round of smoke accurately just in front of one of our tanks and then firing into the smoke with armour-piercing shot. Within fifteen minutes seven Shermans were on fire within Turner's position.

The worst of this fierce conflict took place in the sector occupied by 239th Battery. Sergeant Bob Smith's gun, which was close to one of our Shermans, was knocked out by a direct hit, and he was blinded for several hours; Bombardier Barnes and Gunner Mercer were killed and Gunner Kane shell-shocked. The stalwart sergeant, in spite of his blindness, moved over to join his friend, Sergeant Ronald Wood, taking Kane with him and nursing him until he recovered. Sergeant Norry's gun, similarly placed close to a Sherman, was also knocked out, but with no serious casualties. A moment later the tank itself was hit and burst into flames with great violence.

In a trench nearby were Lance-Bombardier Voce, Baer's driver, and Gunner Fred Beeson, his soldier-servant. They saw a man screaming with the agony of burns, trying to escape from the turret. They leapt from their trench, clambered on to the burning tank and bore him to their trench. There, some time afterwards, he died.

Quite clearly, it was out of the question for the armoured brigade to stay in this death trap. It was certainly not the 'firm base' it was intended to be. Very rightly, they withdrew to hull-down positions on the *Oxalic* ridge, leaving a void of a mile and a quarter between themselves and the garrison, who were not sorry to see them go.

As they withdrew, they were attacked by some German tanks and guns from the north in the Kidney area and this gave the gunners of 239th Battery an opportunity to have their first shoot. A Mark IV was clearly visible at about 1,800 yards. The range was extreme for a 6-pdr and Sergeant Binks, when urged to shoot by Mike Mosley, the RB company commander, rightly declined. This was completely against his training. A little later, when the Mark IV moved, Binks, to the mild annoyance of his own watching Troop commander, was persuaded by Mosley to 'have a go'. With his third shot Binks hit and halted the tank, which was immediately towed away by another.

At about the same time (9 a.m.) considerable movement of Italian troops gave indications that they were about to attack the garrison on the south with infantry. Turner ordered the Scout platoon of C Company to 'see them off'. The carriers did so accordingly, engaging the enemy infantry with small arms so effectively that many were killed and wounded and the rest ran away westwards. Two captured British 6-pdrs were then seen being towed into position. These also the carriers engaged and put the towing vehicles out of action. 'During the next half-hour,' Flower recorded, 'many excellent sniping targets were offered by small groups of Italians as they tried to run away'. With their bren-gun ammunition running low, rifles only were used.

Turner, 'hopping mad' at being shelled by his friends, as he continued to be for some time, and exasperated by the lack of a FOO, became seriously concerned also for the wounded. If the doctor could not come up, somehow an attempt must be made to get the more seriously wounded back to him, whatever the risk. Turner accordingly ordered Captain Peter Shepherd-Cross, accompanied by Sergeant Sampher, to make a dash in three bren-carriers.

The loading of the wounded into the carriers was done under fire and the little convoy was shelled all the way back. Shepherd-Cross's carrier actually sustained a direct hit from a 75-mm but miraculously was not seriously damaged. The little convoy got safely home. It was Shepherd-Cross's intention to bring back Picton, together with more ammunition, which was urgently needed. He found Tom Pearson standing by with a convoy trying to get through, as he continued to do most of the day, but whenever he attempted to cross the ridge the convoy was immediately lashed with fire which it could not hope to get through.

The garrison was, therefore, now alone and cut-off, with virtually no hope of relief. Turner and Bird went round the position telling the men so and that they would have to stick it out. The officers were answered by little grins and Cockney jokes. The men closed more firmly up to their weapons, bracing themselves, entirely confident. What had happened so far had been a sharp enough experience, but not a severe test. They had no doubt that such a test would come.

The continued resistance of the island outpost had become a serious nuisance to the enemy, who now evidently decided that they must wipe it out. Two further direct attacks upon it were mounted at 10 o'clock. They were part of a two-pronged offensive operation ordered by Colonel Teege from behind Hill 37. One prong of this operation was directed against 24th Armoured Brigade, who had just retired. This was to be carried out by some twenty-five to thirty German tanks of the Stiffelmayer Group. To make this attack, however, the German tanks would be exposed to dangerous flanking fire from Turner's outpost and Teege accordingly ordered the Italian element of this battle group to attack the garrison and wipe it out. This attack was entrusted to Captain Preve, of 12th Battalion, 133rd Tank Regiment, Littorio Division. He set out from Hill 37 with thirteen M13 tanks.

On seeing them advance, Turner ordered the guns of Sergeants Brown and Dolling to be moved to the west sector at once. The detachments responded without hesitation, but the soft sand caused the wheels to sink to their axles. Carriers were then called in and, there being no proper towing-hook, the trails of the guns were hitched up with tow ropes. The awkward manœuvre, naturally, drew enemy fire at once and Lieutenant R. M. Salt and three men were killed.

The Italian attack was, however, easily beaten off. Four tanks were hit quickly. The remainder did not attempt to press the attack and withdrew. While this attempt was in progress, the German tanks of the Stiffelmayer Group were seen to move out of their hull-down positions behind Hill 37, driving eastwards across the southern front of the garrison. Their intention to attack 24th Brigade was clear to Turner and his men.

The riflemen, having disposed of the Italians, at once engaged the Germans, who presented broadside-on targets at about 1,000 yards. Thereupon the German tank commander detached half his strength directly towards the garrison. Notwithstanding this threat, the riflemen continued to engage the broadside-on tanks attacking 24th Brigade, and the latter were similarly presented with broadside-on targets by the tanks attacking the garrison. In this spirited 'cross ruff', as Turner described it, not fewer than eight German tanks were set on fire, several others were hit and the remainder withdrew behind Hill 37.

By now it was nearly 11 o'clock in the forenoon and the position had become extremely hot in both senses of the word. The desert was quivering with heat. The gun detachments and the platoons squatted in their pits and trenches, the sweat running in rivers down their dust-caked faces. There was a terrible stench. The flies swarmed in black clouds upon the dead bodies and the excreta and tormented the wounded. The place was strewn with burning tanks and carriers, wrecked guns and vehicles, and over all drifted the smoke and the dust from bursting high explosive and from the blasts of guns. Six more carriers had been hit and set on fire. The 6-pdrs of Sergeants Hine and Dolling had been knocked out and only thirteen remained in action. Sergeant Swann sent the tough little Hine to take over the gun of Corporal Cope, who had been hit. Several of the detachments were down to two or three men and officers were manning guns to replace casualties. Other detachments were doubling up. Thus, one of the guns was manned by Lieutenant A. B. Holt-Wilson, Sergeant Ayris and Rifleman Chard – a very tough team who later in the day were to handle their gun with exceptional daring.

But the offensive spirit had firmly seized upon all ranks. The bursting shells that shook the ground and the heavy shot that smashed a gun or carrier, or that took the breath from one's lungs with the vacuum of its close passing, could not shake that spirit. Every kill was acclaimed. At last they had got a weapon that could knock-out the panzers. Gone was any thought of 'lying doggo', any conception of mere defence of a 'pivot of manœuvre'. They eagerly engaged every target within range. The gunners of 239th Battery, who so far had had only one target, buried their dead on the spot, manned their brens and rifles and occupied themselves with 'rabbit shooting'. On three sides of the island there was enemy movement of every sort – parties on foot, trucks, staff cars, motor-cycles. Turner, Bird and other officers moved about from gun to gun throughout the morning, so also did Rifleman Burnhope, giving to the wounded, including a few German wounded found in the position, such succour as his scanty medical stores allowed.

The most serious concern, however, was the shortage of 6-pdr ammunition. Bird and the great-hearted Corporal Francis – the 'young Old Bill' as Bird called him – set about transferring the heavy green boxes from one gun to another by jeep, unconcerned by the heavy burst of fire which this blatant movement invited. The shortage was particularly acute on the south-western sector, facing Hill 37, where Lieutenant Jack Toms's guns were sited.

It was precisely from this direction that another attack was mounted at 1 o'clock, and again by Italian tanks. Believing, no doubt, that there could now be little left of the garrison after so long a drubbing, and having seen no gunfire for some time, eight tanks and one or more Semovente self-propelled field guns (of

105-mm calibre) advanced on the position, firing their machine-guns vigorously.

Here there was now only one gun in action that could bear. It was that commanded by Sergeant Charles Calistan, the finely-built young athlete from the East End of London. He was alone, one of his detachment lying wounded and the others having, on his orders, crawled away to fetch more ammunition. Seeing his predicament, Turner himself and Jack Toms ran to join him. Calistan took post on the left of the gun as layer, Turner on the right as loader, and Toms behind as No. 1.

Turner ordered fire to be held until the enemy tanks were within 600 yards. The sergeant and the two officers then opened a devastating fire. Five of the eight tanks and the Semovente were hit very quickly one after the other and burst into flames. The three remaining tanks still came on, however, with great spirit, machine-gunning hard, and there were only two rounds of ammunition left.

Toms ran to his jeep, which was a hundred yards away, and quickly loaded several boxes of ammunition from a gun out of action. He drove back with the machine-gun bullets from the three tanks streaming down on him. It was an almost suicidal act. The jeep was riddled and burst into flames ten yards short of Calistan's gun. Turner ran to the jeep. So also did Corporal Francis, who had doubled over from Hine's gun to give a hand. Turner, Toms and Francis lugged the ammunition from the burning vehicle and dragged it to the gun.

At this point a shell splinter penetrated Turner's steel helmet and wounded him severely in the skull. He keeled over sideways beside the gun, the blood streaming down over his eyes.

Toms and Calistan carried on, joined now by Corporal Barnett as loading number. The three remaining Italian tanks, their machine-guns blazing, were now within 200 yards. The silent gun seemed to be at their mercy. Their bullets were beating like rain upon the gun-shield and kicking up spurts of sand in the shallow pit. Calistan, who all this time had been keeping them in his sight with the utmost unconcern, while he waited for the ammunition, laid with coolness and deliberation.

With three shots he killed all three tanks, which added their conflagrations to those of the other six.[1]

He then coolly turned round and said: 'We haven't had a chance of a brew all morning, but the Eyeties have made us a fire, so let's use it.' He thereupon poured some water into a billy-can, which he set on the bonnet of the burning jeep, and brewed-up some tea. To the wounded Turner, it was 'as good a cup as ever I've tasted.'

This must, without doubt, have been a disconcerting blow to the enemy. An intercept of his wireless disclosed that he was seriously concerned by this island of resistance just before he was to launch his big counter-attack. No further tank activity, however, took place for another three hours, but in the meantime the shelling continued.

Turner, having lain down for a while under a camel's thorn bush near Calistan's gun, insisted, against all persuasion, on visiting his guns once more, but the effort was too severe and he had to be taken down into the small headquarters dug-out where Marten and the wireless were. Even from here he occasionally sallied out to give encouragement and example, but later in the day he began to suffer from the hallucination that he was defending a harbour against hostile warships. On seeing a tank, he would exclaim 'Open fire on that destroyer.' It was, indeed, a very good simile and an hallucination of the sort that showed the spirit in the man. At length his officers had to restrain him physically.

The long, hot afternoon that followed under almost continuous shell and mortar fire, with no chance of hitting back and with the desert floor dancing in the rays of the furnace overhead, was perhaps the hardest part of the day. After the fatigues of the long night, the strain of the gruelling hours under the sun became accentuated by hunger and thirst; there was no chance to eat anything and those who did not have full equipment 'on the man' had nothing to drink either. Before long Bird, Toms, Liddell, Flower, Irwin and Crowder had all been wounded. In the tiny command-post dug-out six wounded officers and men, two other officers and two signalmen

1. Calistan, with the DCM and the MM to his name, was later given a commission, but was killed in Italy. He had been recommended for the Victoria Cross.

were crowded together with a million flies. No officer was left on the western sector and command fell to Sergeant Brown. It became impossible to move about in the position except at a crawl, but in A Company's sector Sergeant-Major Atkins crawled round from time to time to give cheer to the riflemen of the motor platoons.

Command and control thus became extremely difficult. Indeed, each sub-unit and even each gun was now acting mainly by instinct on its own initiative, an initiative that needed no spur. The Scout platoons, performing an equally valiant if less vital service, had been urged by the same spirit, engaging the enemy constantly with bren or rifle, but having their carriers hit one after another. By 4 p.m. the carriers of C Company, having fired 45,000 rounds, had no more ammunition.

Meanwhile, at the headquarters of 1st Armoured Division, Raymond Briggs was following events, as disclosed by the radio, with mixed feelings. Naturally impelled to send help to the hard-pressed garrison, he had, on the other hand, to weigh carefully the new fact, of which he had become aware at 10.30 that morning, through wireless intercepts, that 21st Panzer Division had come up from the south overnight and that their headquarters had actually been located only a little west of Kidney. He must expect to have to face them very soon, as well as the remains of 15th Panzer and the Littorio. To do so, he must conserve his armour. He had, therefore, to choose between the disagreeable alternatives of losing the Rifle Brigade or losing more tanks. He decided that he must leave the garrison to fight it out themselves. Never was a calculated risk more stoutly justified by those exposed to it.

Greater trials, and with them greater triumphs, were still to come. Once more the garrison was attacked by its friends. This time it was 2nd Armoured Brigade, whose tanks breasted the eastern horizon at about 4 o'clock and whose gunners, 11th RHA, subjected the garrison to the most vicious shelling by the 105-mm guns of their Priests. As Turner said afterwards, during an 'unpleasant' day, this was the 'most unpleasant' thing of all.

Though the garrison did not know it, this was the hour that Rommel had decided upon for his counter-attack and the area immediately to their north was one of the two principal points of thrust ordered by Rommel. Soon after this unpleasant shelling experience, the garrison could plainly see a powerful force of seventy German and Italian tanks, accompanied by self-propelled guns, forming up in the area west of Kidney Ridge, facing eastwards towards the British lines.

They were in two groups, one behind the other. In the most forward group could be seen thirty Germans and ten Italians and in their rear were another thirty Germans. The riflemen and the gunners watched them mustering at about 1,200 yards and it was evident that a big action was about to begin. They sat tight in their pits and trenches speculating what might be their part in it. They had not long to wait for the answer.

At 5 o'clock the first of these groups advanced south-eastward in clouds of dust to attack 2nd Armoured Brigade. The German tanks in this group were almost certainly from the newly arrived 21st Panzer Division, for the course of their advance took them within a few hundred yards of the watching garrison, broadside-on, and, as Turner was to say, 'it is inconceivable that the tanks which had been engaging us all day should have been so unwise.'

Advancing in an open phalanx, the tanks shaped course to pass the north-east sector and it was now that the gunners of 239th Battery got their real shoot.

They had four guns left in action. Four small guns against forty tanks. From left to right, they were those of Sergeants Hillyer, Cullen, Binks and Wood (with whom was Smith). Their two subaltern officers were in the centre and a trifle in rear, Baer nearest to Cullen's gun, Willmore moving shortly to Hillyer's. Each sergeant took post a trifle to the flank of his gun, to observe and correct fire. They were in a shallow dip of the ground by themselves and could not see the Rifle Brigade guns from a kneeling position, but knew that Sergeant Newman was just to the left of Hillyer. They were very well concealed, Wood's gun being invisible from fifty paces ahead.

Guns loaded, layers following the leaders of the oncoming tanks in their sights, the detachments knelt low behind the small shield, between the widely splayed legs of the split trails. Thrilled and fascinated, the gunners watched the immensely impressive spectacle as the powerful force roared slowly athwart their front, the sand billowing from the tracks. Baer ordered his guns to hold their fire till he gave the word.

They heard Newman's gun bark on the left but still kept silent. 500, 400, 300 yards. Then Hillyer, seeing a tank turn in to attack Newman, fired on his own initiative and scored. Accordingly, at 200 yards, Baer gave the order to open fire.

Binks fired immediately. The red tracer darted to the target and a Mark III leapt into flames. On Cullen's gun there was a momentary delay as his layer's hand, seized with excitement, froze on the gun. Cullen promptly knocked him aside and took over himself. Extremely cool and resourceful, he immediately clean knocked-out two tanks. Wood, on the right, did not fire at once. Baer darted over to him and found that the breechblock, fouled by sand, would not close. He knocked it up with an empty cartridge case and Wood fired. For the remainder of the action Baer stayed in the pit, he and Bombardier Percy Walker knocking up the breechblock for every round until it cleared.

All four guns were now scoring. Their shots struck home like hammers on an anvil, glowing red as they drilled through the steel walls. In two minutes a dozen tanks were crippled, half of them in flames. The nearest column then turned to face the guns with their frontal armour and attack them. As they came on, they struck with every weapon in their armoury – with machine-gun, high explosive and the shrill scream of close-passing armour-piercing shot. The gunners, filled with exaltation at their swift success, stuck to their guns and gave shot for shot. A great long-gunned Mark IV Special bore straight down upon Cullen, approaching to within 100 yards, 'hideously menacing', its machine-guns blazing and its bullets penetrating the gunshield. Cullen stood fast and he and Binks hit it together.

A minute later Binks's gun, after having knocked out four tanks, was smashed to pieces by a direct hit. Except for himself, all his detachment were killed or mortally wounded, one of them having his head severed from his body. Cullen, a model of steady hand and heart, was also hit, together with his excited layer, Gunner Evans. On the gunners' left, some of Irwin's platoon also engaged vigorously. Three tanks and a self-propelled gun fell to Sergeant Pearson, but his own gun and Sergeant Brett's were, in turn, knocked out. Meantime, bursts of fire from the Rifle Brigade machine-gunners streamed out on the enemy tank crews as they sought to escape.

These few guns it was, therefore, that brought Rommel's counter-attack to a standstill on this sector. Surprised and shaken, with half his forty tanks halted in confusion and several of them burning fiercely, and finding himself now attacked frontally by 2nd Armoured Brigade as well, the enemy commander called off his attack, withdrew and took cover in low ground to the west of Kidney Ridge, twenty-five minutes after he had begun his intended attack.

This, however, was only the first phase of the afternoon action. On observing the reverse to his comrades ahead, the commander of the enemy second wave, which was advancing in their rear, detached 15 Mark III tanks in a direct assault upon the island outpost. They came in head-on, advancing cautiously on the northern sector and making brilliant use of ground in their approach. It was the most dangerous attack that had yet been made against the garrison and only two guns – those of Sergeant Hine and Sergeant Miles – now remained that were in a position to oppose them. It looked very much, indeed, like the end of things. Seeing the critical situation, Lieutenant Barry Holt-Wilson, who, as we have noted, had been manning a gun in another sector with Sergeant Ayris and Rifleman Chard, swung it right round from front to rear. The three guns had an average of only ten rounds of ammunition left.

Sergeant-Major Atkins, from his slit trench at A Company's little command post, watched enthralled. He felt as though he were witnessing a Wild West film, with tanks for horses. He saw his machine-gunners with their weapons closely following the turrets of the panzers, ready to burst into fire the second that the tank crews leapt out. He saw the guns of Hine and Miles likewise following their targets in their sights and, as the panzers drew closer and closer, he asked himself: 'Why the hell don't they open fire?'

Because of the enemy's shrewd use of small folds in the ground, effective fire could not be brought to bear until the range was very short indeed. As they came on, the panzers lashed the detachments with machine-gun fire, especially that of Sergeant Miles. Miles was hit and his detachment forced into their slit trench. It certainly looked like the end. The juggernauts were almost on top of them.

Sergeant Swann, however, whose gun had been knocked-out earlier, seeing Miles's gun unmanned, crawled out from his position thirty yards away under the stream of bullets and manned it alone. The guns of Hine and Holt-Wilson stood their ground in the most determined fashion and at about 200 yards all three opened fire. Swann continued to load, lay and fire alone, until Miles's detachment, inspired by his leadership, jumped forward and joined him.

As in all the previous encounters, the effect was shattering. All four of the leading tanks were knocked out. Two others in the rear of the leaders were also knocked out. All six went up in flames. Last to be destroyed was a Mark III that Swann hit at 100 yards and as he did so Wintour, watching from the battalion command post, and giving physical expression to the exhilaration that filled every man who witnessed the spectacular action, leapt up and down with excitement, shouting:

'He's got him, he's got him, he's got him!'

The remaining nine tanks of this assault force promptly backed and took up hull-down positions about 800 yards away, whence, immune from the fire of the 6-pdrs, they kept up a galling fire with their machine-guns. From the last tank that Swann had knocked out a man was heard screaming with agony and his screams were heard in all the remaining hours to come.

The three guns that had repulsed this dangerous attack were now left with only three rounds each. Squatting in their gun-pits, the detachments, expecting the attack to be renewed, made ready to use them up to the very last. So certain had it appeared that the position was going to be overrun that Marten, on orders from Turner in the command post, had burnt all codes and maps.

The enemy, however, Germans and Italians alike, had now had quite enough. The scene of desolation in and around the island outpost was staggering. Nearly seventy tanks and self-propelled guns, all but seven being of the enemy, lay wrecked or derelict, many still burning and the black smoke from their fuel trailing forlornly across the desert. To these were added the shattered remains of several tracked and wheeled vehicles. Hanging out of the open turrets of the tanks, or concealed within their bowels, were the charred corpses of their crews who had been unable to escape the flames. Around them sprawled the bodies of those caught by the riflemen's machine guns. Within or immediately on the perimeter of the island were seven British tanks and one German, and the wreckages of sixteen bren-carriers, several jeeps and ten guns. Five other guns had been damaged; out of the original nineteen, not more than six remained that could be relied upon to engage.

Within this panorama of desolation and death there still remained, however, some 200 gallant men, red-eyed, coated with dirt and sweat, hungry and thirsty, but their spirit even higher than when they had first set out. Within their desert keep, as the crimson sun began to damp down its fires and to tinge with blood the funeral plumes of smoke from the dead tanks, they waited calmly with their few remaining guns and their last rounds of ammunition for a final attack that never came.

They waited also for night, which, whatever might be its fresh perils, they had been told would bring them relief. There had been good wireless communication all day with 7th Motor Brigade and Marten had been talking freely to Charles Wood, but at 5.40 Bosvile himself spoke on the air and said:

'Friends will come and take your place at dinner time. You are to wait until they are happily settled in your place. Your carriages will then arrive and take you home.'

Marten asked: 'Will it be an early dinner or a late one?', and was told:

'The fashionable time.'

This typical radio cross-talk meant, though Turner and Marten did not know it, that one of the Sussex battalions of 133rd Lorried

Infantry Brigade had been ordered to relieve the garrison at about 9 o'clock that night. The codes having been destroyed, Bosvile could give them no more information.

When last light came at 7.30 the enemy tanks to the north-west were seen to pull out from their hull-down positions and move farther back to go into night leaguer. Twenty minutes later they were seen nicely silhouetted against the pale evening sky and such guns as could bear in that direction, in a spirit of jubilant defiance, shot off the last of their ammunition against them, scoring one hit at 1,200 yards.

Some hours before this, Turner had been overcome by the heat and the effects of his head wound. The company commanders and the adjutant therefore held a conference when darkness had fallen to determine the measures to be taken. Their chief anxiety now was that the enemy might mount an attack by infantry, which they had small chance of withstanding. However, they made such preparations as they could, contracting their perimeter, and decided meantime to evacuate the wounded as soon as it was fully dark, without waiting for their relief.

No attack actually developed, but soon afterwards the enemy could be seen and plainly heard very close in on three sides collecting wounded and towing away the tank casualties considered repairable. The man wounded when the last tank was hit was still screaming. No offensive action was taken against these parties, however, as the garrison's own wounded were being collected for evacuation. For this purpose there remained three jeeps, six bren-carriers out of the twenty-two that had started, and one lorry, which had been unaccountably left in the position the night before and which, lying in a hollow to the east, had miraculously survived. So also had Baer's White scout car, riddled with bullets and shell splinters.

It was now 9.30 and there was no sign of the relief. Holt-Wilson went round the whole position and removed the breech-blocks of every RB gun that still remained serviceable; Baer did the like for the RA guns.

At 10.30 our artillery started shelling the German leaguer to the north-west. The enemy thereupon broke leaguer and his tanks began making straight for the garrison, forming a new leaguer very close to it. There was still no sign of relief, the Sussex battalion having, in fact, been completely misdirected by the same sort of map-reading discrepancies which had led Turner's force itself astray. Bosvile accordingly gave Marten permission to withdraw.

At 11.15, weary in body but not in spirit, the gallant company withdrew in good order, leaving behind them the bodies of their comrades who had won the soldier's highest honour.

One 6-pdr was successfully towed out by the gunners of 239th Battery – that of Sergeant Ronald Wood.

This heroic action illustrates not only the typical minor mischances and pitfalls of battle and of desert battles in particular; it illustrates not only the splendid fighting spirit and battle discipline of the two units that took part; it illustrates also the helplessness of tanks against good anti-tank guns, stoutly manned, even when sited on ground of no natural advantage.

The immediate lesson that was read to the whole of the Army was that, when equipped with their own 6-pdrs, the infantry could themselves see off a tank attack and inflict severe losses upon the enemy. The battalion and their Royal Artillery comrades, in resolutely holding ground that in itself was worthless, had that day struck one of the stoutest blows that helped to win the Alamein victory. They had destroyed or disabled more enemy tanks than had so far been destroyed or damaged in any single unit action and had shot one of the most crippling bolts in the destruction of Rommel's counter-attack of that day.

The action gained such fame throughout the desert, becoming somewhat embroidered in the retailing, that a Committee of Investigation was appointed a month later to examine the ground, count the still remaining carcasses of the enemy tanks and sift all the evidence critically. Their inquiry was searching. They analysed the performance of every single gun. Taking into consideration the number of wrecks that had by then been removed by ourselves or by the enemy, the committee concluded that the minimum number of tanks burnt and totally destroyed was thirty-two – twenty-one German and eleven Italian – plus five self-propelled guns, and that certainly another fifteen, perhaps twenty, tanks had been knocked out and recovered, making a grand total of fifty-seven. A few tracked and wheeled vehicles had also been destroyed. Only a very few of the tanks recovered could have been repaired before the battle ended.

This phenomenal success had not been won without its cost in flesh and blood, but, speaking relatively, the cost had not been grievously severe. Of the total force of less than 300 who had started out from the Highland lines, seventy-two riflemen and gunners had been killed or wounded, to which number were to be added some RE casualties, not ascertained. The figure would have been very much higher if they had not been well trained in the principle of 'dig or die' and in the craft of concealment.[1]

Montgomery was naturally delighted. This was just what he wanted. In due process of time there came the Victoria Cross for Victor Turner, the DSO for Bird, the DCM for Sergeants Calistan and Swann and Rifleman Chard and the Military Cross and the Military Medal for those who were selected from the many more who earned them among that gallant company.[2]

REPULSE OF THE COUNTER-ATTACK

The action by 2nd Rifle Brigade battalion group was, however, the only significant success of 1st Armoured Division on the 27th. The armoured brigades, as we have seen, were unable to penetrate the enemy crust and progress more than a few hundred yards towards the Rahman Track. Their tanks and artillery, however, continued to inflict a great deal of damage and they were well placed to meet Rommel's own attack under Von Thoma. This broke down everywhere as completely as it had done at the *Snipe* position.

Even before the counter-offensive was launched, the Stukas, the

1. 1st Armd Div. War Diary, however, gives the casualties as over 100.

2. This account of the action has been compiled mainly from the report of of the Committee of Investigation, the official report after the action by Bird and Marten (incorporating a report by Flower), the accounts by Turner in *The British Army Journal* and *The Rifle Brigade Journal*, the personal narratives to the author by Turner, Bird, Marten, Baer, Roper-Caldbeck, Atkins and Swann, and various other sources in matters of detail.

CR 42s and the Messerschmitts 109s which were to support it in the air, were met and engaged by sixteen American Kittihawks and twenty-four British Hurricanes and the enemy formation was completely broken up with the loss of five aircraft at a price of three Hurricanes in the Allied Squadrons. In the more westerly of Von Thoma's two main thrusts the operations were under 21st Panzer Division and it was the Rifle Brigade's unexpected stand that was primarily responsible for its failure.

The other main thrust, against the Australians on Point 29 again, was assigned to the formidable 90th Light Division, fresh from its long rest in reserve. Their attack was crushed at the start by very heavy and well-directed artillery fire in great volume, backed by some devastating bombing by ninety British and American day-bombers. So crushing was the artillery fire and the bombing that 90th Light, fine fighting troops though they were, never closed with the Australian infantry.

The counter-attack was watched by Rommel himself. 'Every artillery and anti-aircraft gun which we had in the northern sector' he recorded, 'concentrated a violent fire on the point of the intended attack. Then the armour moved forward. A murderous British fire struck into our ranks and our attack was brought to a halt by an immensely powerful anti-tank defence. *There is, in general, little chance of success in a tank attack over country where the enemy has been able to take up defensive positions.*'[1]

To his wife he wrote characteristically: 'No one can conceive the burden that lies on me.'

When Von Thoma reported the situation to him at eight o'clock that evening, the only orders that Rommel was able to give were that all positions must be held and that no major penetration of the front by the British could be allowed.

THE 'WOODCOCK' AFFAIR

There is a postscript to be written to these hard-fought operations of D plus 3 and D plus 4 and that an unhappy one.

1. *The Rommel Papers.* Italics not in original.

First Armoured Division was due to be relieved by 10th Armoured Division on D plus 5, 28 October. As a first step in the relief, Lumsden had ordered up 133rd Lorried Infantry Brigade, under Brigadier Alec Lee, with its battalions of the Royal Sussex Regiment to take over the tasks of 7th Motor Brigade on the night 27th/28th. This involved the relief of the *Snipe* garrison and the capture of *Woodcock*.

Arriving at short notice on a front unknown to them, the Sussex Brigade were unhappy victims of a confused situation and of the inexperience of the armour commanders in infantry assault operations. Parts of three divisions – 51st and 1st and 10th Armoured – were sitting on the same piece of desert and the armour were astray on the map. Lee, on arrival at Bosvile's headquarters, which was under fire, could get no information. After some hours Lumsden and Gatehouse themselves arrived and told him that he could expect no assistance in his preparations. They said that all he had to do to take *Woodcock* and *Snipe* was to 'walk through', but that he would be given ample artillery support and that the two armoured brigades would be up at first light. It was very obvious to Lee that Lumsden and Gatehouse were acting under pressure from the Army Commander.

Not liking the situation at all, Lee and his battalion commanders set out to fulfil their mission as best they could that night. As we have briefly recorded, the attempt to relieve *Snipe*, which was made by 5th Battalion of the Royal Sussex, went astray. The battalion reached what it believed to be the right piece of desert and dug in. The attempt on *Woodcock* was a sadder story. It was made by the 4th Battalion, of which Lieutenant-Colonel Ronald Murphy had taken command only a few days before.

The attack was to begin at 10.30 in the dark hours before the moon rose, supported by a very simple artillery plan prepared by Ebbels, but severe congestion in the minefield gaps caused the battalion to be twenty minutes late at the start. On the right of the attack confusion attended the operation from the outset. Here the battalion found their advance obstructed very soon after it had begun. But it was not the enemy who obstructed them, but 1st Gordon Highlanders, across whose newly-won position at *Aberdeen* the battalion's axis had been directed. There was an unfortunate clash. One of Lieutenant Harry Gordon's sentries, on challenging, was shot through the head. The light of a burning truck then showed the advancing figures to be British, 'coming on in very good order and aggressive spirit.'

The advance was resumed after the mistake had been discovered, but shortly afterwards the battalion found itself being heavily fired on from the left. The reserve company was sent to suppress this opposition but was nearly annihilated in the attempt.

At length, Murphy judged that he must have reached *Woodcock*. He halted and ordered immediate consolidation. At 5.29 a.m. he reported that he was in possession. He seems, in fact, to have reached the eastern edge of *Woodcock* and to have come to a stop in between some German and Italian units.

At 6 a.m. Murphy reported by air that tanks could be heard near by. Soon afterwards he and the FOO of 104th RHA both went off the air.

At dawn, 2nd Armoured Brigade was moving round on their northern flank, as they had done the day before, but, before they could intervene, the enemy suddenly attacked with tanks and overran the Sussex, with a loss of 47 killed (including Murphy himself) and 342 missing. A little later a patrol of 10th Hussars discerned, at a distance of two miles, the melancholy spectacle of the prisoners being marched away to captivity.

The brigade had been hustled into these assaults with too little forethought. Like those of 7th Motor Brigade on the night before, the operations had been laid on with insufficient opportunity for reconnaissance, with much confusion about map locations and with inadequate measures for ensuring that the assaulting troops were correctly guided to their unrecognizable objectives in the dark obscurity of the desert.

Thus amid signal triumphs there were frustrations and occasional bitter losses. Yet these reverses were purely local and all the time the battle was being steadily won. Rommel began to lose the battle the moment he attempted the tank counter-offensive. His armour was as much at the mercy of the British anti-tank guns as ours were at his. His tactics were merely those of the battering-ram. In the last two days he had lost another 100 tanks, of which about 75 were German. He was doing exactly what Montgomery wanted. Which particular patch of desert Rommel chose for his self-immolation was of little consequence.

On 28 October the relief of 1st Armoured Division by 10th began, but for the remainder of the day 2nd Armoured Brigade remained in action, steadily continuing the work of attrition. Major K. J. Price, of 9th Lancers, in a skilfully handled squadron attack, demonstrated how, on a limited scale, anti-tank guns could be overcome. Putting down a smoke screen to mask a battery of 88s on his flank, he swung his squadron in a half-circle in the cavalry manner and, at a cost to himself of three tanks, overran a German company position that contained three 50-mm anti-tank guns and two heavy mortars.

In another series of small engagements by the regiment, Sergeant F. Edwards, with Corporal Nickolls as gunner, handling their tank with brilliant skill and coolness, stalked and destroyed eight of the enemy, to the delight of the watching Gordon Highlanders. Montgomery himself listened to the progress of this engagement on the radio and afterwards telephoned his congratulations and his instructions for Nickolls to be recommended for the Military Medal.

That night Briggs handed over his front to Gatehouse, and 1st Armoured Division pulled out for a very brief refit and reorganisation in readiness for the new blow that Montgomery was preparing. *Lightfoot* was over for them. In four and a half gruelling days of continuous fighting they had not got very far on the ground, but they had inflicted great damage to the enemy. Their claim to have knocked out 186 enemy tanks so far was a trifle on the high side, but certainly up to this time they had been by far the largest tank destroyers. Of these, 94 were known to have been completely burnt out or to have been destroyed by the Royal Engineers in their nightly sallies for that purpose. A very high proportion of the kills was to the credit of the 6-pdrs of the riflemen of 7th Motor Brigade and the gunners of 76th Anti-Tank Regiment, pre-eminently at *Snipe*. Added to these tank victims were fifty-five guns of all sorts destroyed and a good bag of prisoners. An enormous amount of damage had been done by the divisional artillery under 'Frizz' Fowler, as, indeed, had been done by all the divisional artilleries and the boldly handled medium regiments of the Royal Artillery. Rommel seems to have been surprised at the fact that British artillery officers accompanied the leading tanks and were able to bring down concentrations of fire with 'tremendous speed' to meet any situation.

First Armoured Division had thus contributed handsomely to the 'crumbling' operation. Though they had not done so quite in the manner anticipated by Montgomery, he sent his able young ADC, John Poston, to convey to Raymond Briggs his personal congratulations on the handling of the division. But whatever emotions or reflections the red-eyed tank crews may have entertained as they drove back through the dusty minefield gaps, with croaking voices and cracked faces, were submerged in an intense desire for sleep.

On the night that 1st Armoured pulled out, the Australians began the northward drive to the coast road that Montgomery had ordered and thither we direct our attention for the next tempestuous four days.

Chapter Sixteen

THOMPSON'S POST

(28 October to 1 November)

The Australian Offensive Renewed – The Rival Commanders – The Third Northward Attack – The Rhodesian Gunners

THE AUSTRALIAN OFFENSIVE RENEWED

The country on the front of 9th Australian Division was not quite so devoid of features as that over which the other divisions of 30th Corps had been fighting and the shape of its frontage had become decidedly awkward. The attack on the night of D Day had hinged on the centre of the divisional front, so that the division faced two ways.

From the sea coast it faced north-west for two and a half miles, as it had done for four months, running across the dreary salt-marshes that lay immediately inland from the snow-white beach, passing just west of the bony crest of Tel el Eisa and crossing the black ribbon of the coast road and the broken thread of the railway before it reached the open desert. Along this coastal sector 24th Brigade stood guard under Arthur Godfrey in a position of defence. A little to the westward of the ruined Tel el Eisa station, at the point where the attack of 23 October had begun, the line pivoted until it faced north, reaching westward to Point 29 since its capture on the night of 25 October. Along this northward face, still deployed on the ground they had won in three nights' fighting, the soldiers of 20th Brigade (of which Victor Windeyer had now resumed command) and 26th Brigade under 'Torpy' Whitehead sat squarely in their rocky 'doovers', supported by the English tanks and guns of 23rd Armoured Brigade Group under Rickie Richards.

Within the angle of this two-directional front stood a strongly fortified enemy outpost system, known as Thompson's Post. It was dug-in on a somewhat pronounced rocky elevation, covered about half a square mile, dominated the bare desert on all sides of it, had a German artillery observation post just behind it at Point 25 and was to prove a thorn in the flesh of the Australians.

Most of the country was flat and sandy, with underlying rock, but north of the road it was somewhat interrupted by the small, rocky hummocks which were a continuation of Tel el Eisa, and here and there were to be seen an occasional palm or wild fig-tree near the road side.

Facing the Australians round this awkward pocket, which the British artillery and the Allied Air Forces made extremely uncomfortable, were 164th Light Division and the Bersaglieri, troops of good quality, together with the still more formidable 'battle groups' of 90th Light, freshly thrust into the line.

Thus the Germans and Italians, though they had had a gruelling ordeal, held all the advantages of the defence. The assaulting Australian brigades, however, – 20th and 26th – had had a scarcely less gruelling time. In the five days they had been in the line, together with 40th RTR under Jim Finigan, they had not only made three winning attacks but they had also, under fire from two directions, decisively beaten off two counter-attacks, including Rommel's 'rivers of blood' attack on the 26th.

They were not alone among the other divisions in these trials of combat endurance, but the fierce and bitter conflicts to which they were now to be committed were made remarkable by the fact that they were begun and carried through by men who already showed in their faces the strain that comes from long endurance of shell fire and who had already been severely weakened by casualties. Thus Second-13th Battalion, a New South Wales unit, had been decimated of officers after completing its capture of the *Oxalic* objective on 24 October. The CO, Lieutenant-Colonel Bob Turner, all the company commanders and nearly all the platoon commanders had been killed or wounded. The assaulting rifle companies began the new operations with strengths of about thirty-five officers and men each – little more than the strength of a platoon – instead of 120.

This was fairly representative of several of the battalions in 20th and 26th Brigades and reinforcements were so lacking that the detention camps and hospitals in the base areas as far away as Palestine were being scoured to make good the casualties.

The blow which Montgomery ordered to be struck by the Australians was calculated to serve two purposes: it would maintain the motive of the initiative, thus forcing the enemy once more to react to his tune, and it would improve the prospects for a breakthrough astride the coast road, which, at that time, seemed to Montgomery the most promising vista. Along that road he saw the powerful impetus of Bernard Freyberg thrusting fast and hard with his spirited New Zealanders as part of the drive he ordained for 10th Corps. He therefore withdrew Lumsden's Corps headquarters into reserve in readiness for that drive, leaving 10th Armoured Division temporarily under Oliver Leese's command in the Kidney sector, where during the next few days it performed some excellent 'crumbling'.

Morshead's task of a northward attack from the shoulder of the bulge was anything but easy to execute. His grand objective was the coast road and he had also to demolish the strong forces in the coastal pocket, which, from its most formidable feature, we may call the Thompson's Post pocket. He intended first to enlarge his tenancy at Point 29. Then, with the aid of Richard's armour, he would strike for the coast road and swing south-eastward to destroy the enemy in the Thompson's Post pocket, who consisted chiefly of 125th Panzer Grenadier Regiment and some Bersaglieri.

In outline, his plan for achieving this purpose was first to capture two enemy positions about a mile to the north-east[1] and to the east-north-east[2] of Point 29, each being a battalion task. This was entrusted

1. 868303.
2. 869301 and 870301.

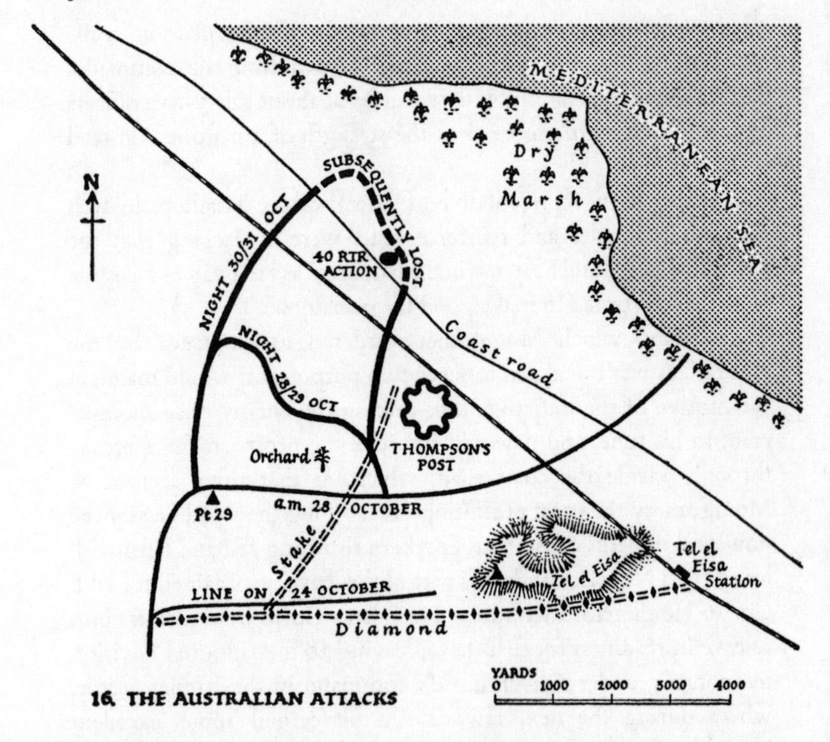

16. THE AUSTRALIAN ATTACKS

to 20th Brigade. Then 26th Brigade and 23rd Armoured Brigade were to advance between the two captured localities and secure the main road, whence they would turn inwards and exploit to clear the pocket. For these operations Richards would have two of his armoured regiments – 40th and 46th RTR – and his gunner regiment, 121st Field Regiment, with their 25-pdrs on 'Bishop' mountings.

It was a complicated operation, involving the Australian CRA, Brigadier Ramsay, in a difficult programme of artillery fire, to support attacks in different directions. However, Oliver Leese gave him every gun he could spare for the task, and Dennis, his Corps artillery commander, handled the complicated disposition with his usual easy skill.

The night was dark and cold under the glittering canopy of stars when 20th Brigade's attack began at 10 o'clock on 28 October.

It was entrusted to Second-13th Battalion (now commanded by George Colvin) and the Queenslanders of Second-15th, under C. K. M. Magno. They were met by some fairly hot shell-fire and suffered painful casualties from S-mines, but gained their objectives and sat firmly on them.

The circumstances in which this attack was launched, and launched successfully, are vividly illustrated by the experiences of B Company of Second-13th, who were posted on the right flank in their attack on 'Fig Orchard'.

A new officer – Captain C. Vincent – arrived to take command of the company just before it was due to attack. George Colvin had already given out battalion orders to the company commanders. At his 'Order Group' there had been only a subaltern to take orders for B Company – Lieutenant Frederick Treweeke. Vincent, on his arrival, had at once to call his own company 'O Group', though he did not yet know the battalion orders. So weak was the company that his O Group consisted of Treweeke, one other officer, one corporal and two privates, and it took place under heavy fire.

They collected together in adjacent holes in the ground. Treweeke, reading from his rough notes, shouted them to Vincent between shell bursts. Vincent, unable to hear him at one point, shouted to Treweeke to come over to him. Receiving no answer, he scrambled over to Treweeke's hole and found him dead.

The dead subaltern's pencilled notes were almost illegible, but, deciphering as much as he could, Vincent took his slender company straight to the battalion forming-up position. Their strength was two officers and thirty men and with these they had to attack on a frontage of 200 yards for a mile and a half in the dark to the 'Fig Orchard' near Thompson's Post. They did this successfully, and sent forward a patrol as well.

In such circumstances, Colvin had no following-on troops for mopping up and before long his battalion command post was being kept under incessant fire by a heavy mortar and two Spandaus in a German position in the left rear. Colvin ordered C Company to deal with them and the mission was entrusted to Lance-Sergeant Reginald McKellar and the remnants of a platoon – ten men.

He was given the bearing to the enemy post and was handed a compass. With no other information or aids than these he set out.

The platoon traversed a minefield of 200 yards depth, reached the barbed wire surrounding the enemy post and was immediately attacked by the two Spandaus, which pinned them to the ground, while the mortar went on firing. McKellar, however, gave the order for the patrol to let fly their hand grenades, of which they carried four each. The patrol then rushed the post and captured the guns and their crews.

There remained, however, the trench mortar, which, from 30 yards away, was still pumping bombs into Fig Orchard. This also they rushed and captured after a hand-to-hand fight in the pit, knocking out one of the crew with the fist and shooting down another who tried to escape.

Another German machine-gun then opened fire on the patrol, killing one of the prisoners, and the patrol began to make their way back, driving their prisoners before them through the minefield at the point of the Tommy gun. McKellar then realized that, if he left the mortar behind, it might be manned again by the enemy. He therefore went back himself with four men, dismantled it, captured another prisoner and made his way back to his company, with the German prisoners carrying the mortar and the machine guns.

It is by such acts of individual initiative, with which the next four days' fighting was vividly illuminated, that actions are often won and dominance over an enemy asserted. Before the night was out the four rifle companies of this battalion had been reduced to a total of 100 and they had lost another CO, Colvin being severely wounded after having commanded the battalion for only four days. The 'orchard of dreadful memory' became a charnel-house reeking with the stench of German dead and a place of sudden death for the Australian infantry and the English tanks. 'Mind the bloody orchard' became the warning to all who had to pass that way.

Thus the first phase of this assault of 28/29 October went well, but of the attempt of 26th Brigade and their accompanying tanks to push right forward to the coast road in the next phase there is a rougher story to tell.

The units selected for this bold thrust were Second-23rd Battalion, commanded by Bernard Evans, and 46th RTR under T. C. A. Clarke. The two units had worked together often before and knew each other well. On this occasion, in order to get tanks and infantry on to the objective together, part of the infantry were carried on the Valentines and part in carriers – a device of very dubious merit. Unfortunately, the start-line, very advanced, had been chosen from the map and was not reconnoitred.

Darkness and clouds of dust obscured the start and 500 yards from the start-line Clarke's tanks began to blow up one after the other on an unexpected minefield. Others were knocked out by short-range anti-tank gunfire, while scalding machine-gun fire forced the infantry to dismount from the tanks. Tanks and infantry soon lost touch with each other and the attack broke down in confusion. The Valentines suffered very severe casualties, Clarke himself being badly wounded right at the start and all his squadron leaders being casualties also; Major Eric Offord took command.

In this turmoil, the two brigadiers, Whitehead and Richards, were following up together close behind the assaulting troops and were caught in the enemy counter-barrage. Whitehead held an impromptu and uneasy conference in a 'doover' but had now small chance of controlling events. Richards sent back for six Scorpions to come forward and flail the minefield. Finigan, who had been supporting 20th Brigade, calmly came up in the midst of the storm to offer the help of 40th RTR, but Richards sent him back. By 4.15 a.m. it was learnt that Evans had halted his battalion and dug in half a mile beyond the start-line, together with all that remained viable of 46th RTR – eight tanks in all. The attempt to penetrate to the coast road had thus not succeeded, but severe damage had been inflicted on the enemy and his position had been pierced at a very sensitive spot. The 3rd Battalion of 125th Panzer Grenadier Regiment had been virtually annihilated and a gap had been blown between what remained of them and Battle Group 155 of 90th Light.

This was excellent 'crumbling' in just the sort of 'dog fight' that Montgomery had purposed and for which 9th Australian Division was so well equipped by nature and by training.

THE RIVAL COMMANDERS

As the news of the new northward thrust came through to the two rival commanders in the early morning of 29 October, and its relationship to the operations as a whole was appreciated, we are presented with a fascinating picture of how they read each other's minds.

Rommel was now at last seriously worried. His tank strength, which had been ravaged in five days' fighting with 1st Armoured Division, was now augmented by forty-six new or repaired tanks, but his German panzers nonetheless were reduced to about half their original numbers and his infantry and artillery were daily being shattered, captured, crazed and exhausted by the sustained pressure of the British offensive. His attempts to throw the British out of the ground they had won had broken on the rocks of their anti-tank guns, their tanks employed defensively, the 'terrible British artillery' and the bolts showered down by the Allied aircraft.

He began, therefore, at last to make preparations for what he should have done several days earlier, instead of playing into the hands of his adversary – a withdrawal to Fuka.

These preparations, however, were hesitant and indeterminate. Rommel was for the moment undecided in mind and he temporized. He still hung on to the wasteful and valueless Thompson's Post pocket, which lengthened his frontage and engaged some of his best troops. He had, however, correctly appraised Montgomery's new intention of making his main thrust along the coast road and he reacted accordingly.

All his German troops (except the Ramcke Brigade) were now concentrated in the extreme north. He withdrew 21st Panzer Division from the line in the Kidney sector and positioned them north of Tel el Aqqaqir, replacing them with the Trieste division, which he brought up from reserve. To the same area he also transferred Battle Group 155 of 90th Light (together with the remnants of 11/125 Panzer Grenadiers), posting them south-east of Sidi Abd el Rahman, the road and track junction marked by the little, lone mosque where his repair workshops were, and whither, he apprehended, Montgomery would direct his attack. He ordered the other units of 125 Panzer Grenadiers to continue holding their dangerous positions in the Thompson's Post pocket and gave command of the coastal sector to 90th Light Division under General Graf von Sponeck.

Thus he still kept a barrier across the road in the pocket and he also built a fence of tanks and guns in front of the approaches to the road south-east of his highly sensitive position at Sidi Abd el Rahman. By this means, he could either continue to resist or he could cover a withdrawal to Fuka.

Montgomery, in his more serene headquarters beside the placid brilliance of the Mediterranean, observed with interest these new dispositions. He saw that his adversary had divined his intention, was answering to his tune and was packing all his strength to cover the approaches to the coast road. On the morning of 29 October there was a conference at his headquarters, at which Alexander was present, together with McCreery, and various courses were discussed. At 11 a.m. Montgomery decided once more to change the tune.

The final blow was not now to be directed at and astride the road. It was to be directed due westward between *Woodcock* and the extreme top corner of the bulge, six miles south of the road, from what had been the Australian sector at the start of the battle and had now been taken over by 51st Division. It would be aimed to break the enemy's last and powerful defences on the Rahman Track above and below Tel el Aqqaqir.

In the meantime, in order to keep Rommel's attention distracted in the Thompson's Post pocket, he ordered the Australians to resume their northward attack on the night of the 30th.

THE THIRD NORTHWARD ATTACK

This third assault by 9th Australian Division was planned to an even more elaborate formula than the previous one, of which it was a continuation. It was to be a strangling operation in three phases. First, resuming the theme of the previous attack, there was to be a thrust north-eastward to secure a position astride the road and the railway. This thrust would then turn at a right angle to sweep down the railway and get behind the enemy in the bottom of the pocket. The third phase was a final push from the coast road to the sea, for which Morshead was obliged to bring in his Pioneer Battalion to augment his attenuated infantry. To these specific objectives were added patrol tasks to Thompson's Post and a point on the coast, but they were not set-piece attacks.

In this night's work, therefore, there were to be assaults in three directions – three short, fierce dashes – with three Zero hours. An enormous volume of artillery fire was to be at Ramsay's disposition for an operation that must have been a gunner's nightmare. For the infantry, the operation meant great skill and dexterity as well as tremendous guts. It was to be an infantry-cum-artillery attack pure and simple, the Valentines of 23rd Armoured Brigade not being specifically committed in the plan but 40th RTR standing by at call. Clarke's battalion, after their mutilation on the night of 28 October, were out of the battle.

As before, the night would be dark, with the moon a little later still. The narrow, thrust-out shoulder of ground from which these multiple attacks were to be launched was swept by fire from three sides and the steadiness of the troops would be tested even before they got to their several start-lines. The German OP on Point 25 had complete command of the front. Large areas of the ground were alive with S-mines and booby traps, so that every step in the dark was made at a man's peril.

Thus an entanglement of thorny problems beset the feet of those about to step out on this night's work, but, if these entanglements were overcome, the remaining battalions of 125th Panzer Grenadiers and their supporting troops would be trapped in the bottom of the pocket and this in turn would certainly lead to a fierce reaction by Rommel.

Before the new battle, Rickie Richards observed to 'Bomba' Wells, Morshead's GSO 1 (with whom, we have noted, he had been at the Staff College): 'If we had put in this solution to the problem at Camberley, we should certainly have been failed!' Wells, tired but cheerful, answered with a friendly grin.

This time it was Second-32nd Battalion, brought in from 24th Brigade, that led off, under John Balfe, setting out behind their powerful barrage in the dark of 10 p.m. on the night of the 30th. The attack went exceedingly well against 1st Battalion 125th PZ Grenadiers, and the Australians, pressing with great dash and determination, won their objective on the coast road[1], but could not mop up all the enemy posts they by-passed. Balfe was wounded and Tom Scott took over.

For the second phase – the right-handed swing and sweep down the railway – the Victorians of Second-24th ('Wangaratta's Own'), under Charles Weir, and the South Australians of Second-48th, under Dick Hammer, came up under a lively fire, formed up on their uncomfortable start-line and advanced to their barrage at 1 o'clock in the morning. They were met by a galling fire from front and flank, suffered heavy casualties and lost touch with each other. Too weak in numbers to press their attack to a firm conclusion and hold their ground, they withdrew to a position in contact with Second-32nd.

In phase three a gallant effort was made to dash for the sea by Second-3rd Pioneer Battalion at 4.25 a.m. It was the first time that the Pioneers had ever been employed as assaulting infantry, but they succeeded in getting half-way, when stubborn resistance brought them to a halt and, realizing they could not stay out there in isolation, they drew back to a tenable position before dawn.

The threatening bastion of Thompson's Post, however, from which a patrol of Second-24th was repelled by fire, remained in enemy hands, and its resolute garrison, encompassed on three sides, continued to be a thorn in Morshead's side, hammering his troops deep in the flank and rear.

Thus, in terms of ground gained, it may be said again that the operations did not achieve their objectives in full. The Germans, under a tremendous volume of artillery fire, had fought back with great spirit and managed to hang on 'with the skin of their teeth'. But the ground was of little value and the enemy losses had been heavy, including 500 officers and men captured, and the greater part

1. Between Eastings 870 and 871.

of 125th PZ Grenadiers, with their associated troops, were all but shut up in their pocket, only a narrow strip of ground along the sea coast remaining by which to maintain a life-line with the main body.

The morning light, therefore, showed that the Australians had driven a narrow tongue-like salient into the enemy salient – a tongue with its root between the orchard and Point 29 and its tip thrust out northward to the salty fringe of the sea-marsh, licking precariously a little beyond the embanked coast road. Across the tongue ran the railway, its rails torn and twisted by shell fire and its embankment, four or five feet high, a major obstacle to vehicles. Between the railway and the road there lay some four furlongs of sand and rock, completely flat, completely bare, lashed almost continuously with observed fire from three sides. The air reeked of high explosive and the stench of dead bodies. Vision was limited to a few yards except when, in the occasional pauses in the storm, the sun broke through the enveloping dust-clouds. Across this fiery salient the Australian infantry, with their artillery FOOs and their anti-tank guns driven up with great daring and much loss, superbly supported by field artillery itself under fire, stood prepared to repel all assaults of their enemy.

Rommel's reaction was exactly what Montgomery expected and wanted, both for his policy of attrition and for the purpose of distracting Rommel's attention away from the intended British point of main effort. Entirely fulfilling the Army Commander's purpose, the Australians 'drew everything on to themselves 'with considerable emphasis, for Rommel's response was immediate, fierce and persistent. The worthless strip of marsh and desert that comprised this pocket was an obsession to him throughout. Instead of withdrawing its garrison and employing their good qualities more economically on a shortened front, as, for example, to the position east of Sidi Abd el Rahman, he threw in everything he could to support them and to restore the coloured lines on his map to their previous shapes.

Graf von Sponeck, commanding 90th Light Division, urged that he should be allowed to make a full-scale infantry attack with the whole of his division; he felt confident of success, but Rommel would not consent.

Four times Rommel strove to hurl back the Australian infantry and the English tanks. First there was an infantry attack by 361st Panzer Grenadiers on the western edge of the tongue early next morning, the 31st. It was met and broken up by strong artillery fire. Rommel then ordered up a 'battle group' from 21st Panzers, composed of a few squadrons of tanks accompanied by self-propelled anti-tank guns and field artillery. This gave him a strong superiority at the point of impact, there being no British armour in this sector to face the heavy German panzers other than the lightweight Valentines of 40th RTR.

During the previous night Finigan had been slowly bringing his Valentines up into the battle by the Stake Track, preceded by the sappers of 295 Field Company, Royal Engineers, weeding the ground of the mines that impeded his progress. By first light he had reached the railway immediately north of Thompson's Post, but, on attempting to advance up the line of the rail to the north-west to support Second-48th, again struck mines. Finigan's own tank was blown up and, on his changing to another tank, that also was blown up. He therefore went his harzardous way on foot, while the Field Company commander made a reconnaissance with the audacious notion of attempting to open a way from the east side of Thompson's Post. That bastion continued to be an impediment to progress. Finigan and Hammer held an uncomfortable conference in the lee of a tank, trying to organize an assault upon it, but Hammer's gallant band of Second-48th, by reason of their tremendous casualties, could no longer be called a unit and were widely dispersed. 'Even if it wasn't broad daylight', Hammer said as he looked over the wild scene, 'I doubt whether I could collect more than sixty or seventy men.'

Therefore Finigan's squadrons went on alone. Pressing with great spirit, they cut the main road and held their ground beyond it all day entirely unsupported.

Soon afterwards some twenty German Mark III tanks (augmented later) were seen to be forming up immediately beyond the road near the tip of the salient, and at 1 o'clock, with the desert shapes dancing in the heat haze, battle was joined between the German heavies and three reduced Squadrons of the English lightweights, at a critical point of the new front.

In that unequal fight the Liverpool men, fighting with the utmost tenacity and skill, assailed by shell-fire from field artillery as well as by the red-hot shots of the panzers, held the enemy at bay beyond the road the whole of the afternoon at heavy cost to themselves. In the midst of the action Finigan was summoned to meet Richards at the Orchard for fresh orders and on his way back to the battle was unhorsed for the third time that day, his mount being knocked out this time by an anti-tank gun at Thompson's Post. His adjutant Wilfred Hargreaves, and his driver, 'Chalky' White, were pinned down to the ground by a Spandau in the same strongpoint, which kept its sights firmly fixed on them. In Finigan's absence, Major Richard MacLaren commanded the tank battle beyond the coast road. When both sides withdrew at last light the gallant 40th Battalion, after breaking the attack and destroying five German tanks, had themselves lost twenty-one.[1] In their eight days of almost continuous action with the Australians, 'Monty's Foxhounds', having begun the battle on 23 October with 42 tanks, lost nearly fifty.

Meanwhile, in this dangerous counter-attack by the German battle group, the infantry had been no less severely engaged. The attack fell mainly on Second-32nd, now commanded by Tom Scott. There was a critical, hard-hitting fight at close quarters in blazing heat and in a storm of fire that shook and smothered both sides. Although there was some local penetration, the Australians held on to their main positions with set teeth as the enemy thrusted, recoiled then thrusted again, the while a pall of smoke and dust totally obscured the salient from observers to the rear and even at times hid one man from his neighbour.

Three hours later the German battle group assaulted once again in the same manner and again with no success. The ragged salient, held by thin ranks of men dazed and numb from mental and physical fatigue, stood firm against the waves that beat upon its rocks, while

1. This fine action by 40th RTR took place at 87123043; one squadron had been sent over to the western flank.

an unceasing rain of shells, bombs and bullets pounded down from Thompson's Post to the sea, and the sand slowly drifted over the bodies of the dead. The whole battle glittered with valiant feats of arms by individual soldiers and small units, not the least of whom were the devoted stretcher-bearers and ambulance men who, under murderous fire, unconcernedly went about their work of mercy to friend and enemy.

A quiet night followed, the soldiers of both sides completely exhausted. The lull was fortunate, for Morshead had decided that that night the battle-torn 26th Brigade must be relieved. To do this, 24th Brigade, from their old coastal position to the east, were ordered round by a long, circuitous and very difficult approach march, which Godfrey's brigade accomplished skilfully.

The 26th had fought to the limits of flesh and blood; one of its battalions was commanded by a captain. Second-24th had been reduced to 140 men. Second-48th had won its third Victoria Cross, again posthumous, the courage of Sergeant Bill Kibby had shone in one heroic act after another from D Day onwards and now, on the night of the 30th, after his platoon had been mown down by machine-gun fire at point blank, he had gone forward alone, hurling grenades, until he himself had fallen.

Not yet convinced of the futility of these attacks on the 31st, Rommel ordered yet another attempt to throw out the Australians on the morning of Sunday, 1 November. His voice was heard by the British wireless intercept service, telling his soldiers that only a small pocket of tired British troops lay in front of them. There was another long, bitter and bloody fight in the sweltering heat and the choking dust. The Australian forward positions were penetrated, but the infantry, as long as they lived, did not give ground and the battle rasped up and down the frayed and blistered edges of the protruding tongue. Ground was lost, retaken and lost again. Arthur Godfrey, commanding his brigade from a small weapon pit, was killed by a direct hit, together with all with him. His brigade-major, Don Jackson, carried on till Bernard Evans was sent to command.

Unsupported by tanks, and their every movement observed by

the German OP on Point 25, the Australians hung on by their teeth to their main positions and the only satisfaction that the enemy could extract from these fierce efforts was to bite off the tip of the tongue beyond the road and re-establish contact with 125th Panzer Grenadiers in the bottom of the pocket. That, however, did not avail them for long.

THE RHODESIAN GUNNERS

Among many memorable actions fought by small sub-units in this fierce fighting in the Australian sector, one that bears witness to the nature of the conflict was that fought by the Rhodesian battery of the Northumberland Hussars (102nd Anti-Tank Regiment, Royal Artillery).[1]

That regiment was one which in earlier days had won fame as tank-killers with little 2-pdrs and they had served through the fiery ordeals of Greece and Crete. The Rhodesians, or 'Rhodeos', as they were affectionately called, were incorporated as their D Battery, 289th in the official serial numbering. They had a pronounced English Yeoman character and flavour, were resourceful, tenacious, self-reliant, cheerful, accustomed to an open-air life and delightful companions and comrades. They were commanded by Major W. H. Williamson, an Englishman of charming personality and gallant spirit.

The Rhodesian Battery, equipped with 6-pdrs, was sent up from the south, where the Northumberland Hussars were serving with 50th Division, to reinforce the Australians on 27 October, but did not go into action until the night assault of the 30th. They then drove up their guns behind the infantry. The night erupted and flashed on all sides and the moon glowed yellow through the clouds of dust that spouted from the bursts of shells. The dim shadow of the rail embankment appeared like a low wall stretching away on either side in the dusty darkness. Williamson disposed three of his Troops astride it, Lieutenant John Bawden's Troop facing north-west towards 361st Panzer Grenadiers and those of Lieutenant Pat Cramer and Lieutenant

1. Commanded at Alamein by the Author.

H. R. C. Callon north and north-east towards 125th. There was no finesse of defilade fire; the guns, sited in the dark, just pointed at the enemy. Just to a flank were the still forms of a clutch of dead Valentines of 23rd Armoured Brigade.

Williamson waited for the morning's early light of the last day of October to correct his guns' positions. But he was never to see that light. He stood near the mangled railway line in the bitter cold, with Lieutenant J. N. D. Woodrow beside him and Bombardier Catella near by. Just as the stars began to pale, a burst of machine-gun fire caught him full in the chest. Catella was killed also and bullets ripped through both armpits of Woodrow's coat.

Command devolved on Captain Guy Savory, the slow-spoken Rhodesian farmer, but he was not in the battery position that day and all the morning the Rhodesians, with no officers but their subalterns, sat tight and expectant in their gun-pits, watching and listening to the conflict ahead as 361st Panzer Grenadiers made their fruitless attack. They were continually under fire, but could do no more than sit and wait, as anti-tank gunners so often had to do, taking casualties, until attacked.

It was not until the more dangerous attacks of the afternoon by the battle group of 21st Panzer Division that they got the chance of a shoot, when the German tanks began to approach closely, and then they quickly killed four of them. Two of Callon's guns, however, in dead flat ground north of the railway overlooked from the OP on Point 25, were knocked out. That night, which was the relatively quiet night when 24th Brigade relieved 26th, Savory moved the remaining two back alongside Bawden's. At the same time the Troop commanded by Pat Cramer was moved forward. The Rhodesians were now mainly in the terrain taken over by Second-43rd Battalion. Savory's little command post was a hole dug into the side of the railway embankment, not far from a small railway hut where Australian medical officers had set up a precarious Aid Post in the heart of the conflict. The Red Cross emblem on this hut and the files of wounded being brought to it were clearly seen by Rommel himself as he watched his troops trying 'to throw back the British'.

On the next morning, which was Sunday, 1 November, at the

warning that the new German attack of that day was imminent, Savory was ordered to bring up the reserve Troop of Lieutenant Paul Jackson, a quiet, spectacled officer, who in peace served in the Native Administration of Southern Rhodesia. To bring up their guns, Savory had to drive three miles in daylight, under direct observation from the Thompson's Post area, by a track appropriately named Guillotine. He ordered the Troop to 'drive like hell, wait for nobody, zigzag and create your own dust'. This they did with such gusto that they arrived in the deployment area with only one man wounded.

The attack was imminent and Jackson's Troop dug in with all speed near the railway on the Thompson's Post side. His own truck was hit and went up in flames as they did so. Savory, going back to his hole in the railway embankment, saw four portees with their 6-pdrs driving forward across the track and for an agonized moment thought they were his own going up in error; but they were Australian guns and within a few minutes he saw every one of them blown to pieces.

This was the beginning of a furious and critical struggle which went on for nearly a day and a half. All Cramer's guns appear to have been destroyed after an onslaught in which Cramer himself, going about from gun to gun with complete unconcern, to the admiration alike of the Australians and his own troops, met his death after an example of steadfast leadership that lives in the memory of all who survived.

The other Troops, more fortunate in their positions, fought with no less spirit. On Sergeant Hotchin's gun all the detachment except himself and Gunner Robert Young were wounded, but the two continued to man the gun together until it was knocked out. John Bawden, tall, stalwart, the picture of a soldierly figure, commanding his Troop with resolution and composure, was an inspiration to them all, in perfect control, at once on the spot when any detachment was in difficulty or danger. He had his guns very well sited, with the result that they did great damage with little loss. In the faint grey light of early morning on 2 November, Sergeant Cary, seeing some enemy guns coming into action at 1,200 yards, engaged them and, after a few misses in the poor light, hit them one after another and set fire either their trucks or their ammunition.

The final exploit of the Rhodesian anti-tank gunners came on the afternoon of the same day. Gunner Peter Vorster sighted a German Mark III tank approaching on a reconnaissance. To the right of it, at long range beyond the road, he saw an 88-mm being towed by its half-track and to the right of that again a captured 6-pdr on the move on its portee.

With successive shots he knocked out the tank, the 88, its tractor and the portee. There followed a demonstration that must be almost unexampled on a modern battlefield. The surrounding Australians, transfixed with admiration for this cool and superlative shooting, stood up in their doovers and burst into cheers, as though they were applauding a century in a Test Match.

Three months later, after the 9th Division had returned to Australia, there arrived through the devious 'usual channels' a report by the CO of an Australian battalion bringing to Montgomery's notice the courageous bearing of the Rhodesian anti-tank gunners and recommending for a very high award the dead subaltern officer, but, since he was dead, the rules of the Army allowed him no more than a Mention in Dispatches. To those who know, this tells its own tale.

Here we take leave of the gallant Diggers and those who supported them. They had, in General Alexander's words, 'fought the enemy to a standstill'. And themselves also. Alamein and Africa were over for them. If they listened with some wistful feelings to the news of the victory so soon to come, to which they had so much contributed, and to that of the subsequent pursuit, in which they were denied a share, their compensation was that they were soon to see their native land again, before setting out to win fresh laurels in New Guinea.

For, as we say goodbye to 9th Australian Division, we turn to see the curtain go up on the last act.

Part III

SUPERCHARGE

Chapter Seventeen

'A REAL HARD BLOW'

(1/2 November)

Morale from the Skies – The Battlefield Picture –
Freyberg's 'Cup of Tea' – 'Like a Drill'

MORALE FROM THE SKIES

While the Australians were 'drawing everything on to themselves', the forces designed by Montgomery for the final blow were being quickly marshalled and re-equipped. Though the infantry available for a further strike was much weakened and although 24th Armoured Brigade was broken up, the losses in tanks were quickly made good, the artillery, albeit tired, were still very much in the ascendant and the air forces were in control of the skies for most of the day.

The enemy's strength had been reduced in all arms. By the end of October his tank casualties amounted to 289, of which 222 were total losses. With the recent augmentations, his tank strength may still have been nearly 300 (the *Papers* say 304), still a formidable force, but forty were still in the south in the Ariete Division. He still, also, had nearly as many anti-tank guns of all sorts as ever and his ammunition supply was far from being as short as Rommel tried to make out. Moreover, his forces were now so disposed that he could concentrate quickly on a narrow front. His most serious shortage was in petrol.

Even more important than the statistical and material conditions of the rival forces was the morale factor and in this the air forces under Tedder's command had been a potent influence. To our own front-line soldiers the spectacle of the immaculate squadrons sweeping overhead with majestic unconcern and the roar of their bombs, shaking the earth and erupting in enormous clouds of smoke and dust, was immensely heartening, materializing in their eyes as a symbol of invincibility.

To the enemy, on the other hand, the cumulative effect of round-the-clock bombing became an ever-tightening strain. 'Air raid after air raid after air raid,' wrote Rommel himself, more than once in person the quarry of the aerial hunters. Continuing when the daylight squadrons finished, the night bombing by experienced teams of RAF Wellingtons and Fleet Air Arm flare-dropping Albacores lengthened the hours of strain and disturbance among the tank leaguers and the concentrations of transport. These, in fact, offered better targets than were normally to be found by day, when, as often as possible, units were widely dispersed.

Indeed, the material damage from aircraft, as contrasted with their effects on morale, was very small, especially against troops and guns dug in. Even tanks suffered little serious damage, except for the rare and fortuitous direct hit. The only tank destroyers we had at that time were Hurricane II Ds armed with 40-mm 'cannon', firing armour-piercing ammunition, and these, to be effective, had to fly very low and so themselves became targets for every kind of enemy weapon. Their use was accordingly confined to the southern front.

Where our aircraft did execute material damage of the greatest value was at sea. There the Wellingtons and Beauforts continued to sink the enemy's fuel and supply ships with admirable regularity; to such an extent that Rommel was obliged to resort to having fuel brought to him from Crete by air, and there, accordingly, 205 Group paid a bombing visit on 27 October.

THE BATTLEFIELD PICTURE

The picture painted for us, however, as we look over the battlefield on the last day of October, is by no means one in which the soldier's dream of victory was clearly written in the sky.

As we have seen, both Germans and Italians had surrendered readily enough on many occasions, but on the whole the enemy, particularly the German enemy, was resisting tenaciously, showing not only his good fighting qualities, but also his swift response to a situation. These responses were not always sound tactically, but they were instinctive on his part, trained as he was to act swiftly and to counter-attack immediately. The local initiative of his junior commanders was very high and he was skilful at swift improvisation and in the economic use of force. His battle drill insisted on the immediate sowing of mines and the deployment of his anti-tank guns wherever they might be needed and for this manœuvre he had a tremendous advantage in the half-track vehicles that towed them. Moreover, these guns, both those of the divisional units and the formidable heavy weapons manned by the Luftwaffe, were served by exceptionally brave and resolute detachments.

We see the enemy now, therefore, contemplating a short withdrawal, but not defeat. His main strength had been disposed between Tel el Aqqaqir and the coast road, apprehending as he did that Montgomery's intention was to advance along the axis of that road. Approximately along the line of the Rahman, or Ariete, Track he threw out a very formidable zareba of anti-tank guns. Forward of this track, he still maintained his positions at *Woodcock* and *Snipe* in the Kidney Ridge area, facing our old *Oxalic* line along its general length.

Such in outline is the picture behind the enemy's front, where Rommel was anxious but not dismayed. Within the British lines, under cover of the storm that was raging on the Australian sector, the picture shows us the swift and secret marshalling behind clouds of dust of the new striking forces. They were working against time, for Montgomery did not intend to slacken the momentum of the offensive, and staff officers, working day and night with their clerks and signallers, were under severe strain.

Thick congestions of traffic built up as divisions, brigades and units began to shape their courses for the allotted routes forward through the old minefields and order themselves in their determined sequences of march. Intricate regulations governed the movements to Traffic Control Posts, Start Points, Regulating Stations and at all these, as well as at cross-routes and the gaps in minefields, the Military Police, under the orders of their Assistant Provost Marshals, stood imperturbable amid the billowing clouds churned up by fleets of vehicles that lurched and clanged over the dusty desert in the stifling heat of day and the bitter cold of night. Backwards to the base flowed the loaded ambulances and the damaged tanks jangling on their transporters; forward from the base flowed up the RASC lorries with ammunition, fuel, rations and stores of all sorts, new tanks and their ready-trained crews. The dead, wrapped in blankets, were laid to rest in their sandy graves. The air hummed with a cabbalistic jargon in English, German, Italian, French, Greek, Urdu and Afrikaans.

Overhead there was a deeper hum as the Allied squadrons swept the skies and occasionally, at dawn or eve, an enemy squadron darted out to rain down sudden mischief or a lone Messerschmitt skimmed the desert like a blackbird across the lawn, gunning whatever target lay beneath and awakening an angry chatter from every bren, rifle and bofors-gun that could be brought to bear in the swift seconds of its passing.

Amid all these physical activities, officers of all arms were deep in conferences, poring over sand models of the next zone of attack, defining objectives and boundaries, determining the methods and timings of attack, debating the rate of advance and studying the now very scanty information from air photographs and other sources of the dispositions of the enemy. The gunners were working out their complicated sums to bring together the fire of more than four divisions in what was to be the densest concentration of artillery yet fired. The armoured car regiments, long awaiting their turn, were making ready to slip out and to kindle the fires of havoc in the enemy rear.

Montgomery had been visiting the divisions to show himself, to feel the pulse of the troops and to apportion praise where it had been due. With his characteristic disregard of the rules of grammar, he wrote home to General Sir Alan Brooke, the CIGS:

A real hard and very bloody fight has gone on now for eight days. It has been a terrific party and a complete slogging match. . . . So far Rommel has had to dance entirely to my tune; his counter-attacks and thrusts have been handled without difficulty up to date. I think he is now ripe for a real hard blow which may topple him off his perch.

FREYBERG'S 'CUP OF TEA'

The 'real hard blow' was planned under the code-name *Supercharge*. In general method it was to be a variation on the theme of *Lightfoot*, with the infantry of 30th Corps attacking at night under heavy artillery cover and the armour of 10th Corps following up as quickly as lanes could be cleared through whatever minefields there were.

There, however, the resemblance ended. The attack was to be on a narrow front of only 4,000 yards and to the same depth, employing two infantry brigades only. There was a waning moon, not rising until 1 a.m., thus leaving only about four and a half hours for gaining the objective and sweeping a way through the mines before getting the armour out into the open. Very little was known of the locations of enemy defences forward of the Rahman Track and, therefore, a different artillery plan was required. For the same reason, and in view of the experience of *Lightfoot*, the tank attack to be launched after the infantry objective had been won would also be covered by a barrage.

Such were the general considerations. We have already seen what sector Montgomery had selected for the blow. It would create a further extension of the bulge, or what Raymond Briggs called a 'funnel', at its northern end. The centre of this attack would carry the infantry within about half-a-mile of the Rahman Track, north of Tel el Aqqaqir, and the armour was then expected to break through the line of guns known to be on the general line of the Rahman Track and to pass beyond.

There was at first some uncertainty about what infantry could be called upon for the initial phase of this momentous attack. Except for the South Africans, no uncommitted infantry divisions were left in 30th Corps who were strong enough for the effort. As we have seen, Bernard Freyberg was seriously concerned at the numerical weakness of his New Zealand infantry (whom Montgomery designed for a special mission in the pursuit), and he said to the Army Commander during the planning for the new operation:

'I will lead any other infantry you like, but I will not take my New Zealanders into another assault.'

Montgomery, however, wanted Freyberg to do the job and he knew his man. He raised the matter again when they next met. First, he told Freyberg that he could have 9th Armoured Brigade again, but Freyberg shook his head; it was a matter of infantry. Montgomery then offered him a British infantry brigade as well, but he still shook his head, although Montgomery could see that he was clearly 'weakening'.

'Very well, Bernard, I'll give you two infantry brigades.'

Freyberg fell. 'I could see,' Montgomery said afterwards, 'that the old war-horse was itching to fight again. This sort of show was very much his cup of tea and I knew he was the right man for it.'[1]

The *Supercharge* opening attack, therefore, was to be made by the New Zealand Division under Freyberg's command, but, except for the Maori Battalion, without New Zealand infantry. The brigades that Montgomery gave them, in addition to 9th Armoured, who were already fast becoming blood-brothers of the Kiwis, were 151st and 152nd Brigades.

The first of these, commanded by Brigadier 'Jos' Percy, a burly figure with greying hair, came from 50th Division in the south and was composed of 6th, 8th and 9th Battalions, Durham Light Infantry, and we shall accordingly call them the Durham Brigade, by which name they went in their own division.

The second of these brigades, commanded by the thorough, sandy-haired Caithnessian, Brigadier George Murray, came from 51st Division, was composed of 2nd and 5th Seaforth Highlanders and 5th Cameron Highlanders and so was often called the Seaforth and Cameron Brigade.

1. Field-Marshal Montgomery to the Author.

For the benefit of those readers who may not be clear about these things and for those writers who certainly are not, it must be emphasized that these were not operational 'brigade groups' in the desert sense, but brigades temporarily allotted to 2 NZ Division, fighting under the orders of the commander of that division and operationally integrated into it, with his normal divisional staff, his full divisional artillery, engineers and medical and other services. In military terminology, the Durham and Highland Brigades were 'under command'; so also were 9th and 23rd Armoured Brigades, the latter, less one battalion, being also added to Freyberg's force for close support of the assaulting infantry and being ordered over from the Australians as soon as Finigan's tank battle was done. (See also page 67.)

The infantry, however, as in *Lightfoot*, were only a means to an end. Theirs was the task to storm the approaches to the citadel. It was for the armour to break in the gates and to destroy the enemy within. The most critical of all tasks was that designed for 9th Armoured Brigade, who were to break open the gate so long locked by the enemy's anti-tank guns, now ranged in strength along and before the Rahman Track. The brigade had, accordingly, been made up to strength with seventy-nine Shermans and Grants and fifty-three Crusaders.

So vital was its task that Montgomery, who on this occasion, as on so many others, could see far, impressed upon Freyberg that he was prepared, if need be, to lose every tank in the brigade, provided they broke that gate. The lean and percipient Army Commander was to be justified not only in the accuracy of his anticipations but also in his judgement of John Currie and his resolute regiments.

After the Rahman Track and the elevated ground beyond it had been seized, the battle would pass to 10th Corps, who were then required to bring the enemy armour to combat and destroy it. Lumsden also had, therefore, been swiftly regrouping. He decided to use only 1st Armoured Division but to strengthen Briggs's hand with the addition of 8th Armoured Brigade under command.

Montgomery's intention was that the new blow should be struck on 31 October – designedly on the night following the Australians' final northward thrust – but forty-eight hours was too short a time for the enormous amount of preparation required. Freyberg asked Leese for a postponement of twenty-four hours and Montgomery agreed.

After many consultations with Oliver Leese, and after a frustrated attempt to reconnoitre the ground from the Australian lines, which even Freyberg found too hot for that purpose, he held a conference of brigadiers and staffs in an unfinished dug-out in the old Alamein line. Wimberley was there, too, a large part of his division being involved.

It was an impressive gathering, composed, with a lone exception, of some of the ablest and most resolute leaders of armour, artillery and infantry in the desert. A sense of drama possessed them all, waxing more keenly as the intent and scope of the design were unfolded. A plaster model was before them, and there, dwarfing them all, Bernard Freyberg expounded his plan, going through the technique of the infantry assault in detail for the benefit of Murray and Percy, whose brigades were working under his command for the first time.

In the two and a quarter miles of desert over which the two infantry brigades had to advance, Freyberg explained, they would face conditions very different from those on the first night of *Lightfoot*. Much was unknown or uncertain. The country was as flat as a table. Only one substantial minefield was known to exist, but mines must be expected anywhere. To whatever position the Boche was driven back, he observed, the mine was his first weapon of defence, and a patrol of 51st Division in the line had observed the enemy sappers drilling holes with compressors in the rock. In further contrast to *Lightfoot*, it was thought likely, Freyberg said, that enemy tanks might be encountered in dug-in positions in the zone of attack.

The enemy troops facing them were 115th PZ Grenadiers to the south and probably 200th PZ Grenadiers to the north, together with the Littorio Armoured Division, but very little was known of their locations and strengths, except that air photos showed them to be a good deal thicker on the right flank, where the enemy was exerting all the pressure he could against the Australians. Accordingly, the emphasis in the artillery plan was to cover as much of the ground as possible by means of a moving curtain of fire.

Other consequences of these uncertainties were that the infantry objective would be merely a line drawn on the vacant map and that our own forward localities were to be evacuated in the zone of attack to provide a firm start-line for the Durham and Highland Brigades. To avoid the kind of nonsense that had occurred in the Kidney sector, a line of stone cairns had been erected on this start-line on a true survey and related to the artillery 'grid'. Thus it was ensured that the infantry would go where they were intended to go and that all arms would be in agreement. Behind the assaulting troops, Gentry's 6th NZ Infantry Brigade would hold the line.

With this firm basis of survey, the artillery would put down the opening line of their barrage on our evacuated front line with all guns, field and medium, while the infantry closed up to it. After five minutes, the medium guns and a proportion of the 25-pdrs would lift their fire on to such enemy battery positions as were known. Then, as the infantry and sappers moved forward, the barrage would roll in front of them in an intensity not seen since 1918, and it would fall in depth. Closest to the leading infantry would be a curtain of 25-pdr shells twenty yards apart, beyond that another curtain of shells every forty yards and farther behind still the 5·5s and 4·5s would throw down their heavier bursts. There would be 192 guns on the creeping barrage – 168 on such targets as were believed to exist. Halfway to the ultimate objective there would be a primary one for reorganization; as before, both these objectives would be defined by the field gunners with smoke shell and the Light AA gunners would fire bofors tracer to mark direction.

To exercise this formidable artillery programme, the artillery of the Highland Division, 1st Armoured Division, 10th Armoured Division, one regiment from the Australian Division and two medium regiments were added to that of the NZ Division and all were placed under command of 'Steve' Weir, the New Zealand

CRA. Here was one of the most striking examples of the centralized control of artillery, which was one of the great battle-winning factors of Alamein and, indeed, of all the operations of Eighth Army under the new order.

Allotting the infantry tasks, Freyberg put the Durham Brigade on the right of the attack. On this side the enemy defences were thickest and here also was the most sensitive flank, fortified by some of his pre-Alamein defences and lying nearest to his counter-attack forces. Under their command he placed the Maori Battalion, with the special mission of wiping out a known strongpoint at the junction with the Australians, near Point 29.

To the Sussex Brigade, borrowed from 10th Armoured Division, and rather oddly placed under Wimberley's command for the night, was allotted a similar task on the other flank, their target being *Woodcock*, where they had suffered such grievous losses early on D plus Five. Close support for the two main assaulting brigades was to be provided by the Valentines of 8th and 50th RTR. The code names for the infantry final objectives were *Neat* for the Seaforth and Cameron Brigade and *Brandy* for the Durhams.

Finally, as the climax and zenith of the NZ Division's battle, John Currie was to follow with 9th Armoured Brigade to attack and break the line of guns dug-in on the Rahman Track. Their ground objective was the long, mounded Aqqaqir Ridge, of which the Tel was the highest part. 'We all realize,' Freyberg said, 'that for armour to attack a wall of guns sounds like another Balaclava; it is properly an infantry job. But there are no more infantry available, so our armour must do it.'

This, it was expected, would be the last barrier. Through the breech in the wall made by Currie's brigade the armour of 10th Corps would push and the baton would then pass to General Lumsden, while the NZ Division prepared for the final phase of pursuit and encirclement.

This was the outline of the plan that Freyberg explained to the tense and expectant commanders and staffs in the Alamein dug-out. He was insistent that the assault had to go forward 'at all costs'. He told them bluntly that the situation after dawn would be difficult,

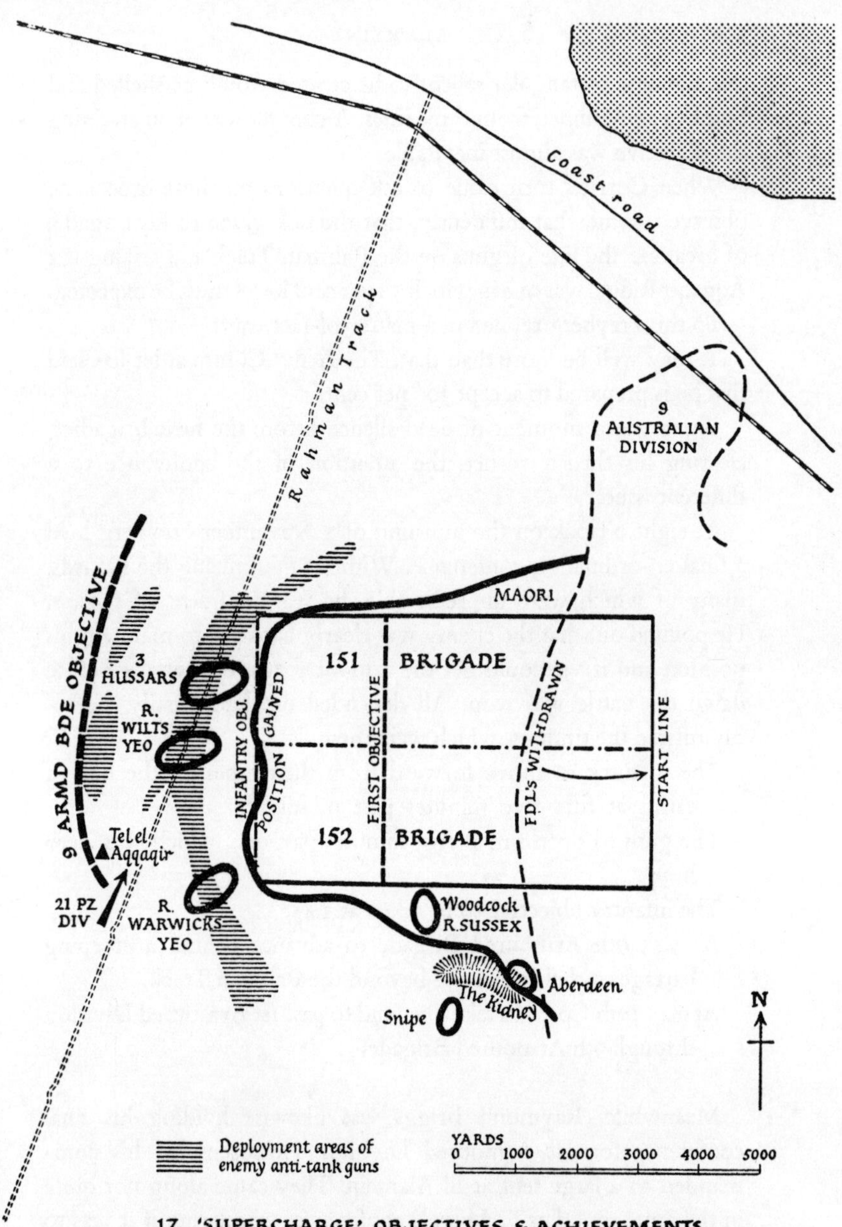

17. 'SUPERCHARGE:' OBJECTIVES & ACHIEVEMENTS OF OPERATIONS UNDER COMMAND 2 NEW ZEALAND DIVISION 2 NOVEMBER

that the new rectangular salient to be created would be shelled and bombed and gunned from three sides. A counter-attack on attaining the objective was almost inevitable.

When Currie's turn came to ask questions on these orders, he observed, somewhat diffidently, that the task given to his brigade, of breaking the line of guns on the Rahman Track and seizing the Aqqaqir Ridge, was one in which 50 per cent losses must be expected.

To this Freyberg replied in a matter-of-fact way:

'It may well be more than that. The Army Commander has said that he is prepared to accept 100 per cent.'

There was a moment of dead silence before the next brigadier, clearing his throat, turned the attention of the conference to a different issue.

At eight o'clock on the morning of 1 November Freyberg held a final co-ordinating conference. Without minimizing the hazards, many of which were unpredictable, he was confident of success. He pointed out that the enemy was clearly hard put to maintain his position and if we could get the armour forward to attack before dawn the battle was won. All depended on that. Finally, he recapitulated the timings, which were these:

The infantry to move forward from their tapes on the line of cairns at fifty-five minutes past midnight.

The guns to open fire at five minutes past one, which was Zero hour.

The infantry objective to be taken at 3.45.

At 5.45 9th Armoured Brigade to advance behind a creeping barrage to their objective beyond the Rahman Track.

At 6.45 10th Corps to take over and to pass 1st Armoured Division through 9th Armoured Brigade.

Meanwhile, Raymond Briggs was likewise holding his final conference for 1st Armoured Division. He assembled his commanders in a large tent at El Alamein. They came along not quite in the same mood as Freyberg's conference, wondering if it was to be 'the medicine as before', but Herbert Lumsden walked in, together with Ralph Cooney, and put them all in a good humour.

'Well, gentlemen,' he said, 'the bet is on. The odds look a bit long but I'm sure we're on a winner.'

Operationally, Briggs's orders (embodied in Operation Order, No. 34) were simple, the greater part of them being taken up with the intricate and tedious business of routes, traffic control, timings, and all the other problems of getting a large volume of fighting vehicles to their right places through the long minefield lanes in the dark. The division, he said, would move up from the rear in three columns by the Australian routes – Diamond, Boomerang and Two Bar – led on each column by the Minefield Task Force under Tom Pearson (who had succeeded Turner in command of 2nd Rifle Brigade). They would carry forward the lanes cut by the New Zealand engineers and reconnoitre for mines forward towards *Recluse*, the code name adopted for the Rahman Track.

Behind them, 2nd Armoured Brigade, on the right of the divisional front, were ordered to advance to a ring contour two miles north-west of Tel el Aqqaqir and 8th Armoured Brigade, under command, were directed on to the Tel itself. In those areas they would stand prepared to meet the attack which he hoped the enemy armour would launch against them. The most likely and the most dangerous direction from which the counter-attack would come, Briggs considered, was from the north and it would most probably be directly against that flank of the New Zealand 'funnel'.

Seventh Motor Brigade were to advance in battalion groups by all three routes to a central deployment area, prepared to meet a counter-attack from the north or north-west. The divisional artillery, having completed their programmes in support of the New Zealand attack, were to move right up to the same area. The armoured cars of 12th Lancers were to advance behind 2nd Armoured Brigade on the northern flank, prepared to slip through and penetrate deeply.

Briggs emphasized, however, that the operations of the armour were not dependent on the success of the infantry. 'Even if 2 NZ Div fail to reach their objective in whole or in part', ran his operation order, '1 Armd Div will fight to reach its objective.'

'LIKE A DRILL'

As before, the prelude to the battle was sung in the air.

On the evening of 1 November, while the assaulting troops below them were moving forward to their battle positions, sixty-eight Wellingtons and nineteen Albacores began a seven-hour attack on targets in the areas of Tel el Aqqaqir, Sidi Abd el Rahman and beyond. Six tremendous explosions and twenty large fires were observed and the signal system at Von Thoma's advanced *DAK* headquarters wrecked. The ruddy glow of their burning could be distantly seen from the British lines, illuminating the palls of smoke that hung over them.

On the ground, the night was exceptionally cold. The Jocks and the Durhams, thinly clad, waiting on their tapes along the line of cairns with their anti-tank and machine-gunners and their New Zealand sappers, shivered a little as they listened to the roar of the distant bombs. The Durhams had had a seven miles night march from Tel el Eisa, ploughing through powdered dust a foot deep, and they arrived looking like ghosts or as though dipped in a huge tub of flour. Hot from their march, they soon felt the two-hour wait in the chill night-air the more keenly.

The night was very dark, the myriad stars providing no substitute for the unrisen moon. Officers and NCOs went briskly up and down the line, checking equipment and correcting the spacing between platoons. On the right of the Durhams, the dusky Maoris were itching to be off in their whirlwind manner. It was too dark to see the shapes of Richards's Valentines that were waiting just a little way behind unless you adopted the desert trick of crouching on the ground.

Farther back still, the trails of 360 field and medium guns were being swung round until all the muzzles converged on the 4,000 yards of frontage ahead of the infantry and the layers were bringing the cross-wires of their sights on to the pinpoint lamps of their night aiming-posts. Fifteen thousand shells stood ready to be fired during the next four-and-a-half hours. Once again every man was looking at his watch as the hands passed midnight and crept into the first minutes of 2 November.

Fifty-five minutes later, with the shrunken moon now diffusing a wan light, the assaulting troops got up from their knees, fixed bayonets and stepped silently across their tapes, guided by compass and regulated by counted paces. Ten minutes later the barrage, a real barrage, burst ahead of them with 'a frightful shattering', standing still on its opening line as the soldiers closed up to it, a shell every twelve yards.

Then, as it jumped forward 100 yards every two-and-a-half minutes with reduced intensity, the infantry and their companions followed it at the set pace, moving into a dense cloud of smoke and dust. They coughed and spluttered as the dust and the fumes of high explosive enveloped them. The moon was blotted out and no man could see more than thirty yards, but, ominously visible above the pall, the enemy's SOS rockets, calling for the fire of his own artillery, shot up along the line. Amid the smoke and smother the notes of the Scottish pipes, filling the momentary pauses between the successive crashes of the shells, 'like linnets in the pauses of the wind', stole stirringly upon men's ears. On their right, where the spectral shapes of the 9th Durhams glided in their blanched accoutrements, they were answered by the hunting-horn of Major Teddy Worrall.

Very different were the fortunes of this night from those of D Day. On the left the attack of the Seaforth and Cameron Brigade went, in Freyberg's own words, 'like a drill'. The brigade attacked with 5th Seaforths, the Caithness and Sutherland men, on the right, 5th Camerons (Ronald Miers) on the left and 2nd Seaforths (Kenneth MacKessack) following. At the last moment Jock Stirling, commanding 5th Seaforths, his arm in a sling from a septic infection, was obliged by his medical officer to leave the field and Major Jack Walford was brought up from the rear to take over just as the battle began. He was a small, almost insignificant figure of a man, but was to show himself a wonderful leader in battle, with a life charmed against all danger.

In this exhibition attack George Murray was throughout in good wireless contact with his battalions, and to Freyberg's tactical headquarters in his Honey tank there flowed throughout the night-hours a series of model signals that told with graphic composure their own story of resistance swiftly overcome and objectives won.

1.48 a.m. We are in touch with both battalions and everything appears to be going smoothly.

2.18 a.m. There is light shelling and moderate machine-gun fire on our front. We have taken some prisoners, a mixture of Italians and Germans. Everything appears to be going according to plan.

2.35 Newly laid minefield discovered.

3.59 On left flank our tanks [*i.e.* 50 RTR] are engaging enemy tanks.

4.17 Both battalions have reached objective and are in action with enemy tanks. Artillery concentration 'Roxbrough' called for and fired.

5.25 Enemy tanks are melting away and battalions are getting supporting arms up. One Italian tank captured intact.

5.35 Reorganization of final objective is proceeding and battalions are linking up. Right gap is through and left, will be open as soon as small minefield is cleared. Our casualties will not exceed 40 per battalion.

Murray's brigade had, indeed, captured all their *Neat* objectives very aptly and on schedule and had executed an operation in full battle conditions better than many a manœuvre on training exercises. Throughout the attack and its subsequent phase the Jocks were balanced, composed and in command of the field. Their communications were sound and when threatened they were able to call for artillery support and receive it promptly. In Freyberg's own words, 'it was a very fine performance.'

The Highlanders' assault, however, was by no means the cakewalk that Murray's matter-of-fact signals seemed to suggest. As Freyberg thought they might, both battalions ran into the dark and forbidding shapes of dug-in tanks during their advance, and when they consolidated on *Neat* it was 'amidst the enemy armour'. In the

Cameron battalion Lance-Corporal Mightens and in 5th Seaforths Sergeant Carnduff's platoon, dropping grenades into the turrets, each captured a tank intact and the commander of the first fell to Mightens's rifle.

Casualties, which had not been severe against an enemy shaken by artillery fire in the assault, mounted rapidly after winning the objective, when heavy and continuous shelling pounded the battalions and where the ground was like iron. Then and in the succeeding hours 5th Seaforths lost twelve officers and 150 men and by the morning's light Lieutenant H. S. Robertson and seventeen men were all that were left of C Company. Captain Murdo Swanson, his leg shot off, lay cracking jokes till he died with the soldier who lay near him. The battalion's MO, Captain Farquhar Macree, went about unconcernedly tending the wounded, was captured and escaped.[1]

On the right of 5th Seaforths, however, the attack of the Durhams, though successful, did not march with the same precision. The opposition on their sector was stronger, particularly in the path of the 8th Battalion on the right, where there was a series of ten or more enemy posts, in depth, and there were many more on the dangerous and strongly-manned right flank, where the enemy had been facing the Australians.

This battalion was commanded by the blunt and forceful Lieut-Colonel 'Jake' Jackson and on his left was the 9th Battalion (Lieut-Colonel Andrew Clarke). Following them was the 6th Battalion, led by Lieutenant-Colonel William Watson. His special and difficult mission, on reaching the first objective, was to execute a right-wheel and face northwards to guard this flank. A New Zealand anti-tank battery was under Brigadier Percy's command.

The Brigade began to take casualties early but were encouraged by the numbers of German and Italian dead who littered the path of their approach and by the shattered men who gave themselves up,

1. So highly do the Seaforths and Camerons prize the memory of their achievements on this night that, largely on this account, the new combined regiment – The Queen's Own Highlanders – now wear *Alamein* on their pipers' accoutrements.

many of them almost hysterical from the fearful bombardment. Other enemy posts, however, overleapt by the inevitable gaps in the barrage, resisted and the advance was marked by a series of fierce little duels by sections and even single men who encountered detachments of entrenched Germans still full of fight. Thus, Private James Brown, of the 8th Battalion, though wounded himself, wiped out or captured a German section post single-handed and in the 6th Battalion RSM Page and Sergeant Albert Dunn accomplished similar feats of arms.

The 8th Battalion of the Durhams, however, was itself very much cut-up. Jackson's own carrier was blown up by a direct hit. Even at the halfway objective, the two leading companies had lost more than 100 men. B Company had lost all its officers and A Company had been reduced to isolated sections. The attack upon the final objective was undertaken by C Company alone, finely led by Captain I. R. English. To that objective, isolated from the rest of the battalion, they hung on nearly all next day under a galling fire and with German tanks within a few hundred yards.

On the dangerous right flank, as was to be expected, 6th Battalion also faced stiff resistance. Here one platoon lost its subaltern commander, all its NCOs and all but five of its men. While attending to their casualties the doctor was himself wounded; he carried on, but, while he was dressing the wounds of RSM Page, both were killed, as well as the medical sergeant. Away on the left, the medical officer of the 9th Battalion (an American) and his sergeant were likewise both killed.

Thus the passage of the Durham Brigade was rough and bloody, yet they reached their final objective within a few minutes of time, and by four o'clock in the morning, with the partial moon beginning faintly to illuminate the scene as the dust of the barrage settled, they were digging into the rock. The New Zealand sappers, making a safe way for the armour, came up behind them and by five o'clock the fighting vehicles of 6th Battalion, led by Maurice Kirby, were up, and soon afterwards the ambulances, crammed with wounded, were making their way back.

Brigadier Percy, however, seems to have been out of communication with his battalions during the later stages and Freyberg, back at his Honey, was anxious, for a firm base for the armoured advance was very important. The situation was not lucid and it was not until nearly 5.30 a.m., with first light less than an hour away, that he felt justified in informing 30th Corps that the new front had been fully won.

Farther still to the right, where the flank of the night's attack hinged on the Australian sector, the Maoris also had a fierce fight for their limited objective. Assaulting with their characteristic fire, they captured the stronghold west of Point 29 that threatened the Durhams' right flank, linked up with the Australians and handed over to them their bag of prisoners. But they took 100 casualties in doing so, including their gallant half-Maori CO, Fred Baker, whose tongue was torn out by a bullet.

On the opposite flank, the Sussex Brigade had the satisfaction of capturing *Woodcock*, with their 2nd and 5th Battalions, thus avenging the bitter experience of their sister battalion there a few nights before.

Thus, although the Durhams' hold at the northern extremity of their new front was tenuous, Freyberg could regard the night's work by his infantry and sappers, superbly supported by the artillery of 10th and 30th Corps under the able handling of his own young CRA, as a brilliant success. Not only had the ground been won as a 'funnel' for the armour, but severe casualties in killed, wounded and prisoners had also been inflicted on the enemy in this battle of attrition; 9th Durhams alone had captured over 400 prisoners. The enemy was, therefore, not nearly so thin on the ground as General Alexander's subsequent dispatch suggests, and they had been overcome in a battle fought in the 'old-fashioned' First World War way – the Freyberg way.

It was a splendid prelude to the momentous attack in the new-fashioned way by 9th Armoured Brigade, which he was itching to see launched against the Rahman Track, now only half-a-mile distant in the centre, while it was yet dark.

Chapter Eighteen

THE CHARGE OF 9th ARMOURED BRIGADE

The unpredictable factors of war, however, denied to Currie's brigade the chance to meet the enemy while it was yet fully dark.

Currie, like Freyberg, knew well that the moon's phase would give him little enough time after the securing of the infantry objective and the weeding of the Devil's Gardens. His target, we may remind ourselves, was the Aqqaqir Ridge, which, running north-and-south, lay one-and-a-half miles west of the infantry objective, with the Rahman Track, lined with telegraph poles, running diagonally across the intervening ground. Like most other features in this part of the Western Desert, the ridge was merely a long swelling a trifle higher than the surrounding ground and the Tel itself was merely the highest point in it, without any distinctive outline.

As may be seen from the map in Figures 17 and 18, the enemy guns and other defences were deployed in a wide crescent and in depth, many along the Rahman Track itself, others in front of it and others beyond. Many were sited, as was their wont, on the reverse slopes of small folds of ground, so that they might catch the attacking tanks at a disadvantage at killing range. There were some two dozen 88s in the screen, most of them in positions beyond the track, together with what the subsequent staff study described as a 'vast number of smaller guns'. To this formidable barricade were added several dug-in tanks, as seen in Plate xxxi.

The barrage for Currie's attack was timed to begin at 5.45 a.m. He had told his three regimental commanders of Montgomery's preparedness to accept a hundred per cent casualties and some of the COs had, in turn, passed it on to their squadron leaders. The deadly seriousness of the operation was thus evident to them all, but they accepted the challenge without cavil. Their only reservation lay in their concern for the time factor. They dismissed from their minds the likelihood that they would all be wiped out and felt confident that, if they could get in among the enemy guns in the dark, they would be successful. But only in the dark. The COs therefore realized how vital it was that they should reach their *Grafton* start-line on time and they determined that they would press their approach march through the minefield and the newly-won infantry positions with all the resolution possible, taking large risks. Currie, shaking hands with a very young tank gunner of the Warwickshire Yeomanry whose fighting eagerness delighted him, said: 'We can't fail.' If his brigade could blow a hole and if 1st Armoured Division could keep close up to him, then the gates of the enemy citadel would be open at last and the battle won.

The gates, however, were not to be opened quite so quickly or so easily. The brigade left its rest area near El Alamein station at eight o'clock in the night of 1 November, faced with an all-night approach march of about eleven miles before reaching their start-line. They numbered 123 tanks, few of which were new. The replacement Crusaders issued to the Royal Wiltshire Yeomanry after their Miteiriya losses were in a deplorable state. Nothing fitted. Nothing worked. Guns, compasses and radios were all faulty.

The brigade moved off in double line-ahead in three regimental groups into the Diamond, Boomerang and Two Bar tracks, each armoured regiment with its infantry company of 14th Sherwood Foresters, who were placed immediately in rear of the leading tank squadrons, and the anti-tank guns from 31st New Zealand Battery. On the right the experienced Peter Farquhar led 3rd Hussars, in the centre Alistair Gibb commanded the Royal Wiltshire Yeomanry, and on the left were the Warwickshire Yeomanry under the strapping figure of Guy Jackson, a man of astonishing physical resilience.[1]

They were soon in difficulty. The darkness of the night and the enveloping clouds of powdered dust, more than a foot deep, churned up by their own tracks, and driven down each column by a head wind, plagued them from the beginning. The drivers, straining to peer through their apertures, were choked with dust and for long periods could see nothing at all. Tanks at times cannoned into each other and at others lost contact and the wheeled vehicles got stuck in the dust-bog.

As they moved up into the battle area of the ground that had just been won by the Highlanders, the Warwickshires were momentarily checked by having to dispose of some anti-tank, or tank, fire from their left flank. On the troublesome right flank the 3rd Hussars group, pressing with great determination and led by the Crusaders of A Squadron, under Captain Richard Heseltine, suffered damaging casualties from the persistent shellfire that was harassing the Durhams. Every one of the wheeled vehicles was knocked out. All the officers of A Company of the Foresters were killed or wounded. The majority of the lights put up to mark the minefield lanes cleared by the New Zealand sappers had been blown to bits, and in the fog-like conditions ten tanks were lost, either blown up on mines as they tried to by-pass the burning wheeled vehicles in their urge to get forward, or else knocked out by shellfire.

The Hussars' group accordingly arrived at the Durhams' shaky front line with no anti-tank guns and with the Foresters so crippled by casualties that, when the time came to form-up for the attack, the intention to intersperse them between the leading tanks, which had been done so successfully in *Lightfoot*, had to be abandoned. In the brigade as a whole, twenty-nine tanks failed to arrive in time for the attack.

Nevertheless, as a result of their determination, the Hussars and the Royal Wiltshires arrived at the *Grafton* start-line on time. The Warwickshires, however, try as they would, could not quite make it.

1. He treated with the utmost casualness the loss of both legs in the Italian campaign and after the war rode again to hounds.

The Hon. Peter Samuel, leading the advance with the Crusaders of A Squadron, had been badly thrown out in time and direction by an inexplicable diversion in their allotted minefield gap, which had led them to a blind end and obliged them all to turn round and return to the point where the lane had forked.

Farquhar and Gibb urged Currie to let them make their attack without waiting for Jackson, in order to get in among the enemy guns while it was still dark. Currie, however, was concerned for the Wiltshires' left flank and with the importance of making the breach as wide as possible. He thought he could accept a slight delay and asked for his barrage to be postponed for half-an-hour. To this Freyberg felt obliged to agree, though it meant communicating the change to fifteen artillery regiments in the various divisions of the two corps.

The regimental commanders collected their squadrons and arrayed them for battle. Farquhar regrouped 3rd Hussars, withdrawing Heseltine's much damaged A Squadron from the van, and replacing it by Michael Eveleigh's B Squadron. All were feeling the fatigue and 'bloodiness' of the all-night march. For Major 'Tim' Gibbs, who led the advance of the Wiltshires, the approach had been a nightmare, for the intercom radio of his Crusader was out of action, and he had sat all night out on the front of the tank, choked with dust, shouting verbal orders to his driver through the aperture.

All, however, were able to get on their marks reasonably well balanced. The spirit of the squadrons was high and the call of a desperate enterprise put every man upon his mettle. The radios crackled as orders passed from tank to tank. The night was noisy with desultory fire from guns and mortars, but no man deceived himself that the growl of the engines and the creaking of the tracks were unheard by the watchful enemy. Unlike the cavalry of old, the iron horsemen could not muffle the jingle of their harness.

John Lakin, commanding a squadron in the Warwickshires, 'marvelled at the quiet calm of every man and officer as they moved dimly and certainly each to his own particular job; for this was no picnic, and the dead and wounded lay all around as clear evidence of what might befall any man'.

The warning of extreme casualties had not been passed beyond squadron leaders. Not every man could be expected to face such odds with easy feelings. There were some, however, who, when they saw the surprising position in the field that their brigade commander now took up, could not fail to draw their own startling conclusions. For Currie decided that, if there were to be 100 per cent casualties, the brigade commander himself could not be excluded. Accordingly, instead of posting himself in one of the accepted positions in the field, from which a brigadier could command, he now placed himself near the van of the attack. He ordered his little brigade major, Pat Hobart, who knew all, to follow him at ten yards' intervals.

Having emerged from their minefield lanes, Currie's regiments spread out frontally into line-abreast by squadrons, disposing themselves in the irregular pattern that, in their cavalry days, they had known as 'artillery formation'. The feeling that this was indeed a cavalry exploit was not far absent and it was surely the cavalry spirit that would be needed this night of all nights. Regimental and squadron commanders went about on foot, giving last-minute orders.

In the two yeomanry regiments the Crusader squadrons, some of them armed only with 2-pdrs, led the array, followed by the heavy squadrons of Shermans and Grants. The three regiments deployed in the same order of battle as that in which they had marched – the white horse of 3rd Hussars on the right, the Prince's feathers of the Royal Wiltshires in the centre and the Warwickshire bear on the left. With the two yeomanry regiments were their companies of the Foresters, in carriers or on foot. In the Wiltshire Yeomanry Captain John Gilbey was astonished to find that a sergeant of the Highland Division had jumped on his tank in the approach march, begging to be allowed to go with him; Gilbey's gunner having become a casualty, the Jock was given some hurried instruction and took the gunner's place for the coming battle. In the rear of Currie's regiments were the light tanks of the New Zealand

Divisional Cavalry, standing by for their special task after gaining the objective.

The regiments formed up and waited, like horsemen with reins hanging loosely from the bit. The engines idled. The dust of movement settled. Tank commanders peered out of their turrets in the wan moonlight and beheld each other's solid shapes on either hand. Ahead lay the seemingly empty night. The desert was a cold, blue-grey vastness, stretching out to the stars beyond Aqqaqir. One could see about 100 yards – dark enough, men reflected, for a reasonable chance that some of them would get through.

Inside each tank all was quiet. The crew, coated with dust, suddenly became sensible to the strain and fatigue that they had already experienced. The driver sat quietly between his steering sticks, awaiting the order in his earphones to start. The gunner, his weapon ready loaded, tested his traverse a last time and relaxed. The wireless sets ceased their chatter for a while; the last order had been given and the next signal would come from the guns.

At 6.15 the guns roared their signal and the barrage burst in front. The drivers, their hands now ready on the sticks, heard the command in their earphones: *Driver, advance*. They engaged gear, let in their clutches and moved forward into the gloom. Tank commanders, their turrets kept open, stood up with head and shoulders outside; but Farquhar, like Currie, preferred to sit out on top of his tank, behind the turret. The leading squadrons closed up to the barrage, driving not very far behind the curtain of smoke and dust. The curtain then began to move forward at a very slow infantry speed, jumping 100 yards every three minutes.

Not far from the van could be discerned the slim shape of their brigade commander, standing right up on the outside of his tank, in his faded mess-cap, looking sharply to left and right. In contrast to his usual manner, Currie was in a deadly mood tonight, set and determined, the tiger in his blood, not ready to tolerate the slightest faltering on the part of any man.

As the tanks went forward, out of the smother small parties of Germans sprang up from their trenches and then ran about distractedly. The Besas and Brownings of the tanks attacked them at once and many were dropped. Others put up their hands and, with a jerk of the thumb from the tank commanders, were ordered to the rear. Others staggered about in all directions, bewildered and crazed by the barrage, and were inescapably run down by the oncoming tanks. Their mouths were seen to move with unheard screams as the great steel treads rolled on to crush them. The dead and wounded who lay in the path were crushed likewise.

Thus, for a while, the British tanks carried all before them. In the north and centre the leading squadrons of 3rd Hussars and the Wiltshires, their machine-guns blazing, reached the Rahman Track while it was still dark and passed well beyond. The remaining squadrons followed, but the night was nearly spent and, as the eastern sky began to lighten, the British tanks were silhouetted against it and the enemy's heavy guns that were disposed in depth opened a devastating fire against their black shapes. In an instant the whole character of the action was transformed. The enemy gunners and infantry who had surrendered ran back to their weapons and manned them. Along and beyond the now discernible telegraph poles there took place what an officer of 3rd Hussars described as 'a desperate and bloody encounter'. Both sides hammered each other 'even at the cannon's mouth', but, whereas the enemy in the open could clearly see the shapes of the British tanks, the gunner inside the tank was as though blindfolded and could at first do no more than sweep the ground ahead with his Browning or his besa.

Of that tempestuous fight at close quarters it is scarcely possible to give a detailed and coherent account, but through the smoke and din we may discern its main outlines as the barrage passed on and as the telegraph poles began to silver in the early morning light. We see a Crusader tank of the Wiltshires driving right across a gun in its pit, straddling the barrel with its tracks. We see others poised on the lip of a gun-pit, wiping out the detachment with their machine-guns. We see nearly all the enemy guns that were closely engaged overcome, shattered or crushed by the tanks or left with no gunners to serve them. We see also the heavy and inevitable price that was exacted by the more distant guns, the big 88s and 7.62s beyond the track, as they opened fire in the biting dawn, now overlaid with a film of mist. One after another the British tanks were knocked out, and as the smoke and flames poured from their hulls the crews leaped out and rolled themselves in the sand to put out their burning clothes, or endured that harsher fate that overcomes those who could not escape.

Certain incidents we can observe a little more closely through the smoke and dust: Currie himself, standing boldly erect, bearing a charmed life, right in among the enemy guns; Pat Hobart close behind him, his staff duties shed, the world to him a sudden bewilderment of gun-blasts, chattering machine-guns, heavy shot that screamed by in red or white darts, or hit and ricocheted with high parabolas into the sky. A tank, narrowly missed several times, moved away a few yards to take evasive action, but the wrath of Currie fell upon its commander instantly. Moving his tank alongside, Currie shouted above the din, as the armour-piercing shot flashed between them: 'Where the hell are you going, you windy little . . .? Get on!'

Such is the general picture of this Balaclava charge. A clearer view of its course of events is given us if we follow first the action of the Royal Wiltshire Yeomanry in the centre, where there was very nearly a complete break-through.

Here, as throughout the approach march, the van was entrusted by Alistair Gibb to the Crusaders of B Squadron under the stalwart figure of Major Tim Gibbs. Alistair Gibb, in pursuance of the Army Commander's order, was prepared to lose the whole of the squadron, but expected to get through on their heels with his heavies.

Major Gibbs began his attack with eleven tanks all in unsound condition. His was the only compass in the whole squadron that worked. His Besa machine-gun was unserviceable, his 2-pdr very nearly so and his radio in very bad shape. At the start he had gone out on foot to give his Troop leaders verbal orders, knowing that, once the attack was launched, he could exercise little control.

The attack of B Squadron was a complete success. They reached the Rahman Track. They got right in among the enemy guns, dug-in tanks and machine-guns before the enemy knew what was happening. There was complete consternation as the Crusaders swept in in the dark. Few of the enemy weapons could be brought to bear. On every side the German and Italian gunners and infantry were throwing up their hands, fearful of being crushed to death. Others were streaming back, leaping into whatever transport was available and making off. Four officers jumped into a staff car and began to move off. Gibbs, having no other weapon at hand that he could trust, took a pot shot at the car with his .45 revolver, and to his astonishment saw it go up in flames.

Gibbs thought that the battle was won. His squadron went up and down crushing the trails of enemy guns. Finding no other opposition, he radioed successfully to Alistair Gibb that the way was clear and then himself drove on for 1,000 yards or more towards the Aqqaqir Ridge.

Then, as the sky paled, the storm burst. In his own words (to the Author) 'the whole world seemed to blow up at once'. The big guns disposed in depth had seen him in the early light. Tom Elson's Troop, which had done so well at Miteiriya, all burst into flames almost simultaneously. In two minutes Gibbs's squadron was reduced to two tanks – his own and that of Lieutenant R. Balding. He took refuge in an enemy gun-pit, to await the arrival of the heavy squadrons of Lord Cadogan and Henry Awdrey.

As he waited Gibbs saw, away on the left flank, a force of armour approaching in the distance in the early morning mist. He took it for the Warwickshires, whom he expected to be just there, and thought that all was well. Intending to collect the crews of the tanks that had been knocked out, he drove out of his protective gun-pit. He was immediately assailed by the tanks approaching from his left flank, which were, in fact, a counter-attack column of 21st Panzer Division. He replied to their fire as best he could with his ineffectual 2-pdr as the leading panzers got to within 400 yards of him, when his own tank, which had been repeatedly hit, was shot up in flames, his wireless operator killed and he himself hit in both legs. He was hit again as he dragged out the dead man. With his gunner and driver, he made for Balding's tank, which, collecting a few more survivors, made its way back miraculously under a hail of fire from everything that the enemy could bring to bear. All but one of those clinging to the hull of the tank were hit again. Gibbs was hanging on to the ankles of Sergeant Wenham in front of him when a bullet shot through his arm and killed the sergeant.

Meanwhile, Alistair Gibb had ordered his heavy squadron to follow through. They had reached the Rahman Track when the dawn storm burst. They in turn became its victims as the armour of the panzers, now within a few hundred yards, added their fire to that of the heavy guns on the slope of Aqqaqir and to the fire of all sorts from the nearer enemy who had forsworn their surrender. Cadogan's squadron was astride the track when, in a few minutes, it was almost completely wiped out. His own Grant was on fire and two of his crew killed. He saw with dismay the whole Troop of Lieutenant Allen Pennell, well beyond the track, shot up in flames almost simultaneously. He began to collect the wounded and tried to get them back, but the infantry of 152nd Brigade were firing at everything on foot that moved in their direction. The other squadron of the Wiltshires met a similar fate and Henry Awdrey was also 'brewed up'.

Alistair Gibb's command tank 'Trowbridge' was hit likewise and its high octane petrol flamed up in the morning air. He, Christopher Thursfield (his adjustant) and the crew leaped out, but the driver was killed by machine-gun bullets as he did so. After having been pinned down for a while by the machine-gun crew that had so lately surrendered, Gibb and Thursfield made a dash for a wrecked truck, in which they found the wireless still working. There Gibb reported to Currie, saying that he had no wireless contact with any of his squadrons but that he thought B Squadron was through. Soon afterwards he was hit in the arm by the fire from our own infantry.

On the Wiltshires' right very much the same course of events attended the forceful attack of 3rd Hussars under Peter Farquhar. In the first spectacular fifteen minutes, Michael Eveleigh's squadron, leading the assault, crashed through and well beyond the line of guns in the most determined manner. Thus Lieutenant Charles Dorman found himself ten yards away from a battery of four

50 mm guns. His Troop knocked them all out. Almost simultaneously Lieutenant Kenny's Troop knocked out another battery of four farther away to his left. Both Troops then came under fire at the hour of first light from the 88s sited farther back or to a flank, and three or four tanks were quickly in flames. Eveleigh, observing a third battery of four guns in action beyond the road, called upon Kenny, Dorman and Lieutenant Hill-Lowe to follow him and attack them. Kenny at once responded but his tank was immediately hit and blown up and he himself never seen again. Dorman's tank was hit, too. Only five tanks were left in that Squadron, but, in the words of their leader, 'it was no use stopping now and the only thing was to keep going'. This they did, but Eveleigh's own tank was soon shot-up in flames by a battery of Italian 47 mm guns at a range of twenty yards. Ejected from the tank by his gunner and wireless operator, Corporals Rafferty and Holton, Eveleigh ran round to the front to extricate his drive and co-driver, Sergeant Good and Trooper Brooks, but found their apertures locked fast by the shock of the hit and the armour plating already red-hot. Seeing the Italian gunners shooting at his other two men with small arms, he emptied his revolver at them. Dorman, observing what had happened from the right, swung round, engaged and wiped out the Italian battery, while Eveleigh made his precarious way back through the field and, sickened by the repulsive smell of burning bodies, was picked up just in time by Farquhar himself with his revolver empty and his ammunition expended.

Meanwhile, Farquhar, observing that Eveleigh's squadron was through, ordered Major Alan Dawes, commanding C Squadron, to move up at once. Like most of the brigade, he had now no wireless contact and to give Dawes his orders he had to dismount and walk over. Observing the concentration of fire now on the remnants of Eveleigh's Squadron, he ordered Dawes to go through on their right, where there was a slight eminence. It was now almost full day.

His orders, however, must have been misunderstood, for when Farquhar returned to his own tank, which was itself being repeatedly hit, he saw to his dismay that C Squadron was going straight into the furnace. He knew they were going to certain death, but could not stop them. In a few minutes Dawes was killed and most of his squadron wiped out. Undismayed, the remainder still went on, led by Second-Lieutenant Chesworth, but nearly all fell to 88s on the northern flank or to a squadron of Panzers from 15th PZ Division, which now came up behind their protective cover. Only two or three tanks in C Squadron came out of that fiery ordeal of fifteen minutes.

Farther south, the Warwickshires, accompanied by their Foresters, had gone a little off-course as a result of the minefield divergence, thereby unwittingly creating a partially open flank for the Wiltshires as the tanks of 21st Panzer Division made their counter-attack. There they fought their own battle. It was begun very quickly when Lieutenant Ted Parish, 'very small but very brave' as his squadron leader described him, attacked and destroyed a battery of four Italian guns. Very soon the whole regiment, as it followed Peter Samuel's Crusader squadron into the fight, was heavily engaged, encompassed by enemy on all sides, fighting the enemy guns, dug-in tanks and machine-guns at close range and dropping grenades on the German and Italian infantry. As the darkness dissipated, the Warwickshires' tanks became outlined against the Eastern sky, so that, as Lakin thought as he glanced to the rear, they looked like 'damned great houses'. They immediately began to take heavy casualties, but stood their ground, doing great damage and sacrificing all but seven of their tanks.

Guy Jackson, though faint with the onset of jaundice, stood up in his tank throughout, surveying the action like a master watching hounds draw a covert and urging on his squadrons with phrases of the hunting field. 'The fox,' he called into his microphone, 'will break cover any minute and the hunt will be on. Don't go back a yard'. Lakin, his own tank in flames, his gunner mortally burned and his driver and loader badly burned also, made his way on foot over to Jackson after 'a hellish half-hour' and found him 'like the rock of Gibraltar, with his big pennants flying bravely', and his over-heated gun firing rapidly at all sorts of targets until it was hit, while Sergeant Court gave him magnificent support.

Thus all along the brigade front the combat waxed to a climax in the cold dawn mist and, as the eastern horizon glowed blood-red in the pre-dawn, Currie, watching anxiously for the arrival of 2nd Armoured Brigade, whom he expected at this moment to break through upon his heels, saw no sign of them in the lightening sky behind.

All that he could see was a world of devastation – devastation of the enemy, indeed, their shattered guns sprawling at crazed angles, their detachments lying dead, but devastation of his own brigade also. As far as the eye could see lay the terrible record – tank after tank burning or wrecked, the smoke of their burning mingled with the cold mist, the crimson shafts from the eastern sky tincturing all objects with the hue of blood. Only here and there could he see a tank still defiantly shooting it out with the more distant guns and the tanks of Africa Corps. He was very angry, very bitter. In fulfilment of his orders, he was ready to sacrifice all if Fisher's brigade had been there to crash through whatever ragged breaches he had torn in the enemy's wall of guns.

It might be thought that, after such a devastating experience, the remaining handful of tanks would have had little further stomach for the fight, but such was far from the facts. They extricated themselves in good order and continued the fight, their offensive spirit unsubdued. The half-dozen heavy tanks of 3rd Hussars, on Farquhar's orders, took post in line facing west and continued to engage the 88s, which had caused most of the damage, and he sent Heseltine with two Crusaders 1,000 yards to the north to keep observation for the threatened counter-attack by 15th Panzer Division. His own battered tank, hit again and again, Farquhar had had to abandon as a wreck. All that then remained of the whole regiment's tanks, fit to continue action, was eight; they had started the battle with thirty-five. Only four officers of the regiment were alive and unwounded; twelve had been killed.

These are but a few glimpses discerned through the smoke of this fiery action, an action unique in military annals, in which the British tanks fulfilled their mission in blood and fire, and one which we may surely call heroic. Nearly every squadron leader's tank in the brigade was destroyed. In the Wiltshires every tank fought its own fight under its officer or NCO and most of them fought it to the death. Virtually every tank in the regiment was lost. One of them had been hit with such violence, at twenty yards' range, that it had been bowled clean over and lay on its side.

When the battlefield was inspected very soon afterwards, thirty-five enemy guns were found knocked out within 100 yards of the burnt-out tanks. Of these, 3rd Hussars claimed seventeen and the Wiltshires fourteen. Some of the tanks were found at the very mouths of the guns. Three hundred prisoners had been taken and there would have been many more if there had been any troops to gather in those who offered surrender in the battle of the gun-line.

In the words of Freyberg himself, 'it was a grim and gallant battle right in the enemy gun-line. Although the 9th Brigade did not reach its objective and had heavy casualties, the action was a success, as the enemy gun-line was smashed'. Montgomery, sending the brigade his thanks and congratulations, told them that their exploit had ensured the success of the operation.

The price paid by Currie's regiments was slightly lower than the Army Commander had allowed for. Out of the ninety-four tanks with which they had gone into battle, they had lost seventy-five and out of some 400 officers and men who had manned them they had lost 230. For the whole night's operation their total tank losses were 103.

The nineteen tanks that remained rallied on the right and continued to fight under 1st Armoured Division in the further operations which we shall presently witness, and in which, still full of fight, they had the satisfaction of knocking out several German tanks.

Nevertheless, it had been a terrible ordeal. Guy Jackson, having brought back what was left of the Warwickshires, collapsed as he got out of his tank. Currie was asleep on his feet. Briggs, who met him later in the morning, found his eager spirit 'worn with fatigue, harassed with distress' at the agony of his regiments and 'very bitter that 2nd Armoured Brigade had not arrived in time'. We shall judge for ourselves in the next chapter how valid his grievance was.

When, a little later, Gentry brought up 6th New Zealand Brigade to take over from the Durhams, he went forward to discover the dispositions of the tanks on his front. He found Currie, fully dressed still, asleep on a stretcher beside his tank, with a dozen or so other tanks dispersed around him. Gentry hesitated to wake him, but decided that he must. He shook him and, when Currie awoke, said:

'Sorry to wake you, John, but I'd like to know where your tanks are'.

Currie waved a tired hand at the little group of tanks around him and said:

'There they are'.

Gentry, puzzled at his reply, said:

'I don't mean your headquarters tanks. I mean your armoured regiments. Where are they?'

Currie waved his arm again and replied:

'There are my armoured regiments, Bill'.[1]

1. This account of 9th Armoured Brigade's attack has been compiled from such records as are available and from the personal narratives, written or oral, of Brigadier P. R. C. Hobart, Lieutenant-Colonel Sir Peter Farquhar, Colonel M. St J. V. Gibbs, Lieutenant-Colonel The Earl Cadogan, Captain C. R. C. Thursfield, Lieutenant-Colonel John Lakin, Major The Hon P. M. Samuel, Major The Marquess of Bath, Major M. Eveleigh, the late Captain C. B. Stoddart and Major-General Sir William Gentry.

Chapter Nineteen

THE HAMMERING OF THE PANZERS

(2 November)

The Battle of Tel el Aqqaqir – Exploiting Success – Rommel's Eyes Open

THE BATTLE OF TEL EL AQQAQIR

Tiger though he was, Currie remained deeply affected for many weeks afterwards by the grievous losses among his regiments in their self-immolating attack. He continually asked both himself and his friends if he had done right. To that question, however, so far as he and his brigade were concerned, there could be but one answer. They had obeyed orders. Freyberg, with professional detachment, remarked:

> It may be argued that it was a costly and incorrect method of using armour, but, if we are to believe General Von Thoma, it may well prove to have been the deciding factor in breaking the German line, though advantage was not taken of the breach until later.[1]

The qualification with which Freyberg ended his comment illustrates the controversy that followed over the immediately subsequent operations of 1st Armoured Division, and their relationship to those of Currie's brigade. To the sorely-tried Hobart and to most others who followed Currie on that morning, the 'crash action'

1. Op. cit.

(to employ a gunner's term, entirely appropriate to Currie) was a fully justifiable use of armour in the circumstances. But to Briggs and others of hard experience:

> The plain truth is that armour cannot charge concealed or semi-concealed guns behind a crest and get away with it. Those have to be dealt with methodically by stalking, HE fire and artillery concentrations and this takes time. If 2nd Armoured Brigade had been closer up, the story would merely have repeated itself.[1]

On the other hand, it might be argued that the loss of impetus initiated by 9th Armoured Brigade endangered the Army Commander's plan. Montgomery did not want Rommel to retreat; he wanted to break through, swing up to the coast, encircle and destroy his enemy. If 2nd Brigade had been right on Currie's tail, they would have suffered severely but might have crashed through. So it can be argued.

In retrospect, we should treat the charge of Currie's brigade as part of the larger and the most momentous action about to be begun by 1st Armoured Division, to the success of which they paid a sacrificial contribution beyond facile assessment. In their Homeric hour they had severely shaken the opposition to Briggs's division. It is beyond question that 3rd Hussars and the Royal Wiltshire Yeomanry made a definite breach in the Rahman Track. Farther south, as Lakin remarked laconically (to the author): 'You may say that we did not make a real breach, but we certainly made a bloody good dent.' It was daylight that defeated the brigade, exposing them to the fire of the heavy guns disposed in depth on the Aqqaqir Ridge to the west and north-west. Farquhar and others still maintain confidently that, had the attack not been postponed for that half-hour, the two regiments could have overrun these also and won their final objective.

General Briggs, as we have seen, had directed 2nd Armoured Brigade to a feature two miles north-west of Tel el Aqqaqir and 8th Armoured on to the indeterminate Tel itself. He had appreciated, from the enemy's dispositions, that the counter-attack would be

1. To the Author.

most likely to come in on the Durham's flank. The whole division (whose order of battle for this occasion is given in Appendix F), moved up from the Springbok Track during the night under conditions which were, if anything, even worse than those which 9th Armoured Brigade had experienced, the dust-fog being so thick that tank commanders had to hold out torches to the rear for the following tank to keep touch. With tanks, artillery, infantry, engineers, ambulances and front line services, they numbered well over 2,000 vehicles. We shall follow first the fortunes of Fisher's brigade in the north.

Here the Queen's Bays, under the very tall and aquiline Alex Barclay, advanced on the right, 9th Lancers, commanded by Gerald Grosvenor, of handsome bearing and distinguished lineage, in the centre and 10th Hussars, under Jack Archer-Shee, tall and willowy of figure, with a good tactical flair, on the left. Each regiment was preceded by its Reconnaissance Troop and accompanied by its affiliated battery of Priests from 11th RHA, its infantry company of the Yorkshire Dragoons and other supporting elements. The 10th were delayed in their approach march through misdirection by a military policeman and the other regiments were about two and a half miles behind Currie's brigade at the moment when his regiments first came under fire from the guns on the Rahman Track. That was too far to take advantage of any breach, if one were made. Fisher had been unable to make wireless contact with Currie and did not know how matters stood ahead of him.

Shortly afterwards, 10th Hussars were engaging in the half-dark the tanks of 21st Panzer Division that had assailed the Wiltshires. Here Archer-Shee's own tank was knocked out; the enemy, having located his tanks' point of emergence from the minefield gap, made it a very hot spot.

All three regiments, however, after passing through the enemy's artillery counter-barrage, moved on steadily in the cold dawn mist, meeting batches of Germans coming in to surrender from the ground overrun by Currie's tanks.

In the gloom of 7 a.m. Gerald Grosvenor met Currie himself, who appears to have just pulled back. Grosvenor records that 'Never before or since have I ever experienced such shelling. The air seemed to be thick with both armour-piercing and HE coming from the front and both flanks. It was not quite light and, what with the smoke, one could see literally nothing, except the flames from 9th Armoured Brigade's burning tanks.'[1]

As Grosvenor drove up, he saw a group of people sheltering in the lee of Currie's tank, but Currie himself was sitting right out on top of the turret, taking less notice of the missiles than if they had been mosquitoes. Grosvenor dismounted from his tank and walked towards Currie, who called down to him:

'Come up and join me.'

Grosvenor did so. Currie waved towards the smoke and flame to the westward and said:

'Well, we've made a gap in the enemy anti-tank screen, and your brigade has to pass through, and pass through bloody quick.'

Grosvenor, gazing out at the angry chaos, replied:

'I have never seen anything, sir, that looks less like a gap.'

Currie made a tart observation and Grosvenor, feeling that this was no time or place to argue, returned to his own tank and reported to his brigade on the air. Archer-Shee, tall and slim, going forward when his tank was knocked out, also met Currie, alone in a group of wrecked tanks; Currie was 'a bit cross' and said: 'You're bloody late.'

Twenty minutes later 9th Lancers were about 1,000 yards short of the devastation on the Rahman Track, across which the flash and counter-flash showed the remnant of Currie's brigade in the last throes of their engagement with the enemy guns. The Bays were a little farther back on their right and 10th Hussars 1,500 yards away to the south-east; engaging the tanks of 21st Panzer Division that were shaping eastward towards them, they saw them off behind their curtain of anti-tank guns.

Briggs himself, moving by the Boomerang route, very shortly came up behind one of the leading regiments. He used two Crusader tanks for his tactical headquarters; one of these was a spare 'charger' and in the other he took only a junior staff officer, signallers and

1. To the Author.

driver. His Main divisional headquarters was some way back, in their Armoured Command Vehicles, in charge of Roger Peake, his GSO 1. Briggs made a practice of having a telephone line laid forward from Main, which he could tap into from his Tac for freedom of speech, though it was frequently broken by shell fire or tank movement.

As he came up, he was very concerned at the inability of 2nd Armoured Brigade to get forward more quickly, but realized that now there was no purpose to be served by attempting to force a way through in Currie's path. It was not his mission to support Currie, but to bring Von Thoma's panzers to battle on ground of his own choosing. That prospect he thought was now probably very near. He therefore wanted room to manœuvre. For that purpose he hoped, as his orders prescribed, to be able to push on beyond the Rahman Track on to the Aqqaqir feature. The hither side of the Track was very exposed, littered with derelicts and cluttered by our own troops; the whole of the terrain captured during the night was being heavily shelled and mortared from front and flanks, and the infantry brigades, among whose forward elements Fisher's tanks were now taking up position, were sustaining mounting casualties.

About this time, and repeatedly during the next hour or so, Fisher reported that his regiments had reached the Rahman Track, but Briggs quite rightly did not accept this report. The squadrons had perhaps been deceived, it appears, by the fact that somewhere, not recorded on the map, a line of telegraph poles branched off from the track. The only tanks actually across the track, which we have already observed to have been obscured by a small undulation, were a few sad and gallant wrecks of Currie's.

At about 7.40 the sun lit the horizon behind the British lines like an enormous gunflash, but failed to dispel the mist and the drifting smoke of burning tanks, which continued for some time to obscure observation and hinder progress. A few minutes later Lumsden arrived at divisional Main headquarters and Roger Peake reported the position to him. Lumsden stayed a little while, listening to the reports coming in by radio, and heard just after eight o'clock that both 9th Lancers and 10th Hussars were engaging enemy tanks, and that the

Bays, who had made contact with the withdrawn survivors of 3rd Hussars, had had to turn north to fight the anti-tank guns attacking them.

Lumsden was not wholly satisfied and ordered that the brigade must press on and this order was passed forward to Briggs. At the same time Lumsden, speaking personally to Briggs by radio, warned him that he must expect a counter-attack by 'everything that the enemy had got' and that he must look particularly to the west and north-west. It was clear that a vital situation might develop very soon.

Twenty-five minutes later (8.45 a.m.), the telephone lines forward now being through, Peake spoke to his general again, telling him of a message received at 30th Corps from 9th Brigade. It said that Currie thought '2nd Armoured Brigade is not really in touch and may ruin a good opportunity'. Several signals were passing from Fisher's three regiments about this time which showed that they knew little about the situation of their 'friends in front' – who were, by now, not very much in front.

Fisher, who had been forward to look at the ground (and had not-much liked what he saw), was therefore told to ensure a good link-up. He was again asked how far he was from the Rahman Track and again replied that 9th Lancers were on it. Briggs was in a sharp mood, fretting at the lack of progress on the ground, though Fisher's regiments were not having an easy time. At four minutes past nine Fisher asked the divisional commander:

'Is it intended that I push on or stay?'

To which Briggs replied: 'Your instructions are to destroy tanks and get into positions where you can.'

A minute later Fisher reported: 'In accordance with orders, Brigade has taken up positions ready to take on attack from west or north. Being engaged by tanks and anti-tank guns.'

Briggs replied: 'Destroy opposition and get on.'

And ten minutes later he said: 'We must have room. You must push on.[1]

1. These and other extracts from divisional and brigade signal logs are not, of course, verbatim records. They are what signallers (some better than others) were able to record in the flow of signal traffic.

The two commanders were obviously not thinking alike. Briggs was thinking ahead, but Fisher was satisfied that he was in good position to meet an attack and wanted to fight where he was. He controlled his regiments shrewdly and kept them all balanced.

By now the remnants of Currie's brigade had come under command and it was clear that no live tanks were across the track. It was equally clear, however, that Fisher's brigade had not reached the track, as they thought they had, and that there was no immediate likelihood of their doing so.

There were still plenty more anti-tank guns to north and south of the fracture made by Currie, as may be seen in Figure 18; there were tanks and guns on the Durham flank and there were the tanks and guns on the Aqqaqir feature which B Squadron of the Wiltshires had observed and which were now engaging 9th Lancers. On the northern flank the Germans' guns were so close that the Bays could clearly see the detachments reloading after each round, until they were disposed of. Fisher came up to see the regiment in his Grant and told them to 'stick it out where they were'. From here also could now be seen the slim, white minaret of the mosque of Sidi Abd el Rahman, a beckoning symbol gleaming in the sun.

That was the situation which had developed since first light and it was not the business of 1st Armoured Division to make any more Balaclava charges. Their assignment was to invite attack by the main strength of the enemy armour, and this they proceeded to do, although not on top of the Aqqaqir Ridge as had been intended.

All this time the watching and probing armoured cars of 12th Lancers had been reporting a great deal of tank, gun and lorry movement behind the enemy's immediate front, clearly in preparation for a powerful blow by large forces. Soon after 9.30 Briggs learnt that the 'Y' service had intercepted a signal from either Rommel's or Von Thoma's headquarters ordering 21st Panzer Division to attack southwards on the Durham flank. Twenty minutes later Fisher's brigade was engaged and almost at once 8th Armoured Brigade also came into the battle picture, as eighteen German tanks shaped to attack the Staffordshire Yeomanry under James Eadie.

Custance's brigade, following behind Fisher's in the approach march, were naturally much later on the scene, and, in accordance with orders, were shaping course to come up on Fisher's left and make for Tel el Aqqaqir. Like Fisher's they were in regimental groups, accompanied by their batteries of 1st RHA and the infantry companies of The Buffs. Their delayed advance was fortunate, in the sense that the Burton men of the Staffordshire Yeomanry observed a panzer attack developing on the Durhams' flank to the north and were able to turn and face it. The panzers appear, from the map references given in the records, to have penetrated on this flank and the Staffordshires, in the middle of the infantry positions in the 'funnel', became involved in a long duel.

Further evidence very soon came in of the enemy's impending main counter-attack from the north-west. From the look-out position in which the Crusaders of 3rd Hussars had been posted by Farquhar, Heseltine observed tanks moving from both north and south to join up and, as one of these columns passed at 1,000 yards, the remnant of Farquhar's regiment, unbowed by their dawn battering in the gun line, destroyed two Germans and three Italians.

Briggs, warning his brigades of the anticipated attack from the north or north-west, ordered 8th Brigade to link up with 2nd, but at the same time to be prepared to assist the Staffordshires. He also ordered 7th Motor Brigade to deploy against the same threat. Currie's band of survivors, still full of fight, were sent to guard the northern flank. A further 'Y' intercept showed that 21st Panzer Division had ordered an anti-tank screen to be deployed to the north-west of the British position, which Briggs rightly saw as intended to be a defensive screen for the deployment of the German armour; indeed a force of forty enemy tanks began to approach in the distance from that direction.

The whole of the northern and western portions of the New Zealand funnel were being so heavily shelled that it called for no little determination, not only for the infantry but also for the armour, to face it; 7th Motor Brigade resolutely deployed, nonetheless, taking many casualties. The detachments of 239th Anti-Tank Battery, who had fought so gallantly under Baer and Willmore at *Snipe*, were with them, together with the rest of their battery, and deployed under trying conditions to meet the new threat.

A new factor now came into the situation. At 10.37 Montgomery himself intervened and spoke on the telephone to Roger Peake at divisional Main headquarters to enquire about the situation and the locations of units. On being informed of them, he directed that 8th Brigade should be relieved from its role facing north, ('I will take care of that', he said) and should be moved westwards round the southern flank of 2nd Brigade.

Briggs gave orders accordingly, but Custance was unable to comply in full immediately as the Staffordshires were still joined in conflict with German tanks, now numbering twenty-six, attacking from the north. However, he dispatched 3rd RTR, under Pyman, followed later by the Sherwood Rangers under Kellett, and himself made a forward reconnaissance towards the Tel to within a few hundred yards of the telegraph poles.

A big armoured battle was now imminent and Briggs's attention became riveted on the north and north-west. He ordered 2nd Armoured Brigade not to give ground and asked if they were knocking out tanks. Fisher replied:

> We are not giving ground. 40 enemy tanks to NW, 30 to West, 18 to SW are keeping at long range behind an anti-tank screen. 11 RHA are knocking out anti-tank guns with some considerable success.

Fisher's regiments had by now moved right-handed from their furthermost points of advance, and were disposed to meet the new threat. Briggs visited them there and afterwards drove south to 8th Brigade and saw Custance.

Then, out of the heat haze, the enemy made his attack. From the north-west and west and, to a lesser degree, the south-west also, his squat, black shapes – panzers and Italians – came on in serried lines to the number of about 120. The two forces, which had already been engaged in intermittent combat since dawn, became locked in a grim and exhausting duel in the heat of the day in which tanks, anti-tank guns and field artillery joined with concentrated intensity on both

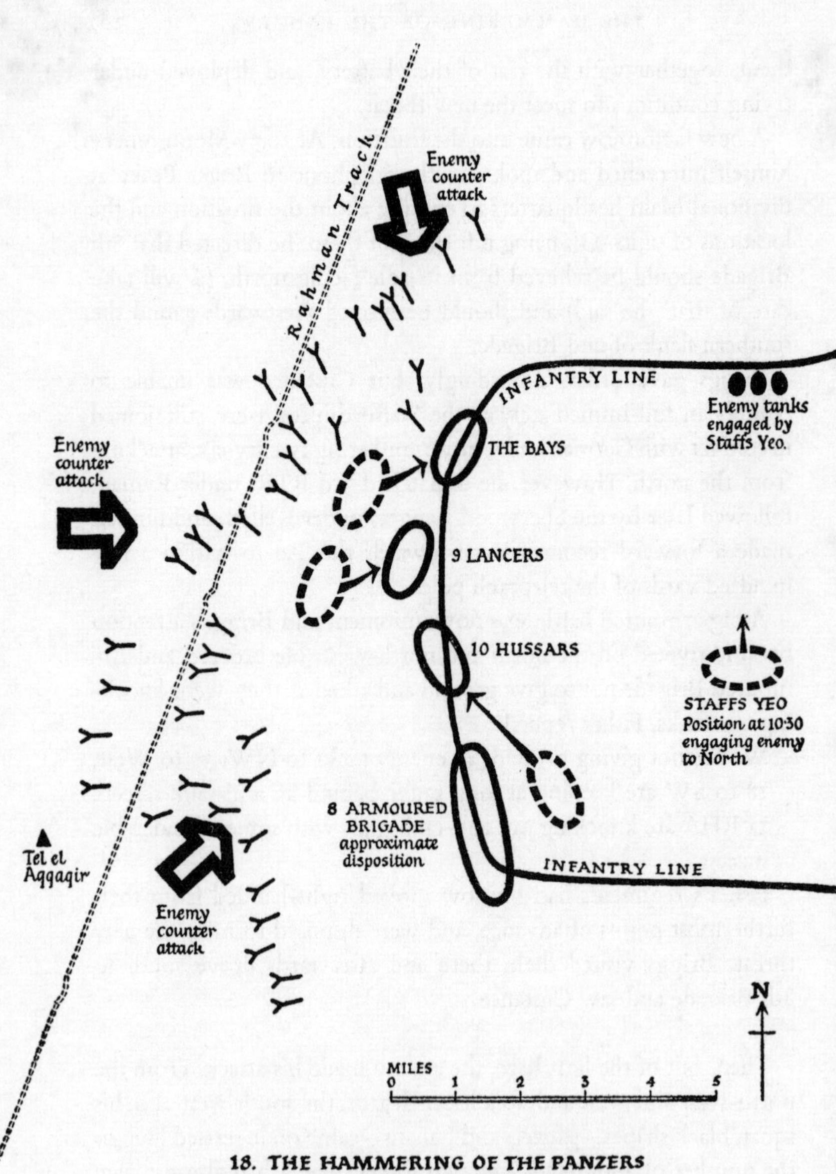

18. THE HAMMERING OF THE PANZERS

Dotted lines show first dispositions of 1 Armoured Division regiments before re-deployment to meet armoured counter attacks. Positions of enemy anti-tank guns notional. Based on the original trace attached to 1 Armoured Division Committee of Investigation report.

sides. This was the vital battle that might make or break the fortunes of the campaign. The British tanks, well enough sited, and aggressively supported by their artillery, stood their ground and dealt out the most fearful punishment, while from the air, in response to Briggs's call, repeated attacks were made on a very large concentration of vehicles observed between the tank battlefield and the mosque of Sidi Abd el Rahman to the north-west.

The desert, quivering in the heat haze, became a scene that defies sober description. It can be discerned only as a confused arena clouded by the bursts of high explosive, darkened by the smoke of scores of burning tanks and trucks, lit by the flashes of innumerable guns, shot through by red, green and white tracers, shaken by heavy bombing from the air and deafened by the artillery of both sides. Upon the British forces in the funnel – tanks, infantry and supporting arms – a 'torrent of shell and shot' was poured in from three sides. In the words recorded by the sober historian of 9th Lancers, 'for hours the whack of armour-piercing shot on armour plate was unceasing'. Overhead, fierce conflicts were fought in the air as the Germans twice attempted to attack the British armour with Stukas, only to be fought off by the RAF.

The long and violent action continued throughout that suffocating afternoon as the enemy made one attack after another in different sectors. B and C Squadrons of 9th Lancers repulsed no fewer than six determined attacks upon them. Again and again the British tanks ran out of ammunition, and each time the replenishment lorries, with great daring, drove out across the shell-swept ground into the heat and clamour of the conflict. The infantry and anti-tank gunners in whose midst this armoured battle was fought – the Motor Brigade, The Yorkshire Dragoons, the Durhams, the Seaforth and Cameron Brigade – suffered considerably. On one occasion the panzers broke across the infantry front, but were quickly forced to pull back. Everywhere else the enemy was met by an inflexible front.

Tel el Aqqaqir, like Thompson's Post, ranks as a battle within a battle. In this exhausting battering match, the biggest and most critical armoured engagement of the campaign, Von Thoma's panzers and their Italian allies were fought to a standstill. It was the hardest hammering they had so far endured and there was to be only one that was harder. By the end of the action sixty-six or more tanks had fallen to the two British armoured brigades. Others fell to the anti-tank gunners, to the survivors of Currie's brigade and to the field and medium artillery. By the end of that day Rommel's strength in tanks had fallen by approximately 117, of which seventy-seven were German.

It was a crippling loss. The enemy's chances of saving himself from ruin were now small indeed. First Armoured Division had not succeeded in making capital out of the sacrificial attack of 9th Brigade and it had made no ground at all, but it had fulfilled a substantial part of its prime mission of 'finding and destroying the enemy armour'. It had also knocked out battery after battery of guns and, when the enemy positions were later overrun, the pits were found full of dead and their weapons broken by the accurate fire of the British artillery. The gunner OPs, pushed right forward among the tanks, had been eagerly calling for fire throughout the day on all manner of targets. Three guns had been knocked out by Jack Tirrell, FOO of B Battery, 1st RHA. The division's own losses in tanks had been no more than fourteen, with a further forty damaged.

Granted the overall superiority in numbers (which did not necessarily mean a superiority at the points of attack), the British armour fought with skill, courage and excellent leadership at all levels, brilliantly supported by 'the terrible British artillery'. They thoroughly deserved their impressive victory. Once again, the tank in attack was seen to be helpless against a determined defence.

It is instructive to remark that the enemy's methods in this vital battle were his usual ones of making a series of probing attacks in different sectors, searching for a soft spot. In these attacks, as soon as the leading tanks were knocked out, the remainder came to a halt, not attempting to press and continuing the engagement by gunfire. They knew that to press against determined resistance was merely to invite destruction. These were also our own methods – methods, indeed, which we had learnt from him but which our infantry and other arms were so apt to criticize without understanding.

Although Freyberg was disappointed at the lack of progress on the ground and the inability to secure the real break-out for which he was itching, both Montgomery and Leese were well satisfied. To Montgomery it seemed significant that Von Thoma had not thrown in his counter-attack with his usual speed and had allowed Briggs to form a strong front for meeting it in good time.

The explanation lay in the fact that Rommel had again been surprised by both the point and the direction of the new thrust. His dispositions had been made for an attack along the coastal axis. He was soon to be once again surprised.

EXPLOITING SUCCESS

Rommel, however, was not yet completely 'knocked off his perch'. He had been dealt a very hard buffet and his wings were beating the air, but he still just managed to hang on by his claws. As long as he could throw out a fence of anti-tank guns he could keep the British iron horses at bay. His difficulty was to know which was the right place, for Montgomery, while still adhering to his general plan, kept hitting him in an unexpected quarter.

Among Montgomery's talents were his skill at exploiting success and his aptitude in creating new reserves to do so. He visited Freyberg's battle headquarters in his tank and made his decisions in the forenoon of 2 November. He had assessed the value of the attack made by 9th Armoured Brigade and scented the first indications of the forthcoming tank battle between Briggs and Von Thoma, but did not wait for it. He decided to strike again immediately, and once more in a new direction, giving his enemy no rest. Exploiting the success of the New Zealand funnel he was now going to strike from it *southwards*.

How the break-out was now to be made was pretty clear to him. While 1st Armoured Division continued their frontal pressure north of Tel el Aqqaqir, the funnel was to be widened in order to launch 7th Armoured Division and the New Zealanders in a swinging movement at its south. Montgomery had brought up 7th Armoured from the south the day before and placed them in Army reserve, strengthening them with the celebrated Queen's Brigade (131st

Brigade) from 44th Division as their lorried infantry. Since this move took place six days after Rommel had moved up 21st Panzer Division from the south, it ought to be pointed out how grossly mistaken is a recent denigrator of Montgomery in describing this move as an example of Montgomery's 'dancing to Rommel's tune'.

To carry out his new intentions, Montgomery now ordered the following measures:

Four infantry brigades to be held in reserve in 30th Corps; these were the Durham Brigade, 154th (Black Watch and Argyll) Brigade from 51st Division, 5th NZ Brigade and 5th Indian Brigade.

Two features south of the funnel to be captured this evening.

Seventh Armoured Division to move to Tel el Eisa and come under command 10th Corps.

Two South African armoured car regiments to prepare for a break-out westwards.

These measures were put in hand with the speed the situation demanded. For the immediate infantry attacks to the south of the funnel, the baton was handed once more to Douglas Wimberley. The objectives were limited, the one being a ring contour known as *Skinflint*,[1] 1,500 yards south of the extremity of the funnel, and the other being *Snipe*, which lay a little more to the east.

Skinflint was duly attacked at 6.15 p.m. by 2nd Seaforth Highlanders and 50th RTR, supported by eight regiments of artillery. *Snipe* was attacked a little later by the Sussex Brigade, also with powerful artillery support. Both attacks 'went like a drill' against small opposition and it was significant that the prisoners taken now were Italians. They were minor operations, but they were to have very important consequences. The funnel had now been widened and from its southern lip would be developed a new attack on the Rahman Track, but this time *south* of Tel el Aqqaqir.

Thus ended a very remarkable series of operations that had been accomplished in about nineteen hours. On this second day of November had been fought two big tank battles, an infantry battle and two minor operations. The enemy had been almost broken. It was the

1. Map ref. 863295.

vital day of the whole of the Battle of Alamein and, as was to be learnt later, it was the most nearly decisive day.

To the swift blows of the soldiers had been added continued blows from the air. The bombers dropped 165 tons of bombs, mainly on enemy positions west of the Rahman Track. Two more ships were sunk in or off Tobruk harbour by Beauforts and American Liberators. The Hurricane squadrons rallied to the help of the British armour, when the attempts were made by the Germans to attack them from the air, once with twelve Stukas and once with forty, both under fighter escort. The first was met by Hurricanes of 33rd and 238th Squadrons and the second by 213th Squadron and 1st Squadron South African Air Force. Both attacks were broken up, the Stukas on one occasion being driven to jettison their bombs on their own troops.

ROMMEL'S EYES OPEN

In spite of the heavy blows dealt to the German Africa Corps that day by ground and air, Von Thoma, who seems never to have fully apprehended the situation until he was taken prisoner, made that evening another somewhat odd report to Rommel. The British forces, he said, were very superior and their air attacks very trying. In his own *DAK* there would be only thirty-five (German) tanks remaining on the morrow. His infantry, artillery and invaluable 88s had been reduced to one-third of their original strength. The 50-mm anti-tank guns had shown that they penetrated the main armour of the Sherman and the Grant at only short ranges and they were gradually being overwhelmed by the British tanks and artillery. The Italians, he said, were of little value, except for their artillery.

In spite of all these gloomy facts, however, he considered that the British advance had been checked and that the front was just holding.

Rommel's eyes, however, were at last more widely open. His forces were being systematically worn down by daily attrition. His losses in tanks and guns that day had been very severe. The indentation of his front was being punched deeper and deeper. He appreciated at last that, if his more valuable troops were not to be destroyed where they stood, he must pull out.

He therefore ordered the first steps to be taken for a withdrawal to Fuka, some sixty miles in the rear, and, on a day of evil omen for them, ordered up the Ariete Armoured Division from the south to assist in covering the withdrawal. He no longer thought in terms of counter-attack, but of erecting a defensive fence to permit a withdrawal in good order. He banked on the hope that the British would follow up sluggishly, as they too often did, but sent a pessimistic report to Germany. To his wife he wrote on the same day: 'The enemy is slowly levering us out of our position.'

Chapter Twenty

THE DAY OF DOUBT

(3 November)

Not Enough Bayonets – Apollo's Bow – No Progress – Hitler Intervenes

NOT ENOUGH BAYONETS

The events of the night following this day of success, however, did nothing to further 'the gradual destruction' of Rommel's forces, but lent some colour to Von Thoma's more sanguine appreciation at that time. It was to be a night in which, as at Miteiriya Ridge, the British waves of impetus seemed in danger of beating fruitlessly against the breakwater of guns.

When darkness came on 2 November, 1st Armoured Division were still not yet across the Rahman Track. Their passage was still barred by the zareba of anti-tank guns that commanded the approaches to the long, low Aqqaqir Ridge. These had got to be shifted by some means before the armour could get on. After a talk with Lumsden, Briggs decided to launch his infantry at the ridge that night. That meant the Rifle battalions of 7th Motor Brigade. They were to capture the track and the high ground beyond it on a front of two miles northward of Tel el Aqqaqir.

The decision was not made until 8.30 at night, so there was no opportunity for reconnaissance. The enemy's positions were not known in detail, but Briggs believed that the opposition would not be stiff. The brigade, after an all-night drive through the dust-bog of the minefield approaches, had been sitting under shell fire all day, and were, even in the best circumstances, far too few in bayonets for the assault of a defended position. Nevertheless, they nearly succeeded.

The three battalions moved up to their start-line and there lay down on the sand for a few hours' uneasy sleep in the cold and the din of war all around them. At 1.15 a.m. on 3 November they made their attack. On the right was the London Rifle Brigade (Lieutenant-Colonel Geoffrey Hunt), in the centre 2nd Rifle Brigade of *Snipe* fame, now commanded by Tom Pearson, and on the left 2nd/60th Rifles, led again by Heathcoat-Amory and directed on to Tel el Aqqaqir itself.

Hastily mounted, the infantry action was carried out with great spirit but was not very well co-ordinated with the artillery. All battalions made a good start as they disappeared into the darkness and on the left the attack of 60th Rifles went well. They crossed the Rahman Track, encountered no guns there and, together with two troops of 6-pdrs of 76th Anti-tank Regiment, dug themselves in on some high ground on the ridge beyond. They believed they were on the Tel itself, but in fact were on some broken ground east of it. At first light they were joined by 10th Hussars, who, together with the anti-tank gunners, saw off an attempted counter-attack by the German armour, the gunners brewing up at least one panzer.

The other two battalions, however, ran into unexpectedly fierce opposition on and along the Rahman Track, where the enemy positions had, no doubt, been reinforced during the night. There was a very tough close-quarters fight in the moonlight right in the gun-line at revolver and bayonet range. The riflemen were leaping into the gun-pits. Gun crews were overcome, infantry and machine-gun positions captured. D Company of the London Rifle Brigade, commanded by Stephen Trappes-Lomax, overran the guns and made contact on their right with 2nd Rifle Brigade, who had got two companies through and were beginning to entrench themselves in the rock. Both battalions had taken prisoners.

Both were, however, far too thin on the ground and the enemy strength had not been accurately gauged. Pearson's battalion had no more than sixty officers and men on the position. A counter-attack by tanks was clearly imminent but the 6-pdrs were barred from coming forward by a heavy counter-barrage, which the enemy now knew exactly where to place. The positions were clearly untenable and Bosvile radioed permission for the two battalions to extricate themselves and withdraw, an operation almost as hazardous as the attack.

Of this action, the historian of the Rifle Brigade, comparing it with the renowned engagement at *Snipe*, remarks: 'One week later, in this trifling, inconsequent, nameless battle, of which no one has ever heard and which ended in undignified retreat, the casualties were nearly as many and individually quite as important.'

Not least of these was Captain Michael Mosley, who had commanded B Company at *Snipe* and who was now killed by a machine-gun burst as he was standing beside Pearson awaiting the order to withdraw. The effort, however, was not in vain, for it served to keep Rommel's attention to the area north of Tel el Aqqaqir while Montgomery was preparing to surprise him by a further series of attacks south of it on the next night.

APOLLO'S BOW

Thus the dawn of 3 November did not appear to break auspiciously for the Allies. Bernard Freyberg, sniffing the powder-laden air that morning and a trifle sanguine, as he sometimes was, thought that the enemy was 'cracking'. Briggs also thought that there would be a big break-out within twenty-four hours. But the time had not quite come.

It was D plus 11 and the physical and nervous strain was beginning to tell on the British as well as on the enemy. They were very close to the zenith of their effort. While the front-line troops naturally had the most to endure, an arduous and exhausting duty was laid also upon all who backed them up. The RASC lorries that brought up ammunition, fuel, rations and stores, as well as the fighting units' own supply echelons, ploughed daily and nightly through the 'bloodiness' of the ever-lengthening minefield gaps, churning and bumping in low gear through the dust-bogs, bleary-eyed from lack of sleep, snatching meals when they could. In a subsequent tribute to them Montgomery wrote: 'The RASC has risen to great heights.'

No one, however, lay under greater strain than the staff officers of formations, who lived under perpetual pressure, divorced from sleep, preparing every day and every night for some operation, each involving concentrated study, planning and quick action. The constant switches of troops which Montgomery required (and which was one of the secrets of his success) alone caused severe staff strains, but Montgomery never spared his commanders or staffs. Many were now beginning to be mentally and physically worn out. We shall see an example of this strain in a divisional commander in the next chapter. For such men as George Walsh, Oliver Leese's BGS, the battle had been ten days of sustained crisis and they had no time to think whether we were winning or losing. 'It was all very well', he said,[1] 'for Monty to express his confidence, but for most of us it was really touch and go to the end.'

The like was true also of all artillery commanders, who had not only to direct the artillery of their own divisions, but also to co-operate every day in the operations of every other division, a task that imposed upon all the most exacting care and the most detailed calculations and planning. Wimberley noted later in his journal that George Elliot, his CRA, was 'by now utterly exhausted, worn out with days and nights of calculating fire plans'.

Accordingly it appeared to few people, if to any at all, that we were about to win one of the great battles of history. Montgomery himself was outwardly the soul of confidence, whatever might be his private thoughts and communications, but victory was not yet convincingly assured. While we certainly could not now lose the Battle of Alamein, we could not win it until we had broken the enemy, and there was no sign yet that we had done so.

Thus, although in retrospect it was to be seen that the first day of *Supercharge* was very nearly a knock-out, to nearly everyone at the end of that day the position was still critical, indeed, seriously critical. Few people are aware today, or ever were aware, how strong

1. To the Author.

this feeling was in quarters by no means inclined to give up easily. Commanders of all grades were beginning to wonder how long they, their staffs and their regiments could stand the strain and they were wondering, in particular, where the troops were coming from for the further infantry attacks that they saw to be likely; 30th Corps never had enough infantry, since the infantry of the three Dominion divisions, for one reason or another, could no longer be employed offensively. Had not some old Roman said that even Apollo's bow was not always at full stretch?

Thus the picture as we see it in review, the picture of a victory imminent, by no means resembles that which was seen by the officers and men who that morning struggled through the dust, sheltered in their shallow trenches from the flying metal and saw the smoke pouring from the stricken tanks. Monty, they reflected, had warned them to expect a vicious and exhausting dog-fight for twelve days. Well, he had certainly been right about the dog-fight; would he be right about the twelve days? This was already the eleventh; would it really be all over in one more?

NO PROGRESS

Unseen events were shaping the course of the battle to a swift climax, but on the surface it seemed a day of frustration. First Armoured Division could not get on, try as they would. The 4/6th South African Armoured Cars, seeking a way through at Tel el Aqqaqir, came to grief on mines and on the innumerable empty gun pits. Eighth Armoured Brigade, dispatched south-westward, came up against a dozen 88s and the remaining guns of 33rd and 604th Panzerjager Battalion, together with the newly arrived tanks of the Ariete Division. The Sherwood Rangers attempted by an audacious dash to cross the track but were seen off. By the end of the day the Division had lost twenty-six tanks.

Thus the defence continued to hold the advantage against tanks, despite weight of numbers. But Montgomery, who had assessed the probable outcome in the morning, had taken measures to prevent the threatened stagnation by developing the more southerly threat he had in mind, in a manner that we shall see in the next chapter.

If there seemed to be stagnation on the ground, there was certainly none in the air. Soon after dawn twenty Stukas, escorted by twelve Messerschmitts, came out of the skies but were intercepted so effectively by Hurricanes of 33rd and 238th Squadrons and by Spitfires of 145th Squadron that they jettisoned their bombs on their own troops. Exactly the same outcome followed from a stronger raid at about noon, which was broken up with great effect by 80th and 127th Squadrons. The enemy's new fighters, however, attacked with some success our fighter patrols in the coastal area and that day we lost sixteen aircraft.

The Allied air effort was now at its peak. The bombers were at their business from dawn onwards, making their main effort on 1st Armoured Division's front. In the twenty-four hours of that day the Desert Air Force pilots made 1,208 sorties and the American Squadrons 125.

The Eighth Army soldier who that day saw his tanks going up in flames and their crews reeling from the furnace that not all escaped, or who prepared himself for yet another night assault, watched with joy these exploits in the skies, but on the ground saw no end to the gruelling dog fight. We were not moving. The rations were hard, the water short, the flies worse than ever they had been in our old lines at Alamein and sleep was short and fitful. It was some time before the soldier learnt that, if we were not moving, the enemy was.

HITLER INTERVENES

The first signs that the enemy might be intending a withdrawal were observed by the Australians. Nothing very definite. A withdrawal from the Thompson's Post pouch would have been no surprise. It was a heavy liability to the enemy rather than an asset and should have been vacated long ago. More significantly, reports then began to come in from 13th Corps down in the south. An increasing quiet and a thinning out of troops. Then came reports from the air of increasing westward movement along the coast road and of backward trickles down the desert tracks. The Australians in the north, 50th and 44th Divisions in the south sent out patrols and by the evening the Australians reported the redoubtable Thompson's Post empty.

The retirement that Rommel had ordered to the Fuka position began at three o'clock. He himself had but a short while arrived at his headquarters, 'only just escaping by some frantic driving a carpet of bombs laid by 18 British aircraft'.[1] He was in an anxious frame of mind, but hopeful that, behind the barrier of guns and armour that he had erected on and westward of the Rahman Track, he would be able to extricate the whole of his forces in an orderly manner. The British armour must be held at bay while his units pulled back in their ordered sequence, the guns and tanks last, maintaining always a strong rearguard.

Half an hour later came a signal from Germany that totally shattered his already uneasy equilibrium. It was a signal from Hitler himself, ordering him 'not to yield a step.' It said:

> In the situation in which you find yourself there can be no other thought than to stand fast and to throw every gun and every man into the battle. The utmost efforts are being made to help you. Your enemy, in spite of his superiority, must also be at the end of his strength. It would not be the first time in history that a strong will has triumphed over the bigger battalions. As to your troops, you can show them no other road than that to victory or death.

A similar signal arrived soon afterwards from Mussolini.

Rommel was stunned and dismayed and for a time did not know what to do. He knew that to obey the order meant the suicide of the army and the end of the Axis cause in Africa. It was, nevertheless, an order and he had not yet learned how necessary it was to circumvent Hitler's orders to military commanders in order to avoid destruction. Before taking action, however, he telephoned Von Thoma and read out Hitler's order to him. Von Thoma replied at once that the German Africa Corps could not hope to escape destruction if it attempted to hold on to its present positions. He suggested a limited withdrawal to Gazel.

Rommel decided then to attempt a compromise. He ordered 90th Light Division and 10th and 21st Italian Corps to stand fast in

1. *The Rommel Papers.*

their present positions, the *DAK* (what was left of it) to withdraw after dark six miles to the west, Ariete Division to take post on their right and 20th Italian Corps (the armoured corps) to conform. This might be said to be a compliance in principle with Hitler's order, but with a readjustment of his forces in order to avoid immediate destruction. The planned general withdrawal to Fuka was off.

At the same time Rommel sent a reply to Hitler in which he emphasized the serious situation to which the Axis forces had been reduced and reporting how heavy were the losses. He ended his signal: *Every last effort will continue to be made to hold the battlefield.*

Montgomery, of course, had no wish to see the enemy make a general withdrawal. He wanted them to continue fighting it out where they stood. Their destruction would then be certain. By staying so long they had enabled him to give them so severe a battering that he hoped very soon to deliver the *coup de grâce*.

By that evening, however, the accumulating straws of evidence presented a picture that Montgomery correctly read as meaning that the enemy was on the brink of a general, not a local retirement. He also correctly appreciated that Rommel's intention was to attempt a stand on the coastal escarpment above Fuka. Montgomery wanted to catch him and cut him off before he got there. He chose this moment therefore to give shape and substance to what was in his mind. In a moment of inspiration he gave surprise orders for a swift follow-up that evening of the successful minor attacks on *Skinflint* and *Snipe* made the evening before.

Through the extension of the funnel that would thus be made, south of Tel el Aqqaqir, he would launch the New Zealanders on the great sweep into open country for which they had been so eagerly waiting and 7th Armoured Division, under the no less eager leadership of John Harding, would be sent by the same path. Both were then to wheel to the right up to the coast to cut the enemy's line of retreat. He gave the orders for this further southward exploitation, the details of which we shall notice in a moment, at noon and he entrusted the sword again to 51st Division.

It was a most skilfully conceived operation, typical of Monty's gift for exploiting success in an unexpected quarter with the aid of swiftly extemporized reserves. It was the stroke that was to blast open the last door of the enemy's strongroom.

Chapter Twenty-One

THE DAY OF VICTORY

The Last Infantry Attacks – Destruction of the Italians – Surrender of the Panzer Commander

THE LAST INFANTRY ATTACKS

The three attacks that Montgomery entrusted to Highland Division on the night of 3 November accordingly took place when Rommel's infantry and guns in the north had been ordered to hold their ground. For these operations, 5th Indian Infantry Brigade had been ordered up from its position to the south of Miteiriya Ridge at very short notice and placed under Wimberley's command. It was led by Brigadier D. Russell, an able commander of buoyant and cheerful disposition who was known by all as 'Pasha' Russell. The three operations are of particular interest, for they provided the avenue for the ultimate surprise which wrecked Rommel's plans and made a nonsense of Hitler's order.

As finally enunciated, the tasks were these:

5/7th Gordon Highlanders (153rd Brigade) and 8th RTR to capture a portion[1] of the Rahman Track two miles south of Tel el Aqqaqir, starting at 5.45 p.m. on the 3rd.

5th Indian Brigade and 50th RTR to capture a stretch[2] of the track four miles south of the Tel, starting at 1.30 a.m. on 4 November.

1. In map square 860293.
2. Contour 45, map square 859290.

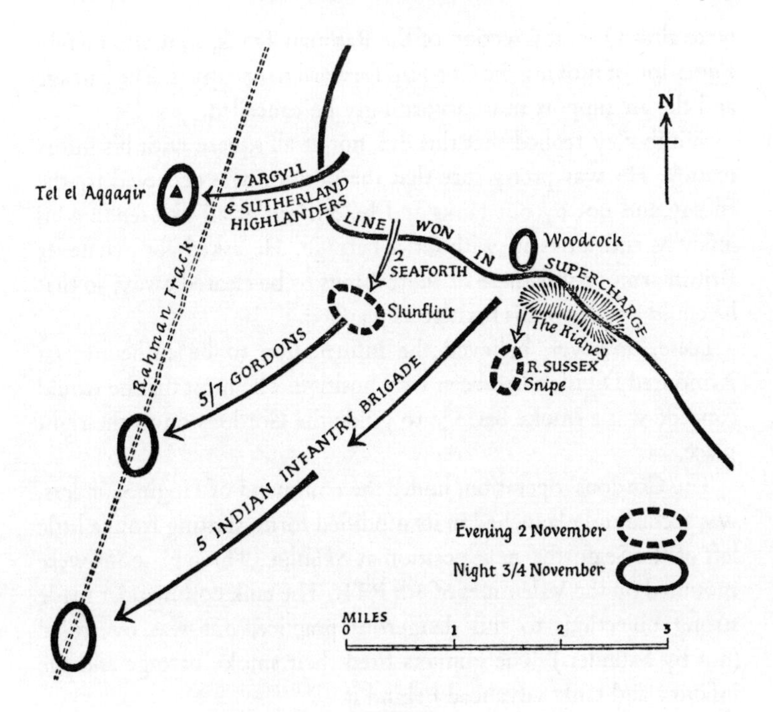

19 THE LAST ASSAULTS

7th Argyll and Sutherland Highlanders (154th Brigade) to capture the Tel itself, starting at 6.15 a.m. on the 4th.

To these 'gate-opening' operations Montgomery attached great importance. They were not easy to launch but were launched with great speed and skill by the commands and staff of the formations concerned. 'Very great credit', Montgomery wrote afterwards, was due to them for the swift and effective execution of the unexpected plan, which again included the co-ordination of a large volume of artillery by Steve Weir. There was, however, one fly in the ointment.

The plans for the first of these attacks had been completed in detail and the gun programmes for the supporting artillery made out when Leese telephoned Wimberley. The Gordons' objective, he said was no longer occupied by the enemy. Eighth Armoured Brigade were already on this section of the Rahman Track, so it was merely a question of moving the Gordons forward to occupy it. The barrage and the air support must accordingly be cancelled.

Wimberley replied that this did not at all square with his information. He was pretty sure that the position was occupied by the enemy and not by our tanks and he did not at all like sending his infantry and tanks in without a barrage. He asked for whatever British armour was there or thereabouts to be cleared away, so that he could put down his barrage as planned.

Leese, however, believed the information to be authentic; 1st Armoured Division had been very positive. The most that he would concede was a smoke barrage to guide the Gordons on to the right place.

The Gordons' operation, under the command of Hugh Saunders, was accordingly launched in its modified form, starting from a little left of the Seaforths' new position at *Skinflint*. Three platoons were mounted on the Valentines of 8th RTR. The tank commander made strong objections to this dangerous practice, but was overruled (not by Saunders). The gunners fired their smoke barrage and the infantry and tanks advanced behind it.

The operation was a tragic failure. The assault was brought abruptly to a halt by a strong and unexpected enemy position on the way to the objective. Saunders tried to call for extempore artillery support, but the wireless links missed. In accordance with orders he had had from Brigadier Murray, he halted, dug in and stood his ground. The two units had ninety-four casualties, including sixteen officers. Of the thirty-two Valentines that went into action, nine were destroyed and eleven other damaged.

It was a sad evening for Wimberley. Watching the tanks come back heavily laden with the bodies of his dead Jocks, he swore: 'Never again.'

Shortly after this he received orders from Leese, by telephone, of the further attacks to be made that same night by 5th Indian Brigade and by the Argylls. Strained and irritable, he said to Leese:

'Must we really go on attacking like this, sir?'

Leese replied:

'Surely you of all people are not going to lose heart at this stage?'

Wimberley wrote later in his journal: 'So many attacks, so many switches of troops. As soon as one show is over, we begin preparing for the next.'

The operation of Pasha Russell's Indian brigade two miles farther south also caused no little anxiety. Much was asked of them. They had first to come right up from the Miteiriya Ridge and were due to attack at 1.30 a.m. on a part of the front of which they had no knowledge, travelling to it by circuitous and strange ways. The dark, moonless night, the press of traffic now trying to push forward and the confusion of tracks and minefields further bedevilled the passage of their lorries. They were spotted by enemy aircraft and dive-bombed. The 3/10th Baluch got bogged in the soft sand. They arrived late at their forming-up position just north of Kidney Ridge, with only two incomplete battalions – 1/4th Essex (temporarily led by Major D. J. M. Smith) and 4/6th Rajputana Rifles. There they were briefed by George Murray, commanding 152nd Brigade, who knew the tactical situation and something of the terrain.

To the confusion of the staffs and gunners of all the divisions supporting him, Russell was obliged to ask for the barrage to be postponed for an hour, while his battalions sorted themselves out and were married to their armour and while he hurriedly re-apportioned their tasks. Yet, in the face of all this, the tired but well-disciplined troops were got to their start-line balanced and in good order. A formidable task lay ahead of them – a night advance into the unknown to a depth of one and a half miles.

When at last, accompanied by 50th RTR, and guided by a powerful barrage, they did attack, the Indian brigade walked straight through, overcoming opposition in what was rightly described as 'a most soldierly performance'. They took 351 prisoners and many anti-tank guns, at a cost of 80 casualties. The brigade reached their objective and consolidated in a dramatic hour, of which the historian of 4th Indian Division has so vividly captured the significance:

> The guns lifted and were done; there was quiet but for the crackle of small-arms fire. Out in front little figures scuttled madly, seeking holes. A carrier platoon went out to bring them in. Then another

noise, thunder out of the east, and more thunder. The roar mounted. The tanks came plunging through, lunging to the west through the gap . . . and wheeling north for the kill. The sun rose on the last of Alamein.

For, all this time, John Harding had been fuming at the delay in getting forward his 7th Armoured Division. The tanks that the Indians saw were those of 22nd Armoured Brigade under Pip Roberts, beginning on that swift 'wheel to the north' that was later that day to have its dramatic climax. At the same time, 4/6th South African Armoured Cars slipped out and, like the Royal Dragoons, who were already doing mischief behind the enemy, began to range the open desert.

The last of the three Highland Division attacks, entrusted by Wimberley to Harry Houldsworth, commanding 154th Brigade, went smoothly and swiftly. The 7th Argyll and Sutherland Highlanders, under Lorne Campbell, supported by seven regiments of artillery firing planned concentrations of mixed high explosive and smoke, advanced on Tel el Aqqaqir and walked through with thirty-one casualties in the face of a little light shelling. The enemy was beginning to melt away. The Argylls captured, intact, the whole apparatus of a divisional headquarters, with signals office and orderly room, documents of the highest importance, large supplies of champagne and chianti and a stock of Iron Crosses with which the Jocks invested themselves. The same morning Saunders advanced with 5/7th Gordons and occupied the position he had been unable to take the evening before. The long, dreary little ridge so devoid of features that had looked down upon a great armoured battle and below which now lay the shattered and blackened remains of some 200 tanks and their sad human remains was at last in our hands.

'That', in the words of Montgomery, 'ended the battle.' The break-out had been accomplished and the hunt was on. He had issued his orders for it the day before. The way was now open for the lorry-borne New Zealanders, complete with their own eager infantry, to launch out on their assigned sweep right-handed to Fuka, accompanied by 9th and 4th Armoured Brigades under command. First, 7th and 10th Armoured Division began to shape their courses to wheel northwards in similar fashion. Down in the south, the divisions of 13th Corps made ready to follow the demoralized Italians who were beginning to melt away, with little food, little hope and no transport; Rommel had abandoned them.

There was still some fighting to be done and there was still plenty of shelling to face. But it was a day in which a tremendous exhilaration filled the whole of Eighth Army. The heavy fatigue slipped off men's shoulders like an abandoned cloak. Wimberley recorded in his journal: 'All very exhilarated in spite of fatigue. Bodies of dispirited prisoners crocodiling in and our armour pouring forward.' On every hand lay the wreckage and the flotsam, human and material, of a broken army. This was victory at last. This was conclusive, undeniable, irreversible victory.

Peter Moore, the fighting sapper, watching the armoured cars swing out that day, called to memory how often before he had seen them drive out in the belief that all the desert was theirs and how each time the terrible clang of shot upon armour had brought disillusionment. Now, as he watched them, he knew that that would never happen again.

It was D plus 12.

DESTRUCTION OF THE ITALIANS

On the morning of that day five divisions of British troops – the three armoured divisions, the New Zealanders and the Highlanders – eager and exhilarated, began to move after the enemy, in the hope of encirclement and quick surrender. About 60,000 men tried to squeeze through the narrow apertures of the minefield lanes and to seek the 'good going' in the desert beyond.

In spite of all the careful staff arrangements, there was appalling congestion. Thus Freyberg, waiting for no man, was ten miles ahead when his 6th Brigade and 9th Armoured were still in the Rahman Track area. Fourth Light Brigade, which should also have got up with him, was still right back at the Springbok Track at dawn and took three hours to cover the twelve miles to the Rahman Track. Wimberley, having visited Tel el Aqqaqir and found the Argylls in great form, forged ahead in his jeep, ahead even of his own leading troops, the divisional Reconnaissance Regiment. Harding's lorried infantry, the Queen's Brigade, were far in the rear, trying to worm their way through the crowded traffic in the old minefields.

Harding did not wait for them. As soon as the Indians had seized their stretch of the Rahman Track, he hurried forward with 22nd Brigade, meeting little opposition until he arrived at a ridge some ten miles south-west of Tel el Aqqaqir. This was the southern flank of the new defensive position which, as we have seen, Rommel had ordered his armoured divisions to hold. Here he had posted General De Stephanis' Italian 20th Motorized Corps, a reasonably powerful force of all arms, of which the preponderant element was the Ariete Armoured Division, so far unscarred by battle. The usual barrier of anti-tank guns bristled along its front, well supported by field artillery and infantry.

Seventh Armoured Division at once attacked. There was a long fight. The Italian armour, in their inferior tanks, together with the artillery, fought it out stubbornly and well, but it was not long before the front as a whole began to crack. The German 3rd Reconnaissance Unit under Major Von Luck tried to come to their aid, but without avail. 'Tank after tank', Rommel himself recorded, 'split asunder or burnt out, while all the time a tremendous British barrage lay over the Italian infantry and artillery.'[1] The Italians were overwhelmed, the Ariete Division shattered and 20th Corps ceased to exist, its broken remnants streaming westward in disarray. The enemy's southern flank was broken and lay wide open.

SURRENDER OF THE PANZER COMMANDER

Meanwhile 1st Armoured Division, to the north of 7th, was pushing back the sterner stuff of the German Africa Corps also and was likewise about to break through. Lumsden had made his way right forward to them during the action and had seen Briggs, who was up in front with 10th Hussars. It is this regiment who act for us the final scene and bring the drama to a symbolic end.

1. *The Rommel Papers.*

Soon after this battle began, Von Thoma, who was a distant witness of it, became very anxious. Fragments of disquieting information reached him, gradually building up a threatening picture, and enormous dust clouds could be seen in the distance to the south, giving evidence of large movements.

At about noon he spoke to Rommel and told him that British tanks, armoured cars and a mass of transport were moving round the southern flank. Rommel refused to believe him. It was 'nonsense', he said. The movements could only be those of armoured cars and they were nothing to worry about. The main British forces were committed frontally and they had nothing available to send round the flank. Rommel's map (seen by Archer-Shee afterwards) still showed 7th Armoured Division down in the south.

Von Thoma, however, was too experienced a soldier to misinterpret the reports and the visible signs. He sent up a reconnaissance aircraft to investigate further, and his fears were amply confirmed. He telephoned Rommel again and Rommel still refused to believe him.

'It is quite impossible,' he said, 'that the British could have gone through the Trieste Division (the motorised infantry of 20th Corps) without my being told.'

He did not know that Trieste had not even stayed to make a report, and were now nothing but a rout.[1]

Nothing, it seemed to Von Thoma, could convince Rommel. He, therefore, decided to go out again on a personal reconnaissance in his tank. According to the somewhat romanticized account of Colonel Fritz Bayerlein, his chief of staff, he was in a fatalistic mood. He took his greatcoat and the small sailcloth bag with which German generals were supplied. He took also his ADC, Hartdegen, with a wireless set.

Some time later Hartdegen returned to Bayerlein and said: 'The general does not want me any more, and he says the wireless is no use now. All our tanks have been destroyed. What has happened to the general I don't know.'

Anxious for the safety of his commander, Bayerlein hurried

1. Eighth Army Intelligence Summary 357.

forward in a small armoured car to find him. Had Von Thoma made up his mind, he wondered, to die, to offer himself to the British guns?

So thinking, Bayerlein tells us,[1] he hurried forward and soon found himself in the thick of the conflict. What in fact he ran into was the concluding phase of the action between 1st Armoured Division and the remains of Von Thoma's once formidable command, the command which had ranged the desert for so long, which had hammered the British from Gazala to Alamein and whose powerful tanks had so often joined battle with the weaker British armour – The German Afrika Corps, pride of the German *Panzerarmee Afrika*. Its pride was now humbled in the flames of their funeral pyre and in the wreckage that strewed the desert waste. In the middle of the wreckage stood its commander, the lean, tall warrior of twenty wounds, 'the epitome of courage', the acknowledged master of tank warfare, the veteran who had fought in the white wastes of Russia, the plains of Poland, the mountains and valleys of Spain and in two campaigns in France.

'A hail of armour-piercing shot,' Bayerlein tells us,[2] 'was whistling all about me. In the noontime haze I could see countless black monsters far away in front. They were Montgomery's tanks, the 10th Hussars. I jumped out of the armoured car and, beneath the burning midday sun, ran as fast as I could towards Tel el Mampsra. It was a place of death, of burning tanks and smashed flak guns, without a living soul. But then, about 200 yards away from the sand-hole in which I was lying, I saw a man standing erect beside a burning tank, apparently impervious to the intense fire which criss-crossed about him. It was General Von Thoma. The British Shermans were closing up . . . Von Thoma stood there, rigid and motionless as a pillar of salt, with his canvas bag in his hand.'

The picture is a little overdrawn, but we can make allowances. The water-colour painted by Henri le Grand, who was serving with 10th Hussars, shows us a less fiery scene, yet dramatic enough.

1. *The Fatal Decisions.*
2. Op. cit.

There had been a brisk engagement between that regiment and the remnant of Von Thoma's command. The Crusader Squadron, under Major R. M. Milbanke, had been leading the advance of the Tenth. They had encountered the German tanks, who, standing back far out of Crusader range, had picked them off one by one and brought them to a halt. Milbanke himself was hit. Archer-Shee then came up with his heavy squadrons and the panzers were forced back. Raymond Briggs's own tank, however, was knocked out by an 88 but not set on fire; the photograph shows it at this moment, with the smoke from some of Archer-Shee's burning tanks trailing down the idle wind. Here and there were the remains of some wrecked or abandoned equipment, but otherwise the scene now was one of the desolate emptiness of the 'open' desert – the dun and rolling desert, limitless, barren, forbidding, roasting under the midday sun – over which the 'black monsters' of the conquering British armour were methodically advancing.

Unexpectedly there appeared over the crest of a dune a single Mark III tank. It was immediately assailed and burst into flames. The commander and crew were seen to leap out, but were pinned to the ground by shellfire from 11th RHA, whose OP tank was right in front. A tall figure was seen to detach itself from the others and walk slowly forward. From the facings that glittered at his shoulder and collar, and by the outsize binoculars that he carried, he seemed to be someone of importance. The shooting stopped. The OP tank of 11th RHA moved forward; so also did the Dingo Scout Car of Captain Grant Washington Singer, a young officer of exceptional charm and outstanding gallantry, who had greatly distinguished himself throughout the battle. He was leading the Reconnaissance Troop, one of whose duties was to collect prisoners. Singer, standing up in his Dingo, was the first to reach the tall, slowly-moving figure. The German, his greatcoat over his left arm, saluted and gave himself up.

Singer took him back in the Dingo to Archer-Shee and reported:

'I've got something here, sir. I don't know what it is, but it looks good.'

The prisoner, who spoke a little English, himself gave the answer. It was General Ritter Von Thoma.[1]

At the same moment some 300 Germans, who had hitherto been concealed in slit trenches right in among Archer-Shee's tanks, rose to their feet, took off their steel helmets, put on their soft caps and surrendered as one man.

With that symbolic episode we must end our story. It was the beginning of the end of the war, though a span of two-and-a-half years still had to run its course before the ultimate collapse of Germany in Europe. In the words of Winston Churchill: 'It may almost be said: "Before Alamein we never had a victory. After Alamein, we never had a defeat".' Hitler or no Hitler, Rommel and his army now fled. 'Anything,' Rommel said, 'that did not reach the road and race off westwards was lost.'

Much indeed was already lost. The tactical defeat was crushing, but the statistical defeat was also immensely impressive. The German divisions had been reduced to skeletons. The Italians had been broken to bits. The Littorio, Trento and Trieste Divisions had been almost wiped out and the Ariete was very soon to meet its doom. In all, the enemy had lost 55,000 men out of the 108,000 with which he had started. Of these, 25,000 had been killed or wounded and 30,000 taken prisoner, among whom were 10,724 Germans. Many more were to be added to the tally as the pursuit went on. More than 1,000 guns of all sorts had been captured or destroyed. In tanks, not less than 320 had been totally lost and many more put out of action.

The British losses, heavy enough in the first infantry attacks, were in the final analysis surprisingly light for a force that was constantly attacking. They totalled 13,560 killed, wounded and missing. Only 2,350 were posted as killed but most of the missing, who numbered 2,260, were also killed. United Kingdom troops incurred 58 per cent of these casualties, the Australians 22 per cent, the New Zealanders 10 per cent, the South Africans 6 per cent.

1. Singer was killed in action next day. Von Thoma, on hearing the news, wrote his father a touching letter of sympathy.

Five hundred tanks had been knocked out, but only about 150 totally destroyed; we still had another 600 or so. One hundred and ten of our guns had been knocked out by shellfire, most of them being anti-tank guns.

In the air, significantly enough, the enemy's losses had been numerically lighter than our own. His amounted to eighty-four; ours to ninety-seven, of which seventy-seven were British and twenty American.

The 4th of November marked the beginning of a new story in the golden annals of Eighth Army. Rommel, for reasons that belong to that story, just escaped absolute destruction for a little longer, but much else flowed to the immediate credit of the Allied accounts. Tedder's pilots were able to push up to the Martuba airfields to cover the critical *Stoneage* convoy to Malta and the valiant isle was saved, never again to be imperilled. The free world rang with the renown of Eighth Army's commander and his soldiers. To Eisenhower's liberation forces about to land in French North Africa the victory gleamed as a signal of promise. To the good people at home it shone as a beacon of hope in their darkness.

To the more immediate concern of the soldiers of Eighth Army and their comrades of the Desert Air Force the day marked not only the conclusion of a resounding victory but also the start of the no less victorious pursuit. That pursuit led them a great deal farther than they had ever imagined: not merely to Tripoli, but even as far as Tunis – the distance from London to Moscow – where, joining hands with Eisenhower's British-American forces, under the tactical command of General Alexander, they forced the final capitulation of the combined armies of Von Arnim and Rommel. Thus was the whole continent of Africa freed of the enemy, the Mediterranean reopened to Allied shipping and a springboard provided for the assault upon Hitler's 'Fortress Europe' itself.

These pages have not been intended as a commentary or critique, except as the incidents of the day demand. They are primarily a narrative. When all is said and done, Alamein stands out as a great feat of arms, a soldier's battle and not merely a general's exercise, which owed its triumph to the guts and fighting spirit of Montgomery's soldiers, to his own high mastery in the technique of the most unforgiving of all professions, to the sustained support of the Allied pilots in the air and to the repeated mistakes, which his adversary so shrewdly invited him to make, of Erwin Rommel.

Appendix A

EIGHTH ARMY ORDER OF BATTLE

on 23 October 1942 (slightly modified and including forward elements only)

Lieutenant-General B. L. Montgomery
(BGS: Brigadier F. W. de Guingand)

HQ EIGHTH ARMY

Formations directly under command included: 1st Army Tank Bde (42 and 44 RTR), who provided Troops to man the Scorpions; 2nd and 12th AA Bdes.

Army Troops included: Tank Delivery Regt, 1st Camouflage Coy, RE, 566th and 588th Army Troops Coy, RE, Eighth Army Signals, 4th Light Field Ambulance, 200th Field Ambulance.

10TH CORPS

(Lieut-General Herbert Lumsden)
(BGS: Brigadier Ralph Cooney)

1ST ARMOURED DIVISION (Major-General Raymond Briggs)

2nd Armoured Brigade (Brigadier A. F. Fisher): The Queen's Bays, 9th Lancers, 10th Hussars and Yorkshire Dragoons (motor battalion).

7th Motor Brigade (Brigadier T. J. B. Bosvile): 2nd and 7th Battalions The Rifle Brigade and 2nd King's Royal Rifle Corps (60th Rifles).

Divisional Troops

12th Lancers (armoured cars)

RA: (CRA, Brigadier B. J. Fowler): 2nd and 4th RHA, 11th RHA (HAC), 78th Field Regt (less Troops with other divisions), 76th Anti-Tank Regt and 42 Light AA Regt.

RE: 1st and 7th Field Sqns, 1st Field Park Sqn. *Attached:* 9th Field Sqn and 572 Field Park Coy.

Others: 1st Armd Div Signals, two companies R. Northumberland Fusiliers, 1st and 5th Light Field Ambulances.

Attached: 'Hammerforce' (artillery and armd cars).

10TH ARMOURED DIVISION (Major-General A. H. Gatehouse)

8th Armoured Brigade (Brigadier E. C. N. Custance): 3rd RTR, Nottinghamshire Yeomanry (Sherwood Rangers), Staffordshire Yeomanry, 1st Buffs (motor battalion).

24th Armoured Brigade (Brigadier A. G. Kenchington): 41st, 45th and 47th RTR and 11th KRRC (motor battalion).

133rd Lorried Infantry Brigade (Brigadier A. W. Lee), added from 44th Division: 2nd, 4th and 5th Royal Sussex Regt and one company R. Northumberland Fusiliers.

Divisional Troops:

The Royal Dragoons (armoured cars).

RA: (CRA, Brigadier W. A. Ebbels): 1st, 5th and 104th (Essex Yeo) RHA, 98th Field Regt (Surrey and Sussex Yeomanry), 84th Anti-Tank Regt, 53rd Light AA Regt.

RE: 2nd and 3rd (Cheshire) Field Sqns, 141st Field Park Sqn; *attached:* 6th Field Sqn, 571st and 573rd Army Field Coys.

Others: 10th Armd Div Signals, 3rd, 8th and 168th Light Field Ambulances.

8TH ARMOURED DIVISION (Major-General Charles Gairdner). This division was reduced to a headquarters staff and some non-operational troops only.

10TH CORPS TROOPS: 570th Corps Field Park Coy RE, 10th Corps Signals, 12th and 151st Light Field Ambulances.

13TH CORPS

(Lieut-General B. G. Horrocks)
(BGS: Brigadier George Erskine)

7TH ARMOURED DIVISION (Major-General A. F. Harding):

4th Light Armoured Brigade (Brigadier M. G. Roddick): 4/8th Hussars, The Greys and 1st KRRC (motor battalion).

22nd Armoured Brigade (Brigadier G. P. B. Roberts): 1st and 5th RTR, 4th City of London Yeomanry and 1st Rifle Brigade (motor battalion).

131 Lorried Infantry Brigade. See under 44th Infantry Division.

Divisional Troops:

Household Cavalry Regt, 11th Hussars and 2nd Derbyshire Yeomanry (armoured cars).

RA: (CRA, Brigadier Roy Mews): 3rd RHA, 4th and 97th (Kent Yeomanry) Field Regts, 65th Anti-Tank Regt, 15 Light AA Regt.

RE: 4th and 21st Field Sqns, 143rd Field Park Sqn.

Others: 7th Armd Div Signals, 2nd and 14th Light Field Ambulances.

Under command: 1st and 2nd Free French Brigade Groups and 1st Free French Flying Column.

44th Reconnaissance Regt (from 44th Division).

44TH INFANTRY DIVISION (Major-General I. T. P. Hughes):

131st Infantry Brigade (Brigadier W. D. Stamer): 1/5th, 1/6th and 1/7th The Queens' (became incorporated in 7th Armd Div on 1 Nov.).

132nd Infantry Brigade (Brigadier L. G. Whistler): 2nd Buffs, 4th and 5th Royal West Kent Regt.

133rd Infantry Brigade. See under 10th Armd Div.

Divisional Troops:

RA: (CRA, Brigadier H. R. Hall): 57th, 58th, 65th and 53rd Field Regts, 57th Anti-Tank Regt, 30th Light AA Regt.

RE: 11th, 209th and 210th Field Coys, 211th Field Park Coy and 577th Army Field Park Coy.

Others: 44th Div Signals, 6th Cheshire Regt (machine-gun battalion), 131st and 132nd Field Ambulance.

50TH INFANTRY DIVISION (Major-General J. S. Nichols):

69th Infantry Brigade (Brigadier E. C. Cooke-Collis): 5th East Yorkshire Regt, 6th and 7th Green Howards.

151st Infantry Brigade (Brigadier J. E. S. Percy): 6th, 8th and 9th Durham Light Infantry.

1st Greek Infantry Brigade Group (Colonel Katsotas): 1st, 2nd and 3rd Greek Battalions, 1st Greek Field Artillery Regt, 1st Greek Field Engineer Coy, 1st Greek MG Coy, 1st Greek Field Ambulance.

Divisional Troops:

RA: (CRA, Brigadier Claude Eastman): 74th, 111th, 124th and 154th Field Regts, 102nd (Northumberland Hussars) Anti-Tank Regt, 34th Light AA Regt.

RE: 233rd and 505th Field Coys, 235th Field Park Coy.

Others: 50th Div Signals, 2nd Cheshire Regt (machine-guns), 149 and 186 Field Ambulances.

13TH CORPS TROOPS: 118th and 124th RTR (dummy tanks)

4th Survey Regt RA (part), 578th Army Field Coy and 576th Corps Field Park Coy, RE, 13th Corps Signals.

30TH CORPS

(Lieut-General Sir Oliver Leese, Bt.)

(BGS: Brigadier G. P. Walsh)

51ST (HIGHLAND) INFANTRY DIVISION (Major-General D. N. Wimberley):

152nd Infantry Brigade (Brigadier G. Murray): 2nd and 5th Seaforth Highlanders, 5th Cameron Highlanders.

153 Infantry Brigade (Brigadier D. A. H. Graham): 5th Black Watch, 1st and 5/7th Gordon Highlanders.

154th Infantry Brigade (Brigadier H. W. Houldsworth): 1st and 7th Black Watch, 7th Argyll and Sutherland Highlanders.

Divisional Troops:

RA (CRA, Brigadier G. M. Elliot): 126th, 127th and 128th Field Regts, 61st Anti-Tank Regt, 40th Light AA Regt.

RE: 274th, 275th and 276th Field Coys, 239th Field Park Coy.

Others: 51st Div Signals, 1/7th Middlesex Regt (machine-guns), 51st Div Reconnaissance Regt, 174th, 175th and 176th Field Ambulances.

2ND NEW ZEALAND DIVISION (Major-General B. C. Freyberg, VC):

9th Armoured Brigade (*United Kingdom*) (Brigadier John Currie): 3rd Hussars, Royal Wiltshire Yeomanry, Warwickshire Yeomanry and 14th Foresters (motor infantry).

5th NZ Infantry Brigade (Brigadier Howard Kippenberger): 21st, 22nd and 23 NZ Battalions, 28th Maori Bn.

6th NZ Infantry Brigade (Brigadier William Gentry): 24th, 25th and 26th NZ Bns.

Divisional Troops:

2nd NZ Divisional Cavalry Regt (light tanks).

NZA (CRA, Brigadier C. E. Weir): 4th, 5th and 6th NZ Field Regts, 7 NZ Anti-Tank Regt, 14th NZ Light AA Regt.

NZE: 6th, 7th and 8th NZ Field Coys, 5th NZ Field Park Coy.

Others: 2nd NZ Div Signals, 27th NZ Bn (machine-guns), 5th and 6th NZ Field Ambulances and 166th Light Field Ambulance (for 9th Armd Bde).

9TH AUSTRALIAN DIVISION (Major-General L. J. Morshead):

20th Australian Infantry Brigade (Brigadier W. J. V. Windeyer): 2/13th, 2/15th and 2/17th Australian Infantry Bns.

24th Australian Infantry Brigade (Brigadier Arthur Godfrey): 2/28th, 2/32nd and 2/43rd Australian Infantry Bns.

26th Australian Infantry Brigade (Brigadier D. A. Whitehead): 2/23rd, 2/24th and 2/48th Australian Infantry Bns.

Divisional Troops:

RAA (CRA, Brigadier A. H. Ramsay): 2/7th, 2/8th and 2/12th Aust Field Regts, 3rd Aust Anti-Tank Regt, 4th Aust Light AA Regt.

Engineers: 2/3rd, 2/7th, 2/13th Aust Field Coys, 2/4th Aust Field Park Coy, 2/3rd Aust Pioneer Bn.

Others: 9th Australian Div Signals, 2/2nd Aust Bn (machine-guns), 2/3rd, 2/8th and 2/11th Aust Field Ambulances.

4TH INDIAN DIVISION (Major-General F. I. S. Tuker):

5th Indian Infantry Brigade (Brigadier D. Russell): 1/4th Essex Regt, 4/6th Rajputana Rifles, 3/10th Baluch.

7th Indian Infantry Brigade (Brigadier A. W. W. Holworthy): 1st Royal Sussex Regt, 4/16th Punjabi Regt, 1/2nd Ghurka Rifles.

161st Indian Infantry Brigade (Brigadier F. E. C. Hughes): 1st Argyll and Sutherland Highlanders, 1/1st Punjabi Regt, 4/7th Rajputs.

Divisional Troops:

RA (CRA, Brigadier H. K. Dimoline): 1st, 11th and 32nd Field Regts, 149th Anti-Tank Regt, 57th Light AA Regt.

RE: 2nd, 4th and 12th Field Coys, 11th Field Park Coy.

Others: 4th Indian Div Signals, 6th Rajputana Rifles (machine-guns), 17th and 26th Indian Field Ambulances and 75th Light Field Ambulance.

1ST SOUTH AFRICAN DIVISION (Major-General D. H. Pienaar):

1st SA Infantry Brigade (Brigadier C. L. de W. du Toit): 1st Royal Natal Carabiniers, 1st Duke of Edinburgh's Own Rifles, 1st Transvaal Scottish.

2nd SA Infantry Brigade (Brigadier W. H. E. Poole): 1/2nd Field Force Bn, 1st Natal Mounted Rifles, Cape Town Highlanders.

3rd SA Infantry Brigade (Brigadier R. J. Palmer): 1st Imperial Light Horse, 1st Durban Light Infantry, 1st Rand Light Infantry.

Divisional Troops:

SA Artillery (CRA, Brigadier F. Theron): 1st, 4th and 7th SA Field Regts, 1st SA Anti-Tank Regt, 1st SA Light AA Regt.

SA Engineers: 1st, 2nd, 3rd and 5th SA Field Coys, 19th SA Field Park Coy.

Others: 1st SA Div Signals, Regiment President Steyn and one coy Die Middelandse (machine-guns), 12th, 15th and 18th SA Ambulances.

Divisional Reserve Group, including 2nd Regiment Botha, was dissolved a week after Alamein began.

30TH CORPS TROOPS and Troops in Corps Reserve:

23rd Armoured Brigade Group (Brigadier G. W. Richards): 8th, 40th, 46th and 50th RTR, 121st Field Regt RA, 168 Light AA Battery, RA, 295th Army Field Coy, RE, 7th Light Field Ambulance.

Armoured Cars: 4/8th South African Armoured Car Regt.

RA: 7th, 64th and 69th Medium Regts.

RE: 66th Mortar Comapny.

30th Corps Signals.

Appendix B

WESTERN DESERT AIR FORCE
Order of Battle

Air Headquarters Western Desert
(Air Vice-Marshal Arthur Coningham)

No. 1 Air Ambulance Unit, DH86.
No. 3 (South African Air Force) Wing
  Squadrons:
    Nos. 12 and 24 (South African Air Force) – Boston.
    No. 21 (the same) – Baltimore.
No. 232 Wing
  Squadrons:
    Nos. 55 and 223 – Baltimore.
United States 12th Bombardment Group
  Squadrons:
    81st, 82nd, 83rd and 434th – Mitchell.
No. 285 Wing
  Squadrons:
    No. 40 (South African Air Force) and No. 208 – Hurricane.
    No. 60 (South African Air Force) – Baltimore.
  Flights, Other units:
    No. 1437 Strategic Reconnaissance Flight – Baltimore.
    No. 2 Photographic Reconnaissance Flight (detachment) – Various.

211 GROUP

  Squadrons:
    Nos. 6 and 7 (South African Air Force) – Hurricane.
No. 233 Wing
  Squadrons:
    Nos. 2 and 4 (South African Air Force) and No. 260 – Kittyhawk.
    No. 5 (South African Air Force) – Tomahawk.

No. 239 Wing

Squadrons:

Nos. 3 and 450 (Royal Australian Air Force) and Nos 112 and 250 – Kittyhawk.

No. 244 Wing

Nos. 92, 145 and 601 – Spitfire.

No. 73 – Hurricane.

United States 57th Fighter Group

Squadrons:

64th, 65th and 66th – Warhawk.

212 GROUP

No. 7 (South African Air Force) Wing

Squadrons:

Nos. 80, 127, 274 and 335 – Hurricane.

No. 243 Wing

Squadrons:

Nos. 1 (South African Air Force), 33, 213 and 238 – Hurricane.

Appendix C

GERMAN ARMY ORDER OF BATTLE

(Based on Eighth Army Intelligence Summary No. 343, slightly amended by later information and given with reserve)

PANZERGRUPPE AFRIKA

GOC (and C-in-C German-Italian *Panzerarmee Afrika*): Panzer-General Georg Stumme
(Chief of Staff: Lieut-General Alfred Gauze)

ARMY TROOPS. Kampstaffel Kiel (Major-General Krause): 221st RHQ (medium and heavy batteries), 612th and 617th Anti-Aircraft Bns.

19TH ANTI-AIRCRAFT DIVISION (Lieut-General Burckhardt): 66th, 102nd and 135th AA RHQs.

GERMAN AFRICA CORPS ('*DAK*')

(Lieut-General Wilhelm Ritter von Thoma)

15TH ARMOURED DIVISION (Major-General Gustav von Vaerst): 8th Tank Regt, 113th PZ Grenadier Regt, 33rd Arty Regt, 33rd Anti-Tank Bn, 33rd Engineer Bn.

21ST ARMOURED DIVISION (Major-General Heinz Von Randow): 5th Tank Bn, 104th PZ Grenadier Regt, 155th Arty Regt, 39th Anti-Tank Bn, 200th Engineer Bn.

90TH LIGHT DIVISION (Major-General Theodor Graf von Sponeck): 155th PZ Grenadier Regt (with 707th Heavy Inf. Gun Coy under command), 200th PZ Grenadier Regt (708th Heavy Inf. Gun Coy under command), 346th PZ Grenadier Regt, 190th Arty Regt, 190th Anti-Tank Bn.
Under command: Force 288, composed of: 605 Anti-Tank Bn, 109th and 606th AA Bns.

164TH LIGHT DIVISION (Major-General Carl-Hans Lungershausen): 125th Inf Regt, 382nd Inf Regt, 433rd Inf Regt, 220th Arty Regt, 220th Engineers Bn, 220th Cyclist Unit, 609th AA Bn.

RECONNAISSANCE GROUP: HQ 15th Lorried Inf Bde, 3rd, 33rd and 580th Recce Units.

RAMCKE (Parachute) BRIGADE (Major-General Bernhard Ramcke): Three battalions of 2nd, 3rd and another Parachute Rifle Regts, Lehrbataillon Burckhardt, Parachute Bty, Parachute Anti-Tank Bn.

Appendix D

ITALIAN ARMY ORDER OF BATTLE

From Eighth Army Intelligence Summary No. 343, abbreviated; names of commanders kindly supplied by Military Attaché, Italian Embassy)

C-in-C (North Africa and Governor-General Libya):
Marshal Ettore Bastico
(Chief of Staff: General Conte Curio Barbaseti di Prun)

10TH CORPS

(Lieut-General Edoardo Nebba; Major-General Enrico Frattini n temporary command until 26 October)

BRESCIA DIVISION (Major-General Brunetto Brunetti): 19th and 20th Inf Regts, 1st Mobile Arty Regt, 27th Mixed Engineer Regt.

FOLGORE DIVISION (Major-General Enrico Frattini): 185th, 186th and 187th Inf. Regts.

PAVIA DIVISION (Brig-General N. Scattaglia): 27th and 28th Inf Regts, 26th Arty Regt, 17th Mixed Engineer Bn.

CORPS TROOPS: 9th Bersagliere Regt, 16th Corps Arty Group, 8th Army Arty Group.

20TH CORPS

(Lieut-General Giuseppe de Stephanis)

ARIETE ARMOURED DIVISION (Brig-General Francesco Arena): 132nd Tank Regt, 8th Bersagliere Regt, 132nd Arty Regt, 3rd Armoured Cavalry Group, 132nd Mixed Engineer Bn.

LITTORIO ARMOURED DIVISION (Major-General G. Bitossi): 133rd Tank Regt, 12th Bersagliere Regt, 3rd Armoured Cavalry Group (part), 3rd and part 133rd Arty Regts.

TRIESTE MOTORISED DIVISION (Brig-General Francesco La Ferla): 11th Tank Bn, 65th and 6th Inf Regts, 21st Arty Regt, 8th Armoured Bersagliere Regt, 52nd Mixed Engineer Bn.

CORPS TROOPS: Part 8th Army Arty Group, 90th Engineer Company.

21ST CORPS

(Lieut-General Enea Navarini; Major-General Alessandro Gloria in temporary command until 26 October)

TRENTO DIVISION (Brig-General Giorgio Masina): 61st and 62nd Inf Regts, 46th Arty Regt.

BOLOGNA DIVISION (Major-General Alessandro Gloria): 39th and 40th Inf Regts, 205th Arty Regt, 25th Engineer Bn.

CORPS TROOPS: 7th Bersagliere Regt, 24th Corps Arty Group, 8th Army Arty Group.

IN ARMY RESERVE

PISTOIA DIVISION (35th and 36th Inf Regts, 3rd Motorized Arty Regt, Bersagliere Bn).

GGFF (Young Fascists) Division (2 or 3 Battalions).

Appendix E

2 NZ DIVISION ORDER OF BATTLE FOR 'SUPERCHARGE'

The following is given from the divisional Operation Order:

9 *Armd Bde*. 3rd Hussars, R Wilts Yeo, Warwickshire Yeo, 14 Foresters, 31 NZ A-tk Bty.

23 *Armd Bde*. 8, 46 and 50 RTR, 121 Fd Regt RA, 168 Lt AA Regt RA, 295 Fd Park Sqn, RE.

2 *NZ Div Cavalry*.

NZ Artillery. 4, 5 and 6 NZ Fd Regts, HQ 7 NZ A-tk Regt, 14 NZ Lt AA Regt.

NZ Engineers. 6, 7 and 8 NZ Fd Coys, 5 NZ Fd Pk Coy, One Fd Coy RE (51 Div).

2 *NZ Div Signals*.

151 *Inf Bde*. 6, 8 and 9 Durham Light Infantry, 34 NZ A-tk Bty, One A-tk Bty (from 30 Corps), Two Coys 27 NZ (MG) Bn.

152 (*H*) *Inf Bde*. 2 and 5 Seaforths, 5 Camerons, One MG Coy (7 Middlesex Regt), One Bty 61 A-tk Regt RA.

5 *NZ Inf Bde Gp*. 21, 22 and 23 NZ Bns, 28 NZ (Maori) Bn, 32 A-tk Bty, One Coy 27 NZ (MG) Bn.

6*NZ Inf Bde Gp*. 24, 25 and 26 NZ Bns, 33 NZ A-tk Bty, One Coy 27 NZ (MG) Bn.

Appendix F

1 ARMD DIV ORDER OF BATTLE FOR 'SUPERCHARGE'

From 1 Armd Div OO No. 34 (slightly modified):

Div Troops. 12 Lancers (Armoured Cars), 2 RHA, 78 Fd Regt RA, 73 A-tk Regt less two Byts and two Tps, 42 Lt AA Regt less one Bty and one Tp, 1 Field Park Sqn, RE, 7 Motor Bde Workshops, 2 Armd Bde Wkshops, 1 and 15 Lt Fd Ambulances less one Sec each, 550, 910, 918, 920 and 925 Coys RASC, 1 Armd Div. Provost Coy.

2 *Armd Bde Group.* Queen's Bays, 9 Lancers, 10 Hussars, Yorkshire Dragoons, 11 RHA, Two Btys 76 A-tk Regt, One Tp each 145 and 231 Lt AA Btys, 1 Field Sqn RE, X Coy R Northumberland Fusiliers.

8 *Armd Bde Group.* Staffordshire Yeo, Nottinghamshire Yeo, 3 RTR, 1 RHA, One Bty each 73 and 84 A-tk Regts, One Bty 53 Lt AA Regt, 2 Fd Sqn RE, 1 Buffs, Z Coy RNF.

7 *Motor Bde Group.* 4 RHA, 76 A-tk Regt less two Btys, 231 Lt AA Bty less one Tp, 2 KRRC, 7 RB, Sec, 15 Lt Fd Amb, Recovery Sec, Bde Workshops.

Minefield Task Force. 2 RB, 7 and 9 Fd Sqns RE, 572 Fd Coy RE, Three Tps Crusaders (2 Armd Bde), Detachments, Div Sigs and Provost.

Appendix G

AUTHORITIES AND SOURCES

Maps. 1 : 50,000 Egypt; Sheets 2, 5, 6, 7, 8, 9 and 10.
1 : 25,000 Tel el Eisa; Sheet 2, with Defence Overprint 18 Oct. 1942.
German map 1 : 100,000, Alamein.

Operation Orders, Intelligence Summaries, War Diaries, Signal Logs, Reports of Committees of Inquiry of the formations concerned and operational reports by various officers.

23rd Armoured Brigade: *Report on Operations.*

1st Armoured Division: *The Passage of Defended Minefields.*

2nd New Zealand Division: *The New Zealand Division in Egypt and Libya.*

ALEXANDER, FIELD-MARSHAL THE VISCOUNT; 'Despatch' (Supplement to *The London Gazette*, 5 February 1948).

AUCHINLECK, FIELD-MARSHAL SIR CLAUDE; 'Despatch' (Supplement to *The London Gazette*, 13 February 1948).

Cabinet Office: *History of the Second World War*, 'The Mediterranean and the Middle East', volume III.

Cabinet Office: *Orders of Battle of the Second World War*, volumes I and II.

DE GUINGAND, MAJOR-GENERAL SIR FRANCIS: *Operation Victory.*

ESEBECK, H. G. VON: *Afrikanische Schicksaljahre.*

General Staff, Middle East: *Middle East Training Memorandum No. 7* – 'Lessons from Operations'.

HARDING, FIELD-MARSHAL THE LORD: *Mediterranean Strategy* 1939–45: Lees Knowles lecture, Cambridge University, 1959.

HORROCKS, LIEUT-GENERAL SIR BRIAN: *A Full Life.*

JARRETT, COLONEL G. B.: *Gun and Cartridge Record*, USA, volume I, Nos. 3–11. *DAK.*

KIPPENBERGER, MAJOR-GENERAL SIR HOWARD: *Infantry Brigadier.*

LIDDELL HART, CAPTAIN B. H. (Ed): *The Rommel Papers.*

LIDDELL HART, CAPTAIN B. H.: *The Tanks* (History of the Royal Tank Regiment).

MCCREERY, LIEUT-GENERAL SIR RICHARD: *XII Royal Lancers Journal*, April 1959. 'Recollections of a Chief of Staff'.

McMeekan, Brigadier G. R.: 'The Assault at Alamein'. *The Royal Engineers Journal*, volume LXIII.

Mellenthin, Major-General F. W. Von: *Panzer Battles* 1939–45.

Montgomery of Alamein, Field-Marshal The Viscount: *El Alamein to the Sangro.*

Montgomery of Alamein, Field-Marshal The Viscount: *Memoirs.*

Regimental and other histories of all units and formations that participated, where they appear reliable.

Richards and Saunders: 'The Royal Air Force 1939–45, volumes I–III (HMSO).

Richardson and Freidin (Ed): 'The Fatal Decisions' (for article on Alamein by Lieut-General Fritz Bayerlein).

South African War Histories Section, GHQ, Pretoria: *Campaigns in the Western Desert, 1 and 2 South African Division:* (Notes for Permanent Staff Promotion Examinations).

Westphal, Major-General Siegfried: 'Notes on the Campaign in North Africa'. *Journal of the Royal United Service Institution*, volume CV, Nos. 6 and 74.

Private Diaries and Journals of Several Officers. Written or verbal narratives of the following:

Lieutenant-Colonel J. P. Archer-Shee, DSO, MC.
Mr J. F. Atkins.
Mr Alan F. Baer.
Lieutenant-Colonel C. N. Barker, OBE, MC.
Major The Marquess of Bath.
Major T. A. Bird, DSO, MC.
Major-General Raymond Briggs, CB, DSO.
Lieutenant-Colonel The Earl Cadogan, MC.
Brigadier L. M. Campbell, VC, DSO.
Brigadier Neville Custance, DSO.
Lieutenant-Colonel M. H. H. Du Boulay, MC.
Colonel G. W. Dunn, CBE, DSO, MC, TD.
Brigadier W. A. Ebbels, DSO.
Brigadier David Egerton, OBE, MC.
Major M. Eveleigh, MC.
Lieutenant-Colonel Sir Peter Farquhar, Bt, DSO.
Colonel J. L. Finigan, DSO, TD, DL.
Brigadier A. F. Fisher, CBE, DSO.
Mr H. Flinn.
Major R. O. G. Gardner, MC.
Major-General Sir William Gentry, KBE, CB, DSO.
Colonel M. St-J. V. Gibbs, CB, DSO, TD.

Major H. A. Gordon, MC.
Colonel Gerald Grosvenor, DSO.
Lieutenant-Colonel J. E. G. Hay, DSO.
Brigadier P. R. C. Hobart, DSO, OBE, MC, ADC.
Lieutenant-Colonel John Lakin, TD, DL.
Major-General A. W. Lee, CB, MC.
Lieutenant-General Sir Oliver Leese, Bt, KCB, CBE, DSO.
Major-General H. M. Liardet, CB, CBE, DSO.
Lieutenant-Colonel K. MacKessack.
Mr F. W. Marten, MC.
Brigadier G. R. McMeekan, CB, DSO, OBE.
Lieutenant-Colonel Sir George Meyrick, Bt, MC.
Field-Marshal The Viscount Montgomery of Alamein, KG.
Brigadier P. N. M. Moore, DSO, MC.
Lieutenant-General Sir Horatio Murray, KBE, CB, DSO.
Brigadier J. A. Oliver, CB, CBE, DSO, TD, ADC, DL.
Lieutenant-Colonel Nicholas Pease, MBE, TD.
Major J. F. M. Perrott, MC.
Lieutenant-General Sir Harold Pyman, KCB, CBE, DSO.
Brigadier R. C. Queree, CBE, DSO.
Major-General G. W. Richards, CB, CBE, DSO, MC.
Major-General G. P. B. Roberts, CB, DSO, MC.
Brigadier W. N. R. Roper-Caldbeck, DSO.
Major The Hon. Peter Samuel, MC.
Lieutenant-Colonel H. W. B. Saunders, DSO.
Major G. R. Savory, MC.
Brigadier I. F. M. Spence, DSO.
The late Captain Clive Stoddart (letters).
RQMS J. E. Swann, DCM.
Colonel C. N. Thompson, CBE, DSO.
Captain C. R. C. Thursfield.
Colonel V. B. Turner, VC.
Mr J. W. Van Grutten.
Major-General G. P. Walsh, CB, CBE, DSO.
Lieutenant-General Sir Henry Wells, KBE, CB, DSO.
Major H. N. Wigan, MC.
Major-General D. N. Wimberley, CB, DSO, MC, DL.

I have also been assisted on divers points by the kindness of Brigadier Philip Masel (Australia), Major-General Sir Ivor Hughes, Lieutenant-Colonel Michael Verey, Brigadier R. C. Cooney, Major The Hon. Peter Samuel, Major J. M. Hay, Lieutenant-Colonel R. F. Wright, Brigadier J. T. S. Tutton, Brigadier W. H. G. Costello, Lieutenant-Colonel J. W. A. Stephenson, Colonel James Hanbury, Captain George Thompson, Brigadier E. H. Grant, Mr Ronald Wood and Captain Quentin Thomas.

Acknowledgements

I am grateful to the following for their kind permission to quote from their works and thank them for their courtesy:

Field-Marshal The Viscount Montgomery of Alamein for extracts from his *Memoirs* and from *El Alamein to the Sangro.*

Captain B. H. Liddell Hart and William Collins, Sons and Company for extracts from *The Rommel Papers.*

Michael Joseph Ltd for extracts from *The Fatal Decisions.*

The Controller, Her Majesty's Stationery Office for the Order of Battle, Western Desert Air Force, in *The Royal Air Force* 1939–45.

Lieutenant-General Sir Francis Tuker and Lieutenant-Colonel G. R. Stevens for the extract from *Fourth Indian Division* in Chapter 21.

Permission on payment of fees was obtained from David Higham Associates Ltd for some quotations from Major-General Sir Howard Kippenberger's *Infantry Brigadier* (Oxford University Press), and from the Controller, HMSO, for using the main structure of Eighth Army's Order of Battle, *Orders of Battle, Second World War.*

C. E. L. P.

A Short Glossary

Besa: Machine gun mounted in British tanks (tanks of American manufacture had the Browning).

BGS: Brigadier General Staff; the senior staff officer at the headquarter of an Army or Corps.

Bofors gun: Light, quick-firing anti-aircraft gun.

Bren gun: Light machine gun.

Bren gun carrier: A tracked and lightly armoured vehicle, mounting a bren gun and used for carrying men, ammunition, etc. across fire-swept ground.

Brew-up': Slang for (a) to make tea, or (b) of a tank, to be set on fire.

Consolidate: To prepare a captured position for defence against counter-attack.

CRA: Commander Royal Artillery; a brigadier commanding all the artillery in a division.

CRE: Commander Royal Engineers; a lieutenant-colonel commanding all RE units in a division.

'doover': Australian term for a trench, small dug-out or hole in ground (American 'foxhole').

FDLs: Forward Defended Localities (old 'front line').

FOO Forward Observation Officer (artillery).

GSO 1: General Staff Officer Grade One. A lieutenant-colonel, senior staff officer of a division; also on the staffs of higher formations.

O Group Order Group, at which a commander gives operational orders to subordinate officers.

RHA: Royal Horse Artillery

Spandau: German heavy machine gun.

Vickers gun: British heavy machine gun.

General Index

Military and air formations and units are indexed separately at the end hereof. The appendixes are not covered. References of no significance are not included.

Index of Military Formations and Units

The Appendixes are not covered. References of no significance are not included.

BRITISH AND ALLIED

For the convenience of the general reader, all battalions, regiments and sub-units (other than air) are grouped under UNITS in alphabetical order, sub-divided into *Armoured, Infantry, Royal Artillery*, etc., in their appropriate categories. Army formations are in their serial numbers under CORPS, DIVISIONS and BRIGADES.

GERMAN

ITALIAN